THE
NAVAL
HISTORY OF
WALES

THE
NAVAL
HISTORY OF
WALES

J.D. DAVIES

For John and Elaine Williams

First published as *Britannia's Dragon* 2013
This paperback edition published 2023

The History Press
97 St George's Place, Cheltenham,
Gloucestershire, GL50 3QB
www.thehistorypress.co.uk

British Library Cataloguing in Publication Data.
A catalogue record for this book is available from the British Library.

ISBN 978 1 80399 485 7

Typesetting and origination by The History Press
Printed and bound in Great Britain by TJ Books Limited, Padstow, Cornwall.

FSC
www.fsc.org

MIX
Paper from
responsible sources
FSC® C013056

Trees for LYfe

CONTENTS

PREFACE

The genesis of this book can probably be traced to a boat trip around Portsmouth Harbour during a family holiday when I was nine years old, the event that triggered my lifelong interest in the Royal Navy and naval history; so in one sense, I have been 'researching' the subject matter of *The Naval History of Wales*, consciously or subconsciously, ever since. In the shorter term, perhaps the greatest delight of writing this book has been the opportunity it has given me to explore almost the whole of Wales, rediscovering many places that I had not visited properly for years (Anglesey, for example, and the Radnorshire borderland) and discovering for the first time parts of the country that, shamefully, I had barely or never known: Flintshire, some of the South Wales valleys, and even much of the Llŷn Peninsula. It also provided me with an opportunity to visit all of the county record offices in Wales that hold significant amounts of naval material, namely those of Anglesey, Carmarthenshire, Gwynedd (Caernarfon), Denbighshire, Flintshire, Glamorgan, Pembrokeshire and West Glamorgan. My thanks to the staff of all of these, who were unfailingly helpful, and to those of the other Welsh record offices, who responded promptly to my queries and in some cases sent me photocopies of material. The national repositories provided a huge amount of material for this book, and their staffs generally provided an excellent service. These were the National Library of Wales, Aberystwyth; the National Archives, Kew; the British Library; the Imperial War Museum; the National Maritime Museum, Greenwich; and two institutions whose inclusion in a book of Welsh history may raise an eyebrow or two, namely the National Archives and the National Library of Scotland. My experience, and the valuable discoveries I made in those repositories, should act as a corrective to the assumption, still sometimes encountered in Wales, that the history of the country can be written without venturing across the border, or even beyond one's local library or record office.

One thing that became strikingly apparent to me when writing this book is that almost every community in Wales has a naval hero, even if s/he is sometimes an unsung one; almost every community in Wales has its naval story. Regrettably but inevitably, it has not been possible to include every one of these in a narrative of finite length, and I can only apologise for what some might regard as unforgivable omissions or for a comparative lack of 'column inches' devoted to their particular local hero. Fortunately, several Welsh museums are particularly attentive to their local naval history. Particular thanks to Sue Baldwin of Tenby Museum, who put its marvellous collection of photographs at my disposal, and to Eric Anthony, Brian Jones and Gareth Williams of Holyhead Maritime Museum, who made me welcome and gave me free rein, even though the museum was officially closed that day!

In writing this book, I have incurred a great many debts of gratitude. Lieutenant-Commander Lawrie Phillips, the editor of the splendid *The Royal Navy Day by Day*, was willing to share with me his unrivalled knowledge of Pembroke Dock and commented upon my chapter on the dockyard's history. Others who provided useful information, ideas or support, or who commented on drafts of particular sections, included Professor Huw Bowen, Alexandra Churchill, Dr James Davey, Dr Reg Davies, Martin Gant, Steven Gray, John Harland, David James, David Jenkins, Lyn John, Professor Andrew Lambert, Dr Peter Le Fevre, Captain John Lowe, Sam McLean, Dr Mark Mathews, Professor Steve Murdoch, Alan Phillips, Phil & Rachael Read, Dr Duncan Redford, Inger Sheil, Mrs Ceinwen Williams and Dr Sam Willis. Thanks also to Jo de Vries, my editor at The History Press, for her help in bringing the book to fruition. Finally, as always my biggest thank you is to my partner Wendy, who put up with my frequent disappearances to distant corners of Wales and provided constant encouragement and support.

At 11 a.m. on Sunday 11 November 2012, when I was putting the finishing touches to this book, I stood at the war memorial at Aberdaron on the Llŷn Peninsula and observed the two minute silence. The tide lapped gently on the beach just behind me. It was both idyllic and moving; but as I paid my respects, and remembered in particular all those who had given their lives in naval service, I was also saddened by the fact that I was entirely alone. Or, perhaps, not quite alone: a few yards away, at the edge of the churchyard nearest to the sea, stands the grave of an unknown sailor of the Great War lost on 13 December 1917 when HMS *Stephen Furness*, an armed boarding steamer, was sunk in the Irish Sea. Unlike the vast majority of headstones erected by the Commonwealth War Graves Commission, which are usually of Portland stone, this one is of Welsh slate. It was undoubtedly a particularly appropriate place to end the journey that led to the writing of this book, and to remember all those whose service, and, in many cases, sacrifice, *The Naval History of Wales* commemorates. *Cofiwch*.

David Davies
Bedfordshire
30 November 2012

The original edition of this book was published in 2013 as *Britannia's Dragon: A Naval History of Wales*. This new version takes account of sources discovered, and books and articles published, since 2013 (notably *Wales and the Sea: 10,000 Years of Welsh Maritime History* (Talybont, 2019), published by the Royal Commission on the Ancient and Historical Monuments of Wales), includes new material omitted from the original, and covers developments between 2013 and 2023. I am particularly grateful to Huw Williams for his comments and suggestions and to Peter Schofield for generously sharing his information about 'Warship Weeks'.

David Davies
Bedfordshire
1 August 2023

A NOTE ON TERMINOLOGY
AND CONVENTIONS

Wales is officially a bilingual country, and its native language is one of the oldest in Europe. These two facts create a minefield for any author who ventures into the field of Welsh history, one of the principal dilemmas being – Welsh names or English? In one sense, my response to this dilemma is rooted in my family history: Welsh-speaking mother from a wholly Welsh background, monoglot English-speaking father with a mother from Worcestershire. Consequently, I make no apologies for adopting a strategy that some might find idiosyncratic. As this book is written in English, and likely to be read primarily by an English-speaking audience, I have used the accepted English versions of most place names: so Cardiff not Caerdydd, Fishguard not Abergwaun. I have preferred to use the historic pre-1974 county names rather than those of the bewildering array of petty fiefdoms that succeeded them, so Anglesey rather than Ynys Môn, Pontypridd located in Glamorgan rather than the county borough of Rhondda Cynon Taf, and Breconshire preferred to both the archaic Brecknockshire and the modern Powys. On the other hand, if the Welsh version is so close to the English as to be referring unambiguously to the same place, then I have preferred the former: hence Caernarfon rather than the various anglicised spellings, Llansteffan not Llanstephan, Rivers Tywi and Dyfi rather than Towy and Dovey, and Owain Glyndŵr rather than the Shakespearean version. But ship names have been retained as the British Admiralty coined and recorded them – so HMS *Fisgard*, *Carnarvon* and *Owen Glendower*, the last of which is perhaps the best possible proof that the Royal Navy, *y Llynges Frenhinol*, was not the imperialist, anti-Welsh institution that some have at times assumed it to be.* Throughout, I have attempted to use the form of a name that is most likely to be instantly recognisable to the greatest number of readers, as well as being the one used most frequently in the source material to which this book refers. Throughout, my final criterion has been to adopt the version of a name with which I feel most comfortable. I am entirely prepared for any brickbats that might come my way as a result from certain bastions of the Welsh language, *yr hen iaith*!

Otherwise, I have followed the usual conventions for a book of this kind; in particular, dates prior to 1752 are given according to the Julian Calendar, which by then differed by eleven days from the newer Gregorian Calendar followed in most of Europe.

---

* The frigate HMS *Owen Glendower* served between 1808 and 1884, while HMS *Glendower*, minus the 'Owen', was a major naval training base at Pwllheli during the Second World War. My point is that even today, it seems inconceivable that, say, the French or Spanish navies would ever name warships or important shore establishments after the leaders of failed Breton, Corsican, Basque or Catalan independence movements; even the United States Navy, which has had no difficulty in naming warships *Robert E. Lee* and *Stonewall Jackson*, has baulked at naming one after Confederate President Jefferson Davis, the great-grandson of a Welshman.

INTRODUCTION

There is no part of the Kingdom that, in proportion to its population, contributes more to the British Navy than Wales. Although we live in the mountains, our mountains are high enough for us to see the sea from almost any part of our little land, and there is the eternal fascination of the sea. It is with the greatest difficulty in the world that farmers can keep their sons from going to sea. They can see the steamers and the sailing ships passing to and fro, and there is for these men the eternal attraction of what is beyond the horizon.

David Lloyd George, Prime Minister of the United Kingdom, 1916–22: debate on the closure of Pembroke and Rosyth Dockyards, House of Commons, 11 December 1925.[1]

Wales is a maritime nation. It may not seem so, to those at the heads of the valleys or in the market towns of rural Powys, but nowhere in Wales is more than about 30 miles from the sea or a navigable river and, even in early times, a Welshman in the very middle of his country could probably have reached the ocean's

edge rather more quickly than his contemporary at the equivalent point of England, Scotland or Ireland. In that sense Lloyd
George, the 'Welsh wizard' (or, to some, the original 'Welsh
windbag'), was very nearly correct in his typically flamboyant
comments. True, Wales generally has relatively short rivers, few
of them navigable for any distance. But there were exceptions,
bringing inland areas within reach of the sea. The country's only
true sea-loch, Milford Haven, once permitted shipping to reach
Haverfordwest, deep in the heart of Pembrokeshire. The River
Dee was navigable all the way to Chester; the Dyfi to Derwenlas,
less than 2 miles from Machynlleth in Montgomeryshire; the
Conwy to Llanrwst and the Mawddach almost to Dolgellau.
Trefriw, just 5 miles or so from the heart of Snowdonia, was once
the biggest inland port in Wales. Quite large ships sailed up the
Tywi to Carmarthen until as recently as 1938 and up the Teifi
to Cardigan until 1957. The Usk was navigable to Newbridge-
on-Usk, the Wye to Brockweir easily, to Monmouth for barges,
and even to Hereford in certain conditions;[2] the maritime trade
of tiny Llandogo, above Tintern, still gives its name to the city
of Bristol's most famous pub. Above all, there is the Severn,
Afon Hafren, rising on the slopes of Plynlimon near Llanidloes.
Although most of its navigable course flows in England, the hin-
terland of the Severn's river ports – Lydney, Bewdley, Bridgnorth
and the rest – extended deep into Wales, and the river itself was
navigable as far as Welshpool, albeit with some difficulty. Thus the
Severn gave Welshmen in even some of the remoter areas a highway by which they could escape to new worlds. When William
Owen of Glensevern near Welshpool joined the navy in 1750, he
rode to Shrewsbury, took a wherry to Worcester, then continued
overland to join his first ship at Sheerness before embarking on a
career that ultimately took him to the East Indies and finally to
Canada, where he attempted to create a new Montgomeryshire
on the shores of Passamaquoddy Bay, New Brunswick.[3]

    For those in the littoral, then, the natural viewpoint for many
centuries was to look outward, towards Somerset, Devon and

Cornwall, Ireland, *Ellan Vannin* (the Isle of Man) and Scotland, with the sea acting as a unifier and a highway, not as a divider or barrier.[4] Seaborne journeys were often much easier than those on the overland routes between the north and south of Wales, or into the upland moors of the interior – and indeed, the difficulties of land travel have continued to shape and bedevil much of the economy, politics and linguistics of Wales to this day. It is possible to catch a train from Swansea to England's mightiest dockyard city, Portsmouth, about 170 miles away, and get there four and a half hours later; to get from Swansea to Pwllheli, in the same country and roughly the same distance away, takes up to eight and a half.[5] Consequently, the Welsh have always used the sea. Welsh mariners even have their own patron saint, Cyric, and it is possible that the legend of 'Davy Jones' Locker' had Welsh origins. But Welshmen's seafaring exploits were never as substantial as those of their Cornish or Breton cousins. The legend that Madoc ap Owain, Prince of Gwynedd, discovered America in about 1170, has long been entirely disproved, although as recently as 1953 a memorial commemorating his 'landing' was erected on the shores of Mobile Bay by the Daughters of the American Revolution.[6] Nevertheless, the first major westward voyage of exploration from Bristol, in 1480, was captained by a Thomas Lloyd, and Cabot's historic voyage to the mouth of the St Lawrence in 1497 was skippered by another Welshman, Edward Griffiths; but there seems to be no foundation in the legend that America was named after Richard ap Meryke or Ameryk, a prominent Welsh merchant of Bristol.[7] Perhaps more prosaic, but rather more significant, was the discovery in 2002 of the 'Newport ship', a large craft dating from the 1460s which seems to have traded between Wales and Portugal. Her discovery served as a timely reminder of the long history and profound importance of Welsh maritime trade.[8]

   Many books and articles have been written about the ports and maritime heritage of Wales, and many more about the merchant crews and skippers who sailed trading craft in their own waters

or much further afield.[9] It has been suggested that in proportion to size of population, there were probably more Welshmen
than Englishmen in the Merchant Navy during Queen Victoria's
reign, while in the first half of the twentieth century the Blue
Funnel Line, based at Liverpool, employed so many Welshmen
that it was nicknamed 'the Welsh Navy'.[10] In that sense, again,
Lloyd George was undoubtedly right: in many of the non-
industrialised areas of the country, like the Llŷn Peninsula
from which he hailed, the Cardigan Bay coast and parts of
Pembrokeshire, the sea was the only viable occupation for many
men, both young and old. Many writers have also been drawn to
the peculiar fact that relative to the size of the country, Wales produced a disproportionate number of 'pirates of the Caribbean',
including three of the most famous – or infamous – of them all,
Sir Henry Morgan, Howell Davis and 'Black Bart' Roberts. Yet
the activities of those Welshmen who protected the merchant
ships upon which their countrymen sailed, or who sought to end
the depredations of the pirates (and Barbary Corsairs, Atlantic
slave traders and so forth), have never been properly recounted.

Because Wales is a maritime nation, it follows that it has also
always been a naval nation; or at least, one upon which naval warfare has always impacted. This, too, is simple fact. For example,
few would deny that sea power was undoubtedly one of the most
important factors that ended Welsh independence, first in the
thirteenth and later in the fifteenth century. The Royal Navy has
even shaped the geography of Wales: one town (Pembroke Dock)
was created directly by and for it, another (Nelson in the Taff
Bargoed Valley) was named after its greatest hero, and there was
a Naval Colliery, actually a complex of four pits, at Penygraig
in the Rhondda. Nearly every Welsh town had pubs called the
Trafalgar or the Lord Nelson or the British Tar. Monuments to
naval heroes constitute prominent landmarks from the Menai
Strait and the Tywi Valley to Breidden Hill near Welshpool and
the Kymin at Monmouth. But such indisputable facts seem to sit

awkwardly with the recent history of the country. Nineteenth-and twentieth-century Wales became overwhelmingly a socialist nation – with both a small and a large 's' – and, moreover, a nation that developed a powerful pacifist tradition.* The strong, undeniable military and naval traditions of Wales co-exist uncomfortably with all of this. Thus, at least some Welshmen felt deeply troubled in 1982 when – barely weeks after Wales had declared itself a 'nuclear free zone' – HMS *Glamorgan* flew the *Ddraig Goch* alongside her battle ensigns during the war against Argentina, whose armed forces included some of Welsh descent, the heirs of the one and only true Welsh colony.[11]

Acknowledging the fact that Wales has a long and proud naval history is certainly not a glorification of war. Nor does it condone decisions taken and policies followed in the past that are now deemed unacceptable to some modern sensibilities. Rather, it is an attempt to tell a story that has simply never been told in its entirety; indeed, much of it has never been told at all. Despite recent worthy attempts by academic historians to dispel Wales' 'amnesia' about its military and imperial history,[12] the neglect of the naval dimension has remained glaring. For example, an authoritative recent book entitled *Wales and War* contains precisely one mention of the Royal Navy, and that only in passing.[13] Likewise, an otherwise deeply moving literary anthology on 'Wales and War in the Twentieth Century' contains not one poem about the navy – other than a brief section in a longer piece, and that entirely disparaging in tone.[14] But then, arguably

---

*   It is significant that Scotland has a National War Museum, whereas Wales does not – although it does have a Temple of Peace instead. (The possibility of adding a naval and military section to the National Museum of Wales was debated during the First World War, but was quietly dropped; while a National Museum of the Welsh Soldier opened only in 2010.) The outstanding National Waterfront Museum in Swansea has much on Welsh maritime history as a whole, but has little about naval history other than some Nelson memorabilia and a model of the Pembroke-built gunboat HMS *Janus*.

it was ever thus. In 1919 a book was published entitled *Wales: Its Part in the War*, but it contained not a single mention of the thousands of Welshmen who had served at sea.

This book is an attempt to redress the balance. It tells the story of those Welshmen (and, latterly, women) who served selflessly and courageously in naval forces, firstly of their own land, later those of the union with England and the United Kingdom, as well as in those of other lands, including Australia, Brazil, Chile, India, and above all, both the United and the Confederate States of America. It is the story of the Welsh contribution to the naval struggles against the Spanish Armada, Napoleon and Hitler, as well as those against General Galtieri and Saddam Hussein. It is the story of the ships that bore Welsh names, from the *Dragon* of 1512 to its original namesake HMS *Dragon* five centuries later, and of the Royal Naval Air Stations on Welsh soil. It is the story of the shore facilities in Wales that supported the Royal Navy, and of the thousands of civilians, men and women alike, who worked within them. Finally, it is the story of the part played by Welsh manpower, resources and enterprise in the achievement of British naval supremacy, which – for good or ill – largely shaped the destiny of the world for the best part of two centuries. Welshmen sailed with Drake, Blake and Nelson, as well as with Cook, Franklin and Scott. The strategy proposed by a Welsh naval officer possibly stopped Napoleon Bonaparte conquering Egypt, and perhaps India thereafter. The decisions taken by a Welshman largely determined the outcome of the Battle of Jutland, the single opportunity for a decisive naval victory during the First World War. The last invasion of mainland Britain occurred when French sea power briefly eluded the naval defence of the Welsh coast. Without Welsh-smelted copper, it is debatable whether Nelson would have won at Trafalgar; without Welsh-mined coal, it is arguable whether the Victorian Navy could ever have imposed the *Pax Britannica*.

That is the story told in this book.

ABBREVIATIONS USED IN NOTES

AA	Anglesey Archives, Llangefni
CAS	Carmarthenshire Archives Service, Carmarthen
CSPD	*Calendar of State Papers, Domestic Series* (accessed via both hard copies and online at www.british-history.ac.uk/)
DRO	Denbighshire Record Office, Ruthin
Eames	A. Eames, *Ships and Seamen of Anglesey, 1558–1918* (Greenwich, 1981 edn)
FRO	Flintshire Record Office, Hawarden
GAC	Gwynedd Archives, Caernarfon
GRO	Glamorgan Record Office, Cardiff
HMC	Publications of the Historical Manuscripts Commission
IWM	The Imperial War Museum, Lambeth
Lyon and Winfield	D. Lyon and R. Winfield, *The Sail and Steam Navy List: All the Ships of the Royal Navy 1815–89* (2004)
MM	*The Mariner's Mirror* (published by the Society for Nautical Research, 1914 to date)
MW	*Cymru a'r Môr/Maritime Wales* (published by Gwynedd Archives, 1976 to date)
NLW	The National Library of Wales, Aberystwyth
NMM	The National Maritime Museum, Greenwich
NRS	Publications of the Navy Records Society (1893 to date)
O'Byrne	W. O'Byrne, *A Naval Biographical Dictionary* (3 vols, 1849; modern reprint, Uckfield, n.d.)

ODNB	*The Oxford Dictionary of National Biography* (print edition, Oxford, 2004; accessed principally online at www.oxforddnb.com)
PRO	Pembrokeshire Record Office, Haverfordwest
THSC	*Transactions of the Honourable Society of Cymmrodorion* (1893 to date)
TNA	The National Archives of England and Wales, Kew
WBO	*Welsh Biography Online* (i.e. the online version of the *Dictionary of Welsh Biography*), http://wbo.llgc.org.uk/en/index.html
Winfield 1603–1714	R. Winfield, *British Warships in the Age of Sail 1603–1714* (Barnsley, 2009)
Winfield 1714–1792	R. Winfield, *British Warships in the Age of Sail 1714–792* (Barnsley, 2007)
	WTS: 10,000 Years of Welsh Maritime History, ed. M Redknap, S. Rees and A.Aberg (Talybont 2019)
Winfield 1793–1817	R. Winfield, *British Warships in the Age of Sail 1793–1817* (Barnsley, 2008)

The place of publication for books is London unless stated otherwise.

Notes

1   *Hansard*, HC Deb 11 December 1925 vol. 189, *c*.868.
2   P. Courtney, 'Towns, Markets and Commerce', *The Making of Monmouthshire, 1536–1780* (Gwent County History, volume 30, ed. M. Gray and P. Morgan (Cardiff, 2009)), pp.262–3.
3   NLW MS 14438.
4   See e.g. R.A. Griffiths, 'Medieval Severnside: The Welsh Connection', *Welsh Society and Nationhood: Historical Essays Presented to Glanmor Williams*, ed. R.R. Davies et al. (Cardiff, 1984), pp.70–89.

5   National Rail timetable for summer 2023.

6   G.A. Williams, *Madoc: The Making of a Myth* (1979), passim.

7   A. Davies, 'Prince Madoc and the Discovery of America in 1477', *The Geographical Journal*, 150 (1984), pp.363–72; Griffiths, 'Medieval Severnside', p.88; D.B. Quinn, 'Wales and the West', *Welsh Society and Nationhood: Historical Essays Presented to Glanmor Williams*, ed. R.R. Davies et al. (Cardiff, 1984), pp.90–1.

8   B. Trett, ed., *The Newport Medieval Ship: A Guide* (Newport 2010).

9   Particular mention must be made of the splendid journal *Cymru a'r Môr/Maritime Wales*, published annually since 1976, and of a number of excellent websites, notably the Welsh Mariners index (www.welshmariners.org.uk), the Gwynedd Maritime Database (freespace.virgin.net/r.cadwalader/maritime/maritime.htm) and the Swansea Mariners website (www.swanseamariners.org.uk). (Accessed: 2012).

10 A. Eames, *Machlud Hwyliau'r Cymru/ The Twilight of Welsh Sail* (Cardiff, 1984), p.13.

11 e.g. www.telegraph.co.uk/news/worldnews/southamerica/argentina/9169222/The-Welsh-Argentine-who-fought-the-British.html. (Last Accessed: 2012).

12 e.g. H.V. Bowen, ed., *Wales and the British Overseas Empire: Interactions and Influences*, 1650–1830 (Manchester, 2011).

13 M. Cragoe and C. Williams, eds., *Wales and War: Society, Politics and Religion in the Nineteenth and Twentieth Centuries* (Cardiff, 2007).

14 T. Curtis, ed., *After the First Death: An Anthology of Wales and War in the Twentieth Century* (Bridgend, n.d.), p.244.

1

SEA OF MY FATHERS

TO 1485

The epitome of ancient Roman maritime technology was probably the trireme; that of early modern Spain, undoubtedly the galleon; that of eighteenth- and early nineteenth-century Britain, the mighty first-rate man-of-war. For good or ill, the epitome of Welsh maritime technology is the coracle. Despite its astonishing qualities, the coracle has always attracted scepticism or downright derision. In 1806, the Scottish traveller George Douglas of Tilquhillie described it thus: 'They seem, to a stranger's eye, most unsafe aquatic conveyances, and very unfit to contend with the angry waters of the vasty deep.'[1] Yet the coracle, which probably predated the trireme, has long outlived it, the galleon, the first rate, and countless other much grander craft, and is still in use (just) on Welsh rivers in the twenty-first century. Its survival could be seen to parallel that of Wales itself, together with its ancient language; in the words of Dafydd Iwan's famous song, '*Er gwaetha pawb a pho-peth, ry'n ni yma o hyd*' ('Despite everything and everyone, we're still here').

Cambria Romana: The Roman Navy and Wales

Neither fleets of coracles nor the frenzied incantations of the druids massed on the shore could hope to defend Anglesey against the formidable amphibious assault that the Romans launched against the island in AD 60, seventeen years after the invasion of Britain by the Emperor Claudius. According to the historian Tacitus, General Suetonius Paulinus was determined to crush this notorious seat of rebellion and created a fleet of flat-bottomed boats to ferry his infantry across the Menai Strait and onto the island; the cavalry either forded or swam their horses across. The druids were slaughtered, their sacred groves were cut down, and the Roman Navy's British fleet, the *Classis Britannica*, reigned supreme in the waters around what would eventually become Wales.[2] Over time, the Romans created a sophisticated naval infrastructure in Welsh waters. There were probably squadrons operating from the Dee, based at Chester, and in the Bristol Channel; local legend has it that there was a Roman 'dockyard' at Porthkerry, near Barry, but the evidence for this appears to be slight.[3] Nevertheless, the first forts built in Wales, at Usk, Chepstow and Cardiff, were all clearly sited with an eye to their maritime potential, both as possible naval bases and as locations that could easily be resupplied by sea. The same was also true of the new legionary fortress at Caerleon, begun in the mid-70s AD, of its northern counterpart at Chester, and of the strings of new forts along the coasts of Wales, such as Caerhun and Caernarfon in the north, Carmarthen, Loughor and Neath in the south, and Pennal in the west.[4] In 2011, the remains of a huge Roman port were discovered at Caerleon; to date, the only one identified outside London, and indicative of the scale and significance of the maritime aspects of Caerleon's legionary headquarters.

In later years, the Roman military and naval defences were reorganised to deal with changing threats and circumstances. In particular, attacks from tribes in continental Europe inspired the construction of the 'Saxon shore forts' in the east, probably with naval squadrons operating from them, and raids from Ireland and the Picts to the north led to enhancements to the defences of the Welsh coast, notably the construction of a large new fort at Cardiff shortly after AD 268, possible improvements at Neath and Loughor, and extensive refurbishment at Chester.[5] During the fourth century, these attacks on the Irish Sea coast of Wales became an increasing problem for the Romans. A new fortified landing place was built at Holyhead, and this was supported by a signal tower, now known as *Caer y Twr*, on Holyhead Mountain.[6] Geography and logic alike suggest that there was probably some sort of base for a Roman seaborne presence in Pembrokeshire, to plug the huge gap between Cardiff and Holyhead, but no evidence of it has yet been discovered.[7] Watch towers were built elsewhere – there is some evidence of a line along the North Wales coast[8] – but the loosening of Roman control over Britain, and the eventual withdrawal to the continent prior to the fall of the Western Empire in 410, meant that the tribes of Wales were effectively left to their own devices.[9]

Celts, Saxons and Vikings

Following the Roman withdrawal, a number of new kingdoms arose in the territory that would ultimately become Wales. These were based partly on the old tribal divisions, but they also reflected the abiding influence of Rome: Paternus, the last Roman governor of North Wales, has been identified by some as Padarn, the first King of Gwynedd and possibly the grandfather of the famous Cunedda.[10] In *c.* 429 Gwynedd was invaded by a Pictish fleet which might have made its landfall in the Dee Estuary.[11] There is little firm evidence to suggest that these early kingdoms possessed substantial fleets, although the *Trioedd Ynys Prydein* (Triads of the Island of Britain), the tantalising mixture

of myth and history set down in manuscript form in the Middle
Ages, makes some intriguing but unverifiable claims:

> The three admirals of the island of Britain: Geraint son
> of Erbin; Gwenwynwyn son of Naf, and March son of
> Meirchion, and under each of these admirals six score ships,
> and six score mariners in each ship … the three roving navies
> of the island of Britain: the navy of Llawr son of Eiryf, the
> navy of Divyg son of Alban, and the navy of Dolor son of
> Mwrthach, King of the Isle of Man.[12]

It has been suggested that sixth-century Meirionydd had its own
naval force, and that in 566–67 its king Gwyddno used this fleet
to overrun Gwynedd and Anglesey.[13] By then, and despite the
best efforts of the shadowy King Arthur, the Britons in the main
part of the island were being driven back by the invaders who
would eventually rename the lost territories England. There
were even some early attacks on the new western heartland
of the dispossessed Britons. According to the Venerable Bede,
Edwin, King of Northumbria (616-33) conquered Anglesey and
the Isle of Man, suggesting that he must have possessed considerable naval resources.[14]

The Anglo-Saxon advance ultimately drove wedges between
the Welsh kingdoms and their surviving Celtic cousins, the
Cornish to the south and the men of *yr Hen Ogledd*, the 'Old
North' of the Welsh chronicles; for many centuries their lands in
southern Scotland formed the true 'North Wales', the border of
which was the great rock of *Clach nam Breatann* overlooking the
northernmost shore of Loch Lomond. Direct contact between
these surviving British/Celtic kingdoms must have been undertaken principally by sea, but there is relatively little evidence of
naval activity in the Irish Sea throughout the half-millennium
known misleadingly as 'the Dark Ages'. However, there is ample
evidence to show that a vibrant and deeply interconnected culture developed around the Irish Sea littoral in the centuries after

the Romans left: there were strong trading links and deeply-rooted religious connections, exemplified by active missionary work across the waters. There were also strong political and dynastic ties. The south-western kingdom of Dyfed even had an Irish dynasty for some centuries from the fifth century onwards; but in turn, the Isle of Man had a Welsh dynasty from the fifth century to the eighth.[15] The petty monarchs of Wales, Ireland, Man and southern Scotland formed alliances, intermarried, and, if they were overthrown, readily found refuge and allies in neighbouring realms, which might then provide the springboards for attempts to regain their thrones – attempts that invariably had to be made by sea.[16]

During the ninth century a new, powerful and deeply disruptive element was added to the already complex geopolitics of the Irish Sea. The first recorded major raid by 'Vikings' – specifically, Norwegians or Norsemen – took place at Lindisfarne in 793. Within a few years, the longships were active on the western seaboard of Great Britain and penetrating into the Irish Sea. By 841, the Vikings had established their own kingdom in Dublin and also had a kingdom of the Isles in the Hebrides, both obvious springboards for raids on the Welsh coast. The first serious attacks (or at least, the first recorded ones) began in about 850; a substantial assault on Anglesey in 855 or 856 was repelled by Rhodri Mawr, King of Gwynedd. In 870 Dumbarton, capital of the 'Welsh' kingdom of Strathclyde, was captured by a fleet of Norse longships, and during the years that followed, many exiles from *yr Hen Ogledd* seem to have made their way to Gwynedd. A Viking fleet operating against Alfred the Great wintered in Milford Haven in 876–77 (its leader, Hubba, gave his name to the village of Hubberston), and in 914 another group of invaders who had been expelled from Wessex sought refuge on Flat Holm. By the end of the ninth century, the Vikings had a permanent foothold in Wales; archaeology has revealed significant remains of a Viking settlement at Llanbedrgoch on Anglesey, while there were probably also settlements on the shores of Milford Haven and on the Gower (hence 'Sweyn's Ey', Swansea), all of which were probably concerned principally with trade.[17] But elsewhere, the attacks continued. In 918, Anglesey was ravaged by 'the folk of Dublin'.[18] There were a few decades of relative peace before large-scale attacks were launched against Anglesey again in 954, Holyhead and Llŷn in 961–62, Tywyn and Aberffraw in 963, Anglesey yet again in 968, 971 and 987, St David's and Dyfed in 982, the entire coast from Cardiganshire round to Morgannwg in 988, and on St David's again in 992 and 999.[19]

The Welsh kings were also facing an ominously powerful new neighbour on their eastern land frontiers. By 930, England had been unified, presenting both a potential threat and an attractive opportunity to the native rulers. Hywel Dda, who had recently united Dyfed and Seisyllwg in the south-west into the new kingdom of Deheubarth, paid homage to King Athelstan and in return received the protection of regular cruises by English fleets in the Irish Sea, which kept the coasts of Deheubarth largely free of Norse raids until Hywel's death in 950; it is perhaps no coincidence that his reign, a reign sustained by naval power, is still remembered as one of the most important in Welsh history, a time when just laws were promulgated during an almost unprecedented era of peace.[20] Accepting the overlordship of England might thus have involved some diminution of sovereignty, but arguably the rewards were worth it. This probably explains the extraordinary scene that was played out at Chester in 973. According to some sources, in that year the English King Edgar took a great fleet on a circumnavigation of 'Britain' (possibly the entire island, but more likely just Wales), summoned eight kings to Chester and had them row him upon the Dee as a symbol of his imperial overlordship.[21] Edgar is widely regarded as the 'founder of the Royal Navy', establishing three standing fleets in different parts of his kingdom. The remarkable ceremony at Chester has caused much argument among historians, but it has recently been suggested that from the Welsh point of view, the submission was both a necessary way of recruiting powerful English naval support in response to the recent Norse depredations and a means of bolstering the authority of the weak incumbents of the north Welsh thrones against their many rivals.[22] From the English point of view, of course, it was a vivid demonstration of the imperial pretensions of the monarchs of the newly united kingdom and would ultimately provide the historical justification for the rather more aggressive claims to overlordship made by later kings, notably Edward I.[23] In either event, the huge fleet that Edgar had in the Dee while the ceremony took place constituted both a promise and a threat for the Welsh kings: paying homage to Edgar might place their coasts under its protection; resistance to the English king might see it unleashed against them.

The Welsh Kingdoms, *c*. 1000–*c*. 1200

The Vikings or Northmen were not simply a destructive influence; they could also be potential allies for the Welsh kings and their rivals, who usually preferred to hire fleets from Ireland rather than maintain substantial navies of their own. Inevitably, these naval concerns were particularly important for the two principal maritime kingdoms, Gwynedd in the north-west and Deheubarth in the south-west. For example, in 980 Cystennin ap Iago, King of Gwynedd, recruited Viking support against the pretender Hywel ap Ieauf, devastating Anglesey and Llŷn before Hywel defeated them in battle. Similarly after Hywel ap Edwin, King of Deheubarth, was driven into exile by Gruffydd ap Llywelyn, King of Gwynedd, he returned in 1044 with a fleet of Dublin Vikings. In a naval battle at the mouth of the Tywi, Hywel's fleet was decisively defeated by that of Gruffydd.[24] In 1049 Hywel's successor as King of Deheubarth, Gruffydd ap Rhydderch, joined forces with a fleet of thirty-six Norse-Irish war vessels which sailed up the River Usk, attacking the lands of the King of Morgannwg before turning their attention to England, destroying an army of levies from Herefordshire and Gloucestershire.[25]

Gruffydd ap Llewelyn was involved in many other naval campaigns during his long reign in Gwynedd, and seems to have been a rarity among the Welsh kings in building up a significant fleet of his own, based at Rhuddlan and (perhaps) also at Portskewett in the south.[26] His development of such a force might have been a consequence of his experiences in the first half of his reign, when he faced a succession of threats from enemies who could call upon Irish naval power. A more serious threat than that of Hywel ap Edwin was posed by Cynan ap Iago, heir of Gruffydd's predecessor as King of Gwynedd, who recruited Irish/Norse fleets to assist him in regaining what he regarded as his rightful throne: in about 1040, he led a Dublin fleet and briefly captured Gruffydd before being forced to retreat, while in 1052 another attempt by Cynan to bring a fleet from Dublin against Gwynedd was thwarted by a storm which dispersed the ships.[27] In 1055, Gruffydd ap Llywelyn allied with Aelfgar, the exiled Earl of Mercia, and the two used a fleet of eighteen vessels brought from Dublin for a campaign against the English that culminated in the plundering of Hereford.[28] Three years later, Gruffydd and Aelfgar joined forces with Magnus Haraldsson, heir to the Norwegian throne, who assembled a fleet from the Hebrides, Orkney and Dublin for an invasion of England to reinstate Aelfgar. This is a particularly obscure episode; virtually nothing is known of the campaign other than the outcome, which was the restoration of Aelfgar to his earldom.[29] But Gruffydd's ambitious interventions in English affairs made him a powerful enemy, namely Harold Godwinson, Earl of Wessex (the future King Harold), who attempted to seize the Welsh king in his *llys* (palace) of Rhuddlan. Gruffydd managed to escape in one of his ships, but in the following May, 1063, Harold sailed a fleet around Wales while his brother Tostig attacked overland, a campaign that culminated in the death of Gruffydd, the destruction of his fleet, and the presentation of the prow of his ship as a trophy to King Edward the Confessor.[30] Gruffydd ap Llywelyn was perhaps the most naval-minded of all the early Welsh rulers, but ultimately it was superior English naval power that brought about his downfall.

At first, the Norman conquest of England in 1066 seemed to make relatively little difference to the Welsh kings, who continued their traditions of murderous petty feuding aided and abetted by mercenary war fleets. In 1075, a dynastic quarrel saw Gruffydd, son of Cynan ap Iago and claimant to the throne of Gwynedd, recruit a fleet of Dublin Norse, together with some Normans from Rhuddlan, and land at Abermenai. After initial success he was defeated near Clynnog Fawr and forced to retreat, sailing first to the Skerries and then to Wexford. Gruffydd, who had a Dublin Norse mother, was particularly keen to call on the assistance of Viking fleets. He did so again in 1076 or 1077, making another landing at Abermenai, and in 1081 he invaded once more with a fleet of Irish and Dublin Norse, this time landing near St David's. There he joined forces with Rhys ap Tewdwr, the recently deposed King of Deheubarth; their armies went on to victory in the Battle of Mynydd Carn, about a day's march from the cathedral city.[31] In 1087, Gruffydd went to Orkney, recruited a fleet of twenty-four ships and sailed into the Bristol Channel, devastating the church of Saint Gwynllyw (now Newport Cathedral). When Gruffydd's erstwhile ally Rhys ap Tewdwr was deposed in the following year he, too, went over to Ireland, assembled a fleet and returned, regaining his throne and giving an 'immense treasure' to the Irish and Scots seamen who had assisted him.[32] Brought up in Dublin and imbued with Viking attitudes (to the extent that his lifestyle was regarded as Norse, not Welsh), Gruffydd ap Cynan clearly had a particularly keen understanding of the potential of the longships, but this probably explains why he preferred to rely on them rather than following the example of his hated predecessor, Gruffydd ap Llywelyn – the man who had denied his father the throne of Gwynedd – in continuing and developing a tradition of native Welsh naval power. After Gruffydd's death in 1137, his sons followed their father's example in calling upon Norse Irish fleets to aid them in campaigns against the Normans and each other. Fatally, then, Gwynedd's policy continued to be based on the assumption that there would always be friendly naval forces somewhere in the western seas that could be called upon to come to the kingdom's aid.

Meanwhile, the customary Viking raids on the Welsh coast continued as before. Bangor was attacked in 1073, St David's in 1073, 1080 and 1091. But the Normans, too, were soon showing a serious interest in Wales: William the Conqueror's pilgrimage to St David's in the same year as the Battle of Mynydd Carn was probably undertaken as much for reconnaissance as reverence. In 1098, Hugh the Proud, Earl of Chester, and Hugh the Stout, Earl of Shrewsbury, launched a massive invasion of the north. Gruffydd ap Cynan retreated to Anglesey and, adopting his familiar strategy, awaited the arrival of a relief fleet from Ireland. This duly appeared, but promptly accepted the significantly larger bribe offered by the Normans and defected. Gwynedd seemed to lie at the enemy's mercy, but fortuitously at that moment a fleet commanded by Magnus Bareleg, King of Norway, appeared off Anglesey. The Normans foolishly attacked it, Magnus retaliated, and Hugh the Stout was killed in a sea battle in 'Anglesey Sound', after which the Normans retreated.[33] Norse fleets remained active in the Irish Sea, and raids on the Welsh coast continued intermittently, until the middle of the twelfth century. Thus it is likely that the Norman castles which were built in the early 1100s to guard every river mouth in South Wales (Ogmore, Kidwelly, Laugharne and the rest) were originally conceived just as much to defend against Norse seaborne depredations as attacks by the native Welsh.

The Conquest

The Norman annexation of South Wales was a gradual process taking more than a century and a half. It was arguably more a slow absorption than a conquest, and was by no means a story of steady and inevitable Norman triumph: the tremendous onslaught of 1093 which came close to obliterating the Welsh kingdoms entirely was followed by a marked native revival in the second third of the twelfth century, which saw large areas wrested back from Norman control.[34] Nevertheless, the old, vulnerable eastern kingdoms of Brycheiniog and Morgannwg disappeared (in about 1070 and 1090, respectively), and even mighty Deheubarth in the south-west lost much of its coastal land, particularly in what had been Dyfed and which ultimately became Pembrokeshire. Sea power played relatively little part in all of this and, indeed, at sea the Normans were much weaker than their Saxon predecessors had been.[35] But there were exceptions, and some surprising reverses for the newcomers. In 1157, Henry II's fleet sailed from Pembroke and attacked Anglesey, but it was repelled off Tal-y-Foel by the forces of Owain Gwynedd (king from 1137–70). Henry attacked Wales again in 1165, hiring a fleet from Dublin, shipping supplies up the Severn to Shrewsbury and sending ships to relieve beleaguered castles like Neath, but once again poor organisation and strategy culminated in English defeat.[36] Meanwhile, some of the Norman Marcher lords were beginning to behave in very much the same way as Welsh kings had always done. In 1102, for example, Arnulf de Montgomery of Pembroke rebelled against Henry I and formed an alliance with the Irish king Muirchertach O'Brian, who commanded the fleets of Dublin and Waterford.[37] William Marshall, Earl of Pembroke, again recruited an Irish fleet for an attack on his Welsh neighbours in 1223.[38]

Pembrokeshire, remote from England, dependent chiefly on the sea and thus in some ways a semi-independent world of its own – the 'Little England Beyond Wales' that survives to this day – also provided the English with a springboard for an ambitious naval expedition against a foreign land, albeit one that would ultimately have far more abiding and disastrous consequences even than the conquest of Wales. In 1171, King Henry II came to Milford to lead an expedition into Ireland, only two years after the first Norman intervention in the country. Henry's landing at Waterford was the first occasion when an English king set foot on Irish soil, and was effectively the beginning of the English crown's long and fateful involvement in Irish affairs. Before embarking, Henry had met with the 'Lord Rhys', ruler of Deheubarth, at Newnham on the Severn and then again at Pembroke to agree a detente which was probably intended to protect the flank of the English expedition as it made its way to Milford to embark.[39] Henry's expedition marked the beginning of Milford's long history as one of the principal ports of assembly for English fleets transporting armies into Ireland. His son John sailed from there with armies in 1185 and, as king, in 1210; further royal expeditions from Milford to Ireland took place under Richard II in 1394 and 1399.

Meanwhile, Gwynedd established its hegemony over the remaining native kingdoms of Wales. Owain ap Gruffydd, known as Owain Gwynedd, the son of Gruffydd ap Cynan and king from 1137–70, took advantage of the relative weakness of Powys and Deheubarth at his accession to make himself the unchallenged principal Welsh ruler. On his death, that mantle passed to Rhys of Deheubarth, but in the early years of the thirteenth century Llywelyn ap Iorwerth, 'the Great', re-established the pre-eminence of Gwynedd, a primacy that was retained under his son Dafydd (reigned 1240–46) and grandson Llywelyn, 'the Last' (reigned 1246–82). By the mid-thirteenth century, though, Wales faced a new and perilous strategic situation at sea. The Irish and the Dublin Norse were no longer the forces they had been – the kingdom of Dublin had been eradicated by the Normans in 1171 – and the decisive defeat of the Norwegians by Alexander III, King of Scots, at Largs in 1263, followed by their expulsion from Man and the Hebrides, meant that the Welsh rulers could no longer hope to recruit friendly fleets to defend them against the English.[40] Without the shield of their traditional naval allies, the Welsh coastline's vulnerability to blockade was all too apparent. An early foretaste came in 1212 when King John sent twenty galleys to harry the Welsh coast, a powerful statement of intent directed against his son-in-law Llywelyn of Gwynedd, who had joined a rebellion against him.[41] If they wished and could afford to concentrate their resources, the English could operate ships from the south-western peninsula, Chester, Lancashire and Ireland, effectively surrounding Wales and potentially throttling every harbour in the country. In that sense, the apparent triumph of Llywelyn of Gwynedd in the Treaty of Montgomery (1267), when he was recognised by the English king as 'Prince of Wales',[*] was always illusory; the failure to build up a Welsh naval tradition, and the over-reliance on allies who no longer existed or cared, meant that conquest was only a matter of time. Even so, it took the English some time to realise the strength of their position. In 1277, Edward I deployed a substantial fleet of twenty-seven large ships based at Chester, most of them drawn from the Cinque Ports of south-east England, and used them to seize Anglesey, thus depriving Llywelyn and Gwynedd of the vital grain harvest. During the final English onslaught in 1282, an even larger fleet was used to seize Anglesey, but an attempt to attack across a pontoon bridge on the Menai Strait ended in disaster and one of the last Welsh victories before the death of Llywelyn at Cilmeri, the final defeat of his brother Dafydd in the following spring, and the obliteration of Welsh independence.[42]

The majority of the huge new castles with which Edward ringed and intimidated the conquered Welsh heartland reflected

---

[*] In Wales, 'prince' – principal ruler – was seen as a higher title than 'king', the latter having been devalued by the proliferation of petty 'kings' throughout the country.

the realities of sea power. Aberystwyth, Flint, Conwy and Caernarfon occupied coastal sites and could be readily resupplied from the sea. Harlech was given an astonishing fortified stairway, the 'way from the sea', which descended the cliff to the shore-line, whose benefit was proved during the Wars of the Roses when the castle withstood a seven-year siege (1461–68), the longest in British history and the inspiration for the battle hymn 'Men of Harlech'. Rhuddlan received a purpose-built dock, and the River Clwyd was canalised for 2 miles to allow seagoing vessels direct access to and from it. Finally, Beaumaris, begun in the aftermath of the great Welsh revolt of 1294, was given both a site that dominated the eastern entrance to the Menai Strait and a sophisticated dock immediately adjacent to the gatehouse. On the other hand, the castles might have looked impressive (as they still do), but in many respects they were largely useless – in isolated locations that did not actually control the surround-ing territory at all. This was demonstrated during the revolt of 1294, when naval forces far larger than those deployed in 1277 and 1282 had to be diverted from Gascony 'to save the king's white elephants from slaughter; the entire overseas empire was put at risk to preserve garrisons of 26 men in Harlech and 30 in Criccieth'. [43] It was also demonstrated by the subsequent history of Harlech. The reason why it was the last of Owain Glyndŵr's fortresses to fall, why the siege of the 1460s lasted so long, and why it was the last fortress in England and Wales to hold out for King Charles I in the first civil war of the 1640s, was that there was simply no point in wasting men, money, weapons and ships in attempting to take a fortress that looked spectacular but which served no strategic purpose whatsoever.

The Last Wars of Independence

Welsh mariners have always been independent-minded; some might even say obstreperous. Early evidence of this came in 1336 when some of them refused to serve the English crown, which had commandeered their ships for service against the Scots and French, unless they were paid in advance for the entire summer's service. This event, which has been described as 'the earliest known withdrawal of labour in the principality, if not Britain', probably centred on ships requisitioned at Beaumaris and Conwy. It led to an effective capitulation by King Edward III, whose evident desperation to get the Welsh ships into action against the Scots overrode any concerns about the creation of a dangerous precedent.[44] Indeed, the crown genuinely feared that Wales was in imminent danger of invasion from the forces of the Scottish King David II. In the previous year, 1335, Owen de Montgomery and Philip de Clanvowe were appointed to organise the defence of the south, the former dealing with preparations on land and the latter with those at sea. Clanvowe requisitioned eight ships for coastal defence, two each from Carmarthen, Swansea, Tenby and Haverfordwest, converting them for naval warfare. The *Nicholas* and *Blithe*, the ships at Swansea, were taken up for ninety-six days, the masters receiving 6*d* a day and the sailors 3*d*; but they never actually left harbour, and the threat of invasion rapidly receded. Nevertheless, Welsh ships were taken up in a similar way at regular intervals during the English crown's interminable wars during the fourteenth century.[45] Naval raids on the Welsh coast continued, too: in 1346, four Genoese galleys full of 'Saracens' (Turks) were harrying the coastline of North Wales, having been hired by King Philip VI of France. Such attacks were barely distinguishable from the frequent depredations of pirates of many nationalities that were endemic during the Middle Ages.[46] The responses to these depredations included the lighting of beacons along the coast and a strategy that foreshadowed the naval policies of six centuries later – the organising of merchant vessels into convoys accompanied by armed escorts.[47]

By now the Welsh had a formidable military reputation, albeit one founded on extreme and random violence which horrified

both chroniclers like Froissart and even some of their own commanders.[48] Many thousands served the English crown during its
Scottish campaigns and the 'Hundred Years' War' against France,
and in an age when the dividing line between land and sea warfare was still somewhat blurred, a significant number served
during what we would now define as naval operations. During
the 1360s, one of them became convinced that he was destined to
be none other than Wales' national deliverer as foretold in bardic
prophecy. Owain ap Thomas ap Rhodri, by-named Owain
Lawgoch, was grand-nephew in the male line to Llywelyn the
Last, and thus the sole surviving direct heir of the royal house of
Gwynedd. He defected to the French, whose king, Charles V,
accepted his pretensions and gave him a fleet and an army which
set out from Harfleur for Wales in December 1369, only to be
dispersed by winter storms. He launched another invasion
attempt from France in 1372, but the expedition succeeded only
in ransacking Guernsey before being diverted by the French to
attack La Rochelle, then in English hands.[49] Owain subsequently
served the French on land, his ambitions of returning to Wales as
a liberating prince increasingly remote, until he was assassinated
by an English spy in 1378.

The next, and rather more successful, candidate for the role of
Welsh national redeemer was the gentleman of Glyndyfrdwy,
now in Denbighshire, who on 16 September 1400 was proclaimed Prince of Wales by a small circle of his friends and
countrymen. Owain Glyndŵr, a descendant of the old kings of
Powys, had served the English crown in war and had participated
in naval warfare, taking part in the Battle of Cadzand off the
Dutch coast in 1387. He seems to have had a clear understanding of the importance of sea power to the prospects of Welsh
survival, and took steps to neutralise the overwhelming English
advantage at sea that had proved fatal during the previous wars
of independence. Above all, Glyndŵr reverted to the practice of
the earlier kings of Gwynedd by seeking to secure powerful naval
assistance from foreign powers. In 1401, Scottish ships appeared

in the Menai Strait and helped the rebels to seize Conwy. The Scots briefly took Bardsey, although one of their ships was chased all the way to Milford.[50] In October 1403, French ships under the 'pirate' Jean d'Espagne were off Kidwelly, and they continued to operate in Welsh waters until April 1404. In July of the same year Owain concluded a formal alliance with King Charles VI. More French ships duly appeared in the Irish Sea, and the results were momentous. The English depended heavily on their ability to resupply their garrisons by sea, the northern castles from Chester, the southern ones from Bristol, with some reliance also on the sea routes from Ireland.[51] Criccieth Castle, which had survived a Welsh siege in 1294 because it could be resupplied by sea, fell to Glyndŵr in 1404 precisely because its supply lines were now cut off. It was followed in short order by Aberystwyth and the mightiest white elephant of them all, Harlech, which became the jewel in the crown of the Glyndŵr rebellion and the seat of the prince's court. In August 1405, a large French fleet of some 120 ships under Jean de Rieux arrived in Milford Haven from Brest, bringing 2,600 soldiers to support Glyndŵr's army. The Franco-Welsh host took Carmarthen and then invaded England, ultimately confronting Henry IV's army at Woodbury Hill in Worcestershire, while Rieux's ships blockaded Tenby and sailed up the Severn to support the army.[52] But a land battle never took place, and the English king fought back. A fleet was assembled from the Cinque Ports and placed under the command of Lord Berkeley, who brought it into the Bristol Channel. Fifteen French ships were destroyed and others fled; it was only with difficulty that the French mustered enough vessels to evacuate their army in 1406.[53]

The assistance of the French fleet was crucial to Glyndŵr's hopes, but the Welsh also took their own initiatives in naval warfare. In 1403, Henry Don, Glyndŵr's swashbuckling lieutenant in south-east Carmarthenshire, captured a Llansteffan merchant's ship at Carmarthen.[54] But the principal effort to create a native Welsh naval force seems to have been due to the somewhat unlikely figure of David Perrot, an elderly merchant of Tenby, treasurer-chancellor of the county of Pembroke and a man only recently entrusted by the crown with provisioning its Welsh castles by sea. Moreover, Perrot was the grandson of an Englishman and seems to have moved almost exclusively in Anglicised circles, yet he threw in his lot with the cause of Welsh independence. But Perrot seems to have been a loyalist of the deposed King Richard II (whom Glyndŵr had also served loyally) and might have helped to arrange the king's Irish expedition from Milford in 1399, so it is possible that his revolt was caused more by dislike of the new usurping regime of Henry IV than any great patriotic sentiment on Perrot's part. He went over to Glyndŵr in the spring of 1403, and within a year he was preparing ships to take on the English at sea. It is somewhat unclear where he operated them from, as his native Tenby, along with Haverfordwest and Pembroke, remained in English hands throughout, but Milford Haven was probably large enough to shelter a rebel fleet well away from the beleaguered English garrisons.[55] Perrot's 'fleet' can only have operated for a very short period of time, and there seems to be no record of its successes or failures (if any), but it probably has some claim to be the only true 'Welsh navy' in the country's history.[56]

Y Mab Darogan

Just before sunset on 7 August 1485, a fleet of ships entered Milford Haven. The vessels made their landfall on the north side of the great waterway, between Dale and St Ann's Head. The leader of the expedition came ashore at Mill Bay, a narrow defile between the cliffs. Behind him came some four to five thousand men, mostly French (or, to be precise, mostly French jailbirds) leavened with a thousand or so Scots and some four hundred English exiles. It was quite clearly a foreign army intent upon conquest, but it was a mightily unconvincing one: a contemporary claimed that it would have been difficult to find a more unimpressive coterie,[57] and it had before it the unfortunate precedent of Jean de Rieux's calamitous defeat in the same waterway eighty years earlier. Nevertheless, the invading army's leader, Henry Tudor, Earl of Richmond – an obscure Lancastrian claimant with a virtually non-existent claim to the throne, but who had still audaciously proclaimed himself the rightful King Henry VII of England – is said to have knelt down, sung the forty-third psalm and kissed the soil of his native land.[58] For by landing in Milford Haven, Henry was literally coming home. He had been born in Pembroke Castle twenty-eight years earlier; moreover, he was the heir of the ap Tudurs who had fought for Glyndŵr, and many Welshmen perceived him to be *y mab darogan*, the son of destiny foretold by the bards. They were useful cards to play as Henry marched through Wales under his red dragon standard, gradually recruiting supporters among his countrymen, invading England, and ultimately winning an unlikely victory over King Richard III at Bosworth in Leicestershire. The English had once imposed a Prince of Wales upon the reluctant Welsh, but now it seemed as though the Welsh had turned the tables in the most spectacular fashion imaginable by placing a Welshman upon the throne of England. As if to emphasise the point, the red dragon now took its place opposite the lion as a supporter of the new Tudor dynasty's royal coat of arms.

Notes

1 National Library of Scotland, MS 10439, fo. 108.

2 Tacitus, *Annals*, XIV, xxix–xxx.

3 D.J.P. Mason, *Roman Britain and the Roman Navy* (Stroud, 2003), pp.30, 117; E. Evans et al., 'A Third-Century Maritime Establishment at Cold Knap, Barry, South Glamorgan', *Britannia*, 16 (1985), pp.57–125.

4 Mason, *Roman Navy*, pp.90, 96, 123–6.

5 Mason, *Roman Navy*, pp.170–3.

6 Mason, *Roman Navy*, p.183; M Redknap, 'Late Roman Coastal Defences', *WTS* 84–5.

7 J. Roche, 'Roman Pembrokeshire', *Journal of the Pembrokeshire Historical Society*, 5 (1992–3), pp.5–13.

8   Mason, *Roman Navy*, p,183.

9   D. Leedham, *In Defence of the Empire: Roman Gwynedd 398–1301* (Chester, 2010), pp.45–6, 66.

10   Leedham, *Roman Gwynedd*, pp.49–74.

11   Leedham, *Roman Gwynedd*, pp.80–94.

12   R. Bromwich, 'Trioedd Ynys Prydain', *THSC* (1969, Part 1), pp.133, 138.

13   Leedham, *Roman Gwynedd*, pp. 190, 320–3.

14   D. Rollason, *Northumbria, 500–1100: Creation and Destruction of a Kingdom* (Cambridge, 2003), pp.42–3.

15   P. Mac Cana, 'Ireland and Wales in the Middle Ages: An Overview', *Ireland and Wales in the Middle Ages*, ed. K. Jankulak and J.M. Wooding (Dublin, 2007), p.20.

16   MacCana, 'Ireland and Wales', p.24.

17   M. Redknap, 'Viking-Age Settlement in Wales: Some Recent Advances', *THSC* (2005), pp.5–35.

18   T. Jones, ed., *Brut y Tywysogion – Red Book of Hergest* (Cardiff, 1955), p.11.

19   C. Etchingham, 'Viking Age Gwynedd and Ireland: Political Relations', *Ireland and Wales in the Middle Ages*, ed. K. Jankulak and J.M. Wooding (Dublin, 2007), pp.150–8; I. Jones, 'Môn's "Black Gentiles": Anglesey and the Vikings', *Anglesey Antiquarian Society Field Club Transactions* (2004), pp.49–51.

20   N.A.M. Rodger, *The Safeguard of the Sea: A Naval History of Britain, vol. 1, 600–1649* (2004), pp. 427–8 (although Rodger wrongly identifies Hywel as a king of Gwynedd).

21   T. Clarkson, *The Men of the North: The Britons of Southern Scotland* (Edinburgh, 2010), pp.184–5.

22   S. Matthews, 'King Edgar, Wales and Chester: The Welsh Dimension in the Ceremony of 973', *Northern History*, 44 (2007), pp. 22–4.

23   G. Molyneux, 'Why Were Some Tenth-Century English Kings Presented as Rulers of Britain?', *Transactions of the Royal Historical Society*, 21 (2011), pp. 67–75.

24   T. Jones, ed., *Brut y Tywysogion – Red Book of Hergest* (Cardiff, 1955), p.25.

25   K. Maund, *Ireland, Wales and England in the Eleventh Century* (Woodbridge, 1991), p. 164.

26   M. and S. Davies, *The Last King of Wales: Gruffydd ap Llywelyn, c. 1013–63* (Stroud, 2012), pp.87–90.

27   B.T. Hudson, 'The Destruction of Gruffydd ap Llywelyn', *Welsh History Review*, 15 (1991), p.342; Davies, *Last King of Wales*, pp.44–5.

28   Davies, *Last King of Wales*, pp.54–61.

29 K. DeVries, *The Norwegian Invasion of England in 1066* (Woodbridge, 1999), pp.140–1.

30 Hudson, 'Destruction of Gruffydd ap Llywelyn', pp.337–8.

31 S. Duffy, 'Ostmen, Irish and Welsh in the 11th century', *Peritia*, 9 (1995), p.395; Jones, 'Môn's "Black Gentiles"', pp.51–3.

32 T. Jones, ed., *Brut y Tywysogion – Red Book of Hergest* (Cardiff, 1955), p.31; J.L. Evans, 'The Viking raid on St. Woolos', *Gwent Local History: The Journal of Gwent Local History Council*, 90 (2001), pp.3–7.

33 Maund, *Ireland, Wales and England*, p.169; Jones, 'Môn's "Black Gentiles"', p.53. S Smith, 'The Battle of the Menai Strait', *WTS*, 96–7

34 R.R. Davies, *The Age of Conquest: Wales 1063–1415* (Oxford, 2000), pp.34–55.

35 Rodger, *Safeguard*, p.49.

36 Rodger, *Safeguard*, pp.40–1.

37 Rodger, *Safeguard*, p.40.

38 Gruffydd, 'Sea Power', p.30.

39 R. Turvey, *The Lord Rhys: Prince of Deheubarth* (Llandysul, 1997), pp.54–8.

40 Rodger, *Safeguard*, pp.74–5.

41 K.L. Gruffydd, 'Sea Power and the Anglo-Welsh Wars, 1210–1410', *MW*, 11 (1987), p.29.

42 Gruffydd, 'Sea Power', pp.35–42; Rodger, *Safeguard*, pp.78–9.

43 Rodger, *Safeguard*, p.77.

44 K.L. Gruffydd, 'The Mariners' Strike of 1336 in North Wales', *Llafur*, 7 (1997), pp.15–20 (quotation from p.15).

45 J.R. Alban, 'The Impressment of Two Ships at Swansea for the Defence of South Wales, 1335', *Gower*, 29 (1978), pp.67–71.

46 K.L. Gruffydd, 'Piracy, Privateering and Maritime Wales during the Later Middle Ages (part 1)', *MW*, 24 (2003), p.33 and passim.

47 Gruffydd, 'Piracy, Privateering and Maritime Wales (part 2)', *MW*, 25 (2004), pp.13–5.

48 A.D. Carr, 'Welshmen and the Hundred Years' War', *Welsh History Review*, 4 (1968–9), pp.22–3, 35.

49 A.D. Carr, *Owen of Wales: The End of the House of Gwynedd* (Cardiff, 1991), pp.23–4, 27–37.

50 R.R. Davies, *The Revolt of Owain Glyn Dŵr* (Oxford, 1997), p.190.

51 R. Griffiths, 'Prince Henry's War: Armies, Garrisons and Supply during the Glyndŵr Rising', *Bulletin of the Board of Celtic Studies*, 34 (1987), p.171.

52 Gruffydd, 'Sea Power', p.50.

53 Rodger, *Safeguard*, pp.114–5.

54 Davies, *Revolt of Owain Glyn Dŵr*, p.200.

55 R.K. Turvey, 'David Perrot: A Pembrokeshire Squire in the Service of Glyndŵr', *THSC* (1990), pp.65–82.

56 Although there is one reference, of dubious provenance, to Llewelyn the Last having a fleet: Gruffydd, 'Sea Power', p.35.

57 Quoted by C. Carlton, *This Seat of Mars: War and the British Isles, 1485–1746* (New Haven, 2011), p.1.

58 R.A. Griffiths and R.S. Thomas, *The Making of the Tudor Dynasty* (Stroud, 1985), pp.129–31.

2

'FROM THE WELSH, GOOD LORD, DELIVER ME'

1485–c. 1688

The very notion of a 'British Empire' defended by a powerful Royal Navy is seen by some as a malevolent phenomenon that emerged gradually between the seventeenth and nineteenth centuries, and many in Wales have comforted themselves by regarding it as an alien, primarily English, creation that was essentially inimical to Welsh traditions and aspirations: in other words, nothing to do with us.

Not so. The term 'British Empire' was coined at a precise moment in time, a six-day period in August 1576, by one man: a Welshman. Moreover, he was a Welsh wizard, too, or at least a mystic, astrologer, mathematician and alchemist. Sitting in his library at Mortlake, surrounded by books and manuscripts appropriated from dissolved monasteries, John Dee, London-born scion of a Radnorshire family named Ddu and a descendant of Rhodri Mawr (or so he claimed), produced in those six summer days a work entitled the '*Pety Navy Royall*, devoted to the Brytish monarchie and its Incomparable Islandish Empire'.[1] In 1578, Dee wrote a further manuscript entitled *Brytannici Imperij Limites* (*The Limits of the British Empire*). These works advocated a strong permanent navy as the means by which Elizabethan England could acquire territories around the world; or rather reacquire them, for Dee attempted to convince his readers that this would be merely the re-creation of the great empire once established by King Arthur and Prince Madoc. Dee might have been something of a charlatan, but there can be no doubt that his idea of a British Empire guarded by an invincible fleet drew heavily upon Welsh tradition and culture as he understood (or invented) it. In turn, he directly inspired many of the great seafarers of the age, notably Raleigh, Frobisher, Hakluyt and John Davis, and although his projects were far beyond the resources of the Elizabethan state, his thinking contributed greatly to the development of an early 'imperialist' mentality.[2]

Officers and Men [I]

One of the first Welshmen to command at sea in the Tudor period was Sir Matthew Cradock of Swansea, a prominent royal official and merchant. In 1483, he was commanding a 'ship of war' for King Richard III, albeit using it for a piratical attack on a Breton vessel lying off Ilfracombe, and thirty years later the ship he had named after himself, the *Matthew Cradock* (one of several that he owned) was taken up for service during Henry VIII's first French war.[3] In 1543, the veteran soldier Rice Mansell of Oxwich was the king's vice-admiral in the west, and in July of that year he commanded six ships which encountered eleven French vessels in the narrow seas, capturing one of them.[4] There were probably Welshmen in the crew of Henry's famous warship, the *Mary Rose*, when she sank in the Solent in 1545. At the time of writing (October 2012), a detailed scientific examination was being carried out at Swansea University on the remains of archers found in the wreck; the formidable reputation that Welsh archers had acquired during such battles as Crecy and

Agincourt makes it a reasonable assumption that at least some of those aboard the *Mary Rose* were from the Principality.

When the Spanish Armada set sail in 1588, intent upon deposing the granddaughter of Henry Tudor, Welshmen formed part of the resistance. There is a persistent tradition (albeit one doubted by modern historians) that Piers Griffith of Penrhyn commanded a ship from Beaumaris that joined Drake's fleet at Plymouth, where the great Devon seaman entertained him and commended his loyalty and spirit.[5] The vice-admiral, Sir William Wynter, was Brecon-born and descended from a family that had been established in the county for centuries, although his more immediate antecedents were in Bristol. By 1588 he was already an old man, but he set out against the Armada in the *Vanguard* (two of his sons joined him in the campaign) and may well have been the man who proposed the fireship assault on the Spanish fleet as it lay at Calais.[6] But there were Welshmen on the other side of the Armada campaign, too, and one of them achieved a belated celebrity status in Victorian England. This was David Gwyn, reputedly a galley slave aboard the great *Vasana* (or, to be accurate, *Bazana*). When, in 1860, the American historian J.L. Motley published his book *The United Netherlands*, which swiftly became an international bestseller, he included a dramatic account of how the *Vasana* encountered a terrible storm in the Bay of Biscay and witnessed the sinking of one of her consorts, the *Diana*. The captain, knowing Gwyn's reputation as a seaman, asked him to save the vessel, which he proceeded to do; but on a pre-arranged signal, his fellow slaves then rose up, produced weapons that they had made in secret from slivers of wood and so forth, killed the soldiers and took over the galley. Realising that something was badly wrong with the *Vasana*, one of her consorts attacked her, but Gwyn and his allies promptly boarded and captured this other galley. He then steered the two vessels to Bayonne, thus depriving the great Armada of their services in the battle to come.

The story was taken up by Sir Lewis Morris of Carmarthen, a poet regarded in his own time as second only to Tennyson and who would almost certainly have become Poet Laureate but for Queen Victoria's disapproval of the fact that he was not actually married to the mother of his three children. In 1887, Morris penned a poem entitled 'David Gwyn', one of his 'Songs of Britain', which concluded by presenting its hero as nothing less than the saviour of his country (on the basis that the galleys might have tipped the scales in favour of the Armada). Unfortunately, the dramatic story was nothing more than a wilful fabrication on Gwyn's part. He was aboard the *Diana*, not the *Vasana*; she did not sink in the open sea but reached Bayonne, only to run aground in the harbour approaches; and there was certainly no slave mutiny. Far from organising a heroic takeover of the galley (a story which begs such obvious questions as why the slaves were unchained and how they managed to fashion so many weapons without being noticed), Gwyn and some others sneaked away overland and somehow managed to get back to England. He was then sent to Ireland to interrogate prisoners from the Armada ships wrecked on that coast, but was soon expelled as 'a liar, a thief, and a lewd person'. Gwyn made his way to the Netherlands and there probably started to spin the increasingly tall tales that eventually found their way into Dutch sources, then to Motley, and so eventually to Morris, who was comprehensively fooled.[7]

The iconic status of the Spanish Armada often clouds popular perceptions of a war which still had sixteen long and often desperately unsuccessful years to run. The naval campaigns of the period 1588–1604 frequently involved combinations of the monarch's ships and those set out by private individuals; sometimes the latter embarked on more or less illegal expeditions on their own account. With the boundaries between state naval enterprise, privateering and downright piracy still somewhat blurred, the opportunities for enterprising 'sea dogs', including Welsh ones, were legion. Regardless of whether he did or did not take part in the Armada campaign, by 1600 Piers Griffith of Penrhyn was regarded as a 'notable pirate', bringing a rich Spanish prize laden with oil, silk and olives into Abercegin near Bangor. His subsequent depredations were indiscriminate enough to lead to his arrest and the confiscation of his lands.[8] Richard Nash, a Carmarthen merchant and possible ancestor of 'Beau' Nash, commanded a ship during Drake's disastrous expedition to Portugal in 1589.[9] William Myddelton of Llansannan embarked on a privateering career in the same year, and captured several exceptionally lucrative prizes; it was said that the cargo purloined from one of them enabled Myddelton and another Welsh privateer, Thomas Prys, to be the first men to smoke tobacco publicly in London. At much the same time, Myddelton was writing substantial amounts of Welsh poetry. He completed a major book of metrical psalms at Escudo de Veragua, Panama, in 1596 while accompanying Drake and Hawkins on their fateful Caribbean expedition, but died shortly afterwards.[10]

The early Stuart period was the golden age of the Welsh naval officer: the Principality produced a stellar succession of bold and successful captains. Unfortunately, they flourished during a period that is unanimously regarded as one of the most mediocre and unsuccessful in the whole of British naval history, and as a result, the names of some of Wales' finest seamen are now largely forgotten. Robert Mansell, one of the greatest of them all, was a younger son of Sir Edward Mansell of Margam Abbey, Glamorgan.[11] Mansell was related by marriage to Thomas, Lord Howard, a cousin of the Lord High Admiral who led the fleet against the Spanish Armada. In 1591, Howard commanded a privateering voyage to the Caribbean and gave a ship to the 20-year-old Mansell, who evidently found the experience to his liking. In 1596, he commanded a ship during the Earl of Essex's expedition to Cadiz, being knighted by Essex for his part in the action, and in the following year he served as the earl's flag captain. In 1601, Mansell was admiral in the western approaches, capturing six vessels laden with Portuguese goods, and in the following year he became Admiral of the Narrow Seas. In September 1602, his ships intercepted six Spanish galleys, driving them into the clutches of a waiting Dutch fleet, which destroyed them. The accession of James I seems to have encouraged Mansell to pursue political ambitions, and in 1604 he became both a gentleman of the Privy Chamber and Treasurer of the Navy, thus placing half the principal offices of the navy in the hands of Welshmen (Sir John Trevor of Trefalun and Plas Teg was the Surveyor). He became an MP, acquired the monopoly on glass production in 1615, and in 1618 was appointed Vice-Admiral of England, the honorary deputy to the Lord High Admiral. Mansell weathered charges of corruption against him and in 1620 was given command of an expedition against the Barbary Corsairs of Algiers, the first major British naval intervention in the Mediterranean. Mansell reached Algiers in November and succeeded in releasing a few of the prisoners, but sickness and shortage of victuals forced him to retire to Spain. He returned to Algiers in May and launched an attack on the harbour, but this achieved little and he was recalled to England soon afterwards. A substantial body of letters describing the Algiers expedition that Mansell wrote to his nephew, Henry Rice of Dynevor (Dinefwr), is held at the county record office in Carmarthen, and these tend to confirm the longstanding critical view of the early Stuart Navy. Mansell experienced endemic administrative incompetence and corruption, and always had to look over his shoulder in case hostile factions at court might be undermining him in his absence.[12] Mansell subsequently fell out with his former patron, the Duke of Buckingham and, although he acted as an important adviser on naval matters through the 1630s, he did not hold command at sea again. He was too old for active service when the Civil War broke out, although it was believed that he still had great authority among the seamen; he died in 1652.[13]

One of those who sailed with Mansell was Sir Sackville Trevor of Trefalun, Denbighshire, brother of Sir John, the Surveyor of the Navy. He first commanded in 1595 and took part in the Cadiz expedition of the following year, rising to be vice-admiral in 1602 when he took four valuable prizes off the Spanish coast. In 1623, he possibly saved the life of the future King Charles I when the latter was Prince of Wales:

> On 12 September Charles, having dined on board the *Prince*, returned to Santander after dark. Seeing that the wind and tide were sweeping his boat out to sea Trevor floated a buoy with a rope attached from the stern of his own ship, which the prince's party seized, rescuing Charles from a perilous situation.

In 1627, he commanded a squadron blockading the Elbe, subsequently capturing a powerful French warship at Texel – the sole naval success of Charles I's disastrous simultaneous wars against France and Spain. Thereafter, Trevor continued to act as an adviser on naval affairs until his death in 1635.[14] He was a contemporary of Sir William St John of Highlight (Uchelolau), Barry, who commanded the *Advantage* in 1607–09. St John was also an associate of Raleigh, a colonial adventurer in Virginia and Guinea, and a relative by marriage of the king's future favourite, the Duke of Buckingham. Trevor, St John and Mansell were prominent examples of the 'gentlemen' captains given commands by the Stuart monarchs, and several other younger sons of Welsh gentry or aristocratic dynasties followed in their footsteps during the seventeenth century.

Thomas Button of Worlton, Glamorgan, entered the navy shortly after Trevor, distinguishing himself in command of a ship blockading the Spanish-held harbour of Kinsale in 1601. Button displayed considerable personal courage several times in his career, once rowing back and forth under fire to inspire the besiegers attacking a rebel-held Scots castle, but otherwise his naval service was remarkable chiefly for quite astonishing levels of corruption:

He exploited successive commands to line his own pockets, keeping his crew under strength to benefit from surplus wages and victuals. This was a common fraud among captains, but Button acquired a reputation for being especially greedy. In December 1605 he also harboured aboard his ship a notorious pirate, whom he permitted to escape and from whom he received two chests of sugar, which he smuggled ashore and sold for £42.

In 1612–13, Button commanded an expedition sent to discover the North-West Passage, surviving a fierce winter by eating white partridges, and subsequently commanded on the Irish coast and as rear-admiral to Robert Mansell during the Algiers expedition of 1620. But Button received very little pay for any of his service and often had to victual his crews from his own pocket, so by the mid-1620s his finances were in desperate straits; he mortgaged his Welsh lands but almost lost them when he was unable to make the repayments, and far from providing the back pay due to him, the Admiralty brought a new set of corruption charges against him. Sir Thomas Button died in 1634, his career a microcosm of the staggering naval failings of the early Stuart period. It was hardly surprising that Button and many others helped themselves when the system was so badly broken; perhaps it is more remarkable that he continued to serve the crown for so long, risking his life several times in the service of a state that treated him so shabbily.[15]

Button was followed into the service by his nephew Captain William Thomas, who, unusually for a Welsh sea officer, commanded warships for Parliament during the Civil War. Thomas Herbert of Montgomery commanded the *Marmaduke* in the Algiers expedition of 1620–01 and the *Assurance* in 1625–26, but he failed to obtain the promotion he craved and sank into a long and melancholic retirement.[16] Sir Henry Stradling of St Donat's was at sea on privateering expeditions in the 1620s and took command of his first royal warship in 1631 before commanding large ships in the Ship Money Fleets of the 1630s.[17] Stradling was forced to leave his command in 1642 when his crew mutinied in favour of Parliament; he then served on land during the Civil War, fighting in the north of England, being captured at the Battle of Rowton Heath (1645) and later joining the South Wales revolt during the Second Civil War of 1648.[18] Stradling then joined Prince Rupert's Royalist fleet based in Ireland, and in April 1649 was appointed by Rupert to command a powerful squadron of four ships with orders to attack Commonwealth shipping; but he died not long afterwards and is said to have been buried at Cork.[19] Rather fewer Welshmen seem to have commanded under the Commonwealth and Protectorate, although Robert Coytmor of Caernarfonshire served as secretary to the Admiralty from 1649, becoming an active and highly regarded figure, and Colonel Philip Jones of Llangyfelach, one of the dominant figures in South Wales politics during the Interregnum, was appointed a commissioner of the Admiralty in December 1653.[20]

Naval Administration

The reigns of Henry VII and his successors opened up new realms of possibilities for ambitious Welshmen. Many flocked to London, seeking opportunities at court or in the machinery of government. The latter included an expanding and increasingly important navy: Henry VII authorised the construction of the first English dry dock at Portsmouth in 1497; Henry VIII established new dockyards at Deptford and Woolwich, built large prestige warships like the *Mary Rose*, and instituted a new form of naval administration under a group of principal officers, the Controller, Treasurer, Surveyor and Clerk of the Acts. In 1598, John Trevor of Trefalun, brother of the naval captain Sir Sackville Trevor, was appointed Surveyor of the Navy, holding the office until 1611. He had started out as secretary to Lord

Howard of Effingham, the admiral who led the fleet against the Armada, and it was Howard's influence that led to his appointment as Surveyor. John was knighted in 1603, one of the hordes to be so honoured following James I's accession.[21] His time in office was marred by serious accusations of corruption, and these have more or less clung to his reputation ever since. Trevor was the principal target of an enquiry into naval maladministration in 1608 and had to seek the king's pardon, but there seems to have been little different about Trevor's conduct in the office of Surveyor to that of many of his predecessors.[22]

Kendrick Edisbury of Marchwiel was another Welshman who prospered in the Stuart naval administration. He began as a clerk to his neighbour Sir John Trevor, and although both were accused of corruption during an enquiry in 1608, no action was taken against them.[23] Edisbury subsequently became deputy governor of the Chatham Chest, the pension fund for seamen, and in 1618 became paymaster of the navy. He gradually built up a reputation for competence that contrasted markedly with the dire ineptitude of the Navy Board and was appointed Surveyor of the Navy in 1632, working tirelessly to root out corruption. But the post of Surveyor was traditionally held by an experienced shipwright who could assess the merits of new ship designs and order appropriate repairs to old ones. Edisbury lacked such a background, which meant that his time in office was also characterised by several important failings – notably his failure to spot the defects in the new second rate *Unicorn*, which needed substantial modification before it was seaworthy. He bought up a significant estate in North Wales but spent little time there, dying at Chatham in 1638. A memorial to him survives at the dockyard town's St Mary's church; Samuel Pepys was once scared witless by the legend that the chamber he was occupying in Chatham Dockyard was haunted by Edisbury's ghost.

Edisbury established something of a Denbighshire dynasty in the naval administration. His son John followed him into the Navy Office, but subsequently developed a more enduring career as a lawyer.[24] Kendrick's great-grandson Richard worked at the newly established Plymouth Dockyard in the 1690s and was desperate to secure the place of clerk of the ropeyard, despite the machinations of Commissioner Greenhill to obtain it for his own son-in-law. His quest for promotion was not unconnected to the fact that he was smitten with a Plymouth merchant's daughter and needed the increased salary to impress his potential father-in-law. Richard mobilised his family and got them to intercede for him with Denbighshire's greatest figure, Sir John Trevor, Speaker of the House of Commons. He even suggested, somewhat impertinently, that Trevor 'might be moved to visit the Comm[issione]rs of Adm[iral]ty at their office & when sitting at the board (which office lies in Sir John's way home, he passing by the door every day in his way to and from the Parliament)'.[25] Edisbury's efforts had at least a partially happy outcome. He did indeed obtain the post of clerk of the ropeyard, but the success or otherwise of his pursuit of the merchant's daughter is unknown.

The Civil War

Civil war broke out in England and Wales in 1642, but it was already well under way elsewhere in the British Isles. Ireland had erupted in revolt in 1641, and this made Wales of exceptional strategic significance for both king and Parliament. Welsh ports would be vital to Parliament if it wished to send armies to crush the Catholic uprising, and to the king if he sought to bring over those same rebels to assist his cause. Initially, it seemed as if Charles had the advantage. Wales was overwhelmingly Royalist and a major recruiting ground for the king's army, but there were small pockets of Parliamentarian support, notably in south Pembrokeshire – including, crucially, Milford Haven. Prince Rupert's capture of Bristol in July 1643 made Parliament's retention of Milford even more essential. Two Royalist ships, the *Fellowship* and *Hart*, arrived in the Haven on 3 August, followed shortly afterwards by a small Parliamentarian squadron returning from Ireland under the command of Vice-Admiral William Smith. There was a brief engagement which ended with the *Fellowship* being taken and the *Hart* run aground and abandoned. This success was more than offset by the disastrous news that the Royalists had taken Tenby. Admiral Richard Swanley, who brought the rest of Parliament's Irish Guard into Milford Haven on 28 August, promptly moved round the coast and lay off Tenby with a formidable squadron of three large frigates – the *Bonadventure*, *Swallow* and *Leopard*, together with six smaller ships – but a bombardment of the town proved futile, and Swanley withdrew. Meanwhile, Parliament's garrison in Pembroke, and its control of Milford Haven, was threatened by a new Royalist fort at Pill, close to the future site of the town of Milford.[26]

On 23 January 1644, Swanley's fleet entered the Haven again, anchored off Pill Fort, and exchanged fire with it. He then deployed two hundred of his seamen to support Colonel Rowland Laugharne's troops in capturing some outlying royalist garrisons. Encouraged by this success, on 22 February he began an ambitious amphibious assault on Pill Fort. Under cover of night, 250 men were ferried across to Newton Noyes and set up a two-gun battery there. The *Swallow* and Swanley's flagship *Leopard* anchored off the west side of the Pill, the *Prosperous* and *Leopard Merchant* off the east, and began a sustained bombardment. Meanwhile, Laugharne moved his men and five field guns to Steynton before advancing on the fort itself on the following day. The pincer attack culminated in the surrender of Pill Fort and the two Royalist ships in the Pill. Swanley then sent three ships under Smith to make another attack on Tenby. The bombardment began on 7 March and lasted for three days. Finally, the main gate through the town walls was stormed by seamen from the *Crescent* and *Swallow*, followed by Laugharne's cavalry. Tenby's fall meant that the whole of Pembrokeshire was back under Parliamentary control. Milford Haven was safe for Swanley's fleet and could serve once again as a base for operations in Ireland, against the Royalist stronghold at Bristol, and ultimately as the foothold from which the Parliamentarians could break out to conquer South Wales.[27]

The strategic importance of North Wales to both sides increased in the autumn of 1643 when King Charles signed a truce with the Irish rebels. Control of the sea passage between Dublin and Chester and Beaumaris became critical, and initially the Royalists held the upper hand. Two thousand troops sailed in eleven ships from Ireland for Beaumaris in November 1643, but bad weather drove them to the Dee Estuary, where the army landed near Mostyn. The convoy was commanded by the Royalist sea captain Baldwin Wake, who subsequently used Beaumaris as a base for his operations and made what were regarded as excessive demands for victuals on the people of the port. By the spring of 1644, Parliament was able to mount a more effective blockade of North Wales' harbours, and their ability to do so was further enhanced when Liverpool fell to them in June. The king's response was to appoint the highly capable sea captain Sir John Mennes as Governor of North Wales, based at Beaumaris, but he proved ineffective in the role, simply antagonising the leading local power-brokers. Following the king's defeat at Naseby in June 1645, the position of the Royalists in North Wales became hopeless, and they finally negotiated surrender terms with the Parliamentarians.[28] Nevertheless, Harlech Castle held out until March 1647, and nominally Royalist Irish privateers continued to operate in Welsh waters until Cromwell's campaign of 1649–50 largely destroyed Irish resistance; the future Lord Protector sailed from Milford Haven in August 1649 at the beginning of a campaign that culminated in the notorious assaults on Drogheda and Wexford.

Parliament's victory in the first Civil War was followed by a bitter falling out among the victors. This culminated in the outbreak of a new war in the spring of 1648, and South Wales was one of its principal theatres. The garrison at Pembroke declared for the king, followed by that at Tenby, and the solitary Parliamentary warship in Milford Haven, the *Expedition*, could do nothing to resist the revolt. Admiral John Crowther's squadron was ordered to the Welsh coast and blockaded Tenby.[29] Parliament's army won an important victory at St Fagan's on 8 May, but Oliver Cromwell himself had already been despatched to take command against the Welsh rebels, and early in June he laid siege to Pembroke. However, his siege guns had been lost in the Severn, so he had to take guns from the warship *Lion* in Milford Haven. They had the desired effect: Pembroke surrendered on 11 June, bringing an end to hostilities. However, desultory naval warfare in Welsh waters continued for some time. In March 1650, John Robinson of Monachdy, Anglesey, and Gwersyllt, Denbighshire, who had served as a lieutenant-colonel in the king's cause, attempted to turn Bardsey into a royalist privateering base, but his efforts came to nothing. Royalist ships operating from the Isle of Man continued to trouble the coast of North Wales until the island's surrender in October 1651.

Arguably the very last engagement of the British Civil Wars took place off Mumbles and at Swansea in March 1660. On the ninth the small Royalist privateer Henrietta Maria, commanded by Captain George Dowdall and sailing under a commission that had been issued by James, Duke of York (the future King James II) at Brussels in the previous July, came into the anchorage. Dowdall was unaware that King Charles II had been proclaimed in London on the previous day and proceeded to capture several ships within Swansea Bay. Complainants hastened to Cardiff to demand action from Colonel Edward Freeman, governor of the castle there. Freeman immediately despatched soldiers to the Mumbles, and went down himself on the following day. He informed Dowdall of the astonishing developments in London, and Dowdall immediately agreed to restore the prizes he had recently taken, and not to attack any more shipping. There matters rested until about the fifteenth, when the fifth frigate Lichfield (24 guns) sailed into Mumbles Road. She was an altogether different proposition to the relatively small Henrietta Maria. Her captain, William Barker, gave the order to open fire, and the Henrietta Maria cut her anchor cable and sailed for the mouth of the River Tawe. The Lichfield pursued her, firing all the time. The Henrietta Maria anchored at Swansea Quay, but still the Lichfield followed. The Royalist ship now cut her other anchor cable and sailed even further upstream, where the larger Lichfield could not follow. The Henrietta Maria sailed 'above the town', but then 'stuck at the Point' and could go no further. Barker sent some forty to sixty men ashore, heavily armed with cutlasses and muskets. They boarded the ship, stripped the crew (beating some of them in the process), broke open chests and boxes, and pillaged the money on board. Barker subsequently sent the Henrietta Maria to Plymouth as a prize. The affair at Swansea was one of the first things that crossed the Duke of York's desk during his earliest days in office as Lord High Admiral, and he ordered Barker to ensure that the contents of the Henrietta Maria were not embezzled (wishful thinking, as the ship had obviously been cleared out at Swansea) and that it should be placed in safe custody.[31]

Officers and Men [II]

After the Restoration, King Charles II and his brother James, Duke of York (Lord High Admiral, 1660–73; later King James II & VII) again encouraged younger sons of royalist aristocratic and gentry families to enter the navy, although their objective was now overtly political: they hoped to enhance the political reliability of an officer corps that consisted principally of veterans who had been commissioned by Cromwell and the Commonwealth regimes.[31] The rise of this new generation of 'gentleman captains' provided opportunities for Welsh families, albeit not to the same extent as in the early Stuart period. One of the first to benefit was Arthur Herbert, a son of Sir Edward Herbert of Aston, Montgomeryshire, King Charles I's solicitor-general, who entered the navy in 1663 and became a captain in 1666, aged about 19.[33] He distinguished himself during the second and third Dutch wars, subsequently (in 1679) becoming admiral of the fleet operating in the Mediterranean against the corsairs of Algiers. Although undoubtedly brave and competent, Herbert was also arrogant, outspoken and remarkably immoral, even by the standards of the Restoration: his cousin Lord Herbert of Cherbury once warned him that his faults were 'of as many ton as your vessel',[34] and he made an inveterate enemy of Samuel Pepys, whose denunciation of Herbert still largely affects posterity's assessment of him.[31] Crucially, however, he kept the favour of the king. When Herbert offered to pay some of the fleet's expenses out of his own pocket, the Secretary of State, Sir Leoline Jenkins of Llantrisant, remarked 'this a Welshman can do'.[35] In 1682, he secured a peace with Algiers that would endure until 1816, and returned home in triumph, becoming the first holder of the honorific post of Rear-Admiral of England.

In 1687, Herbert astonished the political world by refusing to agree to the Catholic King James II's scheme to remove the legal penalties against his co-religionists, despite the fact that his dependence on the income from his offices and the king's favour was common knowledge. This sudden manifestation of Herbert's previously little-glimpsed conscience led to his dismissal and to a period of exile with his family in Wales, but in 1688 he secured his place in history by playing a pivotal part in the 'Glorious Revolution'. Dressed as a common seaman, he carried to William of Orange the letter from several prominent politicians that invited the Dutch prince to invade England; he then commanded William's invasion fleet, which made landfall in Torbay on 5 November. James' flight and William's accession to the throne led to honours being showered on Herbert.

He became First Lord of the Admiralty, and after a drawn battle against the French in Bantry Bay in May 1689, he was created Earl of Torrington. But on 30 June 1690, his fleet encountered the French again, in the English Channel off Beachy Head. Herbert's combined Anglo-Dutch fleet suffered heavy losses and retreated up the Channel, a strategy that Herbert justified by coining the expression 'a fleet in being': in other words, the French could not invade or take other decisive action as long as he kept his force intact. Even so, the king and public opinion was furious. The government was desperate to make Herbert a scapegoat in order to divert attention from its own part in the fiasco, but the court martial that tried him consisted largely of officers who had risen under his patronage. He was acquitted, but King William's displeasure ensured that it was a pyrrhic victory. Herbert never served at sea again, spending a long retirement on his Surrey estates and dying in 1716.

Other Welsh captains of the Restoration age included Arthur Laugharne, who held five commands between 1661 and 1665 (including, appropriately, that of the *Pembroke*). He was the son of the Parliamentarian army officer who had played an important part in securing South Wales for Parliament before changing sides in 1648 and holding Pembroke Castle against Cromwell.[36] His son Arthur also rose to command, but was killed in 1667 when commanding the *Colchester* in action against a French ship in the West Indies. Charles Royden of Isycoed, Denbighshire, had a career distinguished only by the extraordinary saga of his command of the frigate *Sweepstakes* in 1677–78: the chaplain was a drunken card-cheat with a penchant for cavorting naked in public with his equally naked wife, while Royden was accused by his Irish lieutenant of having called him 'spy, knave, rascal, and Irish dog and toad ... to which I replied ... that I was no more an Irish toad than he a Welsh one ...'[37] David Lloyd of Ffosybleiddiad, Cardiganshire, commanded five ships between 1677 and 1689, supposedly obtaining his first command by bribing a servant of the king's mistress, the Duchess of Portsmouth.[38]

He followed James II into exile and became Groom of the Bedchamber to the former king at the palace of Saint-Germain. Lloyd also became an active Jacobite conspirator, attempting to 'convert' the Admiral of the Fleet, Edward Russell, although he eventually returned to Britain and lived quietly in London.[39]

It is likely that several other Welshmen commanded warships in the second half of the seventeenth century. No fewer than five Joneses held captains' commissions, along with a Richard Griffith, but no definitive Welsh connections have been established for any of them. Other Welsh gentlemen served at sea without formal rank. When the second Anglo-Dutch war broke out in 1665, many aristocrats and gentlemen flocked to volunteer to serve in the fleet; one of them was Sir Edward Broughton of Marchwiel, a veteran soldier, drinker and debauchee, who was killed at the Battle of Lowestoft on 3 June 1665.[40] John Williams of Edwinsford, near Talley, is commemorated by a memorial high on the wall of Saint Peter's church, Carmarthen, which records that he 'behaved himself with resolution worthy of a gent[leman] in an action eminent for its inequality of seven Algerines against one single ship, the *Kingfisher*'. This refers to an engagement against the Barbary Corsairs in May 1681, when the *Kingfisher* (an early 'Q-ship', a warship disguised as a merchantman) came under attack off the coast of Naples; her captain was killed, but despite the odds, the Algerine squadron was successfully fought off.

Contrary to popular mythology, the majority of men serving in the sailing navy were usually volunteers, rather than pressed men – certainly during the late seventeenth and eighteenth centuries, albeit rather more so in peacetime than in wartime. Even at Trafalgar, perhaps only a sixth of British seamen were pressed, and the proportion of pressed men on individual ships during wartime from the 1660s through to 1815 varied from perhaps 5 to 45 per cent, very rarely exceeding 50 per cent, depending on a wide range of factors such as the location of the ship, the popularity of the captain, the time of year, the condition of both the war and the national economy, and so forth.[41] The navy might have been a harsh and perilous environment, but it provided a much more substantial daily diet than that available ashore, reasonable pay (even if payment was often tardy) and, in wartime, the chance of enriching oneself through prize money or promotion. Although there was as yet no naval uniform, sailors were usually kitted out from a standard list of slops, and this included one peculiarly Welsh item that became ubiquitous throughout the 'Navy Royal' – the Monmouth cap, a knitted woollen cap manufactured exclusively in the town, which was the standard headgear of the British naval sailor throughout the Restoration period. That said, the picture was not entirely black and white. Many men 'volunteered', and thus qualified for joining bounties, rather than running the risk of being pressed; it was very much a case of bowing to the inevitable and making the best of it. And when the navy expanded rapidly, as it did at the start of each war, the proportion of pressed men always increased rapidly as ships sought to make up their numbers.

During the seventeenth century, and on even into the nineteenth, men joined individual ships rather than the navy *per se*. Thus seamen often volunteered to serve under captains whom they knew and trusted, usually men who were well known in their home areas or who had built up a strong reputation for treating their crews well. Welsh captains, like those from other parts of the British Isles, often had their own 'followings', volunteers who would accompany them from ship to ship.[42] When men needed to be pressed, it was customary until the eighteenth century for local authorities to raise a set allocation laid down by the Privy Council (a process quite separate from the more familiar 'press-ganging' carried out by ships' officers). In 1678, for example, an order was raised to recruit 10,160 men in this way, of whom 380 were to be drawn from South Wales and 280 from the north. These figures compare quite favourably with those of obviously maritime counties in England (for example, Essex and Sussex, which were also allocated 380 each, and even Cornwall, allocated 370).[43] The great problem affecting Welsh recruitment was the country's distance from the principal dockyards and theatres of naval warfare, particularly during the Anglo-Dutch wars when the focus was principally on the North Sea. In 1678, men from the south were sent to Portsmouth and those from the north to Hull or London, and simple geography might therefore have been as considerable a disincentive to naval service as perceptions of bad pay, poor victuals and harsh discipline. Geography also made it relatively easy to evade the press: by June 1672, only sixty-five men had been pressed by the vice-admirals in North Wales because so many men had simply disappeared into remote inland areas. Language created another barrier. In March 1665, 200 pressed Welshmen arrived at Portsmouth, but many of them could not speak English; nor could one of the eleven men from Wrexham (itself an unlikely source of naval seamen) who were pressed in 1672.[44]

Direct pressing by ships' captains was somewhat more successful. In 1678, 100 men were sent from Milford and another 150 from Swansea, the latter being said to have gone 'with a strange cheerfulness'. Welshmen could also be recruited outside Wales, especially if the merchant ships on which they were serving were intercepted by a pressing tender or were in a port where a 'hot press' was in force.[45] Many of these Welsh volunteers and pressed men fell victim to naval warfare or to those even less discriminating killers, storm and disease. Richard Evans of Lledrod, Cardiganshire, perished aboard the flagship *Royal Charles* at the Battle of Texel on 11 August 1673, and Joseph Vaughan of Llanelli, able seaman aboard the *Lion*, was killed during the same engagement. Both were entitled to bounties for death in service, which were paid to their widowed mothers in their hometowns.[46] Wounded seamen were entitled to charity from the Chatham Chest, the navy's system of outdoor relief. In 1675, only three Welshmen were recorded among the 632 pensioners, rather fewer than the number present at several fairly small English towns (such as Gravesend and Deal), but this was probably an inevitable consequence of geography; distance made it difficult for Welshmen to apply for, and to receive, such bounty.[47]

The Name of the Dragon: 'Welsh' Warships

Famously, King Charles II had no legitimate children, although he fathered a large brood of royal bastards, the eldest of whom was James Scott, offspring of the king and a comely Pembrokeshire wench named Lucy Walter. In November 1662, the boy was created Duke of Monmouth, and in quick succession during 1666–67 two warships were named *Monmouth* after the youth who would eventually become known as 'the Black Duke'. One was a royal yacht, assigned for the young duke's personal use; the other, a 66-gun third rate ship-of-the-line launched at Chatham in 1667, had a far more distinguished career, fighting in twelve battles before finally being broken up a century after she was first built. The two *Monmouth*s were among the first warships to perpetuate Welsh place names. The sixth rate *Pembroke* had been launched in 1655, named less after the town than Cromwell's successful siege of its castle in 1648. Even so, it retained its name under the restored Stuarts, who were after all descendants of the Tudor king born in Pembroke Castle, and was lost in a collision in Torbay in 1667. The name *Cardiff* was given to a renamed Dutch prize, taken in 1652; the ship was sold in 1658 and the name was not used again for over 250 years. The name of the 22-gun sixth rate *Fagons*, launched in 1654 and named after the Parliamentary victory at St Fagans near Cardiff in 1648, was evidently considered less politically correct after the Restoration, so she was swiftly renamed *Milford*. In 1667, a 54-gun fourth rate named *St David* was launched at Cornpill near Lydney in the Forest of Dean, which formed part of the port of Chepstow. She remained in service until 1690, serving in home waters, the Mediterranean and the Caribbean; probably her finest hour came in 1672 when she led the expedition that captured Tobago from the Dutch and carried out a number of other operations in the West Indies.[48]

In 1647, the navy launched what was already its fourth warship named *Dragon*, following ships of 1512, 1542 and 1593.

Built at Chatham, the *Dragon* took part in the principal actions of the first two Anglo-Dutch wars and was commanded by Arthur Herbert in the Mediterranean from 1669–72, before being rebuilt in 1690. She then served throughout the French wars, serving principally in the Mediterranean and West Indies in that of 1689–97 and in the Channel and North Sea in the War of the Spanish Succession. She was finally wrecked off Alderney in 1711.[49] Meanwhile, Wales had become the graveyard for one of the most iconic ships of the Restoration age. The *Mary* was the first British royal yacht, a gift to Charles II from the city of Amsterdam upon his restoration. By 1675, she was serving as a despatch vessel between Dublin and Holyhead or Dawpool, near Chester, but on 25 March she was wrecked on the Skerries. Her remains were discovered in the 1970s, and subsequent excavations brought up a wide variety of finds, including nine of her guns, the ship's anchor, silver sword guards, hilts and pommels, shoes, rings, silver spoons, coins, ceramics, a pewter chamber pot and a skull.[50]

The Welsh Tradition of Piracy and the Naval Defence of Wales

Relatively remote from central authority, comparatively unguarded, and yet sitting astride some busy shipping lanes, the Welsh coast was both an attractive stopover and a lucrative target for enemy raiders in both war and peace. It was also home to pirates of the home-grown variety, who often operated with at least the tacit co-operation of the local authorities.* Their 'pedigree' can be traced back far into the Middle Ages, when

---

* Technically, piracy lies outside the scope of this book, but it would be remiss to omit it entirely. The subject has been covered in impressive detail by Terry Breverton in *The Book of Welsh Pirates and Buccaneers* (St Athan, 2003).

the Marcher Lordships often provided safe havens for 'ship thieves'.[51] By the sixteenth century, the likes of Bardsey, Caldey and St Tudwal's Road were the haunts of local pirates, and eminent figures like the Bulkeleys and Wynns in the north and Sir John Perrot in the south-west were accused of being implicated in, or even actually instigating, pirate attacks from which they allegedly profited.[52] Probably the most notorious Welsh pirate of the Tudor age was John Callice, a former haberdasher's apprentice from Tintern. After spending a short period in the navy under Sir William Wynter and Sir John Berkeley, Callice was active as a pirate for roughly a decade from 1574 to 1585, exploiting to the full his many connections among the gentry and civic elites of South Wales.[53] He operated off the Welsh coast but also as far afield as France, often bringing his prizes into Cardiff or Newport, where the local authorities more or less openly colluded with him.[54] During 1586–87, over half a dozen pirate ships were operating off Wales, raiding ships passing to and from Ireland and then disposing of the goods at Milford Haven, Carmarthen and Cardiff, again probably with the collusion of the local authorities.[55] The stories of Callice and the comradeship of the maritime outlaws must have entered local and even family folklore.[56] Sir William Morgan, Vice-Admiral of Monmouthshire and thus nominally a royal official tasked *inter alia* with suppressing piracy, was actually one of Callice's principal accomplices and a beneficiary from his depredations. He was also a relative of the notorious 'pirate of the Caribbean' Sir Henry Morgan, who would be born at Llanrumney in 1635. Perhaps such tales even reached Little Newcastle, a small village off the beaten track a couple of miles from the main road between Haverfordwest and Fishguard, where the infamous buccaneer Bartholomew Roberts – 'Black Bart' – was born in about 1682.

The Welsh coast and shipping lanes were also frequently visited by raiders from further afield. In 1537, Breton and French vessels were said to be plaguing the coast, robbing ships 'and coming on land to steal sheep'.[57] In 1610, Thomas Salkeld briefly declared Lundy a pirate kingdom with himself as its monarch, using it as a base to attack both coasts of the Bristol Channel. During one attack on Milford Haven, he burned much of the village of Dale.[58] During the 1620s and 1630s, many pirates and corsairs from Dunkirk, St Malo, Biscay and North Africa plagued the coasts of south-west Britain and Ireland, some of them again occasionally using Lundy as a temporary base for their operations. Anglesey and other coastal areas regularly requested naval protection, but rarely received it. The veteran Glamorgan captain Sir Thomas Button, commanding the tiny *Ninth Whelp*, was at Holyhead in 1631, and in 1633 he was suc-ceeded in the same ship on the same station by the scholarly Captain Thomas James from Wern-y-Cwm near Abergavenny, who cruised the Irish Sea and occasionally escorted convoys to Milford and Bristol. But Button, James and their successors had an impossible task: there were too few ships to patrol too large an area, while the likes of the *Ninth Whelp* were much less nimble than the craft they were meant to capture, so many of their pursuits of pirate ships proved fruitless.[59]

The problem of pirate incursions into Welsh coastal waters remained an issue throughout the seventeenth century. Sallee Rovers, from the pirate republic in Morocco, were said to be operating in the seas around Lundy in 1635, while in 1684 the Basque pirate Fermin de Alberro anchored in Welsh waters prior to seizing a richly laden ship just out of Bristol.[60] During the 1630s, such raids provided the justification for King Charles I's imposition of 'Ship Money', which was nominally intended to pay for additional naval protection against piracy but which the king's opponents believed was to form the basis of a system of non-parliamentary taxation. Perhaps because they suffered more directly and more frequently from pirate activ-ity, Welsh counties proved rather more enthusiastic to pay the controversial exaction than some of their English counterparts, particularly those inland counties where political opposition to the king was strong: Monmouthshire paid all its charge for 1635 by Christmas of that year, while in 1638 the arrears of South Wales and North Wales were 1.8 per cent and 2 per cent, respectively, compared with 45 per cent in Herefordshire, 54.5 per cent in Warwickshire and a whopping 64.6 per cent in particularly obstreperous Bedfordshire. In 1639, when payment had virtually collapsed throughout huge swathes of England, North Wales still paid 61.6 per cent of the amount demanded of it, very nearly the joint highest amount received from any part of the country (Hampshire raised 62 per cent), while South Wales paid 44.1 per cent and Monmouthshire 53.3 per cent. The three Welsh regions made up half the 'top six' payers of Ship Money, in marked contrast to the ten English counties that raised nothing whatsoever.[61]

Piracy was not the only security concern for the Welsh coast. Throughout the Tudor era, Wales was seen as a potential back door for an invasion of England; after all, the Tudors owed their possession of the throne to precisely that strategy. Rumours of imminent Spanish descents on Milford Haven were legion during the long war from 1585 to 1604 and the subsequent conflict of 1625–29, but despite repeated calls for the fortification of the harbour, little was done to supplement the two blockhouses built by Henry VIII in the 1540s.[62] During the seventeenth century, Milford Haven served as a minor victualling facility, supplying the small frigates that operated on the Irish coast. Otherwise, Wales was a low priority for naval protection, especially during the Anglo-Dutch wars when it was distant from the main theatre of warfare. In 1666, though, the French joined the Dutch, and Breton privateers attacked the colliers sailing between South Wales and the south-western peninsula of England. The 12-gun *Martin* was stationed at Milford in 1666 to guard against such attacks, but such token efforts proved largely ineffectual.[63]

Privateering

The distinction between piracy and privateering could be a very fine one. In theory, privateering was a legitimate and entirely legal element of naval warfare, with privately owned 'warships' effectively being licensed by the state by means of letters of marque and reprisal, which permitted them to attack specified enemies during periods of open warfare. But it was never quite as simple as that, particularly during the Tudor and early Stuart periods, and there were always distinctly dubious 'states' from which unscrupulous men could obtain letters of marque: one of John Callice's last voyages was on a 'privateer' licensed by Don Antonio, the pretender to the Portuguese throne (which had been annexed by Spain in 1580), and which used this authority to attack more or less any shipping trading with, or carrying goods from, the Iberian Peninsula.[64] However, privateering was never as significant an 'industry' in Wales as it was in, say, Scotland during the Anglo-Dutch wars or the Channel Islands during the French wars after 1689. Even so, a number of Welsh ships still obtained letters of marque and took part in the naval warfare of the age. Thomas Panton of Beaumaris was one of the co-owners of the *Peter*, which set out in 1665.[65] In the following year a group of gentlemen from south-east Carmarthenshire and the opposite bank of the River Loughor set out on the *Revenge*, commanded by Henry Mansell of Stradey near Llanelli, a 12-gun privateer which seized four French prizes in 1667.[66]

During the Seven Years' War (1756–63) the 20-gun *St David*, 'commanded by Captain Reeves Jones [and] fitted out by a Society of Ancient Britons', set out from Beaumaris. She sailed in April 1757 and swiftly took a larger French privateer after a two-and-a-half hour engagement during which twenty-nine Frenchmen were killed (as opposed to only five Welshmen).[67] At much the same time, Ned Edwards of Holyhead, who had served in the navy in the 1740s, took command of the privateer *Viscount Falmouth*, which issued recruiting posters in Welsh and sailed against the French in

North America, while David Jenkins of Carmarthenshire, who had moved to Truro, commanded the privateer *Duke of Cornwall*.[68] One of the most notorious British privateers of the mid-eighteenth century also had an Anglesey connection. Fortunatus Wright, a Liverpool man who had married Mary, the daughter of William Bulkeley of Brynddu, set himself up as a merchant in Leghorn, but the loss of one of his ships to a French privateer led him to adopt such a course for himself. He took many ships in 1746–47, and when the next war broke out in 1756, Wright again set out as a privateer, rampaging across the Mediterranean and almost bringing about a rupture in diplomatic relations between Britain and Tuscany. Then, quite suddenly, Wright simply disappeared: his ship probably foundered in a storm. Mary, who had been badly treated by her husband and cheated of his fortune by her stepdaughter's husband, made her way back to Anglesey and took refuge with her father, whose diary provides a record of Wright's activities and the travails of the marriage.[69]

Notes

1   G.A. Williams, *The Welsh in Their History* (1982), p.13. For Dee's Welsh origins, see G. Parry, *The Arch-Conjuror of England: John Dee* (New Haven, 2012).

2   I am grateful to Professor Andrew Lambert for these points.

3   I. Jones, 'Sir Matthew Cradock and some of his Contemporaries', *Archaeologia Cambrensis*, 6th series, 19 (1919), pp.395–6, 410–11.

4   D. Loades, *The Making of the Elizabethan Navy, 1540–90* (Woodbridge, 2009), p.19.

5   J.C. Appleby, 'Griffith, Piers (1568–1628), Pirate', *ODNB*.

6   J. Simon, 'The Wyntour Family', *Brycheiniog*, 13 (1968–69), pp.100–1; D. Loades, 'Winter, Sir William (*c.* 1525–1589), Naval Administrator', *ODNB*.

7   J.K. Laughton, ed., *State Papers Relating to the Defeat of the Spanish Armada* (NRS, 1894), pp.lxxviii–lxxix.

8   Appleby, 'Griffith'.

9   earlywelshleigh.blogspot.com/2017/04/richard-nash-abt-1530-aft-1597-son-of.html

10   G.A. Williams, 'Midleton [Myddelton], Wiliam (*c.* 1550–1596?), Poet and Sailor', *ODNB*.

11 Unless stated otherwise, this account of Mansell's career is based on A. Thrush, 'Mansell, Sir Robert (1570/71–1652), Naval officer and Administrator', *ODNB*, and www.historyofparliamentonline.org/ volume/1604–1629/member/mansell-sir-robert-15701-1652

12 CAS, Dynevor Additional MS 73.

13 D.E. Kennedy, 'Naval Captains at the Outbreak of the English Civil War', *MM*, 46 (1960), pp.189–90.

14 R. Wisker, 'Trevor, Sir Sackville (1567–1635), Naval Officer', *ODNB*.

15 A. Thrush, 'Button, Sir Thomas (*c.* 1575–1634), Naval Officer', *ODNB*.

16 G.G. Harris, 'Herbert, Thomas (b. 1597, d. before 1643), Naval Officer', *ODNB*.

17 M. Baumber, 'Stradling, Sir Henry (d. 1649?), Naval Officer', *ODNB*.

18 Baumber, 'Stradling'.

19 GRO, D/D TD13.

20 A. Eames, 'Sea Power and Caernarvonshire, 1642–60', *Caernarvonshire Historical Society Transactions*, 16 (1955), pp.47–49; S.K. Roberts, 'Jones, Philip, appointed Lord Jones under the Protectorate (1617/18–1674), Politician and Army Officer', *ODNB*.

21 A.H. Dodd, 'Trevor family of Trevalun, Denbs., Plas Têg, Flints., and Glynde, Sussex', *WBO*.

22 H.A. Lloyd, 'Corruption and Sir John Trevor', *THSC* (1974–5), pp.77–102.

23 Unless stated otherwise, this paragraph is based on A. Thrush, 'Edisbury, Kenrick (*d.* 1638), Naval Administrator', *ODNB*, and C.M. Rees, 'Kendrick Edisbury of Marchwiel and Deptford (*c.* 1580–1638), Surveyor of His Majesty's Ships 1632–8', *Old Denbighshire*, 52 (2003), pp.53–79.

24 Rees, 'Kendrick Edisbury', p.77.

25 FRO, D/E1323 (quotation from letter of 11 Mar. 1694), FRO D/E/1323/519.

26 J.R. Powell, *The Navy in the English Civil War* (1962), pp.43–45.

27 Powell, *Civil War*, pp.58–61; original report in *Documents Relating to the Civil War*, ed. J.R. Powell (NRS 1963), pp.128–35.

28 Eames, pp.61–85.

29 Powell, *Civil War*, pp.148–51.

30 'Robinson family, of Conway, Caerns., Monachdy, Anglesey, and Gwersyllt, Denbs.', *DWB;* Eames, pp.87–9.

31 TNA, HCA 13/73, fos. 520–1; ADM 2/1732, fo. 1

32 J.D. Davies, *Pepys's Navy: Ships, Men and Warfare 1649–89* (Barnsley, 2008), pp.94–9.

33 Unless stated otherwise, the following account of Arthur Herbert
    is based on my summary in 'Wales and Mr Pepys's Navy', *MW*,
    11 (1987), pp.106–8, and P.J. Le Fevre, 'Arthur Herbert, Earl of
    Torrington, 1648–1716', *Precursors of Nelson: British Admirals of the
    Eighteenth Century*, ed. Le Fevre and R. Harding (2000), pp.19–42.
34 NLW, MS 9346B.
35 Bodleian Library, Oxford, Rawlinson MS A228, fo. 67v.
36 Longleat House, Coventry MS 98, fos. 52–3.
37 Bodleian Library, Oxford, Rawlinson MS A181, fo. 340.
38 E. Chappell, ed., *The Tangier Papers of Samuel Pepys* (NRS 1935), p.134.
39 J.D. Davies, 'Captain David Lloyd, RN', *MW*, 12 (1989), pp.27–8.
40 N. Tucker, *Denbighshire Officers in the Civil War* (n.d.), pp.21–3.
41 N Rogers, *The Press Gang: Naval Impressment and its Opponents in
    Georgian Britain* (2007), pp.4–5; N.A.M Rodger, *The Command of
    the Ocean: A Naval History of Britain 1649–1815* (2004), pp.395–400;
    Davies, *Pepys's Navy*, 111.
42 Davies, *Pepys's Navy*, p.112.
43 TNA, ADM1/5138, p.916.
44 Davies, 'Wales and Mr Pepys's Navy', pp.104–5.
45 Davies, 'Wales and Mr Pepys's Navy', pp.104–5.
46 TNA, ADM 17/13.
47 TNA, ADM82/12, fos. 351–2.
48 D.G. Shomette and R.D. Haslache, *Raid on America: The Dutch Naval
    Campaign of 1672–4* (Columbia, SC, 1988), pp.90–2.
49 Winfield 1603–1714, pp.91, 130.
50 M. Tanner, *Royal Yacht Mary: The Discovery of the First Royal Yacht*
    (Liverpool, 2008). S Rees, 'The Royal Yacht *Mary*', 'Finds from
    the *Mary Yacht*', WATS, 188–9, 242–3. The *Mary* was not the only
    warship to come to grief on the Welsh coast in this period: the sixth
    rate *Increase* was wrecked near Swansea in March 1650.
51 K.L. Gruffydd, 'Piracy, Privateering and Maritime Wales during the
    Later Middle Ages (part 1)', *MW*, 24 (2003), pp.24–30 and passim.
52 J.C. Appleby, *Under the Bloody Flag: Pirates of the Tudor Age* (Stroud,
    2009), pp.33–5, 59, 92.
53 D. Mathew, 'The Cornish and Welsh Pirates in the Reign of
    Elizabeth', *English Historical Review*, xxxix (1924), pp.342–3; T.
    Breverton, *The Book of Welsh Pirates and Buccaneers* (St Athan, 2003),
    p.109.
54 Appleby, *Under the Bloody Flag*, pp.147–58, 162.
55 Appleby, *Under the Bloody Flag*, p.223.
56 Appleby, *Under the Bloody Flag*, p.146.
57 Appleby, *Under the Bloody Flag*, p.37.

58 HMC *Salisbury MSS*, xxi. 209–13; *CSPD 1603–10*, 17 April 1610, deposition of William Young.

59 Eames, pp.40–53.

60 *CSPD 1635–6*, 18 March 1636; bertan.gipuzkoakultura.net/es/5/ing/8.php

61 A.A.M. Gill, *'Ship Money during the Personal Rule of Charles I: Politics, Ideology and the Law 1634–1640'*, (PhD thesis, University of Sheffield, 1990), pp.339, 357, 358.

62 See e.g. *CSPD 1591–4, 1595–7, 1598–1601, 1625–6*, indices sv 'Milford'.

63 Davies, 'Wales and Mr Pepys's Navy', pp.110–11.

64 Appleby, *Under the Bloody Flag*, p.190.

65 TNA, HCA 25/9.

66 J.D. Davies, 'The *Revenge* of Llanelli: A Welsh Privateer of the 17th century', *MW*, 21 (2000), pp.45–51.

67 D C Jenkins, 'Before it's Forgotten', *The Carmarthenshire Historian*, XI (1974), 82

68 Eames, pp.148–52; carmarthenshirehistorian.org/cgi-bin/twiki/view/Historian/BeforeItsForgottenVol11

69 K. Breen, 'Wright, Fortunatus (*d.* 1757), Merchant and Privateer', *ODNB*.

3

DRAGON RAMPANT

c. 1688–1793

In 1781, the 'gentlemen of Montgomeryshire' erected a pillar on Breidden Hill overlooking the broad vale of Severn and the town of Welshpool. It was inscribed in English on the north face and in Latin on the east and south, but that on the west, the longest of the three inscriptions, was in Welsh. The pillar was erected to celebrate the achievements of Admiral George Brydges Rodney, although ironically his greatest triumph of all, the Battle of the Saintes, came in the year after the monument was unveiled. But 'Rodney's Pillar' was also intended to express the pride that the gentlemen of Montgomeryshire felt at the part their county had played in Rodney's triumphs, for this nearly landlocked and remote shire was a hugely important source of wood for the Royal Navy: it was said that many great ships of the age were built largely from Montgomeryshire timber.[1] The pillar is still a prominent landmark as one enters Wales along the A458 from Shrewsbury and the A483 from Oswestry, and it is not alone. On the summit of the steep hill known as the Kymin, overlooking Monmouth, stands a peculiar little 'naval temple', built by local subscription in 1800. It is one of the first public

monuments to show Britannia holding a trident rather than a
spear, reflecting the greater perceived importance of the navy at
the time,[2] and it carries plaques commemorating sixteen admirals who had distinguished themselves in the French wars of the
eighteenth century, including Nelson, Duncan, Hood, Howe,
Jervis and Rodney, together with the rather more obscure John
Gell – but Gell was very much a local naval hero, having captured a fabulously rich treasure ship in 1793 before retiring to
Crickhowell, where he died in 1806.[3] Further west, the Tywi
Valley between Carmarthen and Llandeilo is dominated by
'Paxton's Tower', erected in 1806 by Thomas Paxton as part
of the campaign of prodigiously expensive bribery by which
he persuaded the electors of Carmarthenshire to return him as
their MP. The tower contained both a rooftop platform from
which Paxton and his guests could enjoy the stunning views and
a comfortable first-floor chamber adorned with stained glass
windows commemorating Nelson.[4] These three monuments
are merely the most grandiose proofs that in eighteenth-century
Wales there was certainly no shortage of pride in the Royal
Navy and in the Principality's connections with it. Naval men
returning home were treated as celebrities: when the Welsh-
speaking Lieutenant William Owen of Glansevern returned to
Montgomeryshire after ten years in the East Indies, his arrival
'was announced by the ringing of Berriew and Llanidloes
bells, and an inundation of ale drawn; the neighbouring gentry
flocked to pay their compliments to a Nabob from the East'.[5]

Officers and Men [I]

A small but steady stream of Welshmen continued to obtain
commissions in the Georgian Navy, and in some cases rose to
very high rank. Thomas Mathews of Llandaff became a captain in 1703 and by 1744 was commanding the Mediterranean
fleet, monitoring its French counterpart in Toulon. In February

the French weighed and put to sea. On the eleventh, Mathews signalled to form line of battle, but the rear squadron under Richard Lestock remained far astern and made no effort to come up to the main fleet. Thus, when battle was joined on the twelfth, Mathews' centre division, particularly his own flagship, the *Namur*, and the van under Vice-Admiral Rowley, bore the brunt of the action. The French escaped and recriminations began at once, with Mathews accusing Lestock of not supporting him and the latter accusing Mathews of making inadequate and contradictory signals. There was a clear political dimension to the Mathews-Lestock dispute. Mathews was part of the Glamorgan Whig elite and was elected MP for Glamorgan at a by-election in January 1745. He was criticised for being proud and aloof, and these traits did him harm during the unprecedented parliamentary enquiry into the battle during March and April 1745: Lestock appeared cool and rational, Mathews 'a hot, brave, imperious, dull, confused fellow', according to Horace Walpole. The subsequent court martial of Lestock in October led to acquittal, while that of Mathews led to his dismissal; he was never employed again, and died in 1751. Although he made many mistakes in the battle, he had the good grace to admit that he had done so; his temper and condescension told against him, whereas Lestock, with his better political connections, was exonerated, despite the weight of evidence against him.[6]

Sir Erasmus Gower, eldest of the nineteen children of the vicar of Glandovan, Pembrokeshire, circumnavigated the world twice by the time he was 26 and had landmarks in New Ireland and the Solomon Islands named after him. He rose in the service as a protégé of Admiral Rodney, and in 1792–94, shortly after his knighting, he commanded HMS *Lion* on a voyage to China, carrying the first British ambassador to that nation, Earl Macartney. In 1797, Gower was briefly ejected from his command of the *Triumph* by the mutineers at Spithead, but was promoted to flag rank shortly afterwards. He later served as Governor of Newfoundland and did much to establish it as a proper colony. He died in 1814 and was buried in Hampshire, but is commemorated by a memorial in Cilgerran church.[7] Other prominent Welsh officers of the eighteenth century included Savage Mostyn of Flintshire, who served as Comptroller of the Navy 1749–1755, second in command of both the North American and Western squadrons in 1755–56 and for a few months as one of the Lords of the Admiralty; and Admiral Thomas Tucker (d. 1766) of Sealyham, Pembrokeshire, reputedly the man who killed the notorious pirate Blackbeard.[8] Pembrokeshire provided a number of other officers who attained distinction. John Vaughan of Trecwn commanded the *Juno* at the siege of Louisburg in 1758 and was eventually promoted to Admiral of the Blue shortly before his death in 1789.[9] Carmarthenshire provided the likes of David Edwardes of Rhyd-y-Gors and William Lloyd of Danyrallt near Llangadog, both of whom rose to flag rank by seniority, although their active careers were relatively undistinguished.

Tudor Trevor, a son of Sir John Trevor of Trefalun, Speaker of the House of Commons, became a captain in 1697, commanded the *Triton Prize* at the Battle of Malaga (1704), and served for many years in the West Indies and the Baltic before becoming Lieutenant-Governor of Greenwich Hospital, where he died in 1740.[10] Thomas Griffin of Dixton Hadnock, Monmouthshire, was a controversial figure whose career was blighted by two occasions on which he failed properly to engage the enemy; in 1750 a court martial found him guilty of negligence and suspended him, although the king subsequently restored him to flag officer's rank. A memorial to him survives on the wall of Dixton parish church.[11] Rather more obviously heroic was Captain Walter Griffith of Llanfechain, Montgomeryshire, who was killed in command of HMS *Conqueror* off Martinique in 1779 when she was surrounded and shattered by three French ships-of-the-line.[12] Finally, Sir Francis Geary, who commanded the Channel Fleet in 1780, was born in Cardiganshire, albeit to a family which moved back to England soon after his birth.[13]

Several Welsh captains inherited or acquired landed estates and, perhaps because their naval service had given them broader horizons than their neighbours, they generally proved to be enlightened landlords. Captain Thomas Lloyd of Cilgwyn, Cardiganshire, commanded the *Vulcan* at the Battle of Ushant (1778), and was known to Nelson during his command of the *Glasgow* in the Caribbean. He eventually retired to run his family estate, became renowned as an improving landlord who did much to enhance agricultural methods in West Wales, and served as sheriff of the county in 1800, the year before his death.[14] Similarly, Timothy Edwards of Nanhoron on the Llŷn Peninsula created a famous garden (which still survives) and was an enthusiast of estate improvement, in marked contrast to the majority of Welsh squires, whom he believed to be 'idle [and] dissipated'. Edwards joined the navy during the Jacobite rebellion of 1745 and served in 1748–50 aboard the *Sphinx* under Captain William Lloyd of Danyrallt, Carmarthenshire. He obtained his first lieutenant's commission in 1755 and became a post-captain in 1759, earning a substantial sum from prize money before going onto half pay at the end of the war in 1763, shortly before he inherited the Nanhoron estate. There he began a major planting programme (principally oak and beech), grew fruit, beautified the garden and improved the grazing before returning to sea in 1777, taking eight Welshmen with him. He took command of the *Cornwall* (74) early in 1778 and took her to New York, then to the West Indies, where the ship was severely battered in the Battles of Grenada and St Lucia, losing twenty-three men in the latter action. With his ship unfit for further service, Edwards was turned over into the *Actaeon* to return to Britain, where he planned to stand for election to Parliament. But it was not to be. He was already sick when he joined the *Actaeon* and died of fever, probably gastric malaria, on 12 July 1780. His younger son, John Browning Edwards, entered the navy and also rose to the rank of captain; Timothy, whose fighting qualities earned him the nickname 'Hammer

and Nails' quite early in his career, is commemorated by a
memorial in Llangian church.[15]

These Welsh officers operated within tightly knit patronage
networks that were often based on nationality and kinship. When
William Owen of Glansevern, Welshpool, joined HMS *Sphinx*
in 1750, shortly after Timothy Edwards had left the same ship,
it was to serve under Captain William Lloyd and Lieutenant
Charles Davids of Brecon.[16] Eight years later, John Williams of
Carmarthenshire, first lieutenant of HMS *Ambuscade*, wrote to
Griffith Phillips of Cwmgwili, stating that he had applied to his
captain, Richard Gwyn, for a certificate to his character, and had
also sent details of his service to Captain John Williams, for many
years commander of one of the royal yachts but since retired to
Plaistow, Essex, hoping that Williams would intercede for him
with Lord Barrington, the influential Secretary at War. Williams
wrote in hopes that Phillips would strengthen his interest with
the Admiralty and 'Mr Rice', the MP for Carmarthen and Lord
Lieutenant of the county. (Unfortunately, this was a sign of just
how mediocre Williams' career had turned out to be; by then
he had already been a lieutenant for nineteen years, and rose
no higher.)[17] Four decades later, the next squire of Cwmgwili,
John George Phillips, MP for Carmarthen, was similarly solicited at regular intervals by his kinsmen and neighbours George
Davies and Henry Vaughan.[18] Thomas Lewes of Gellidywyll,
Carmarthenshire, was a close friend of Sir John Stepney of
Llanelli, eighth baronet, and had acted as an unofficial secretary to Stepney when the latter was ambassador in Saxony. This
connection enabled Lewes to solicit the patronage of Stepney's
friends the Duke of Beaufort and the Earl of Carlisle; he was
promoted to captain in 1782 and died in command of the
Hannibal in the West Indies in 1795.[19]

Richard Morris of Llanfihangel Tre'r Beirdd, Anglesey,
Navy Office clerk and founder of the Honourable Society
of Cymmrodorion, promoted the careers of several kinsmen
and neighbours, notably his brother John, nephews William

and John Owen, and Ned Edwards, who went on to captain a
successful privateer during the Seven Years' War.[20] Timothy
Edwards of Nanhoron was an assiduous promoter of his countrymen and revelled in the age-old Welsh obsessions with
genealogy and who might be related to whom. For instance, he
described Captain Christian, the commander of a packet boat,
as 'half a Welshman. His mother was a Hughes related nearly to
Lloyd of Havod-dinas and the Lewises of Llysddylais. In short
he is very clever and an honour to any country that he may have
first breathed in. Which has occasioned my bringing him on the
stage a propos.' He also helped other countrymen:

> Tell Captain John Williams his son is a fine lad and I have rated
> him a midshipman. When you see Mrs Ellis Nanney, tell her
> I have advanced Jones the Postmaster's son to a Master's berth,
> near £3 a month. There is a lad of the name of Williams in
> the *Prince of Wales*. He says Mr Williams of Llangian is his
> friend and guardian. He applied to me for money and I lent
> him two guineas … There is a son of Mr Jones the parson
> of Newborough [*Anglesey*]. He applied to me for money on a
> bill drawn by Councillor Parry. I had none to give him. He is
> now in *Conqueror* & very bare of clothes and other necessaries.
> If he is sober I will endeavour to serve him when he has been
> long enough in the navy to merit some promotion.[21]

Such connections were essential for success: as one member of
a Merionethshire family which sent several members into the
navy observed, 'promotion is very tedious and uncertain in the
navy unless seconded by a powerful interest.'[22]

The eighteenth century also saw the beginnings of Welsh
naval 'dynasties'; in other words, the development of a tradition of naval service across several generations. John James of
Rhayader, a master in the navy, bequeathed his estate to his
nephew of the same name, who distinguished himself by carrying away the body of General Wolfe from Quebec before

commanding the *Hawke* sloop on anti-smuggling operations in New York in the 1760s. John II served as lieutenant of the *Levant* in the Mediterranean before the inheritance from his uncle enabled him to retire to Mid Wales. In turn, John II's eldest son went into the East India Company's service and his two younger sons into the Royal Navy. Hugh, a midshipman, died of yellow fever at the age of 19, but Horatio James became a lieutenant at the end of the Napoleonic Wars and eventually held several commands, culminating in that of the Pembroke-built steam vessel *Tartarus* from 1834–37.[23] But perhaps the most successful Welsh naval dynasty was the Mends family of Haverfordwest.[24] Their very name is proof of Wales' deep-rooted maritime connections: the family was almost certainly established by a Mendez from Spain who moved to Pembrokeshire in the fifteenth century. Robert Mends joined the navy in 1779, losing his right arm at the siege of Yorktown when not yet 14; he was subsequently wounded in the head by a large splinter and severely burnt by a powder explosion. Knighted in 1815, Mends commanded the Dublin Sea Fencibles, the prison hulks at Portsmouth, and two 'Welsh' warships, the *Abergavenny* and *Owen Glendower*. He died aboard the latter on the Gold Coast in September 1823 while serving as commodore of the squadron tasked with stamping out the slave trade (*see Chapter 8*). All three of his sons followed him into the navy: one, a midshipman on the *Glendower*, died three months after his father; the others reached the ranks of captain and rear-admiral.[25] Thirteen of Robert's siblings joined the army or navy. One of them, William Bowen Mends, born in 1781, was on the active list for sixty-two years, dying as a full admiral in 1863, and three of his sons, in turn, became naval officers. One, Sir William Robert Mends, had a markedly successful naval career despite having his left hand crushed by a block, leading to the loss of several fingers and lifelong attacks of neuralgia. He distinguished himself during the Crimean War (*see Chapter 8*), and later ran the Admiralty's transport department for twenty years, organising the Indian troopship system and the expeditions taking troops to Abyssinia, Egypt and the Zulu wars.[26]

'Welsh' Warships

A new crop of Welsh warship names appeared in the wake of the Glorious Revolution of 1688. There were several more *Pembroke*s, the most distinguished of which was the third, which took part in the battles of Vigo (1702) and Marbella (1704).[27] Although the ship herself was lost in 1709, her bell survives in the unlikely setting of a church porch in Otorohanga, New Zealand, despite disappearing for a few days after being stolen by metal thieves in June 2011. The first ship to be named after the Isle of Anglesey, albeit spelled *Anglesea*, was launched in 1694. She was also the first warship to be built by the new royal dockyard in Plymouth, and had a long and active career.[28] However, the *Anglesea* launched in 1742 was taken by the French three years later, the acting captain shot for surrendering her, and then served in her captors' navy as *L'Anglesea*.[29] There were several more *Dragons* and *Severns*, none of which had particularly distinguished careers, while a sixth rate named *Newport* was launched in 1694, though it is probably more likely that it was named after the town on the Isle of Wight than that on the Usk.[30] Meanwhile, the name *Milford* had an appalling run of bad luck. Two in succession were captured by the French, who put them into service as *Le Milford*, while the third, launched in 1705, was wrecked on Cape Corrientes, Cuba, in 1720.[31] The *Milford* of 1759 was launched into the waterway after which she was named (*see Chapter 6*), and took four French and four American privateers during a notable career.[32]

The name of *Monmouth* was a more or less permanent fixture on the navy lists of the eighteenth century. The ship of 1667 was notionally 'rebuilt' in 1716–19, actually a euphemism for the building of a new ship with some of the timbers of the old, and was finally broken up in 1744.[33] By then a new *Monmouth* was already in service. Built at Deptford, she distinguished herself in the two Battles of Cape Finisterre in 1747, and in 1758 took the much larger 84-gun French ship *La Foudroyant*. One of her last captains before she was broken up in 1767 was Augustus Hervey, the renowned naval Casanova.[34] Hervey also commanded the navy's next *Dragon*, launched at Deptford in 1760, and took part in the bombardment and capture of Havana in 1762. She was not a particularly successful ship and saw little service after 1763, eventually being sold in 1784.[35] The navy's next *Monmouth*, launched at Plymouth in 1772, had a distinguished career, fighting in fleet actions in both the West and East Indies. Ultimately, though, this *Monmouth* suffered a grim fate: in 1796 she was renamed *Captivity* and became one of the infamous prison hulks at Portsmouth, serving as such until she was broken up in 1818.[36]

The 1760s saw the introduction of two new 'Welsh' names for warships, *Prince of Wales* (see Chapter 6) and perhaps the oddest choice of all, *Druid*. The first of the latter name was a sloop launched at Harwich in 1761, but which served for only twelve years before being sunk as a breakwater at Sheerness. The *Druid* launched at Bristol in 1783, a fifth rate frigate, proved to be a successful ship which took five French warships and privateers during her time, as well as acting as a royal escort. Her roll call of captains included two of the best of the age, Edward Codrington who would later command the British fleet at the Battle of Navarino and Philip Broke who commanded HMS *Shannon* to victory over USS *Chesapeake* during the War of 1812.[37] Broke was unimpressed with the *Druid*, describing her as a 'point of honour ship' – too large to run and too small to fight.[38] Another manifestation of Welsh mysticism on the Navy List was the second *Merlin*, an 18-gun sloop launched in 1767. She had a very active career before being abandoned and burned in the Delaware River in October 1777 while under American fire.[39]

Officers and Men [II]

On the lower deck, the old maxim about joining the navy and seeing the world appealed to young Welshmen with a sense of wanderlust and adventure. Richard Morris' brother John's reason for joining the navy was simple: 'I am resolved now to be one amongst them *i ladd Ysbaengwyns* [to kill Spaniards]', although he was soon disillusioned by poor victuals, unhealthy conditions aboard his ship, and a lack of correspondence from his friends in Anglesey. In the event, his ambitions went unfulfilled: he died of sickness aboard the *Torbay* in the West Indies in 1741, one of many who succumbed to the fevers of the Caribbean.[40] Young men's naval and military ambitions have often caused discord within families. In 1743, for example, Vaughan Thomas of Posty, Pembrokeshire, ran away to join the navy, entering himself on the ship's books of the *Princess Amelia* at Plymouth. His father sent him a letter that plumbs the depths of emotional and financial blackmail:

> we are all glad to hear that you are well, your mother and sister and self lost years at the reading of your letter. We expected to hear that you designed to return homewards, your mother has been ill of the rheumatism ever since you parted … there is not a day or night but that she sheds tears about your going away, pray if possible return home … We are informed that it is like to be very troublesome both at sea and land and that several worthy men have lately lost their lives at the West Indies, we desire you to consider both of the times and of the hot season, as to what your mother and myself proposed to give as the present you may assure yourself of it if you return home and settle with us. Pray let us hear how you were received when you went first on board, and what post you have had, we thought that you had no need of going into a man of war but leave such a place to those that had most need of having a sufficiency provided as we thought

for you here. We desire you to consider seriously of it, and as
to your having any preferment at sea, I think you are too old
and besides one that never used the sea, and as to what [*illegible
– 'disputes' or 'troubles' clearly intended*] have been between us
here, your mother and self desires it might be forgotten …[41]

Vaughan did not pursue a naval career, although whether his
change of heart was due to this letter or to disillusionment with
his experiences aboard ship will probably never be known.

The press gang remained a feature of Welsh life during wartime. In 1756, a regulating captain was appointed at Pembroke,
and Welshmen would almost certainly also have been taken
up by those stationed at Liverpool, Bristol, Shrewsbury and
Gloucester.[42] Lieutenants in charge of press gangs had always
received 10 shillings for every able and ordinary seaman they
recruited, but in the Seven Years' War (1756–63) they also got
5 shillings for each landsman. Private citizens who reported able
or ordinary seamen were rewarded with 40 and 30 shillings,
respectively; from 1762 parish constables who apprehended an
able seaman received five pounds for his pains.[43] These shore-
based recruiters were complemented by press gangs afloat,
who took pressing tenders into ports to hunt for men. This
was only done on a systematic basis in the west of Britain from
1755 onwards, when press gangs were based at Chester and
Liverpool. Volunteers and pressed men from South Wales were
often conveyed to Plymouth by tenders sailing from Swansea,
Carmarthen, Cardiff or other ports, and even such a relatively
short voyage could be perilous. In the morning of 28 November
1760, the pressing tender *Caesar* sailed from Mumbles Road
carrying a crew of one officer and thirteen men, together with
about eighty pressed men who were probably shut in below
decks to prevent them overpowering the crew. The *Caesar*
struggled to make headway in poor conditions, and at two in the
afternoon she turned back for the safety of the Mumbles anchorage. But the watch seems to have mistaken Pwlldu Head at the

east end of Oxwich Bay for Mumbles Head, and at about five she ran onto the rocks of the former. About seventy perished, the vast majority being the pressed men below decks. The mass grave of those who perished aboard the *Caesar* is still marked by a circle of limestone rocks in a gully called Grave's End on Pwll Du Head, overlooking the spot still known as 'Caesar's Hole', and the story of the wreck entered into Gower folklore.[44] The site is unmarked; the new 'Wales coast path' runs not far above, with a clear view down onto the circle, but unless the site is marked properly, virtually every walker passing that way will remain in ignorance of what passed, and what is commemorated, just a few yards below.

It was hardly surprising that pressing was universally detested, and it was sometimes resisted with extreme violence. In 1759, an attempt to press the crew of a ship at Carmarthen led to a ferocious battle which saw the defeat of the press gang at a cost of one man dead and many seriously wounded on both sides.[45] But Lieutenant William Owen of Glansevern could see both sides of the argument. When he pressed men at Shrewsbury (the navigable Severn being defined as 'the sea'), he observed that it was:

> a hard case to act a part so repugnant to one's own nature and temperament. But ... however unconstitutional it may be to deprive this useful class of people of their liberty above all others, it is an act of necessity that cannot be dispensed with ... Seamen were now much wanted, and seamen were to be procured at all events to bring affairs to a happy crisis.

Moreover, the press gangs were often literally risking life and limb to carry out their unpopular duties: Owen's gang was confronted by seamen who had armed themselves with 'cutlasses, kitchen tongs, pokers, spits and pitchforks'.[46] Another party of potential recruits appropriated the last boat moored at Eastham on the Wirral, and as it pulled away from the quay and Owen's press gang, they 'gave three loud huzzahs, very politely slapped their posteriors and bade us kiss their a[rses]'.[47]

In these circumstances, it is perhaps surprising that Owen was as discriminating as he was during his pressing expeditions through Shropshire, the Cheshire borders, down through Welshpool, Newtown, and to the fairs at Montgomery and Llanidloes. When he stopped four seamen on the English side of the border, Owen dismissed two immediately, as one was the master of a vessel and the second had a bad arm; the third escaped, so he only recruited the fourth, 'a very decent young man' from Caernarfonshire named William Jones, 'and whose unhappy fate I often regretted' – Jones was one of the men put aboard the *Scorpion*, which was lost with all hands a few months later.[48] Press officers had to be careful that they did not exceed the strict limit of the law, or else press substantial men whose recruitment might enrage the local community. At Llanidloes Fair in May 1762 Owen pressed Jeremiah Pryce, but only after Pryce had mocked the press gang, saying he was a better seaman than any of them and insulting Owen himself, whereupon the lieutenant personally impressed the man and despatched him to Shrewsbury. When Owen returned there, he found that Pryce had hired an attorney to prove he was a freeholder, whereupon he was discharged. But as Owen observed, 'the man declared himself a seaman, and I was not obliged to know him to be a freeholder'; thus Owen could not have simply snatched any man attending Llanidloes Fair, only trained seamen of a certain social status. When he later returned to the area, he found Pryce was always civil to him and expressed his regret that he had not joined the navy when given the opportunity, 'as it would have prevented his marrying a vixen who proved his ruin'. Pryce and Owen subsequently became great friends.[49]

Unsurprisingly, communities often used the press as a means to offload their undesirables onto the navy. Thus in July 1779, Richard Codd, a prisoner at Haverfordwest, was delivered

to the tender mercies of the press gang.[50] But by no means all
Welsh sailors serving in the navy were the dregs of their locali-
ties. Many were respectable, and in some cases propertied,
citizens. One such was Richard Bowen of Ilston, Gower, who
died aboard HMS *Fox* in the Firth of Forth during the Jacobite
rebellion of 1745, and who presumably owned the property
in the parish of Llanrhidian that passed to his widow; another
was Richard Leach, who owned a house in Pembroke when
he died aboard HMS *Chester* in 1748.[51] Others became reasonably prosperous through naval service. In 1726, John Levett
of Haverfordwest was able to bequeath £80 that he had saved
during his time aboard the *Dunkirk* and *Diamond*; Thomas John
of St Nicholas, Glamorgan, came home with the same sum after
taking part in the capture of Havana in 1762.[52] The sailor who
retired from the sea with enough money to set up his own pub
was something of a stereotype in the eighteenth and nineteenth
centuries, but there were plenty of cases in point: one was Tom
Cleaves of Swansea, formerly the boatswain of one of Nelson's
ships, who was the landlord of the Plume of Feathers in his
hometown when the admiral visited it in 1802. 'Sion ab Ifan
Edwart' of Bodorgon, Anglesey, sometime captain's steward of
the *Buckingham*, came home with enough money to set up his
Irish wife in her own shop.[53] Others established themselves as
schoolmasters. Edward Lloyd of Llanddarog, Carmarthenshire,
son of a Methodist preacher, served aboard the *Burford* at the
taking of Guadeloupe in 1759 and of Belleisle in 1761; he subsequently worked as a schoolmaster in different parts of Wales,
settling in Neath in 1777. He remained there for almost forty
years and was still 'in harness', teaching the youth of the town,
at the age of 76.[54] After the Napoleonic Wars, William Francis
taught navigation at Amlwch, while a one-legged naval veteran named Brown became the schoolmaster at Llandysilio,
Montgomeryshire, where 'he was said to have wielded the ferule
with great vigour'.[55] On the other hand, many Welsh seamen
died in abject poverty. When the will of William Hughes of

Holyhead, who had been serving aboard HMS *Worcester*, was proved in 1779, it was baldly endorsed 'pauper'.[56]

A number of Welshmen served as naval surgeons and chaplains. Herbert Jones of Llanengan, Llŷn, who was surgeon of the *Swan* in 1746, later served in the East Indies and made a small fortune from prize money, enabling him to buy a substantial estate on Anglesey; by contrast, his exact contemporary George Williams, never in the right place at the right time to enrich himself to the same degree, did not even make enough from his naval service to sustain his wife and seven children.[57] Thomas Phillips of Radnorshire spent only two years in the 1780s as a naval surgeon before moving into the East India Company's service. In later life he became a major benefactor of St David's College, Lampeter, and the founder of one of Wales' greatest public schools, Llandovery College. Other Welsh naval surgeons included David Samwell, whose colourful career is recounted below; Edward Evans, who is commemorated on a memorial at Llanidloes church; William Llewelyn, who started a medical practice in Tai-Bach when he retired from the navy in 1810; and David Williams of Disgwilfa, Llanybydder, whose naval service included a stint on the infamous prison hulks at Chatham.[58]

The Welsh naval chaplain was such a common feature of the sailing navy that he became a stereotype. In his popular book *The Marine Officer*, Sir Robert Steele wrote of his ship's chaplain, 'a native of Wales, as pastoral and as without guile as the herd on the hill ... to tell the truth, our Cambrian was better in the bottle than in the wood.'[59] The ubiquity of Welsh clergy in the navy is unsurprising; many Welsh parishes were very poor, and naval service was one way of supplementing a meagre income. None did so more successfully than John Deere, son of a minor gentleman of Penlline, who was alleged to have swum ashore from the wreck of Sir Cloudesley Shovell's fleet in 1707 despite being laden down with a huge amount of treasure, and to have left £10,000 when he died over half a century later.[60] Several Welsh chaplains had rather less profitable but still distinguished careers. Thomas Morgan of Devynock, Breconshire, was a graduate of Jesus College, Oxford, and became a naval chaplain during the 1790s. He was at Spithead when the great mutiny broke out in 1797; his sympathies were with the men, but he played an important part in quietening the discontent. He subsequently served as chaplain and secretary to Admiral Sir Charles Cotton, finally becoming chaplain of Portsmouth Dockyard where he served from 1817 until his death in 1851.[61] Jeffrey Holland, Rector of Penmorfa, near Porthmadog, became chaplain of the 74-gun *Audacious* in 1793 and saw action in the battle of the Glorious First of June in the following year. He went home to Llŷn in 1797, but returned to the colours in 1805 as chaplain of the *Warrior*, serving until 1810.[62] John Jenkins of Llangoedmor, Cardiganshire, served as chaplain successively of HM ships *Agincourt*, *Theseus* and *Bellerophon* from 1799 to 1804, principally because the debts he had run up during his previous curacy on the Isle of Wight had become unsustainable. John surprised himself by enjoying naval life, which is more than can be said of his brother Jeremiah, who served as a naval surgeon at much the same time, but by 1806 was bored of the 'dull and stupid routine' of the navy.[63] John Jenkins finally returned to his native land, becoming vicar of Ceri, Montgomeryshire (hence his bardic name, Ifor Ceri) and gaining a reputation as an eminent antiquarian who was a leading light in the establishment of *eisteddfodau* during the 1820s.[64] Other Welsh bards who saw service as naval chaplains, albeit only briefly, were Evan Evans, 'Ieuan Fardd' (1731–88), 'undoubtedly the greatest Welsh scholar of his age', and Edward Hughes of Nannerch.[65]

The Welshmen serving in the navy retained a pride in their identity that manifested itself in time-honoured ways. Captain Thomas James from Wern-y-Cwm near Abergavenny, commanding an expedition looking for the North West Passage, recorded that on St David's Day he and his crew 'kept holiday

and solemnised it in the manner of the ancient Britons'.[66] On
1 March 1679, the English chaplain of the *Royal Oak*, in the
Mediterranean, noted in his diary 'St Taffy's Day: and many in
our ship do wear leeks'[67] – the very fact that leeks were aboard so
very far from home is revealing in itself. Aboard Captain Cook's
ship, the *Resolution*, in the Pacific, naval surgeon David Samwell
of Nantglyn, Denbighshire, marked St David's Day in 1777 by
penning a poem in honour of the occasion:

Cyn codi'r Haul tirion ar Wyneb yr Eigion
Rhôf allan Benillion yn union fy Nôd
Ceir clywed f'Awenydd ar godiad Boreu ddydd
Yn cyfarch Gwyl Ddafydd gwiw ddefod.

[Before the gentle sun rises on the face of the ocean
I shall pronounce verses, my specific intent,
Muse shall be heard at the start of day break
Greeting St David's Feast-day, fine ceremony.][68]

Samwell, an irrepressible womaniser whose bardic name was
Dafydd Ddu, was a prominent member of London Welsh society; like many London Welshmen before and since, he much
preferred the life of the capital and regarded the prospect of
returning home to live in Wales with horror. Samwell was
one of those who took part in the rituals on Primrose Hill
on Midsummer day 1792, when Iolo Morgannwg founded
the modern Eisteddfod. But Samwell did not entirely live
up to the peaceful principles of the Gorsedd. According to
one of his biographers, 'by temperament Samwell was manic
and often violent'; when he disagreed with a verdict at the
Corwen Eisteddfod of 1789, he promptly challenged one of
the adjudicators to a duel.[69] When he went back to sea aboard
HMS *Marlborough* in 1793, he wrote to his friend and fellow
bard, Gwallter Mechain (Walter Davies):

I wish you and some other pious gownsmen of Oxford would pray to the Lord to send a good prize into our clutches the first cruise we take; our whole thoughts are fixed on the Mammon of Unrighteousness, alias, a rich French East Indiaman – God forgive you exclaims Mechain, Amen says Dafydd Ddu.[70]

'Wenglish', the practice of transforming English words into new 'Welsh' ones by changing the odd letter here or there, is usually derided by linguistic purists, notably those from the northern heartlands. But perhaps it has a longer and more respectable pedigree than is sometimes assumed: the Anglesey bard Richard Morris, founder of the Honourable Society of Cymmrodorion in 1751, was a clerk in the Navy Office from 1748 to 1775 and regularly translated the name of his workplace into 'Welsh', not as *swyddfa'r Llynges*, but as 'nafi offis'.[71] Like his fellow bard and London Welshman David Samwell, Morris evidently saw no difficulty in working for the Royal Navy. The third and fourth verses of the Cymmrodorion anthem lambasted the French and Spanish, so by implication, Britain's principal weapon against those inveterate foes could only be a force for good, one which right thinking Welshmen ought to exalt. Moreover, the second half of the eighteenth century was the high point of interest in the Madoc legend: following in the footsteps of John Dee, authors like Theophilus Evans produced books which presented the story of the Welsh discovery of America as a certainty, and tales of Welsh-speaking Indian tribes spread like wildfire.[72] On his voyages in the Pacific, Samwell seems to have regarded himself as following in a noble tradition of Welsh explorers of the past, although whether such a tradition really entailed having sex with as many local women as possible is a moot point. For bards, therefore, the Royal Navy could be seen as the power that would finally enable the isles of Britain – and thus, by implication, the Ancient Britons, the aborigines of the isles, the Welsh – to fulfil the destiny mapped out for them by Madoc, King Arthur and John Dee.

The Naval Defence of Wales, *c.* 1650–1793

During wars against the French and Spanish, and even more so during the seventeenth-century wars against the Dutch, Wales was a comparative backwater in naval warfare, geographically removed from the main spheres of action. But warfare in Ireland altered the case dramatically. In the Middle Ages, then during Elizabeth I's campaigns there, and later during Cromwell's campaign from 1649 to 1652 and William of Orange's from 1689 to 1692, Wales was very much the front line. Her harbours became vital to the transportation of armies to Ireland, and the prospect of invasion if the government armies suffered a fatal reverse across the Irish Sea seemed a very real one. Thus the naval forces deployed off the Welsh coast could be quite substantial. Admiral Arthur Herbert's entire fleet was in Milford Haven in April 1689.[73] In February 1690, the fourth rate *Charles Galley* came into the same anchorage, landed some passengers from Ireland, replaced her main yard and then sailed in company with two other fourths, Sir Cloudesley Shovell's flagship *Monck*, and three smaller ships, calling at Beaumaris before going on to Liverpool.[74] By June of that year, when the French fleet was at sea, a squadron consisting of one third rate, four fourths, three fifths and lesser craft was on station in the Irish Sea, with a second third rate, the *York*, detached for convoy duty between Ireland and St David's Head.[75] But by 1692, large naval forces had been withdrawn from the area, and French and Jacobite ships were able to play havoc. In June of that year, the naval vessel *Hart Ketch* and four merchantmen were captured barely eight hours after they had sailed from Milford, and others escaped only by the skin of their teeth. The government's correspondent Walter Middleton, writing from Laugharne, observed that 'there is not a vessel dare stir out of Milford but they are taken by King James' privateers'; two vessels lying off Lundy were preventing all cross-channel trade between England and Wales and threatening the entire trade of the Severn, including the valuable Virginia ships bound for Bristol, so that:

> we are not safe in our beds for them. You cannot imagine the clamour and noise the people makes here, that they have not men of war ordered to cruise in their channel, whereby they may have their coast trade free to them to endeavour to get monies to pay their taxes, which are very heavy upon these parts …[76]

As Middleton's letter suggests, apart from the brief periods of war in Ireland, the naval presence on the Welsh coast was minimal and intermittent. During the Anglo-Dutch wars and the Anglo-French wars of 1689–1713, ships were appointed to convoy collier fleets from Welsh ports while others undertook cruiser duty off the coast.[77] In 1703–04, the fifth rate *Rye* and sixth rate *Penzance* were cruising between Milford and Lundy with the brig *Discovery* working closer inshore between Milford and Swansea.[78] During the eighteenth century, smuggling became endemic in the Bristol Channel, with Gower and the islands of Barry, Sully and Flatholm becoming 'the gentlemen's' favourite haunts, and was equally common in Anglesey.[79] Consequently, the navy was requested to provide small craft for anti-smuggling operations on the Welsh coast. It has been claimed that this service began with the sloop *Hawke* in the 1730s, but the sloop *Cruizer* was operating from Milford, 'employed against the smugglers', as early as 1722–25.[80] By the mid-1750s, the *Hazard* and *Saltash* sloops were cruising off the South Wales coast on 'quarantine' (anti-smuggling) duty.[81] In the mid-1760s this role was fulfilled by the *Lord Howe* cutter, and her log book gives an insight into both these unsung naval operations in Welsh waters and the nature of Welsh maritime trade at the time.[82] After first arriving on station in the spring of 1763, she cruised between Saint David's Head and Bardsey, usually chasing or checking two or three sails a day. On 17 August

1764, for instance, the *Lord Howe* chased a ship into Pwllheli harbour and sent a boat in after her; she proved to be the *Royal Oak*, bound from Cardigan for Wicklow. In a typical week in July 1765 she spoke with sloops bound from Newry to Barmouth, Belfast to Milford, Waterford to Caernarfon, and from Dublin to Pwllheli, Cardigan, Barmouth and Aberystwyth. The *Lord Howe* sometimes ventured as far north as Holyhead and the Skerries, or crossed over to Dublin. When not at sea, she usually moored off Neyland Point in Milford Haven, obtaining a new main foresail and storm jib from Hubberston, or else at Beaumaris, where she spent part of the winter.

Later in the eighteenth century, the potential vulnerability of the Welsh coast to attack led to the construction of several new fortifications. Fort Belan, built in 1775, was unusual in that it was privately funded by the local landowner, Thomas Wynn of Glynllifon, and intended to defend the western entrance to the Menai Strait.[83] The shots that the American privateer *Black Prince* fired at Fishguard in 1779 led to the construction of a fort overlooking Fishguard harbour and mounting eight 9-pounder guns. The depredations of French and American privateers in Welsh waters had a devastating impact on the tiny ports along the coast, with many of their ships being lost to enemy raiders.[84] To defend against these attacks, warships were stationed in Welsh waters, but they were usually too few and of the wrong kind: in 1777 the *Exeter*, 64, was on station alternately at Milford and Cork, a huge ship that would be virtually no use for chasing the small, nimble ships favoured by American and French privateers.

Hearts of Oak

Early in the sixteenth century, the monks of Llantarnam Abbey in Gwent felled 'twenty great oaks' to build 'a ship for the maintenance of the navy'.[85] However, Welsh timber was a relatively minor source of supply for the Royal Navy until the 1690s:

simple geography dictated that it was remote from all the royal dockyards and transport costs were therefore frequently prohibitive. The decision taken in 1689 to establish a new royal dockyard at Plymouth transformed the situation. Suddenly Wales was one of the nearest, and thus cheapest, sources of timber to a major yard, and unlike the New Forest, which traditionally supplied Portsmouth, the Welsh forests were virtually untapped. The building of major warships on the new site that would later be named Devonport began with the fourth rate frigate *Anglesea* in 1694, and by the 1780s the dockyard was building such leviathans as the *Royal Sovereign* and also repairing many of the navy's largest ships. The establishment of the 'western squadron' and the near-permanent blockade of Brest during the great wars with France in the eighteenth century made Plymouth Britain's most important dockyard, with a constant turnaround of ships coming in for repair and refit, and an elaborate supply chain was established between Wales and Devon.

Glamorgan and Monmouthshire provided large amounts of ship-timber to the eighteenth-century navy. In 1729, Bussy Mansell of Briton Ferry contracted to supply naval timber, and in 1732 he signed another contract by which he undertook to supply nearly 5,000 loads to the yard at Plymouth; this included timber that would provide sternposts, keelsons, half beams and floor riders for ships of 50 to 100 guns.[86] During the 1740s, Britain was embroiled in a major European war; shipbuilding was accelerated, and demand for timber increased concomitantly. Bussy Mansell signed further contracts for the supply of timber to the navy in 1742 and 1746, some of it coming from the Clydach area.[87] In 1747, naval agents surveyed timber throughout South Wales, leading to the signing of several other lucrative contracts.[88] From 1748 to 1750, for example, the Glamorgan estates of Lord Mansell of Margam Abbey provided substantial amounts of timber to Plymouth Dockyard, including the ribs for its new dock gates.[89] Logs were moved overland by whatever means were appropriate to the terrain, then floated or shipped down rivers (and, later, canals) to the sea side; in August 1750, for instance, twenty loads of timber, including five dock gate ribs, were moved 16 miles by land to the water's edge at Aberavon Pill, where they were loaded onto John Roberts' vessel, which regularly carried Glamorgan timber to Plymouth.[90]

Other supplies came from further east. During the mid- to late 1740s, timber from the Abergavenny and Monmouth areas was being shipped to the Plymouth yard from Chepstow.[91] In June 1750 a typical large shipment from Chepstow included timber that could provide one second futtock and two top timbers for a 90-gun man-of-war, eleven and three respectively for a 70-gunner, and four and six respectively for a 50.[92] The Chepstow timber merchant William Williams regularly supplied substantial quantities to the navy during the 1760s and 1770s, drawing on woodlands in Monmouthshire, Gloucestershire and Herefordshire.[93] But Welsh weather and the state of the rivers often interrupted the trade. In March 1753, a gale blew one of the timber barges on the Wye from its moorings and wrecked it; that same summer, there was often too little water in the river to permit transit.[94] In 1785, continual frosts (in May!) and scarcity of water in the Severn again made it difficult to get timber down the Wye.[95] Most of the timber shipped from Chepstow went to Plymouth, but some went further afield, especially in later years; in 1808, shipments sailed from the Wye for the 74-gun *Cressy*, under construction at Frindsbury on the Medway.[96]

The north, too, contributed substantial quantities of timber for the navy. During the Seven Years' War (1756–63), when demand was particularly high, £50,000 worth of forest oak was cut down on the Gwydyr estate and floated down the River Conwy.[97] Perhaps surprisingly, remote and largely land-locked Radnorshire and Montgomeryshire came to be particularly important sources of supply for the navy, especially as the more accessible coastal counties were gradually denuded of their trees. Felling of oak was taking place on the Lymore estate in the 1660s, and it was said that Pencerrig in Radnorshire

provided the keelson for the famous *Royal George*, launched at
Woolwich in 1756 (not necessarily the best advertisement for
Welsh timber, as the ship's bottom fell off in a catastrophic acci-
dent in August 1782 that led to the loss of about 900 lives).[98] The
eighteenth century saw a steady increase in the exploitation of
Montgomeryshire's woodlands, including those in the parkland
of Powis Castle; indeed, by the 1770s fierce competition was
driving up the price. Pride in their county's contribution to the
navy probably inspired the gentlemen of Montgomeryshire to
erect Rodney's Pillar, and anecdotal evidence suggests that it
also manifested itself in other ways:

> Strangers have, it is said, often listened with attention to gen-
> tlemen of the county inquiring anxiously into the conduct
> and fate of the *Windsor Castle*, the *Impregnable*, the *Brunswick*,
> and other men-of-war, in some particular naval engagements,
> and were led to imagine that they had some near and dear
> relations holding important commissions aboard; but, upon
> further inquiry, found the ground of the curiosity to be no
> other than that such ships had been partly built of timber that
> had grown upon their estates, as if the inanimate material
> contained some magic virtue![99]

Radnorshire and Montgomeryshire timber was shipped to
the dockyards from Derwenlas near Machynlleth, floated
down the Severn, or (after its opening in 1797) taken along
the Montgomeryshire Canal to Chester and Ellesmere Port
for onward shipment. All three of the ships mentioned in
the anecdote above were built at Deptford between 1786 and
1790, an indication of the extent to which the Welsh county
also supplied that yard. The French wars from 1793 onwards
led to another spate of felling, notably on the Vaenor estate
where one of the trees cut down for the use of the navy was
68 inches in girth and 73 feet tall.[100] (Vaenor was said to have
provided almost all of the timber for the *Arethusa*, built at

Bristol in 1781 and one of the most successful frigates of the Revolutionary and Napoleonic Wars.) The actual process of converting trees for naval use was lengthy and laborious. When the Golynos oak near Bassaleg, containing some 2,426 cubic feet of timber, was felled in 1810, it took five men twenty days to strip off the branches and fell the tree itself, then two sawyers spent 138 days cutting the main stem into quarter boards and cooper's staves, the branches into six futtocks, one floor timber, three upper piece stems and about twenty knees.[101] Although it was expensive to get timber from central Wales to the royal dockyards, the exhaustion of the more accessible supplies left the navy little alternative; by the 1790s over-cutting was endemic and little attention was being given to conservation or new planting.[102]

Copper-Bottomed

The potential advantages of sheathing ships' bottoms in copper had been known for many years, but expense and scarcity told against it. In 1759, though, the Navy Board ordered the first in a series of trials which continued through the 1760s, and the successful results led to the general adoption of copper sheathing throughout the Royal Navy during the 1770s.[103] It swiftly became apparent that copper sheathing gave the Royal Navy a tremendous advantage, one that it would largely retain until after 1815. Coppered ships were faster, more manoeuvrable, and needed to spend less time in dock to repair the ravages caused by the ship-worm *teredo navalis*: 'effectively, copper increased the size of the fleet by a third'.[104] Thus there can hardly have been many more fortuitous coincidences than 'the great discovery' on 2 March 1768, when a Derbyshire miner, Jonathan Roose, discovered a vast reserve of copper ore at Parys Mountain on Anglesey. From 1776 to 1783, Britain was at war with the fledgling United States of America and then with its allies, France,

Spain and the Netherlands; unsurprisingly, the demands on Parys Mountain and the other Welsh copper mines rocketed. By 1780, the Amlwch solicitor Thomas Williams, *Twm Chwarae Teg*, the canny 'copper king' who developed much of Parys, had his own smelters at Swansea and Ravenhead, Lancashire, as well as developing Amlwch into the second largest town in Wales and the world's principal copper port. Much Parys copper was shipped coastwise to the copperworks at Swansea, Llanelli and Neath, or along the coast to Greenfield, where it was offloaded and transported overland to Holywell. There, a copper forge, wire mill and rolling mill were built and a stronger copper bolt that did not fail was invented;[105] failing bolts were an endemic problem on British warships during the American war and might have been the cause of the catastrophic loss of the *Royal George* at Spithead in 1782. By 1800, *Twm Chwarae Teg* was said to be conducting half of the entire British copper industry, with capital of just under a million pounds.[106] His achievement, and the importance of copper sheathing to the Royal Navy, is still remembered: in 2004, five copper plates from HMS *Victory* were purchased for display at Amlwch, while two others are on display at Greenfield.[107]

Notes

1   M. Lincoln, 'Origins of Public Maritime History', *Journal for Maritime Research*, 4:1 (2002), p.57.

2   P. Borsay, 'New Approaches to Social History. Myth, Memory, and Place: Monmouth and Bath 1750–1900', *Journal of Social History*, 39 (2006), pp.871–3.

3   J.K. Laughton, rev. A.W.H. Pearsall, 'Gell, John (*c.* 1740–1806), Naval Officer', *ODNB*. Gell is buried at Llangattock, where he had built the John Nash-designed Llanwysg House in the year before his death.

4   An example of the windows survives in the Carmarthenshire county museum at Abergwili.

5   NMM, COO/1, pp.14, 35.

6   P.A. Luff, 'Mathews v Lestock: Parliament, Politics and the Navy in Mid-18th Century England', *Parliamentary History*, 10 (1991), pp.52–5; D.A. Baugh, 'Mathews, Thomas (1676–1751), Naval Officer', *ODNB*.

7   I. M. Bates, Champion of the Quarterdeck: Admiral Sir Erasmus
    Gower (1742–1814) (Pomona, Queensland, 2017).

8   J.K. Laughton, rev. R. Morriss, 'Mostyn, Savage (*c.* 1713–1757), Naval
    Officer', *ODNB*. Tucker, then a master's mate aboard the *Pearl*, was
    certainly present when Blackbeard perished. See: R.E. Lee, *Blackbeard:
    A Reappraisal of His Life and Times* (2002), p.139.

9   J. Charnock, *Biographia Navalis: Or, Impartial Memoirs of the Lives and
    Characters of Officers of the Navy of Great Britain, from the Year 1660 to the
    Present Time* (1794), v. 509.

10 Charnock, iii. 173–7.

11 J.K. Laughton, rev. R. Harding, 'Griffin, Thomas (1692/3–1771),
    Naval Officer and Politician', *ODNB*; https://memorials.rmg.co.uk/
    m2030/, M2030.

12 J.K. Laughton, rev. A.G. Jamieson, 'Griffith, Walter (1727–1779),
    Naval Officer', *ODNB*.

13 R.J.B. Knight, 'Geary, Sir Francis, first baronet (1709/10–1796), Naval
    Officer', *ODNB*.

14 F. Jones, 'Lloyd of Gilfachwen, Cilgwyn and Coedmore',
    Cardiganshire: Journal of the Cardiganshire Antiquarian Society, 8 (1976),
    pp.89–90.

15 D.B. Ellison, *Hammer and Nails: Capt Timothy Edwards, Nanhoron*
    (Caernarfon, 1997); quotation from p.101.

16 NLW, MS 14438.

17 CAS, Cwmgwili MS 75.

18 CAS, Cwmgwili MSS 329, 330, 335, 363, 741.

19 NMM, LEW/1; F. Jones, 'Gellidywyll', *Cardiganshire: Journal of the
    Cardiganshire Antiquarian Society*, 8, (1979), pp.385–6.

20 Eames, pp.135–54.

21 Ellison, *Hammer and Nails*, p.156.

22 NLW, MS 1897E/73.

23 NLW, Penralley MSS 19, 165–628, 173, 178; D.H. Williams,
    'Commander Horatio James, RN', *Transactions of the Radnorshire
    Society*, 61 (1991), pp.9–19.

24 Unless stated otherwise, this paragraph is based on L. Phillips, 'Some
    Pembrokeshire Sea Officers (Part Two)', *Journal of the Pembrokeshire
    Historical Society*, 9 (2000), pp.5–6.

25 J.K. Laughton, rev. R. Morriss, 'Mends, Sir Robert (1767?–1823),
    Naval Officer', *ODNB*.

26 O'Byrne, ii. 754–5; J.K. Laughton, rev. A. Lambert, 'Mends, Sir
    William Robert (1812–1897), Naval Officer', *ODNB*

27 Winfield 1603–1714, pp.124, 174–5; Winfield 1714–92, p.120.

28 Winfield 1603–1714, pp.132–3. The *Anglesea* was actually built by a private contractor using labour and materials from the dockyard.

29 Winfield 1714–92, pp.170, 172.

30 Winfield 1603–1714, pp.135, 198. *Newport* was captured by the French in 1696 and taken into their navy as *Le Nieuport*.

31 Winfield 1603–1714, pp.175, 177, 181.

32 Winfield 1714–92, pp.231.

33 Winfield 1714–92, p.44.

34 Winfield 1714–92, pp.51–2; T. Clayton, *Tars: The Men Who Made Britain Rule the Waves* (2008), passim.

35 Winfield 1714–92, p.63.

36 Winfield 1714–92, pp.103–4.

37 Winfield 1714–92, p.217.

38 J. Brighton and P.B.V. Broke, junior, *Sir P B V Broke … A Memoir* (1866), p.56.

39 Winfield 1714–92, pp.276–7, 285.

40 Eames, pp.136–46.

41 PRO, D/CT/419.

42 S. Gradish, *The Manning of the British Navy during the Seven Years' War* (1980), p 56.

43 Gradish, *Manning*, pp.57–9.

44 W.N. Jenkins, 'The Last Hours of the *Caesar*', *Gower*, 26 (1975), pp.19–27.

45 M. Mathews, 'Tales of the Sea: Glimpses of Maritime Wales and the Wider World from South East Glamorganshire, 1762–95', *MW*, 26 (2005), p.25.

46 NMM, COO/1, pp.16–17.

47 NMM, COO/1, p.19.

48 NMM, COO/1, p.19.

49 NMM, COO/1, pp.16–17.

50 PRO, PQ/7/2/30.

51 W.C. Rogers, 'Some Place Names in the Lordship of Gower', *Gower: Journal of the Gower Society*, 18 (1967), p.78; R. Thorne, 'The Leach family of Castlemartin', *The Pembrokeshire Historian*: Journal of the Pembrokeshire Local History Society, 7 (1981), p.32. See also the many wills of naval officers and seamen held by the National Library of Wales.

52 NLW online wills, http://hdl.handle.net/10107/149861; M. Mathews, 'Tales of the Sea: Glimpses of Maritime Wales and the Wider World from South East Glamorganshire, 1762–95', *MW*, 26 (2005), pp.26–7.

53 E. Gill, *Nelson and the Hamiltons on Tour* (Gloucester, 1987), p.42; Eames, p.158.

54 Anon, 'Edward Lloyd, Neath', *Bathafarn: The Journal of the Historical Society of the Methodist Church in Wales*, 24 (1969), pp.38–40.

55 Eames, p.183; T. Pryce, 'History of the parish of Llandysilio', *Collections, Historical & Archaeological Relating to Montgomeryshire*, 32 (1902), pp.55–6.

56 NLW online wills, hdl.handle.net/10107/739975.

57 Eames, pp.155–7.

58 NLW MS 6683D.

59 Sir R. Steele, *The Marine Officer: Or, Sketches of Service* (1840), i. 153.

60 P. Jenkins, *The Making of a Ruling Class: The Glamorgan Gentry 1640–1790* (Cambridge, 1983), p.37.

61 'Morgan, Thomas (1769–1851), Navy Chaplain', *WBO*.

62 T. Morris, 'Penmorfa Panorama (1782–1833)', *Caernarvonshire Historical Society Transactions*, 24 (1963), pp.108–25.

63 NLW, MS 1897E, pt 1, fos. 15, 16, 21; pt 2, fos. 113, 114, 115, 122.

64 M. Stephens, 'Jenkins, John [Ifor Ceri] (1770–1829), Church of England clergyman and antiquary', *ODNB*.

65 'Evans, Evan (Ieuan Fardd or Ieuan Brydydd Hir 1731–1788), Scholar, Poet, and Cleric', and 'Hughes, Edward ('Y Dryw';1772–1850), Eisteddfodic Poet'; both *WBO*.

66 Quoted by Eames, pp.48–9.

67 G.E. Manwaring, ed., *The Diary of Henry Teonge … 1675–9* (1927), p.241

68 N. Thomas, J. Newell and M. Fitzpatrick, eds., *The Death of Captain Cook and Other Writings by David Samwell* (Cardiff, 2007), 131–2.

69 G. Phillips, 'Samwell, David [Dafydd Samuel; pseud. Dafydd Ddu Feddyg] (1751–1798), Naval Surgeon and Poet', *ODNB*.

70 E.G. Bowen, *David Samwell (Dafydd Ddu Feddyg), 1751–98* (Cardiff, 1974), p.89.

71 J.H. Davies, ed., *The Letters of Lewis, Richard, William and John Morris of Anglesey, 1728–65* (Oxford, 1908), passim.

72 G.A. Williams, *Madoc: The Making of a Myth* (1979), pp.78–9 and passim.

73 HMC, *Finch MSS*, ii. 202.

74 B.S. Ingram, ed., *Three Sea Journals of Stuart Times* (1936), pp.126–7.

75 TNA, ADM8/2, navy list of 1 June 1690.

76 HMC *Finch MSS*, iv. 272. See A.G. Crosby, 'By Tempest and Piracy: The Loss of Mersey Salt Vessels off Pembrokeshire, 1697–1715', *Journal of the Pembrokeshire Historical Society*, 12 (2003), pp.59–66.

77 TNA, ADM8/1.

78 TNA, ADM8/7, 8.

79 For the latter, see Eames, pp.113–32.

80 G. Smith, *Smuggling in the Bristol Channel 1700–1850* (Newbury, 1989), pp.133–49; TNA, ADM8/15.

81 TNA, ADM8/29.

82 TNA, ADM51/3871.

83 M. Stammers, *A Maritime Fortress: The Collections of the Wynn Family at Belan Fort, c. 1750–1950* (Cardiff, 2001), p.4 and passim.

84 See e.g. L. Lloyd, *A Real Little Seaport: The Port of Aberdyfi and its People 1565–1920* (Caernarfon, 1996), pp.58–67.

85 D.H. Williams, *White Monks in Gwent and the Border* (Pontypool, 1976), p.90.

86 TNA, ADM106/859/57, 60; NLW, Penrice and Margam MSS 6668–9.

87 NLW, Penrice and Margam MSS 6673–4, 6676–7.

88 TNA, ADM106/1041/43, 159, 333, 382.

89 TNA, ADM106/1079, 88, 94, 119, 153, 164, 177, 185, 190.

90 TNA, ADM106/1079/75, 104, 172.

91 TNA, ADM106/1003/257, 279, 296, 315, 342; 106/1018/202; 106/1047/159.

92 TNA, ADM106/1079/138.

93 TNA, ADM106/1138/34, 150; 106/1161/68; 106/1193/267, 303; 106/1206/321.

94 TNA, ADM106/1110/273, 275, 293.

95 TNA, ADM106/1284/180.

96 TNA, ADM354/231/219, 220.

97 W. Linnard, *Welsh Woods and Forests: A History* (Llandyssul, 2000), p.99.

98 R.C.B. Oliver, 'Pencerrig', *Radnorshire Society Transactions*, 39 (1969), p.37.

99 Anon, 'Montgomeryshire Oak Timber', *Collections Historical & Archaeological Relating to Montgomeryshire and its Borders, Issued by the Powys-Land Club for the Use of its Members*, xvii (1885), pp.383–4.

100 For a timber auction at Vaenor in 1804, see S. Rose, ed., *The Naval Miscellany*, vii (NRS, 2008), pp.199–200.

101 Linnard, *Welsh Woods and Forests*, pp.98–9.

102 Linnard, *Welsh Woods and Forests*, pp.100–1.

103 R.J.B. Knight, 'The Introduction of Copper Sheathing into the Royal Navy, 1779–86', *MM*, 59 (1973), pp.299–309; J.M. Bingeman, J.P. Bethell, P. Goodwin and A.T. Mack, 'Copper and Other Sheathing in the Royal Navy', *International Journal of Nautical Archaeology*, 29 (2000), pp.220–1.

104 Bingeman, Bethell, Goodwin and Mack, 'Copper and Other Sheathing', p.222.

105 K. Davies, 'The Eighteenth Century Copper and Brass Industries of the Greenfield Valley', *THSC* (1979), pp.212–13. S Hughes, 'Defending the Welsh Coast', WATS, 205.

106 A.H. Dodd, *The Industrial Revolution in North Wales* (Cardiff 1971), pp.156–7.

107 news.bbc.co.uk/1/hi/wales/north_west/3607591.stm.

4

THE LAST INVASION OF BRITAIN

WALES, NELSON AND NAVAL
DEFENCE, 1793–1815

The French Revolution triggered an upsurge of radical sentiment throughout Britain, and Wales was no exception. In 1795–6, a series of riots against recruitment into both the army and navy took place across a swathe of North Wales, from Barmouth through Bala to Denbigh.[1] Resistance to naval impressment continued intermittently: there were riots against the press gangs at Carmarthen in 1803 (when a mob of local women liberated the pressed men) and Fishguard in 1811.[2] Such evidence seems to accord with the traditional narrative of a small, oppressed people resisting the unjust exactions of its much larger, warmongering neighbour. Yet Wales' relationship with the Royal Navy during the long French wars of 1793–1815 was actually complex. For example, one of the most prominent Welsh radicals of the age was John Jones of Cerrigydrudion, Denbighshire, known as '*Jac Glan y Gors*'; yet Jac saw no dichotomy in composing odes in praise of Nelson. Similarly, John Williams, sometime vicar of Nantmel, Radnorshire, and schoolmaster at Ystrad Meurig, Cardiganshire, wrote *Nautical Odes … Designed to Commemorate the Achievements of the British Navy*.[3] Several Welsh poets published pieces in their native tongue to mark naval victories: Robert Roberts celebrated the Glorious First of June, 1794, while Edward Pugh and Hugh Jones extolled John Jervis' victory at Cape St Vincent in 1797.[4] George Stephens' poem '*Cân o glod i'r Arglwydd*' ('Song of Praise to the Lord'), published at Carmarthen in 1799, actually sang the praises of no fewer than seven named British admirals.[5] Nor were the poets alone. Welsh towns celebrated naval victories enthusiastically: Carmarthen, which was particularly patriotic, did so with 'bells ringing all day' and 'general illuminations'.[6]

The Black Legion: Fishguard, 1797

The story of the French landing at Fishguard in February 1797 is relatively well known and needs no detailed repetition here.[7] In December 1796, an expedition under General Lazare Hoche and the Irish nationalist leader Wolfe Tone arrived in Bantry Bay but was unable to land due to atrocious weather. Hoche had also envisaged two supporting diversionary expeditions, one to the north-east of England and one to the south-west. The latter was to attack Bristol or else land on the west Welsh coast, disrupting commerce, diverting British forces and, it was hoped, encouraging the local peasantry to rise enthusiastically in the cause of Liberty, Equality and Fraternity. Despite the failure of the Bantry invasion and the cancellation of the raid on the north-east due to bad weather, this one remaining French expedition went ahead. It was commanded by a wealthy Irish-American landowner, William Tate, a close friend of Wolfe Tone who had served as an officer in the Fifth South Carolina Regiment of the Continental Army during the American War of Independence.[8] Tate's force consisted of about 1,200 men, many of whom were former prisoners, with several Irishmen among the officers. The very dark brown die used for their uniforms gave them their nickname, *La Légion Noire*, the Black

Legion. Transporting them into Welsh waters was a squadron of four ships under Commodore Jean-Joseph Castagnier. He had two large and new frigates, *La Vengeance* and *La Résistance*, the latter on her maiden voyage, together with the corvette *La Constance* and a lugger. Flying Russian colours, Castagnier's squadron left Brest on 16 February 1797 and attempted to make for Bristol, but adverse winds forced the French to abandon their principal target and make instead for their secondary objective, Cardigan Bay.

At noon on Wednesday 22 February, the French rounded St David's Head, now flying British colours. These did not fool the eagle-eyed Thomas Williams of Trelythin, a retired naval seaman who recognised the approaching ships for what they were and raised the alarm. At four that afternoon the French anchored off Carreg Wastad Point, 3 miles west of Fishguard, and began to disembark. The lugger sailed into Fishguard Bay to reconnoitre the town, but Fishguard Fort opened fire and the French vessel withdrew in alarm. However, the sloop *Britannia* strayed unwittingly into the middle of the invasion fleet and was captured. Meanwhile, the local defence forces began to mobilise, first the Fishguard and Newport Volunteer Infantry, then the Pembrokeshire Yeomanry under Lord Cawdor, which fortuitously was mustered for a funeral that day (albeit at Castlemartin, some 30 miles away as the crow flies). Captain Edward Longcroft, the navy's regulating officer at Haverfordwest, committed about 150 sailors drawn from his press gangs and the local revenue cutters, one of which, the *Speedwell*, had allegedly encountered the French squadron prior to the landing. Cannon were brought ashore from the revenue cutters to reinforce both the defences of Haverfordwest and Lord Cawdor's little army.[9] That force, reinforced by the local volunteers falling back in the face of the superior French numbers, totalled some 600 men by the time it reached Fishguard in the evening of the 23, but plans for an immediate attack had to be abandoned due to the difficulty of manoeuvring in the darkness. However, morale in the French ranks was crumbling rapidly, despite their great superiority in numbers, partly because of the departure of the reassuring presence of Castagnier's ships, which sailed to harry trade off Dublin. According to one of the great Welsh legends,[10] the French loss of nerve was abetted by the appearance of large numbers of local womenfolk wearing traditional dress of red shawls and black hats, which the jittery Black Legion spied from a distance and assumed to be the uniforms of a vastly superior regiment of the regular British Army. The French asked for terms, but Cawdor would accept only unconditional surrender. Tate finally agreed to this in the afternoon of 24 February, and the last invaders of Britain surrendered ignominiously on the sands of Goodwick Bay.

One aspect of the Fishguard invasion that has been almost entirely neglected in previous accounts is the Royal Navy's response, which can only be described as a catalogue of confusion. The French were able to land partly because of a disastrous intelligence failure at the Admiralty and in the government as a whole, which was convinced that any French assault would be directed either at Ireland once again or else at some place on the east coast of England. (The main body of the Pembrokeshire Militia was in Felixstowe, not Fishguard, as the former was felt to be a much more likely target of a French invasion.[11]) In any case, February was hardly a likely time for any invasion to take place, and the navy had relatively few ships at sea. Consequently, the Admiralty's first response to reports of the Fishguard landing was sceptical and tentative. On 24 February it sent sailing orders to its most famous and successful captain, Sir Edward Pellew of the powerful frigate *Indefatigable*, both still basking in the glory of their stunning victory off the Breton coast five weeks earlier when *Indefatigable* and another frigate had destroyed the French ship-of-the-line *Droits de l'Homme*. At first, Pellew, with *Indefatigable* and two smaller frigates under his command, was directed into the Bristol Channel. On 25 February, though, with financial panic taking hold in the City of London, the Admiralty countermanded this and ordered Pellew to sail instead for Brest, changing its mind again on 2 March when it ordered him to cruise off Worm's Head and thereabouts, 'for the protection of the trade and annoyance of the enemy, intelligence having been received that they have seven frigates on that part of the coast.' But if they had left, he was to proceed 'and sweep round the coast of South Wales in quest of three French frigates which landed a body of troops at Fishguard the 22nd ulto.'[12] These orders must have caught up with Pellew when he was already at sea, for he had finally sailed from Plymouth on 2 March, almost a week after the French surrendered. On 6 and 7 March, *Indefatigable* cruised off St Ann's Head, and on 8 March she was 4 miles off Strumble Head, but it was clear that the emergency was long over. Pellew's squadron rounded Land's End again on 10 March and anchored in Carrick Roads at Falmouth on 14 March.[13]

However, Pellew's cruise was not the sole naval response to the Fishguard invasion. On 22 February, the navy's regulating officer at Haverfordwest, Captain Edward Longcroft, placed an urgent letter aboard the *Valiant* lugger, addressed to Vice-Admiral Robert Kingsmill, commanding the Cork station and flying his flag in HMS *Polyphemus* (or, as the lower deck called her, the 'Polly Infamous'). Longcroft announced the landing of the French and that every effort was being made to oppose them, despite the fact 'we have not one man of war in the harbour'; in evident panic, he pleaded that 'as the enemy are making a landing 15 miles from this place, I request you must sail instantly'. Kingsmill, an elderly and hugely experienced officer, ordered the *Valiant* back to sea to reconnoitre, but at first he, too, was sceptical; fishing vessels were coming into Cork from the Welsh coast averring that they knew nothing of a French landing, and Kingsmill believed that any appearance by French ships had to be a feint to conceal an attack elsewhere. On 27 February, Kingsmill received certain intelligence that there really were French ships in the Irish Sea and that they were now said to be near Wicklow Head. Although he was still convinced that

Ireland must be their principal target, Kingsmill finally ordered to sea a powerful squadron commanded by Captain Michael de Courcey in the 44-gun frigate *Magnanimous*, accompanied by the *Doris*, *Romney*, *Penguin* and a cutter, but this was really a case of bolting stable doors, as de Courcey's squadron failed completely to intercept Castagnier's ships.[14]

However, the hasty naval response to the French invasion achieved a belated but spectacular success on 9 March when two of the ships that had landed the invading force at Fishguard, the frigate *La Résistance* and the corvette *La Constance*, were captured by HM ships *Nymphe* and *San Fiorenzo*. The French ships had spent too long on the Irish coast and had been damaged by bad weather, although Commodore Castagnier himself successfully made it back to Brest in his other frigate, *La Vengeance*. *La Résistance* was taken into the Royal Navy and renamed *Fisgard*, the archaic version of the name that the Admiralty preferred to Fishguard. She was put into commission under Captain Thomas Byam Martin who, as Sir Thomas and Comptroller of the Navy from 1816 to 1831, would later be one of the principal movers in the creation of Pembroke Dock, Wales' only royal dockyard. The *Fisgard* swiftly distinguished itself, capturing the frigate *Immortalité* in 1798 and later taking part in actions at Corunna, Curaçao and Walcheren.[15] The name *Fisgard* would remain on the Navy List until 1983.

The Sea Fencibles

A Sea Fencible corps was first established in 1798 and greatly expanded in 1803 to counter the perceived threat of French invasion. The Fencibles, a kind of maritime reserve force, were to patrol potential landing sites and to man the small armed fishing and coasting craft that would be used to oppose the French assault. They were to comprise men not eligible for service in the navy, such as fishermen and men engaged in some of the

coastal trades, and members of the Sea Fencibles would be protected from the press – perhaps the most important incentive for
men to volunteer. Inevitably, the Sea Fencibles quickly became
a refuge for many who wished to avoid being pressed into the
navy proper.[16] In 1803, the Welsh coast was divided between
three Sea Fencible districts. One, which covered the south coast
from the Wye to the mouth of the Bristol Channel (a location
undefined), had its headquarters at Swansea and subsidiary rendezvous at Cardiff, Newport, Chepstow, Aberavon, Neath,
Penclawdd, Llanmadoc, Oystermouth and Port Eynon; during
October 1805, the month of Trafalgar, the numbers mustered
at each of these locations were respectively 220 (Swansea), 54,
52, 127, 37, 86, 47, 103, 99 and a suspiciously large body of
179 at tiny, remote Port Eynon, giving a total for the district of
1,004 men. The district was commanded by Captain Richard
Jones, a Swansea man. The second area, examined in more
detail below, extended from Kidwelly to Cardigan. Anglesey,
with its principal rendezvous at Holyhead and subsidiary rendezvous at Rhoscolyn and Beaumaris, was commanded by
Captain Richard Byron, a cousin of the notorious poet.[17]
Some Welshmen also came under the Chepstow district which
extended from Westbury on Severn to Beachley, then up the
English side of the River Wye, but there were obvious gaps in
the geographical boundaries of the districts, notably the omissions of the Burry Inlet, much of Cardigan Bay, Llŷn, and much
of the North Wales coast. The Sea Fencibles were given their
own uniform, very similar to that of sailors in the regular navy,
and were armed principally with pikes.[18]

On 11 July 1803, Charles Tyler of St Nicholas, Glamorgan,
an experienced captain who had previously commanded the
Trimmer sloop when it was based at Milford Haven in the 1780s,
received an Admiralty order to form a Sea Fencible corps in an
area extending from Kidwelly to Cardigan. Tyler commanded
two junior captains, John Chesshyre, who had responsibility for the coast from Kidwelly to Tenby and established his

headquarters at Laugharne, and Henry Probyn who covered the coast from Solva (later St David's) to Cardigan where he had his base. Tyler himself oversaw the central part of the district, including Milford Haven, and had his headquarters at Haverfordwest, the rendezvous for the entire district. Probyn in particular immediately encountered difficulties: men failed to come forward, especially at Fishguard, because 'some evil disposed persons have insinuated as soon as they are enrolled, they will be sent to man the ships'.[19] Nevertheless, by November Tyler commanded 772 men, the major recruiting grounds being Cardigan, Tenby and Lawrenny (the latter presumably the rendezvous for men from the upper reaches of Milford Haven, including Haverfordwest).[20] There were suspicions that many of the Sea Fencibles were smugglers – hence, perhaps, the surprisingly large numbers recruited in the Gower, a notorious den of smuggling – so it was ironic that one of their principal duties, apart from obstructing the anticipated invasion, was to interdict smuggling. In February 1805, a party of Tyler's men swooped onto Rhossili Beach, seizing over a hundred barrels of brandy, rum, gin and wine.[21]

In 1803–04, the threat of invasion seemed to be at its greatest. Napoleon's *Grande Armée* was known to be massing at Boulogne, and in Wales, as elsewhere, new countermeasures were hastily put in place. At Milford, the dockyard artificers formed themselves into an artillery company and manned the new batteries being thrown up around the harbour.[22] In October 1803, a signal station was built at St Ann's Point, commanded initially by Lieutenant Rice Morgan, and in February 1804 twelve 26-pounder cannon were set up at Milford, manned principally by the Sea Fencibles.[23] New coastal batteries were hurriedly thrown up to protect other Welsh harbours. There was already a battery at Mumbles, built some time before 1791 and enhanced in 1803, Swansea Corporation meeting half the cost of the new armament.[24] In 1803–04, cannon were also placed at such locations as Swansea and Machynys (Llanelli), the former following a meeting of the town's ship owners and merchants which was also attended by Captain Richard Jones of the Sea Fencibles.[25] At Caernarfon, seventy-eight masters and mates of coastal vessels in the port signed a petition to the Admiralty stating their intention of forming a new corps to be called the Caernarfon Marine Volunteers, which (unlike the Sea Fencibles) would appoint its own officers from within.[26] Ultimately, of course, the French did not come, and as the threat of invasion receded, so did the emphasis on coastal defence; the guns were removed from the Mumbles and the Swansea Burrows in November 1805.[27] Finally, the Sea Fencible corps itself was disbanded on 10 February 1810.

Sick and Hurt

During the Revolutionary and Napoleonic Wars, Swansea was probably the closest thing Wales had to a 'naval base', Milford Haven aside. As well as being a centre for the impress service, a naval victualling port and later the headquarters and rendezvous for the Sea Fencibles, the town was also an agency of the Sick and Hurt Board, the branch of the naval administration that cared for wounded and sickly seamen. Meticulous records of this service were kept and still survive, detailing the men who were cared for in the town, their conditions and their billets. The numbers involved varied depending on how many ships were operating in the vicinity, but they could be surprisingly large: in the second quarter of 1797, for example, thirty-five naval seamen were billeted with local landlords and landladies like Elizabeth James, who had no fewer than twenty-two men under her roof. Several men were listed as having 'fever' or 'consumption', two had dropsy and one each an ulcerated leg and a 'swelled testicle', but the other significant health issue was listed baldly as 'venereal', afflicting eight of the men. In 1805, three of the men aboard the pressing tender *Cleveland*, based at the port, were listed as suffering from 'itch'.[28] The navy also impacted on Welsh communities in other ways. Many of the men who joined the service were unmarried or orphans, but others left families behind, and these sometimes needed the support of their parishes. When Thomas Pugh of Castell Caereinion went into the navy in 1795, the Forden Poor Law Guardians ordered 2 shillings a week to be paid to a 'weekly nurse' to look after his two young daughters, his wife being dead.[29]

Nelson in Wales

In 1802, Wales played host to the most famous admiral and most infamous *ménage à trois* of the age. In the afternoon of 25 July, Horatio Nelson, accompanied by Sir William and Emma Hamilton, disembarked at Monmouth quay, having travelled by boat from Ross-on-Wye. The hero was greeted by a salute of cannon and the band of the Monmouth and Brecon Militia playing *See, The Conquering Hero Comes* and *Rule, Britannia*.[30] Nelson had come to Wales to take advantage of the brief period of peace with Napoleon's France that followed the signing of the Treaty of Amiens, and at the behest of Sir William Hamilton, who had inherited substantial lands in Pembrokeshire from his first wife. Sir William wished to convince Nelson of the potential of Milford Haven as a naval base, and thus, not coincidentally, as a potential source of enhanced revenues for the financially stretched Hamilton and his nephew-cum-agent, Charles Greville. For Emma (who had also been Greville's lover at one time), the Welsh tour was a kind of homecoming; although she had been born a couple of miles over the border at Ness on the Wirral, she was brought up at Hawarden, Flintshire, her mother's family home. The party's reception at Monmouth proved to be a foretaste of what was to come. A huge crowd packed Agincourt Square and cheered Nelson to the heavens when he spoke from the Beaufort Arms before breaking into a spontaneous rendition of *God Save the King*. The next day the party moved on via Abergavenny to call on Nelson's old friend Admiral John Gell at his mansion of Llanwysg. Then it was on to Brecon before a detour to Merthyr Tydfil (or 'Myrter Tydder', as Nelson wrote it), where they stayed on the night of 27 July.[31] Nelson recognised in the crowd a former shipmate, Will Ellis, and gave him a guinea to 'splice the mainbrace'. He offered the same reward to anyone who would toast him in Welsh, and the parish clerk proceeded to do so: '*Yfwn i arwr y Neil! Croeso i Cymru!*' ('Drink to the hero of the Nile! Welcome to Wales!')[32] The next day they inspected the iron foundries of Richard Crawshay, which were making guns for the navy, before resuming their journey and spending the night of the 29 July at the Castle Hotel, Llandovery. The party then travelled on to Carmarthen, where they stayed at the Ivy Bush on the night of the 30 July.[33] Nelson and the Hamiltons left early in the morning of 31 July, passing through St Clears, Narberth and Haverfordwest to the new town of Milford, where they arrived in the evening.

The following day, 1 August, was the fourth anniversary of Nelson's great victory at the Nile. Hamilton and Greville marked the happy coincidence of the hero's presence by staging several days of festivities. The party stayed at the New Inn – inevitably renamed the Lord Nelson shortly afterwards, the name it bears to this day – and at a dinner in his honour, the admiral delivered a suitably gushing speech. He began by praising his old friend Thomas Foley, the Pembrokeshire captain who had served with him at the Nile and Copenhagen (see Chapter 5), before moving on to extol the virtues of Milford as one of the best harbours in the world. He hoped the government would intervene to develop it properly, a sentiment which must have been music to the ears of Hamilton and Greville. Nelson subsequently laid the foundation stone of Saint Katherine's church and, as a memento of the battle, presented to it the truck of the mainmast of the French flagship *L'Orient*, destroyed at the Nile.[34] The party went to Haverfordwest on 6 August, and Nelson and Foley were granted the Freedom of the Borough on the following day. A two-day stay with Foley's brother was followed by a visit to Stackpole hosted by Lord Cawdor, of Fishguard fame, before a stay at Tenby attended by the customary adoring crowds and culminating in a Grand Ball at the Lion Inn.

Nelson and the Hamiltons set out for home on 13 August, going via St Clears and Carmarthen to Swansea. Here the customary procession into the town was suddenly interrupted by three blasts on a boatswain's whistle. Nelson sprang up, crying 'It's Tom Cleaves' whistle, by God!', and leapt from his carriage for an emotional reunion with his former shipmate, then the landlord of the Plume of Feathers inn. The party subsequently stopped at another pub, the Mackworth Arms, where the landlord, Mr Roteley, presented his son Lewis to the admiral. The boy was intent on a career at sea and impressed Nelson, who subsequently recommended him; three years later Lewis Roteley was a Royal Marine officer aboard HMS *Victory*, and witnessed the fatal shot that killed the great admiral.[35] On the following day, 14 August, Nelson and Sir William Hamilton were given the Freedom of Swansea, and Emma led the audience in *Rule, Britannia!* Leaving Swansea, the party passed through Pyle to Cardiff, thence to Newport and Chepstow, where they arrived on 17 August. They returned to Monmouth on the following day, thus completing their full circle in Wales. On 19 August, they went up to the 'naval temple' on the Kymin, then attended a grand banquet in their honour. Nelson responded to the toast with a generous speech, after which Emma sang her own version of the national anthem, with new words exalting her lover:

Join we great Nelson's name,
First on the roll of fame,
Him let us sing,
Spread we his praise around,
Honour of British ground,

Who made Nile's shores resound,
God save the King.[36]

Watkins, the landlord of the Beaufort Arms, subsequently produced some fine vintage claret that had been laid down in his cellar for years, and informed Nelson that he had raised a glass of it to his honour after the Battle of the Nile. 'Poh,' said Nelson, 'that was nothing! I always did beat the French, and I always will, Watkins, whenever they give me an opportunity of meeting with them.'[37] The sojourn in Monmouth concluded with a little sightseeing in the town on the following day before the party left for Ross-on-Wye and thus crossed the border back into England, eventually returning home to Merton on 5 September 1802.

The news of Nelson's death, little more than three years after he concluded his tour, had a profound impact on the Principality, particularly in the parts he had visited. Sir William Paxton erected his great tower to the admiral's memory in the Tywi Valley, overlooking the route he had taken from Llandovery to Carmarthen; at Milford, Lord Cawdor organised an annual sailing race in Nelson's honour. Within a month of Trafalgar, the new Swansea newspaper, *The Cambrian*, had announced a poetry competition, the subject inevitably being the death of Nelson.[38] At Carmarthen, the Trafalgar thanksgiving service on 5 December culminated in a collection for the wives and widows of battle casualties which raised some £60, supplementing the £50 that the corporation had already voted towards their relief.[39] Llanelli celebrated the initial news of the victory by firing guns and ringing bells, but this was followed a month later with a day of thanksgiving 'observed with a becoming reverence', the Dead March from Handel's *Saul* being performed with muffled drums.[40] Further afield, Montgomery, too, marked the admiral's death with solemn music and a sermon; but Trafalgar's curious dual status as both a great national triumph and a cause of profound mourning was demonstrated by the fact that the town also held a grand dinner for the gentlemen and a ball for the ladies, who wore 'laurel, with black feathers' to acknowledge the twin imperatives of the occasion.[41] The bards rushed into print to sing the praises of the dead hero, as their predecessors had done for Urien Rheged and Llywelyn Olaf. John Thomas, whose '[*Cerdd*] *o ddiolchgar goffadwriaeth* ...' ['Song of Thankful Commemoration'] was published at Trefriw in 1805, claimed that over 30,000 French and Spanish sailors had been drowned (in other words, more than the entire complement of the enemy fleet), but this exaggeration aside, he explicitly acknowledged the part played by the English and Welsh together in humbling the enemy, as well as having an unsubtle dig at the Emperor Napoleon:

> Y Ffrancod digrefydd sy ffinion aflonydd –
> I wledydd maent beunydd yn boen;
> Ond Saeson a Chymry a ddarfu'n dychrynu –
> Mae Boni'n darn grynu'n ei groen.

> ['The unreligious Frenchmen are savage and merciless –
> They are constantly troublesome to countries;
> But the English and the Welsh gave them a fright –
> Boney is shaking in his skin.'][42]

Nelson's tour, and particularly his two visits to Monmouth, eventually had a curious sequel. Georgiana Rolls, Lady Llangattock, was the widow of a prominent local politician; their youngest child Charles would ultimately achieve global fame as the Rolls of Rolls-Royce. The family lived at The Hendre, a vast Gothic pile near Monmouth. Lady Llangattock, a fanatical Nelson enthusiast, assembled there a huge quantity of ephemera and important artefacts relating to her hero. When she died in 1924, she bequeathed the collection to the town of Monmouth, which thus became the somewhat unlikely setting for one of the most intimate naval museums in Britain and one of the finest Nelson collections in the world. Now part of a larger Monmouth museum, the collection includes the admiral's fighting sword – bought just before Trafalgar, but which he either forgot or decided deliberately not to carry – and the surrendered blades of the French and Spanish admirals Villeneuve and Cisneros.

The Bishop and the Telegraph

The outpouring of popular enthusiasm that attended Nelson's tour of 1802 was not universal. Scandalised by the *ménage à trois*, several prominent figures, ranging from the Duke of Marlborough to the Vicar of Carmarthen, went out of their way to avoid the admiral and his mistress. One of the most eminent of these refuseniks was Lord George Murray, the Bishop of St David's since February 1801, who conspicuously failed to invite Nelson and the Hamiltons to his episcopal palace at Abergwili, near Carmarthen. Perhaps Murray had mixed feelings, for his entire life had been governed by an insatiable interest in all things naval; and indeed, by 1802 he had already made his own remarkable contribution to the eventual triumph of 'Nelson's Navy'.[43] The Right Reverend George Murray was a younger brother of the third Duke of Atholl and the sibling always destined for a career in the Church, but despite this, his passion for the navy shone through from an early age. On 17 October 1794, he wrote to the Admiralty to propose the creation of a shutter telegraph system, based on lines of signal stations connecting the various royal dockyards to the Admiralty building in Whitehall. Murray's system consisted of two columns mounting six shutters in a vertical frame 20 feet high, giving sixty-three changes and, therefore, the flexibility to spell out any message.[44] When all shutters were open, the station was at rest; when all were closed, it was ready to transmit. Murray's telegraph was tested successfully during 1795.[45] The Admiralty was suitably impressed, and early in December a contract was agreed to build the first telegraph lines.[46] The London to Deal telegraph was completed by 27 January 1796, with the fastest messages taking seven minutes. In March, Lord George was given the direction of the entire Admiralty telegraph system, and two machines were erected on the roof of the Admiralty building itself, one facing east, the other south.

The Admiralty telegraph – the first telegraph in Britain – quickly became an indispensable part of the Royal Navy. Ironically, perhaps its most famous use was not for the purpose Murray feared, namely communicating news of an invasion from the coast to London, but for the transmission of one item of news in the opposite direction. At first light on 6 November 1805, the shutter devices on the roof of the Admiralty building were closed prior to the transmission of the news that Lieutenant Lapenotière of HMS *Pickle* had brought to the secretary of the Admiralty at one that morning, having ridden insanely from Falmouth in barely thirty-eight hours. Thus Bishop Murray's invention carried to Portsmouth the news that Vice-Admiral Horatio, Viscount Nelson, who had sailed from there on 15 September, had destroyed the Franco-Spanish fleet at Trafalgar, but had died at the moment of victory. Bishop Lord George Murray did not live to witness the event. He had died suddenly on 3 June 1803, aged only 42. His brief episcopate is now almost forgotten in Wales, but in modern histories of data transference, Murray's telegraph is now accorded a place of honour as one of the key steps in the long evolutionary process that led eventually to the Internet and the World Wide Web.

Forging the Sinews of War

Naval ordnance had been manufactured in Wales for many years. From the 1590s to about 1609, for instance, the Pentyrch ironworks in the Lower Taff Valley cast several hundred tons' worth of the guns called sakers, minions and demi-culverins, although these were principally destined for foreign countries and the domestic mercantile market rather than the royal ordnance store at the Tower of London.[47] The great French wars of the eighteenth and early nineteenth centuries coincided with the remarkable growth of the South Wales iron industry, and the great foundries at Merthyr and in the other valleys found a ready market in the navy. During the American war of 1776–83, a number of foundries were established at Merthyr to cast cannon and cannonballs for the navy; Richard Crawshay, the man principally responsible for the expansion of Merthyr, first came to the area to run one of them. The Dowlais ironworks obtained ordnance contracts during the Napoleonic Wars, as well as one for bar iron for the royal dockyards (although this was threatened by much cheaper Swedish competition).[48] Crawshay's works at Cyfarthfa was one of the stops on Nelson's tour of South Wales in 1802, and a carronade – a short-range 'smasher' weapon with a short barrel – cast at Cyfarthfa in that year is preserved at the National Museum of Wales.[49] Welsh coal also found a market in the navy long before the adoption of steam power and the huge expansion of the South Wales coalfield; it was being supplied in significant quantities to Plymouth Dockyard as early as 1745.[50]

North and West Wales' industries also benefited from the wars. Copper from Parys Mountain continued to meet the navy's demands, which were so great that new mines were opened on more marginal sites such as Penrhyn Du, Llanberis, Drwsycoed, Aberglaslyn and Llandudno.[51] The Wilkinson iron works at Bersham, which had produced huge amounts of cannon and shot during the Seven Years' War (despite rumours that they were supplying the French too), increased production again during the Revolutionary and Napoleonic Wars.[52] Other suppliers of ordnance to the navy included Robert Morgan of Carmarthen, who produced cannon there during the Seven Years' War, and Alexander Raby, whose furnace near Llanelli (which still survives) was, by 1800, producing 36-pounder carronades as well as swords, muskets, cannonballs and more conventional cannon.[53] Raby-manufactured 12-, 18- and 32-pounder guns could be found on several famous ships of the Napoleonic Wars, such as the Trafalgar participants *Thunderer*, *Swiftsure* and *Colossus*, together with, appropriately, the frigate *Owen Glendower*.[54] Local merchant ships like the *Catherine* and the *Mary Ann* were used to transport Raby's ordnance to London, but the long sea voyage was inevitably hazardous: the *Mary Ann* was captured by the French in April 1804.[55]

The Protection of Welsh Trade and the Dangers of the Coast

In March 1804 the Admiralty ordered armed ships to be taken up for the defence of Welsh coastal trade, and the Swansea brigs *Endeavour* and *Morriston* were duly brought into service.[56] They regularly escorted convoys to and from the port; in September 1805, for example, the *Endeavour* brought in vessels from Falmouth and Plymouth, the usual ports-of-call for the Swansea convoys, and in the same month the *Morriston* sailed from Mumbles with a convoy of coasters.[57] Other gun brigs subsequently served on the station, such as the *Conquest*, which left Swansea with a convoy in January 1813, and the *Bloodhound*, which took a French brig during Napoleon's 'hundred days' before Waterloo. However, the Welsh coast remained a perilous environment, the dangers of enemy attack being arguably only as threatening to shipping as Welsh weather and the treacherous nature of much of the coastline. A potent reminder of this came on 24 January 1808, when the fifth rate frigate HMS *Leda*, en route from Cork, encountered a strong westerly gale and heavy seas which caused serious damage to the ship. Captain Honeyman made for Milford Haven, but she ran aground on the rocks of West Angle Bay in heavy rain whilst attempting to enter the harbour. The wreck gradually broke up, although various artefacts from it have come to light over the years. *Leda* was a particularly important vessel, the lead ship of the navy's largest and most successful class of sailing frigates. Forty-six more succeeded her, including two which survive to this day, the *Trincomalee* at Hartlepool and the *Unicorn* at Dundee.

From 1812 onwards, Britain was also fighting an unexpected new enemy: the United States of America. The ostensible reason for war was the American objection to the Royal Navy's claim to search neutral ships and press 'British' seamen out of them. One such case was that of Thomas Prichard Thomas of Bryncroes, Caernarfonshire, who probably thought he had put behind him any prospect of being pressed into the Royal Navy when he emigrated to the United States in 1795 and became a naturalised citizen of the fledgling nation. In June 1796, how- ever, while serving on a merchant ship plying from New York to Liverpool, he was pressed into HMS *Prevoyance*, and shortly afterwards lost his right leg in a brief fight with a French ship. Thomas made a second, successful, attempt to emigrate in 1800, but cases like his ultimately became one of the principal causes of the 'War of 1812'.[58] A particularly important catalyst of that conflict was the clash on 22 June 1807 between USS *Chesapeake* and HMS *Leopard*, when the latter attempted to enforce the Royal Navy's claimed right to search American ships for desert- ers. The American warship swiftly surrendered to *Leopard*'s captain, Salusbury Pryce Humphreys of Montgomeryshire, but his triumph was short-lived; to mollify the Americans, he was given no further command.

Following the outbreak of hostilities proper, American pri- vateers attacked shipping in Welsh waters, and in the summer of 1813 they were joined by a warship of the still relatively tiny United States Navy, the brig USS *Argus*. She was commanded by a newly-minted American naval hero, William Henry Allen, who had distinguished himself in the encounter between USS *Chesapeake* and HMS *Leopard* in 1807 and in the action of 1812 when USS *United States* captured HMS *Macedonian*. In late

July and early August 1813, Allen's *Argus* took or destroyed twenty-two merchant ships in St George's Channel and the Irish Sea.[59] But on 14 August 1813, a few miles off St David's Head, the *Argus* encountered the larger and more heavily armed brig HMS *Pelican*. Allen was hit early on in the left thigh by a 32-pound shot. The action lasted only forty-five minutes before the *Argus*' stars and stripes were hauled down in surrender, with many of her crew dead or wounded.[60] Allen was taken to Plymouth but died of his wounds a few days later; he was given a funeral with full military honours. But the depredations of the American privateers continued, causing growing problems for Welsh ports and shipowners. Over a hundred ships were lost to such daring raiders as the *Chasseur*, *Neufchatel* and *Wasp*, as well as to the USS *Argus*, and insurance rates more than doubled. In August 1814, the merchants of Swansea petitioned for additional naval protection; the Admiralty sent reinforcements, namely fifteen sloops and gun-brigs that were sent into the southern Irish Sea between October 1814 and January 1815, but no special provision was made for Swansea. It was only the coming of peace early in 1815 that ended the American depredations in Welsh waters.[61]

Prisoners of His Majesty

Naval prisoners of war had been held in Wales on a number of occasions: during the War of Independence, for instance, captured American seamen were imprisoned at Pembroke.[62] During the Napoleonic Wars, French naval officers who had given their parole were quartered in towns all over Britain, and in the latter stages of the wars many were to be found in the six Welsh parole towns, Abergavenny, Brecon, Llanfyllin, Montgomery, Newtown and Welshpool, as well as in Bishop's Castle, just a mile over the Shropshire border. At Abergavenny they even had their own Masonic Lodge, '*Enfants de Mars et de*

Neptune', one of the most prominent members of which was de Grasse Tilly, son of the Admiral de Grasse who had played a notable part in the American War of Independence.[63] During the period 1812–14, 148 paroled French officers were quartered at Welshpool. Most of them were naval men, drawn from men-of-war like *Le Brave* (a 74 captured in 1806) and frigates like *Le Libre* and *La Guerrière*. Others had been captured on sloops, gunboats and privateers. Several had fought at Trafalgar in the *Berwick* and *Swiftsure*, British prizes which were retaken by Nelson's fleet: they included Achille Lafore, lieutenant of the former, and Nicolas Navare, second surgeon of the latter.[64] A further 150 French prisoners could be found in Llanfyllin. Although most were army officers captured at the Battle of Badajoz, many were from two Dutch-manned French warships, *La Wiser* and *La Traave*, both of which were captured in October 1813. The prisoners made an impact on the town in many ways; they fathered several illegitimate children, and a few stayed on after the war or returned in due course (in one case, to marry the rector's daughter).[65]

François Husson, captain in the French Marine Artillery, was captured in 1806 when the frigate *Le Président* was taken on her way back to Brest from the West Indies. He was paroled to Brecon, where a total of eighty-six French officers were quartered between 1806 and 1812. Husson died in April 1810, aged 48, and his grave, with its headstone in French, can still be seen in the churchyard of Brecon Cathedral.[66] The French naval officers at Brecon had a lasting influence in other ways. Many were Breton, and one taught French and another mathematics to a young local man, Thomas Price of Cwm-Du, who went on to become an eminent clergyman, antiquarian, and a driving force in the establishment of *eisteddfodau* throughout Wales. Price's early contact with the Breton prisoners of war also led to him developing a lifelong interest in all things Breton.[67] His was not the only naval contact with Wales' Breton cousins. One Welsh sailor, probably serving aboard HMS *Ripon* in 1813–14, was employed to interpret for Breton fishermen, who spoke no French, when his ship's captain – Sir Christopher Cole, soon to be MP for Glamorgan – wished to interrogate them.[68]

Notes

1   G.A. Williams, *The Search for Beulah Land: The Welsh and the Atlantic Revolution* (1980), pp.28, 132.
2   N. Rogers, *The Press Gang: Naval Impressment and its Opponents in Georgian Britain* (2007), pp.45–6; *The Cambrian*, 27 Apr. 1811.
3   Ff. Payne, 'Exploring Radnorshire', *Transactions of the Radnorshire Society*, LXXIX (2009), p.127.
4   F.M. Jones (ed.), *Welsh Ballads of the French Revolution* (2012), pp.144–8, 186–95.
5   *Welsh Ballads of the French Revolution*, pp.234–9.
6   E. Dale-Jones, 'Admiral Nelson Slept Here', *The Carmarthenshire Antiquary*, XXXV (1999), p.39.
7   The most recent accounts, upon which my summary is based, are: R. Quinault, 'The French Invasion of Pembrokeshire in 1797', *Welsh History Review*, 19 (1999), pp.618–42; R. Rose, 'The French at Fishguard: Fact, Fiction and Folklore', *THSC* (2002), pp.74–105.
8   J.D. Ahlstrom, 'Captain and Chef de Brigade William Tate: South Carolina Adventurer', *The South Carolina Historical Magazine*, 88 (1987), pp.183–191.
9   J.E. Thomas, *Britain's Last Invasion: Fishguard 1797* (Stroud, 2007), pp.73–4.
10 One which has a much greater element of truth than is sometimes assumed: Rose, 'The French at Fishguard', pp.93–101.
11 Quinault, 'French Invasion', p.623.
12 TNA, ADM3/118, fo. 117.
13 TNA, ADM51/1210, pt. 3.
14 TNA, ADM1/614, Kingsmill's letters to Nepean with enclosures by Longcroft et al., 26, 27 Feb., 1 Mar. 1797.
15 P.J. Payton, *The Story of HMS Fisgard* (Redruth, 1983), pp.1–4.
16 N. Rogers, 'The Sea Fencibles, Loyalism and the Reach of the State', *Resisting Napoleon: The British Response to the Threat of Invasion, 1797–1815*, ed. M. Philip (Aldershot, 2006), pp.43–4, 46–8.
17 Listings of Welsh Sea Fencibles: TNA, ADM28/90-3 (Chepstow to Gower), 97–9 (Kidwelly to Cardigan), 100 (Holyhead and north Wales); analysis of South Wales district from ADM28/92.
18 J. Penny, 'The Severn District Sea Fencibles, 1803 to 1810', *The Regional Historian*, 6 (2002) (available online

behind paywall at regionalhistorianuwe.org/2000/09/22/
the-severn-district-sea-fencibles-1803-to-1810/).

19 NMM, IGR/2, Tyler letters, 16 July, 13 Aug. 1803, and order to him,
11 July 1803.

20 NMM, IGR/2, Tyler letters, 26 Nov. 1803, 2 Oct. 1804.

21 *The Cambrian*, 22 Feb. 1805.

22 TNA, ADM106/3186, Barrallier letters, 21 Oct. 1803, 21 Mar. 1804.

23 NMM, IGR/2, Tyler letters, 19 Oct., 3 Nov. 1803, 27 Feb. 1804.

24 A. Saunders, C.J. Spurgeon, H.J. Thomas and D.J. Roberts, *Guns
Across the Severn: The Victorian Fortifications of Glamorgan* (Aberystwyth,
2001), p.39.

25 *The Cambrian*, 7 July 1804.

26 P.K. Crimmin, 'Local Defence in the Napoleonic Wars',
Caernarvonshire Historical Society Transactions, 34 (1973), pp.87–91
(quotation from p.89).

27 *The Cambrian*, 2 Nov. 1805.

28 TNA, ADM102/757.

29 J.G. Morris and M.N. Owen, 'Forden Union during the Napoleonic
Wars 1795–1816', *Collections, historical & archaeological relating to
Montgomeryshire*, 37 (1915), p.97.

30 E. Gill, *Nelson and the Hamiltons on Tour* (Gloucester, 1987), pp.22–3.
Unless stated otherwise, the remainder of this section is based on
Gill's book.

31 The dates of their stops, largely omitted in Gill's book, are provided
by E. Dale-Jones, 'Admiral Nelson Slept Here', *The Carmarthenshire
Antiquary*, XXXV (1999), pp.35–44.

32 Gill, *On Tour*, p.28.

33 N. Evans, 'Lord Nelson Remembered', *The Carmarthenshire Antiquary*,
XLI (2005), p.137.

34 D. Miles, ed., *A Pembrokeshire Anthology* (Llandybie, 1983), pp.72–3.

35 Gill, *On Tour*, pp.42–3.

36 Gill, *On Tour*, p.55.

37 C. Heath, *Descriptive Account of the Kymin Pavilion…to which is now first
added, Lord Nelson's Visit to Monmouth…* (Monmouth, 1802?).

38 *The Cambrian*, 16 Nov., 23 Nov., 21 Dec. 1805, 12 July, 27 Dec. 1806,
4 Aug. 1810, 10 Aug. 1811.

39 N. Evans, 'Lord Nelson Remembered', *The Carmarthenshire Antiquary*,
XLI (2005), pp.141–2.

40 *The Cambrian*, 16 Nov., 14 Dec. 1805.

41 J.D.K. Lloyd, 'Montgomeryshire in the Nineteenth Century',
Montgomeryshire Collections relating to Montgomeryshire and its Borders, 58
(1964), p.94.

42 *Welsh Ballads of the French Revolution*, pp.264–9 (extract from p.269).

43 Unless stated otherwise, the following paragraphs are based on my article, 'Lord George Murray, Bishop of St David's and Progenitor of the Internet', *The Carmarthenshire Antiquary*, XXXVII (2001), pp.51–61.

44 G. Wilson, *The Old Telegraphs* (1976), pp.17–32; T.W. Holmes, *The Semaphore: The Story of the Admiralty-to-Portsmouth Shutter Telegraph and Semaphore Lines* (Ilfracombe, 1983), pp.29–36. Murray's original model of his shutter telegraph is now at the National Maritime Museum.

45 Blair Castle, Perthshire, Atholl papers, 59/216.

46 TNA, ADM106/2220, p.660.

47 P. Riden, 'Early ironworks in the Lower Taff Valley', *Morgannwg: Transactions of the Glamorgan Local History Society*, 36 (1992), pp.73–6.

48 E.A. Havill, 'William Taitt and the Dowlais Ironworks', *THSC* (1983), p.111; National Archives of Scotland, GD51/2/947. S. Hughes, 'Defending the Welsh Coast', WATS, 206.

49 www.gtj.org.uk/en/small/item/GTJ31599/ (last accessed: 2012)

50 TNA, ADM106/1020/44, 100.

51 A.H. Dodd, *The Industrial Revolution in North Wales* (Cardiff 1971), pp.164–9.

52 Dodd, *Industrial Revolution*, pp.135, 136, 139.

53 For Morgan, see L.J. Williams, 'A Carmarthenshire Ironmaster and the Seven Years' War', *Business History*, 2 (1959), pp.32–43.

54 TNA, WO45/54, 23 May, 17 July 1800, ADM160/154.

55 *The Cambrian*, 24 Mar., 7, 14 Apr. 1804.

56 *The Cambrian*, 31 Mar. 1804.

57 *The Cambrian*, 21, 28 Sept. 1805. *The Cambrian* contains many other reports of convoy movements to and from Swansea.

58 B. Hughes, 'The Impressment of Thomas Prichard Thomas in 1796', *MW*, 17 (1996).

59 'Allen, William Henry (21 Oct. 1784–18 Aug. 1813), US Naval Officer and Hero of the War of 1812', *American National Biography*.

60 TNA, ADM51/2660.

61 P.K. Crimmin, 'A Swansea Petition of 1814', *Morgannwg: Transactions of the Glamorgan Local History Society*, 18 (1974), pp.31–44.

62 E.H. Turner, 'American Prisoners of War in Britain, 1777–83', *MM*, 45 (1959), p.201.

63 F. Abell, *Prisoners of War in Britain, 1756 to 1815* (Oxford, 1914), pp.357–64.

64 TNA, ADM103/609.

65 M.Ll. Chapman, 'Napoleonic prisoners of war in Llanfyllin', *Montgomeryshire Collections Relating to Montgomeryshire and its Borders*, 71 (1983), pp.70–85.

66 M. Ford, 'Captain François Husson', *Brycheiniog*, 25 (1992–3), pp.93–5.

67 H. Hughes, 'Thomas Price (Carnhuanawc), Cwm-du, 1787–1848', *Brycheiniog*, 34 (2002), p.137.

68 J.D. Harding, *An Essay on the Influence of Welsh Tradition upon European Literature* (1840), p.18.

5

THE WELSH IN NELSON'S NAVY

1793–1815

In February 1797, the 17-year-old John George, son of the landlord of the Blue Boar Inn, Haverfordwest, watched the Castlemartin Yeomanry assemble in Castle Square before marching out against the French invaders at Fishguard. A few days later, John watched again as the French were marched into the town as prisoners of war. Perhaps it was these experiences that decided him on his career path, for two years later he left home and became a lieutenant in the Royal Marines. He took part in the Battle of Copenhagen in 1801, one of Nelson's greatest victories, remembered above all for the admiral's placing his telescope to his blind eye so he could claim not to have seen a recall signal; his famous remark, 'I do not see the signal', was addressed to his friend Captain Thomas Foley, originally of Ridgeway near Haverfordwest but then the owner of the Abermarlais estate in the Tywi Valley. A quirk of fate then saw John George appointed in 1803 to HMS *Fisgard*, the captured French frigate that had led the force which invaded Wales: as he noted at the time, 'I think it is rather apropos in my embarking in the ship that landed the troops in the neighbourhood of Fishguard & taking her name from it afterwards, and being on the spot at the time myself.'[1] Ultimately, however, the young man became one of the many Welsh casualties of the Napoleonic Wars. On 3 October 1808, while boarding a prize in the West Indies, Lieutenant John George was killed in action at the age of 28.

Officers and Men

William Paget was the second son of the Earl of Uxbridge of Plas Newydd, Anglesey, and a nephew of Captain Paget Bayly, RN, who died in 1804. Despite his youth and frequent absence abroad, William served as MP for Anglesey from 1790 (when he was 21) until his death.[2] His naval career was brief, but glorious. Off Mykonos, Greece, on 16 June 1794, his 50-gun HMS *Romney* took on the French *La Sibylle*, a 48-gun which actually had a much bigger crew than Paget, and defeated her. But within four months, Paget was dead, aged only 25, allegedly as a result of the reopening of a wound inflicted on him by an 'assassin' at Constantinople a decade earlier.[3] A splendid painting of his prize, *La Sibylle*, still hangs in 'Lord Anglesey's Bedroom' at Plas Newydd. Another Anglesey captain had a significantly longer career. Robert Lloyd of Tregaean joined the navy in 1779 at the age of 14, and in 1783 he had the good fortune to join the crew of the *Hebe*, commanded by Edward Thornborough, one of the navy's most brilliant seamen. By 1794 he was one of Thornborough's lieutenants aboard the *Latona* in the great victory of 'the Glorious First of June', subsequently becoming first lieutenant to Thornborough aboard the *Robust*. Lloyd became Master and Commander of the *Racoon* in 1796, monitoring and disrupting French invasion preparations in the English Channel. He became a post-captain in 1799 and joined Thornborough again in 1801, this time as his flag captain in the *Mars*. In 1807, he commanded the *Hussar* at the bombardment of Copenhagen, then the *Guerrière* and *Swiftsure* before taking command of the *Plantaganet* in 1812. Lloyd took her to the American coast and played a prominent part in the blockade of the Chesapeake and Delaware. On 26 September 1814, he was in Fayal Roads in the Azores when an unknown ship, later identified as the American privateer *General Armstrong*, opened fire on the *Plantaganet*'s pinnace. Viewing this as an infringement of neutrality, Lloyd sent all the boats available to him to attack the American vessel, which was eventually burned. The British losses were very high (twenty-four killed, forty-six wounded) and the Portuguese governor blamed Lloyd for infringing his country's neutrality; he was even criticised from the British side, for provocation in sending a boat towards the American ship and for not complaining to the governor before attacking. To this day, some in America regard him, entirely wrongly, as a stage villain of the blackest sort.[4] Even so, Lloyd – who was actually a notably compassionate captain – remained in command of the *Plantaganet* until she paid off in 1815, after which he retired to Anglesey, became a prominent figure in island society, married a wife forty-five years his junior who 'took care of him, limited his grog, and checked his swearing', and measured out an 'Admiral's Walk' exactly the same length as his quarterdeck on the *Plantaganet*, before dying a Vice-Admiral in 1846.[5]

Charles and Edward Hamilton were sons of Sir John Hamilton, first baronet of Trebinshun House, Breconshire, a naval captain who obtained his title for his gallant service during the Battle of Quebec in 1775. Sir John, originally a Kentish man descended from the Scottish earls of Abercorn, acquired Trebinshun a few years later. Both of his sons followed him into the navy, and the younger, Edward, played the key part in the sequel to one of the most notorious mutinies in the history of the Royal Navy. In September 1797, the *Hermione* was seized by her crew, who murdered their officers and handed the ship over to the Spanish. The entire navy regarded the event as a terrible stain on its reputation that had to be avenged, and in October 1799

Edward Hamilton was in a position to do so. Commanding the *Surprise* (32), he was on station off Porto Cabello, Venezuela, where the *Hermione* (44) was moored. Hamilton launched a surprise cutting-out raid before dawn and, despite coming under heavy fire, his party succeeded in taking the ship and towing her away. The Spanish had 119 killed and ninety-seven wounded, the British only twelve wounded – an astonishing imbalance. Hamilton was severely wounded but was knighted for his pains. On his way home, he was captured by the French and was said to have been interviewed by Napoleon himself. He married Frances Macnamara of Llangoed, Brecon, was created a baronet in 1818 and died a full admiral in 1851.[6] His elder brother Charles, who inherited their father's baronetcy and Trebinshun House, also had a distinguished naval career and achieved admiral's rank, as well as serving a term as MP for Honiton.[7]

Most Welsh officers of the war years had rather less spectacular or controversial careers than those of Paget, Lloyd and the younger Hamilton.* John Thomas was a younger son of the vicar of Llandyssul, of whom it was said that 'his pranks as a boy kept Llandyssul alive'. He rose to become captain of the *Trident* during the Battle of Martinique and other actions in 1780, later commanding the *Ulysses* in an action against the French *La Surveillante* in June 1781. He amassed a considerable fortune in prize money during the wars, used some of it to buy the mansion of Llanfechan, was eventually promoted to Admiral of the White, and on his death in 1810 was buried in Llanllwni

---

★   Another prominent officer of the period was Sir Thomas Williams (1761–1841), who was knighted for capturing a French frigate in 1796 and was married to Jane Austen's cousin, hence his frequent appearances in her letters and diaries. Although he appears in an essay on 'Some Famous Welsh Leaders in War' (by General Sir Henry ap Rhys Price, *THSC* (1946), 149), it has proved impossible to confirm or disprove a Welsh connection for him. See J.K. Laughton, rev. A. Lambert, 'Williams, Sir Thomas (1761/2–1841), Naval Officer', ODNB.

church. Another beneficiary of the prize system was Captain John Turnor of Llangoedmor, Cardiganshire, who obtained some £12,000 from prizes taken during the capture of Toulon (1793); he died in the East Indies in 1801 when commanding the *Trident*. George Bowen was the son of a prominent Methodist landowner of Llwyngwair, Nevern, Pembrokeshire, and wrote regularly to his parents and brothers to inform them of the progress of his naval career. Bowen commanded the *Trusty* during the Anglo-Russian invasion of North Holland in 1799 and might have had an illustrious career ahead of him, but he died in 1800, aged only 38.

Midshipman Bowen Robert Robertson of Milford was serving aboard the *Woodlark* in November 1805 when she was shipwrecked near Calais. He was taken prisoner but made several attempts to escape, 'on one occasion he had actually reached the coast, when he was apprehended, carried back several hundred miles in chains, and confined on bread and water.' He finally made a successful escape in March 1811 and returned to sea, but after the end of the war, 'although anxious for employment' he obtained none. He returned to Pembrokeshire and became a magistrate for the county. William Nowell of Nottage, Glamorgan, had become a lieutenant in 1776 and distinguished himself during the American war, taking over command of the 74-gun *Hercules* when his captain was killed during the Battle of the Saintes (April 1782) and immediately implementing a new method for firing the guns by loading two round shot next to the cartridge, with only one wad outside, which greatly speeded up the process of reloading. In 1792, Nowell commanded the *Ferret* in the West Indies and became entangled in the vicious civil war between the white and former slave populations on the island of San Domingo, witnessing a man being roasted alive by the whites and negotiating the release of a lieutenant who had been taken by the former slaves while being surrounded by an angry armed mob of 300 of the latter. Illness subsequently prevented Nowell developing the stellar career that might have lain ahead of him; he held several relatively undistinguished commands, ultimately rose to flag rank by seniority, and died in 1828.

For some Welshmen of relatively low birth, the navy provided a chance of social mobility that would have been very difficult to achieve in any other sphere, particularly if one happened to be in the right place at the right time. For instance, Charles Papps Price from Hay-on-Wye had worked his way slowly through the ranks and by 1798 was a 48-year-old lieutenant, commanding the garrison on the St Marcouf Isles. These barren rocks off the Cotentin Peninsula had been captured a few years earlier to provide a base for naval operations against the French coast, but in May 1798 the French made a concerted attempt to win them back. Price led a determined resistance which successfully fought off the attack, and was rewarded with promotion to commander. Another who rose far higher than his birth might have suggested was James Llewin Lloyd, a sailmaker's son from Pembrokeshire. He was commissioned as a lieutenant in 1799 and served as such aboard HMS *Dreadnought* at Trafalgar. He died aboard her a few months after the battle, bequeathing his possessions to his two spinster nieces in Pembroke. Rowland Bevan was the grandson of a tenant farmer at Oxwich, Gower. In 1794 he was second lieutenant of the *Brunswick* during the battle of the Glorious First of June, and wrote a letter to a friend which remains one of the most vivid accounts of the action; he died a post captain in 1836 and was buried in St John's Church, Cardiff.[17]

The outbreak of the war with France in 1793 had led to an upsurge in patriotic fervour throughout Wales and the establishment of loyalist associations, partly as a counterblast to the various radical organisations that still adhered to the original ideals of the French Revolution. One of these, formed in Whitford and Holywell in Flintshire during the winter of 1792–93, had as its principal aim the establishment of a fund to reward men who volunteered for the navy. This proved remarkably successful, raising over £200 by April 1793. The association offered 2 guineas each to the first twenty able-bodied men to volunteer, followed by 1 guinea each to subsequent recruits. There was an enthusiastic take-up: forty-six Flintshire seamen joined the navy and obtained the bounty in 1793. So successful was the scheme that outsiders were sneaking into the county and claiming to be locals in order to qualify for the money.[18] Wrexham, too, promised two guineas or one 'to those ancient Britons, natives of this country, who are ready to come forward and defend the wooden walls of Old England, against her natural and inveterate enemy'.[19]

Despite the best efforts of Wrexham, Flintshire and the authorities elsewhere in Wales and Britain, by the mid-1790s the service was suffering from a serious manning crisis and needed to take desperate measures. One of them was to make up the numbers in ships' crews with soldiers; the 69th Regiment of Foot, one of the lineal ancestors of the Royal Welsh, served in the fleet at the battle of the Glorious First of June, 1794.[20] Another was the passing, in 1795, of two Quota Acts, laying down recruitment targets for each county and seaport:[21]

County	Number of Men
Anglesey	34
(Beaumaris	196)
Breconshire	41
Caernarfonshire	36
Cardiganshire	36
(Aberystwyth	69)
(Cardigan	139)
Carmarthenshire	67
(Llanelli	32)
Denbighshire	73
Flintshire	38

Glamorgan	76
(Swansea	85)
(Cardiff	14)
Merionethshire	43
Monmouthshire	58
(Chepstow	38)
Montgomeryshire	69
Pembrokeshire	46
(Milford Haven	70)
Radnorshire	26

These figures are somewhat deceptive. 'Beaumaris', for example, meant the entire limits of the port jurisdiction, which stretched as far as Amlwch to the north, Pwllheli to the west, Conwy to the east and Barmouth to the south. Commissioners charged with meeting the quota requirements were appointed at these places, holding their meetings in prominent local inns. Drawn chiefly from the local shipowners, they immediately came into conflict with the Admiralty by proposing the payment of bounties (and expenses for themselves) that were, somewhat suspiciously, even higher than those paid in London.[22]

The pressures of simultaneous recruitment demands for the army and navy eventually led to the riots of 1795–96, described previously. However, during the spring and summer of 1795, the first weeks and months that the Quota Acts were in force, many reacted by volunteering in significant numbers, contrary to the still widely held myth that those Welshmen who served in Nelson's navy were all press-ganged unwillingly into the armed service of a foreign oppressor. One of those who came forward was Robert Jones of Llanfair, Meirionnydd, an 18-year-old labourer, for whom the navy would probably have held out far better prospects for advancing himself than anything available in his home area; the £10 and 10 shillings that he earned as a bounty for volunteering must have seemed like a fortune.[23] Slightly further north, Caernarfonshire men volunteered in some numbers. They included the likes of Richard Edwards, slate quarryman of Llandygai, David Hughes, shoemaker of Llansanffraid Glanconwy, and Robert Roberts, blacksmith of Llanbeblig.[24] Those who volunteered in Anglesey included labourers from Llangefni and Llandyfrydog, but also the likes of a miner from Cornwall, a shoemaker from Blackburn and a gardener from Waterford. Such landmen were deeply resented by the seamen already in the service, who had been paid nothing like the same levels of bounty.[25] Nationally, though, too few volunteers came forward and local authorities were compelled to send convicts and other undesirables into the navy instead.

The navy did employ the press gang in Wales, with impress service bases at Haverfordwest, Pembroke and Swansea, but in theory its remit was still formally limited to those who 'used the sea'; although this term was defined broadly, and could thus include the likes of river bargemen and oyster fishermen, it was still very rare indeed for press masters to live up to their stereotypical image of raiding respectable inns and tearing unsuspecting, innocent young landsmen from the arms of their sweethearts. A large man-of-war was the most technologically sophisticated and deadly structure of the age, and in an ideal world the last thing a captain wanted was a crew made up of ignorant landmen who literally could not tell one end of a rope from the other. But there were exceptions, especially in times of dire emergency and desperation like 1795–96 and 1803–05. One such case was that of Evan Evans, bailiff of Ynysymaengwyn near Tywyn, who was pressed, shot in the face (hence his nickname of *Boch Fawr*, 'Big Cheek'), but went on to serve aboard HMS *Alcmene* and ultimately received £10 per annum as a pensioner of Greenwich Hospital, becoming something of a celebrity in Ardudwy by regaling all and sundry with tales of his naval service.[26] In August 1793, a press gang chased a much larger party of heavily armed seamen to Rhymney, but the men were determined to resist; the presence of fifty or sixty townspeople decided the press gang in favour of prudence.[27] Another incident was recalled by a Llanelli centenarian, reminiscing in 1889 about what seems to have been the period 1795–96, who remembered how fear of the press gang coming from Swansea led the inhabitants to lock their doors and barricade their windows.[28] Such incidents, so much more dramatic and colourful than the more common but mundane process of men simply volunteering for naval service, passed into popular memory and helped shape the myth of the all-pervasiveness of the press gang.

Whether pressed men or volunteers, many Welsh recruits were shipped directly to the fleet, usually at the nearest dockyard in Plymouth; in 1804–05, for example, the *Cleveland* made several voyages from Swansea, carrying newly raised men for the navy.[29] Men could sometimes escape naval service if they found a qualified substitute willing to take their place. In March 1809, David Edmonds, a shoemaker of Swansea, advertised in the local press for just such a willing volunteer.[30] The impress establishment at Swansea was closed down in 1814 and hastily reopened after Napoleon escaped from Elba, only to be discontinued once again a couple of months later, following Waterloo.[31] The total numbers raised by impressment and voluntary means were substantial. The most detailed 'head count' of Welshmen in the navy during the Napoleonic Wars suggests that over 3,300 served in the few years on either side of the Battle of Trafalgar, 793 of them from Pembrokeshire, 512 from Glamorgan, 326 from Anglesey and 304 from Caernarfonshire. These figures are likely to be a significant underestimate of the actual total.[32] Inevitably, many of them never came home. In 1800, John Williams, rector of Begelly in Pembrokeshire, wrote to the Admiralty to try to establish the fate of three local men who had gone into the navy: the saddest case was that of Richard Morgan, whose widowed mother had not heard from him in the six years since he joined the *Caesar* in 1794.[33]

Welshmen were present at all of Nelson's triumphs. Richard Jones of Swansea was first lieutenant of HMS *Defence* at the Battle of the Nile, although Nelson's order to him to stay aboard her because the captain was ill cost him a promotion that he believed himself entitled to.[34] He subsequently commanded the Sea Fencibles in the Swansea area and went on to hold several important commands at sea. James Morgan was wounded during the action; he survived and lived on near Fishguard to the grand old age of 96, finally dying in 1835.[35] The poet David Williams of Lampeter, *Dewi Farfog*, also served at the Nile.[36] Perhaps the last surviving Welsh veteran of the battle was Captain John George Phillips of Cwmgwili, Carmarthenshire, who was aboard the *Minotaur* and died in 1869, aged 85.[37] The truck of the French flagship *L'Orient*, which blew up during the Battle of the Nile, was subsequently lodged in St Katherine's church, Milford Haven, but was later transferred to the National Maritime Museum.[38] John Henry Martin of Ludchurch, Pembrokeshire, who had sailed with Captain Cook (see Chapter 7), commanded the bomb vessel HMS *Explosion* at Copenhagen. Other Welshman present at the same battle included John Rees of Cilymaenllwyd near Llanelli, a midshipman serving aboard HMS *Ardent*, and Thomas Mansel of Muddlescwm, Kidwelly, who was a midshipman with Foley aboard the *Elephant* and lived long enough to become a full admiral on the retired list, dying in 1869. Wales would have provided the third-in-command at Copenhagen had not Holywell-born Admiral Thomas Totty's flagship *Invincible* been wrecked on her way to the campaign. Nevertheless, Totty did serve briefly with Nelson before being appointed commander-in-chief of the Leeward Islands station, where he promptly succumbed to yellow fever.[39]

Several Welsh captains achieved distinction in the latter stages of the Napoleonic Wars. Conway Shipley of Bodrhyddan, Rhuddlan, was 11 years old when he first saw action, during the battle of the Glorious First of June, 1794. In March 1804, he obtained command of the 14-gun sloop HMS *Hippomenes*, and only three days later captured the vastly superior French privateer, *L'Égyptienne*, of 36 guns, after a fifty-four-hour chase and a three-hour battle. Shipley was promoted post-captain at the age of 22, but was killed on 16 April 1808 when in command of HMS *Nymphe*, leading an attempt to 'cut out' a French corvette from Lisbon harbour.[40] His sword is still displayed at Bodrhyddan Hall, and a monument over his grave at Paço d'Arcos is still kept in good repair, and it has even been suggested that Shipley might have been one of the models for C.S. Forester's Horatio Hornblower.[41]

Another Welsh-connected captain to have a brief but meteoric career in the latter stages of the war was Lord William Stuart, a son of the first Marquess of Bute. Stuart was elected MP for Cardiff at the age of 24, but was largely an absentee MP. He commanded the Milford-built *Lavinia* during the Walcheren expedition of 1809, leading a squadron of ships past the batteries of Vlissingen and contributing to the surrender of that town, but died at sea in July 1814.[42] George Lloyd of Dan-yr-Allt, Carmarthenshire, whose brother and only son also went into the navy, was in command of HMS *Castilian* in June 1814 when she went to the rescue of HMS *Avon*, which had been badly damaged in battle against the USS *Wasp*, and forced the American warship to flee.[43] Thomas Walbeoff Cecil, third son of William Cecil of Dyffryn and captain of HMS *Electra*, gained a moderate degree of notoriety in April 1814 when, during a duel in Jamaica, he shot dead his fellow captain Hassard Stackpoole. Lord Byron quoted the affair as proof that in duels, the best shot did not always win. Cecil was said to be almost entirely ignorant of the rules of duelling, but simply fired more quickly than Stackpoole. He died only six months later, of a broken heart for having killed a fellow creature, according to some, but probably rather more prosaically of yellow fever.[44]

The Welshmen in the navy 'networked' with each other and kept up their contacts with home. Lieutenant John George was an avid letter writer, corresponding regularly with his sister at the Blue Boar in Haverfordwest, but he turned down her offer to send him some local ale: 'a drink of Welsh ale is certainly a very great treat to me, but only consider what a quantity we must have so as to give 13 of us a taste & after all to have no thanks of it.' At Gibraltar in December 1801, he found himself part of 'a fine round Welsh party' with Captain Probert of the *Cambrian* and several other countrymen; when he got to Port Royal, Jamaica, in 1806, he found that the master-attendant of the dockyard was a townsman of his, an Owens of Haverfordwest.[45] Several Welshmen sent home letters that slipped seamlessly from English to Welsh and back again. Even when serving aboard HMS *Amethyst* in the Bay of Biscay in 1800–01, Thomas Williams, *Twm Pedrog* of Llanbedrog near Pwllheli, penned Welsh poems (in the form known as *cywydd*) and sent them to his parents and the Pwllheli bard John Roberts.[46] Another Welsh poet in Nelson's navy was John Jones of Llanasa, Flintshire, who had worked in the cotton mill at Holywell before joining the navy at the age of 16; he served for ten years, reading and writing poetry during his time aboard the *Barbadoes*, *Saturn* and *Royal George*. After the war he went to work in a mill in Stalybridge, Lancashire, where his writings earned him the nickname 'Poet Jones'.[47] Less 'Welsh', but considerably more influential, was Charles Reece Pemberton, born in Pontypool to a Welsh mother and an English father, who was press-ganged in 1807 and served for seven years, later becoming a noted actor, lecturer and writer, who penned a devastating radical critique of the navy of his day.[48]

John Richardson, a naval surgeon from Flintshire, was delighted to find that among his mess mates aboard the *Mars*, 'one is my country man, a fine [?] bold jovial tar as ever stepped on board a ship, who is a midshipman, his name is Bevan, he comes from Swansea South Wales.' Even allowing for an element of placating maternal worries about her son, Richardson's spirited letters to his mother provide a corrective to the still widespread popular perception of the Nelsonian navy as some sort of floating hell, as well as throwing a few vicious barbs in the direction of our European neighbours:

we are all in high health & spirits, what should prevent it, when we live in clover, though blockading up an enemy's port, having plenty of fresh grub, fruit and onions, and to crown all good Lisbon and Port wine to drink, who would not fight to protect so good a sovereign and country, who supplies us so bountifully, is it possible we could suffer so noble and gracious a monarch to be molested or overrun with those infernal damn'd rascals the French, who are worse than pirates, indeed nothing more than the scum of the earth, what other appellation can you make use of? The Spaniards not much better ...[49]

However, Andrew Phillips must have felt distinctly lonely aboard the frigate *Artois* in the late 1790s: his captain described him as 'quiet and sober', and also as 'a Welshman [who] cannot speak English well'.[50]

Foley at the Nile and Copenhagen

Thomas Foley, perhaps Wales' greatest naval hero, was born in 1757 at Ridgeway near Narberth, Pembrokeshire, the second son of a local landowner and nephew to a captain in the navy of the same name who had sailed round the world with Anson. He entered the navy at the age of 13, became a lieutenant in 1778 and commanded small vessels until promoted post-captain 1790. In 1793, he was appointed flag captain of the *St George* under Rear-Admiral John Gell, and thus shared in the fabulous windfall of prize money that accrued to Gell's squadron when it took the Spanish prize *San Iago*. Foley remained in the *St George* when the squadron command passed to Admiral Hyde Parker, but by February 1797 he was flag captain of the *Britannia*, in which he took part in the Battle of Cape St Vincent.

In May 1798 Foley, commanding HMS *Goliath* (74), was sent to join Nelson's fleet in the Mediterranean, and thus came into close contact with the Royal Navy's new hero for the first time. Foley was 6 feet tall and had a commanding presence; he would have dwarfed the minute Horatio Nelson. Together with the other captains who would become known collectively as 'Nelson's band of brothers', they pursued the French Toulon fleet across the Mediterranean. They were unable to catch it in time to prevent Napoleon landing an expedition in Egypt with the intention of using it as a stepping stone for a campaign to dislodge the British from India, but on 1 August Nelson's fleet approached the French fleet, then lying in Abu Qir (or Aboukir) Bay near Alexandria. The French were at anchor in the bay, but their position seemed to be very strong. Nevertheless, Nelson ordered an immediate attack without forming the line of battle, allowing his captains to use their initiative – especially Foley, who had been chosen to lead the line. Foley noticed something that Nelson, much further back in the line, could not see: namely that the French ships were at single anchor, so there had to be sufficient depth of water between themselves and the shore for the ships to swing freely. Therefore, he reasoned, there also had to be enough water for ships to sail down the *inside* of the French line, which Foley rightly assumed would be unprepared for an attack from that side. Knowing that Nelson would wish him to use his initiative, he led the way inshore while Nelson's ships attacked the outside of the line. 'At the climax of the battle, an apocalyptic explosion ripped apart the French flagship, the massive *L'Orient*, adding a stunning *son et lumière* to a defining moment. In all, eleven of the thirteen French battleships were taken, sunk or burnt.'[51] Foley's *Goliath* took just ten minutes to cripple the French *Conquérant* at a cost of twenty-one killed and forty-one wounded. The stunning victory, which became known as the Battle of the Nile, wrecked Napoleon's plans for the conquest of Egypt, and perhaps India too, cemented Nelson's place as the new national hero, and led to the beginning of a close personal friendship between Nelson and Foley. Indeed, the admiral, who was ever keen to claim as much credit as possible for himself, always fulsomely acknowledged the Welshman's pivotal role in bringing about the victory of the Nile.[52]

Thomas Foley remained in command of the *Goliath* in the Mediterranean until the end of 1799, then spent 1800 commanding the *Elephant* in the endless, tedious blockade of Brest. Early in 1801, he was ordered to the Baltic to rejoin Nelson, second-in-command under Hyde Parker of the pre-emptive expedition against the Danes at Copenhagen. Nelson shifted his flag to the *Elephant*, a more manoeuvrable ship, and on the night before battle was joined he and Foley dined together, arranging the plan of attack for the next day. The battle fought on 2 April 1801 proved to be a hard-fought affair against a Danish enemy enraged by what they saw as a flagrant violation of their neutrality. Nelson's squadron took a battering, and after three hours of battle, Hyde Parker, watching from his flagship, hoisted signal no. 39, 'Discontinue the Action'. Now occurred one of the most famous events in the making of the 'Nelson legend', which cemented Foley's part in it. Upon seeing the signal, Nelson was furious: 'Leave off action', he exclaimed, 'now damn me if I do!' Turning to Foley, he said, 'You know, Foley, I have only one eye and I have a right to be blind sometimes.' Lifting the telescope to his blind eye, he said, 'I really do not see the signal.' Unlike Hyde Parker, Nelson could see that the Danes were nearly beaten, and only a little more time was needed to secure a successful outcome. His ships, and those of the rear-admiral's division, duly ignored Hyde Parker's signal and completed a famous victory.[53]

In 1795, Foley had used his prize money from the *San Iago* capture to buy the Abermarlais estate near Llangadog, Carmarthenshire, and on 31 July 1802 he married Lady Lucy Anne Fitzgerald, the youngest daughter of the Duke of Leinster, who had been something of a radical Irish nationalist in her younger days.[54] Ill health forced Foley's retirement from the sea after the Battle of Copenhagen, but he wrote regularly to Nelson and other old friends; Nelson wanted him to join his fleet in the Mediterranean, but Foley was not well enough to do so. Although Nelson and Emma Hamilton did not visit Abermarlais in 1802, they met Foley in Pembrokeshire and dined with him and his elder brother at the original family home, Ridgeway near Haverfordwest. The Duke of Clarence, later King William IV, came to Abermarlais in 1825, and was received under a triumphal arch erected at the entrance.[55] On most days, though, Foley spent his mornings in his library, looking out over the Black Mountains, or else perambulated upon the raised terrace outside the dining room: 'traditionally it is said to have matched the dimensions of the quarter deck of one of Foley's ships and that he paced methodically around it to recall his sea-going days, viewing the surrounding countryside through his telescope. Those who remember the house still refer to "Foley's quarter deck".'[56] Naval appointments were few and far between. Promoted rear-admiral in 1808, he was appointed commander-in-chief in the Downs in 1811 (with William Nowell of Wenvoe as his flag captain aboard the *Monmouth*). Knighted in 1815, Foley solicited unsuccessfully for the post of Treasurer of Greenwich Hospital before being appointed commander-in-chief at Portsmouth in 1830.[57] He died on 9 January 1833 and was buried in the Royal Garrison Church, Portsmouth, in a coffin of oak taken from the *Elephant* when she was broken up in 1830.

'Welsh' Warships in Action

The second HMS *Prince of Wales*, a 90-gun second rate, was launched at Portsmouth in 1794. She served as the flagship of Sir Robert Calder in his action off Cape Finisterre in 1805, and subsequently as that of Admiral Gambier in the bombardment of Copenhagen, 1807; she was broken up in 1822. In 1795, the navy acquired its one and only HMS *Abergavenny* when the East Indiaman *Earl of Abergavenny* was purchased, renamed and fitted out as a 56-gun fourth rate frigate which spent virtually her entire naval career as guardship and flagship at Port Royal,

Jamaica, before being broken up in 1807.[58] A new *Monmouth* was launched in 1796. She was an East Indiaman that had been purchased on the stocks, and she first saw action at the Battle of Camperdown in 1797. A long career followed before she was eventually broken up in 1834.[59] The first warship to bear the name *Cambrian* was launched at Bursledon in February 1797. Perhaps surprisingly, she did not honour the part Wales had played in defeating the last invasion of Britain; she was named and went down the ways nine days before the French landed at Fishguard. Her first captain was the possible Welshman Sir Thomas Williams, and during the first few years of the 1800s she captured several enemy privateers in the Channel. *Cambrian* served in the Mediterranean in the latter stages of the Napoleonic Wars and returned there in 1820, taking part in the Battle of Navarino in 1827. Not long afterwards, on 31 January 1828, she was wrecked off Grabusa while in pursuit of some pirate schooners.[60] In 1798, a new *Dragon* was launched at Deptford. She was on the American coast in the War of 1812 and destroyed the USS *Adams* in September 1814. The *Dragon* ultimately ended up in the land which her name honoured, as from 1829 to 1842 she was hauled ashore at Pembroke Dock, serving *inter alia* as the Royal Marine barracks (*see Chapter 6*).

A clutch of geographically-named 'Welsh' warships were built in the latter stages of the Napoleonic Wars. A new *Milford* was launched in its namesake town in 1809 (*see Chapter 6*), another *Pembroke* in 1812, another *Severn* in 1813, and no fewer than four new Welsh names joined the Navy List in 1814: *Conway*, *Menai*, *Towey* (*sic*) and *Wye*, all small sixth rate frigates.[61] None of these ships had lengthy or notable careers in the post-war years, although the *Pembroke*, which was hastily converted to steam power in 1854–55 for use as a floating battery in the Crimean War, ultimately became a base ship at Chatham in 1873 and thus later gave her name to an important naval shore establishment (see Chapter 8). The *Severn* was on the American coast during the War of 1812 and later took part in the bombardment of Algiers (1816) before being broken up in 1825.[62] The smaller 'rivers' served a commission or two on foreign stations, particularly in the Americas or the East Indies, before *Conway* and *Towey* were broken up in the 1820s; the *Menai* and *Wye* both survived until the 1850s, the former as a receiving ship and then a gunnery target at Portsmouth, the latter as a convict hospital ship at Sheerness and Chatham.[63]

The most remarkable new 'Welsh' name to adorn a warship was that bestowed on the fifth rate frigate launched in a private shipyard at Paull, near Hull, on 19 November 1808. His Majesty's Ship *Owen Glendower* was a 36-gun Apollo-class vessel, but there seems no clear-cut reason for the singular choice of name. The First Lord of the Admiralty at the time of her building, Lord Mulgrave, had no obvious Welsh connections; nor did any other member of the board he headed, the most eminent member of which was the precocious 24-year-old Lord Palmerston, the future Prime Minister. Perhaps one of the Admiralty lords had a particular liking for Shakespeare's *Henry IV*, *Part I*, for the navy's first HMS *Hotspur*, part of the same class, was launched just over a year later. On the other hand, there was no homogeneity or apparent logic to the names allotted to the class of which the *Glendower* formed a part: some of her sister ships included *Curacoa*, *Belvidera*, *Maidstone*, *Shannon*, *Surprise* and *Stag*. In any event, the *Owen Glendower* had a long and illustrious career. She saw action almost immediately after first commissioning, taking part in the capture of the Danish island of Anholt in 1809. She later distinguished herself in operations against the slave trade (see Chapter 8), and was commanded by one of the best officers of the Regency era, Robert Cavendish Spencer, whose brother, the future fourth Earl Spencer, served as her lieutenant. She was also the first ship of Robert Fitzroy, who later commanded the *Beagle* during Darwin's expeditions. *Owen Glendower* also served as the flagship of both Sir Samuel Hood and Sir Thomas Hardy, of 'kiss me' fame; the negotiations that culminated in the independence of Peru largely took place aboard her (being concluded on another 'Welsh' warship, the *Conway*).[64] Her ultimate fate was ignominious, however: in 1842 she became a convict hulk at Gibraltar, housing a number of the 'Tolpuddle Martyrs'.

Trafalgar

At the heart of the story of the Battle of Trafalgar is a classic piece of political incorrectness, from a Welsh perspective at any rate: Nelson's immortal signal, 'England expects that every man will do his duty'. One wonders how the famous message was received by the likes of Thomas Twiney of Carmarthenshire, coxswain of the *Victory*, Marine Private David Davis of Llanfihangel-y-Creuddyn, Cardiganshire, aboard the *Defence*, or Ordinary Seaman John Williams of Holyhead on the *Temeraire* (let alone by the five Scots captains and the fourteen hundred Irishmen throughout the fleet).* Arguably, Nelson should have known better, given his fairly recent tour of Wales, his friendship with Foley and the Flintshire upbringing of Emma Hamilton; but Nelson was a typical product of the English middle class of his time, unthinkingly conflating 'English' and 'British' out of simple carelessness.[65] Nevertheless, the signal epitomises a school of thought which perists to this day, and which sees Trafalgar as being essentially an English victory fought by an overwhelmingly English fleet. Paradoxically, it suits both grumpy letter writers from the Home Counties and radical Welsh nationalists

---

* The point is well made by Bernard Cornwell in *Sharpe's Trafalgar* (2000), where the hoisting of the famous signal is greeted by Sharpe's Welsh friend Llewelyn in these terms: '"What about the Welsh?" Llewelyn asked with an equal indignation, then smiled. "Ah, but the Welsh need no encouragement to do their duty. It's you bloody English who have to be chivvied."' Captain George Hope of Linlithgow, commanding HMS *Defence*, deliberately failed to pass on Nelson's signal, perhaps reckoning that it might not go down well with the seventy Scots, fifty Irishmen and ten Welshmen in his crew.

alike to perpetuate this particular canard.[66] In recent years, some of the Welsh ambivalence towards Trafalgar might also be attributable to the fact that 21 October is coincidentally the anniversary of the Aberfan disaster in 1966, one of the most traumatic events in the entire course of Welsh history.[67]

In reality, the contribution of the Welsh at Trafalgar gives credence in spades to the old maxim about lies, damned lies and statistics. About 620 Welshmen, probably more, served in the battle. In absolute terms, this seems a tiny number: it constituted roughly 3–4 per cent of the fleet's manpower, compared with about 9 per cent from Scotland and 25 per cent from Ireland. But when the figures are compared to the actual populations of the four home countries at the start of the nineteenth century, a very different picture emerges. Wales seems to have made up about 3.6 per cent of the population of the British Isles, which means that its contribution to the manning of the Trafalgar fleet is perfectly respectable. Rather more than respectable, in fact: about 0.115 per cent of the entire Welsh population served at Trafalgar, which means that relative to overall population, proportionately more Welshmen fought in the battle than Scots and Irishmen. Moreover, marines made up nearly a fifth of the English contingent (as opposed to only some 14 per cent of the Welsh), so if seamen alone are counted, there were proportionately more Welsh mariners at Trafalgar than English ones, too.[*] Interestingly, these figures are confirmed by analysis of the crew of HMS *Victory*, which has been picked over in more detail than any other. The thirty Welshmen aboard her (3.66 per cent of the crew, in line with expectations) formed a larger proportion of the national population than the Scots and a much larger one than the far more trumpeted Irish contingent, running the 515 Englishmen very close – in relative terms, of course.[68]

Almost a fifth of the Welsh contingent, about 110 men in all, came from Pembrokeshire, with 80 to 100 from Glamorgan, 50 to

[*]   See Appendix 1

60 from Carmarthenshire, about 52 from Caernarfonshire and the same from Anglesey. Most came from obvious maritime towns like Swansea, Cardigan and Holyhead.[69] But there were exceptions, such as James Brown, a 16-year-old ship's boy from Radnor serving aboard the *Tonnant*; ordinary seaman Valentine Price and 14-year-old Midshipman Alexander Martin, both of Hay-on-Wye, aboard HMS *Prince*; and John Thomas of Wrexham, a quartermaster's mate aboard the *Sirius*. The oldest Welshman at the battle was Quartermaster Peter George of Milford, aged 56, aboard HMS *Spartiate*; the youngest were 12-year-old William Wynne Eyton of Leeswood, Flintshire, a Volunteer First Class aboard HMS *Neptune*,[70] along with two 13-year-olds, Thomas Thomas of Cardiff aboard the *Tonnant* and Midshipman John Hoskins Brown of Kidwelly aboard the *Prince*.

Midshipman Francis Edward Collingwood, born at Milford in 1785, both appears in Arthur Devis' famous painting of the death of Nelson and was long reputed to have been the man who avenged the fallen admiral by shooting dead the French sharp-shooter on the fighting top of the *Redoubtable*.[71] Peregrine Bowen of Pope Hill, Pembrokeshire, was an 18-year-old midshipman aboard the *Prince*, the only British ship at Trafalgar that suffered no casualties, and later commanded one of the Admiralty steam packets between Liverpool and Dublin.[72] Hugh Cook of Penally, Pembrokeshire, was First Lieutenant aboard the *Agamemnon*. After leaving the navy in 1812, he set up a charity for the pensioned sailors of Tenby and their widows; the fund lasted until 1970, although by then its payments were worth just 10 shillings each.[73] David Lewis of the *Conqueror*, a Montgomeryshire man by birth, later became deputy harbour master at Aberystwyth, where he was nicknamed 'the old commodore'; he died in 1850, and his gravestone can still be seen near Aberystwyth castle.[74] One of the Welshmen serving aboard HMS *Victory* was Thomas Johns, who wrote to his father in Kidwelly after the ship had returned to Portsmouth. He provided a graphic account of the *Victory*'s part in the battle:

She [the Spanish flagship *Santísima Trinidad*] fired into our bows, and seven ships beside her, ten or fifteen minutes before we returned it, which we did at the last with effect, on opening a tremendous fire on both sides in the midst of them. Engaging the French and Spanish admirals, one on each side, we was so involved in the smoke and fire not to be seen by any of our frigates, looking on for about half an hour, and, they thought we was blown up or sunk, having no less than five ships [attacking us] at a time …

Johns said of the death of Nelson, 'every hero in the fleet shed a tear on hearing the news of his death.'[75] Another South Walian who wrote home with a nearly contemporary account of Trafalgar was Lewis Roteley, second lieutenant of the Royal Marines aboard HMS *Victory*, who had joined the service following his meeting with Nelson in Swansea in 1802. He was severely wounded but succeeded to the command of the remnant of the Marine detachment after his superiors were killed; Roteley's first order was for his men to concentrate their fire on the fighting tops of the *Redoubtable*, from which the shot that killed Nelson had come.[76] He subsequently retired to Swansea and was very much of a local celebrity until his death in 1861, no doubt in part because he had somehow acquired a particularly macabre relic of Trafalgar – the breeches that Nelson wore during the battle. Roteley's memorial in St Mary's church, Swansea, still survives, having narrowly escaped destruction in the Luftwaffe's devastating attacks in 1941.[77]

Inevitably, some of those who fought were either killed or suffered terribly. Able Seaman John Bevan of Swansea was killed aboard the *Mars*, Ordinary Seaman John Griffiths of Llanfihangel-y-Pennant aboard the *Dreadnought*. Evan Pritchard of Llannor, serving aboard the *Conqueror*, drowned in the great storm that blew up during the days following the battle. Twenty-four-year-old marine James Davis of Pembroke was aboard the *Belleisle*, the most severely damaged ship in the

British fleet: he lost his right leg below the knee, and subsequently obtained an annual pension of £6 13s 4d. Philip Fisher of Chepstow served on the famous 'fighting *Temeraire*'. He lost his left leg above the knee during the battle, and was awarded a pension of £8.[78] Meanwhile, the Welsh youngsters who fought in the battle encountered mixed fortunes. William Peregrine of Milford Haven, midshipman aboard the *Tonnant*, died the year after Trafalgar, aged only 16.[79] William Wynne Eyton had an undistinguished naval career before retiring to Flintshire and dying in 1857; Francis Edward Collingwood went into the revenue service on the Irish coast, never rising above the rank of commander; Alexander Martin had no post at all after 1815. On the other hand, John Hoskins Brown wrote *The Shipmaster's Guide* and went on to become Registrar-General of Seamen and the effective founder of the Royal Naval Reserve.[80]

Other veterans of Trafalgar fell on hard times. One anecdote, perhaps too good to be true, related how one of them fetched up in Cowbridge on 'a begging expedition' and was much feted by the locals in the Bear Hotel. Hearing of this, 'a town officer who made himself obnoxious to the inhabitants by the manner in which he performed his duties' marched into the pub and

> with all the pomp of bumbledom asked Nelson's shipmate, 'What did Nelson say before his last battle? Was it not "England expects that every man will do his duty"? It is now my duty to arrest you for begging in this town'. 'Aye, mate, but what did Nelson say after that? Was it not "Give it them, lads!"?' And in a voice of thunder the old sailor cried out 'Avaunt there!' and struck the officer until he tumbled to the other end of the room. He then quitted the town as fast as his aged legs could carry him.[81]

Richard (or Lewis) Hughes of Holyhead, a veteran of HMS *Mars*, fell just short of the service time needed for a naval pension, so he stayed at sea until he was well into his seventies and then retired to his home town to live on a bare 1*s* 6*d* a week from the Sailor's Fund, although he did receive occasional support from his countryman Captain Robert Mends.[82] Griffith Owen, originally of Amlwch, who served aboard HMS *Conqueror* at Trafalgar, fared slightly better, ending up as a fruit seller near Conwy railway station, advertising his stall by a sign which proclaimed his service under Nelson. Conversely, some Welshmen brazenly jumped on the bandwagon by pretending to have been at Trafalgar: these included John Hatton of Chepstow, Evan Herbert of Aberaeron and James Morgan, sometime landlord of the 'Nelson's Victory' pub in Pontypool.[83]

Wales provided no Trafalgar captains, although one could certainly be termed an 'adopted' Welshman.* Charles Tyler, son of an Irish army officer, spent five years in the 1780s commanding a sloop based at Milford Haven, married a local girl and settled down to raise a family at Underdown, near Pembroke.[84] In March 1805, he moved on from commanding the Sea Fencibles of south-west Wales to take command of the *Tonnant*, a French prize taken at the Battle of the Nile in 1798 (and on whose deck Francis Scott Key would later write *The Star Spangled Banner*). Perhaps unsurprisingly, *Tonnant* had one of the largest single contingents of Welshmen at the battle – thirty-one, beaten only by the *Conqueror*'s thirty-seven, and rather more than the twenty-five on the *Victory* and the twenty-eight on the 'Fighting *Temeraire*'. Tyler later served as commander-in-chief at the Cape of Good Hope, reached the rank of admiral of the white, and spent the last eighteen years of his life as tenant to his Pembroke-born son George, a fellow naval officer, in the mansion house of Cottrell Park, near St Nicholas in the Vale of Glamorgan, which George had obtained via a somewhat byzantine inheritance.[85] Charles Tyler is buried in St Nicholas church, where a grand marble wall monument commemorates him; George went on

---

*   And a second Trafalgar captain – or at least, acting captain – is also
    buried in Wales: see Appendix 1.

to become a vice-admiral and MP for Glamorgan. Wales might even have laid claim to the third in command of the British fleet at Trafalgar, but in December 1804 Rear-Admiral George Campbell – brother of Lord Cawdor of Fishguard fame – was relieved of his command by Nelson, under whom he had commanded the rear squadron during the lengthy Toulon blockade.[86] Campbell suffered from severe depression (probably what would now be termed post-traumatic stress disorder), and was remarkably open about it: in one of his letters to Nelson shortly before he struck his flag, he remarked that 'I never was more unhinged in my life.'[87] Campbell recovered sufficiently to be elected MP for Carmarthen in 1806, but he eventually committed suicide in 1821 when serving as port admiral at Portsmouth.[88] His monument and that of Thomas Foley, who succeeded him in the same post a few years later, are only a few feet apart on the south wall of Portsmouth's Royal Garrison Church, and Admiral Thomas Totty of Flintshire was also buried in the same place (although his memorial is in Westminster Abbey), thus making it the somewhat unlikely location of the closest thing Wales has to a national naval mausoleum.

It is not clear when the last Welsh Trafalgar veteran died, as the newspapers of the time tended to be less assiduous in recording the passing of Nelson's men than those of the survivors of Waterloo. It might have been John Hoskins Brown, who died in 1864 and is buried in Camberwell Old Cemetery; on the other hand, the last certain British veteran of Trafalgar died in 1885, the last of all (a Spaniard) in 1892, so it is possible that the last Welsh veteran lasted into the 1870s or 1880s and died unnoticed.

Tell it to the Marines

Lewis Roteley and John George were just two of many Welshmen who served in the Royal Marines during the eighteenth century and the Napoleonic Wars.[89] The corps had been established in 1664 as the Lord Admiral's regiment, but after various disbandings and reformings, it was established on a permanent basis in 1755 and given the 'Royal' label in 1802. The Marines proved attractive to Welsh recruits, including some from inland areas who might not have considered conventional naval service. One such was Henry Davies of Llanycrwys near Lampeter, who was aboard HMS *Repulse* in the Mediterranean in 1807. Deeply religious, Davies summed up his world view in an affecting piece of doggerel:

> Henry is my name and Davies is my nation
> Llanycroys is my dwelling place and Christ is my salvation.[90]

John Jones of Ruthin joined the Marines at much the same time, thus following in a family tradition: his father had been in the same service, and was said to have witnessed the death of Nelson at Trafalgar. However, the son was converted to Quakerism in about 1821 and managed to win a release from the Marines, albeit with much difficulty. He returned to Ruthin and became a well-known figure in the local area.[91] Another Welsh Marine was Edward Lord of Orielton, Pembrokeshire, who went on an expedition to Tasmania as a young officer in 1803, then called Van Diemen's Land, served briefly as acting Lieutenant-Governor, and became so wealthy and influential that he has been called 'the most spectacular character in the first twenty years of Van Diemen's Land's history'.[92] However, the most remarkable Welsh Marine of the age was William Prothero, who spent five months serving aboard the frigate *Amazon* in 1760–61 before it was discovered that he was, in fact, a she, 'an eighteen-year-old Welsh girl who had followed her sweetheart to sea'.[93]

Notes

1   D. Miles, ed., *Lieutenant John George, Royal Marines: Letters 1799–1808* (Llandybie 2002), passim (quotation from p.138).
2   www.historyofparliamentonline.org/volume/1790-1820/member/paget-hon-william-1769-94

3   P.C. Davies, 'An Anglesey Naval Captain of the Eighteenth Century:
    The Short but Bright Career of William Paget', *Anglesey Antiquarian
    Society and Field Club Transactions* (2003), pp.10–21.

4   bobrowen.com/nymas/warof1812paper/paperrevised2006.html

5   Eames, pp.161–78 (quotation from p.177).

6   O'Byrne, i. 450–1; J.K. Laughton, rev. A. Lambert, 'Hamilton, Sir
    Edward, first baronet (1772–1851), Naval Officer', *ODNB*.

7   J.K. Laughton, rev. R. Morriss, 'Hamilton, Sir Charles,
    second baronet (1767–1849), Naval Officer', *ODNB*; www.
    historyofparliamentonline.org/volume/1790-1820/member/
    hamilton-sir-charles-1767-1849

8   D.J. Davies, 'Llanwenog', *Transactions and Archaeological Record,
    Cardiganshire Antiquarian Society*, 12 (1937), p.48; H.R. Evans,
    'Llandyssul Church', *Cardiganshire: Journal of the Cardiganshire
    Antiquarian Society*, 1 (1951), p.123.

9   T.R. Roberts, *Eminent Welshmen: A Short Biographical Dictionary of
    Welshmen who have Attained Distinction from the Earliest Times to the
    Present* (Cardiff, 1908), i. 535.

10 NLW, Llwyngwair MSS 15697–704.

11 W.I. Morgan, 'George Bowen, Llwyn-Gwair a'i deulu', *Bathafarn: The
    Journal of the Historical Society of the Methodist Church in Wales*, 23 (1968),
    pp.14–5.

12 O'Byrne, iii. 987.

13 J. Marshall, *Royal Naval Biography: Or, Memoirs of the Services of all the
    Flag-officers, Superannuated Rear-admirals, Retired-captains, Post-captains,
    and Commanders…* (1828), i. 598–608.

14 T.R. Roberts, *Eminent Welshmen: A Short Biographical Dictionary of
    Welshmen who have Attained Distinction from the Earliest Times to the
    Present* (Cardiff, 1908), i. 429–30; M.E.S. Laws, 'The Defence of
    St Marcouf', *Journal of the Royal Artillery*, 75 (1948), pp.298–307.

15 *The Complete Navy List of the Napoleonic Wars* (CD resource by
    P. Marione); TNA, PROB11/1449/176.

16 R.P. Evans, 'The Flintshire Loyalist Association and the Loyal
    Holywell Volunteers', *Flintshire Historical Society Journal*, 33 (1992),
    pp.54–61.

17 S. Willis, *The Glorious First of June: Fleet Battle in the Reign of Terror*
    (2011), 196–7; 'Memorial Inscriptions: St John's Church', Cardiff
    Records, 3 (1901), 510–45, accessed at www.british-history.ac.uk/
    report.aspx?.compid=48176.

18 B. Lavery, *Nelson's Navy: The Ships, Men and Organisation, 1793–1815*
    (1989), p.126.

19 N.A.M. Rodger, *The Command of the Ocean: A Naval History of Britain 1649–1815* (2004), 442.

20 Willis, *Glorious First of June*, 119; displays at the Museum of the Welsh Soldier, Cardiff Castle.

21 B Lavery, *Nelson's Navy: the Ships, Men and Organisation, 1793–1815* (1989), 126.

22 Eames, pp.179–80.

23 GAC, XQS/1795/50.

24 GAC, XQS/1795/34–55, 278–86.

25 Eames, pp.178–9, 181.

26 L. Lloyd, *A Real Little Seaport: The Port of Aberdyfi and its People 1565–1920* (Caernarfon, 1996), p.66.

27 H.M. Thomas, ed., *The Diaries of John Bird 1790–1803* (Cardiff, 1987), p.90.

28 A. Mee, ed., *Carmarthenshire Notes*, I (Llanelli 1889), p.3.

29 *The Cambrian*, 19 May, 16 June, 11 Aug., 8 Dec. 1804.

30 *The Cambrian*, 11 Mar. 1809.

31 *The Cambrian*, 7 May 1814, 22 Apr., 24 June 1815.

32 www.welshmariners.org.uk/index.php. The figures for the other Welsh counties are: Breconshire 42, Cardiganshire 197, Carmarthenshire 235, Denbighshire 119, Flintshire 132, Merionethshire 146, Montgomeryshire 43, Monmouthshire 164 and Radnorshire 17.

33 National Archives of Scotland, GD51/2/107/1, 2.

34 NMM, CRK/8/22, Jones to Nelson, 25 Nov. 1800.

35 *The Cambrian*, 11 Apr. 1835.

36 G. Matthews, '"The Heroes of Former Days Have Not Been Forgotten": Evidence from the Newspapers of Wales Regarding Welsh Sailors at the Battle of Trafalgar', *MW*, 27 (2006), pp.36–7.

37 *The Cambrian*, 30 Apr. 1869; O'Byrne, ii. 899.

38 J. Bartlett, 'Milford's Lost Memorabilia', *Pembrokeshire Life* (Jan. 2005), p.20.

39 P. Evans, 'Thomas Totty, RN, a Flintshire Admiral, part 1', *Hen Achau* 88 (2006), pp.39–42; 'Thomas Totty, RN, a Flintshire Admiral, part 2', *Hen Achau* 89 (2006), pp.10–4.

40 N. Tucker, 'Bodrhyddan and the Families of Conwy, Shipley-Conwy and Rowley-Conwy', *Journal of the Flintshire Historical Society*, 20 (1962), pp.14–7.

41 Tucker, 'Bodrhyddan', p.16; DRO, NTD 308.

42 www.historyofparliamentonline.org/volume/1790-1820/member/stuart-william-1778-1814. His elder brother Lord George Stuart also served as a captain, eventually dying as a rear-admiral.

43 O'Byrne, ii. 665.

44 *The Complete Navy List*; lordbyron.cath.lib.vt.edu/doc. php?&choose=LiteraryChron.1824.Cecil.xml

45 D. Miles, ed., *Lieutenant John George, Royal Marines: Letters 1799–1808* (Llandybie 2002), pp.100, 165.

46 NLW, Elizabeth Baker MSS 395, 398; Cwrtmawr MS 480C, I-III.

47 D.L. Thomas, rev. M.C. Loughlin-Chow, 'Jones, John (1788–1858), Poet', *ODNB*.

48 A.F. Pollard, rev. N. Banerji, 'Pemberton, Charles Reece (1790–1840), actor and public lecturer', *ODNB*; I. Land, *War, Nationalism and the British Sailor, 1750–1850* (Basingstoke, 2009), pp.124–9.

49 FRO, D/KK/575, letters of 27 Aug. 1795 and 18 Mar. 1798.

50 'Station and Quality of the Artois ship's company', MS in the Richard Endsor collection. I am grateful to Richard Endsor for allowing me to consult this fascinating document.

51 A. Lambert, 'Nelson's Band of Brothers', *ODNB*.

52 R.J.B. Knight, *The Pursuit of Victory: The Life and Achievement of Horatio Nelson* (2005), pp.270–1; compare with J. Sugden, Nelson: The Sword of Albion (2012), pp.90–1, 869–70.

53 O. Feldbæk, *The Battle of Copenhagen 1801* (Barnsley, 2002), pp.191–3.

54 L. Chambers, 'Fitzgerald [married name Foley], Lady Lucy Anne (1771–1851), Radical', *ODNB*.

55 J.B. Herbert, *Life And Services Of Admiral Sir Thomas Foley, GCB, Rear-Admiral Of Great Britain* (Cardiff 1884), pp.17, 33–4, 38.

56 T. Lloyd, 'Admiral Sir Thomas Foley', *The Carmarthenshire Historian*, 20 (1985), p.45.

57 British Library, Additional MS 51803, fos. 194–6.

58 Winfield 1793–1817, pp.23–4.

59 Winfield 1793–1817, p.104.

60 Winfield 1793–1817, p.133.

61 I have taken the view that the *Dee*, and subsequent ships of that name, was named primarily for the river in Scotland.

62 Winfield 1793–1817, p.134.

63 Winfield 1793–1817, p.240.

64 www.ageofnelson.org/MichaelPhillips/info.php?ref=1651

65 S. Conway, 'War and National Identity in the Mid-Eighteenth Century British Isles', *The English Historical Review*, 116 (2001), pp.872–3.

66 For English perspectives, search for 'Trafalgar' in English nationalist internet forums, and see the letter by David Ashton in *The Independent*, 22 March 2012; journals.le.ac.uk/ojs1/index.php/mas/article/ view/84/99, especially p.141, gives a considered view of English attitudes.

67 welshremembrancer.blogspot.com/2011/10/remember-21-october-is-trafalgar-day.html

68 The Welsh proportion of 3–4% is consistent from ship to ship and station to station throughout the Napoleonic Wars: J.S. Bromley, ed., *The Manning of the Royal Navy: Selected Public Pamphlets 1693–1873* (Navy Records Society, 1974), pp.352–3; C.L. Mantle, *The Apathetic and the Defiant: Case Studies of Canadian Mutiny and Disobedience, 1812–1919* (2007), p.76.

69 I have averaged out the slight variations in the major sources. For these, see Appendix 1.

70 G. Dean and K. Evans, *Nelson's Heroes* (the Nelson Society, 1994), pp.90–1.

71 L. Phillips, 'Some Pembrokeshire Sea Officers (Part One)', *Journal of the Pembrokeshire Historical Society*, 8 (1998–99), pp.10–11.

72 Dean and Evans, *Nelson's Heroes*, pp.33–4.

73 J. Bartlett, 'The Charitable Sea Captain', *Pembrokeshire Life* (Nov. 2005), pp.30–2; Phillips, 'Some Pembrokeshire Sea Officers (Part One)', pp.7–8.

74 Dean and Evans, *Nelson's Heroes*, pp.106–7.

75 CAS, MS Museum 510, published *inter alia* in N. Evans, 'Lord Nelson Remembered', *The Carmarthenshire Antiquary*, XLI (2005), p.142; G. Matthews, '"The Heroes of Former Days Have Not Been Forgotten": Evidence from the Newspapers of Wales Regarding Welsh Sailors at the Battle of Trafalgar', *MW*, 27 (2006), pp.32–3.

76 Matthews, 'Heroes of Former Days', pp.31–2.

77 *The Cambrian*, 30 Aug. 1845; Dean and Evans, *Nelson's Heroes*, pp.130–1.

78 www.welshmariners.org.uk/search_rn.php

79 E.O.C. Goddard, 'Pembrokeshire Midshipmen at Trafalgar', *MM*, 69 (1983), p.96.

80 G.H. Gardner, 'On the Formation of Reserves of Officers and Seamen for the Royal Navy, and the Evils and Inadequacy of Impressment to Provide the Same', *Journal of the Royal United Services Institute*, 15 (1871), p.602.

81 *Western Mail*, 22 Dec. 1876.

82 *North Wales Chronicle*, 16 November 1861

83 Matthews, 'Heroes of Former Days', p.35.

84 J. Richards, *Cottrell: Cottrell Park, St Nicholas, Vale of Glamorgan* (Cardiff, 1999), pp.75–92.

85 Richards, *Cottrell*, pp.72–3.

86 CAS, Cawdor MS 2/285.

87 NMM, CRK/3, fo. 15. Compare his description of his symptoms in other letters to Nelson, fos. 13, 14, 17, 18.

88 www.historyofparliamentonline.org/volume/1790-1820/member/campbell-george-1759-1821

89 Many examples can be found in the Royal Marines attestation papers, TNA, ADM157.

90 CAS, CDX713.

91 E.W. Jones, 'William Jones of Ruthin', *National Library of Wales Journal*, 26 (1990), p.407.

92 D. Miles, 'Lord of Orielton, 1781–1859', *Journal of the Pembrokeshire Historical Society*, 14 (2005), pp.21–9.

93 D. Cordingly, *Heroines and Harlots: Women at Sea in the Great Age of Sail* (2001), pp.63–4.

6

HIS MAJESTY'S ROYAL DOCKYARD

PEMBROKE DOCK, 1814–2008

Milford Haven is one of the natural wonders of Wales, and its vast harbour has long attracted the attention of writers. William Shakespeare certainly knew of it – in Act 3, Scene 2 of *Cymbeline*, Imogen addresses Pisanio:

> Then, true Pisanio … Say, and speak thick … how far it is
> To this same blessed Milford: and by the way
> Tell me how Wales was made so happy as
> To inherit such a haven …

Scene 4 of the same act is set in 'country near Milford Haven', where Pisanio tells Imogen that 'The ambassador, Lucius the Roman, comes to Milford Haven tomorrow.' *Cymbeline* is not one of the Bard's best works, and as dramatic poetry, 'Milford Haven' does not possess quite the same ring as, say, Dunsinane, Elsinore or Verona. Getting a mention in one of Shakespeare's works, but one of the least successful, typifies the entire naval and maritime history of a harbour which always seemed to be on the verge of greatness, but somehow never quite achieved it.

Eventually it received the accolade of having a royal dockyard established within its precincts, but it proved to be Britain's smallest and one of its shortest lived. Even so, the new town of Pembroke Dock, established to service that dockyard, became a permanent feature on the map of Wales. To this day, though, it suffers from something of an identity crisis, with attempts to change its name surfacing from time to time: apparently, in 'sea blind' twenty-first-century Britain the word 'dock' has negative connotations.[1]

The Navy and Milford Haven

From Tudor times, wars and war scares led to calls to fortify the strategic natural harbour of Milford Haven, but in practice little was done. Blockhouses were erected at Dale and Angle by Henry VIII's order of 1539, a fort was built at Pill during the civil war, and in the 1750s another was commenced at Pater, one of three planned to guard the upper reaches of the haven; but it was not completed, and the other two were not even started.[2] Ultimately, Milford Haven was too remote, and despite the obvious dangers inherent in leaving such a large harbour virtually undefended, successive governments continued to regard its comprehensive fortification as an unjustifiable expense. As early as 1626, one commentator had summarised the harbour's advantages and disadvantages succinctly: 'though it be most spacious & commodious, etc, … it is in a poor country, very far from London, and the passage full of impediments, as rivers, woods etc, and a blow given there, so far from the east, will never prove mortal.'[3] Nevertheless, subsequent visitors often expressed astonishment that the Royal Navy did not take more advantage of the remarkable natural harbour and that the British state did not fortify it properly.[4]

During the Seven Years' War of 1756–63 both the royal dockyards and the major private shipbuilders were fully stretched.

This led to a search for virgin sites where new ships could be built, and two contracts were signed to build warships at Neyland. Richard Chitty built the frigate *Milford*, launched in 1759; much of the timber for her came from 6,620 trees on the Golden Grove estate in Carmarthenshire, floated downstream to Carmarthen (guided by the local coracle men) and then stacked on the quayside to await onward shipment to Milford Haven.[5] Henry Bird and Roger Fisher subsequently contracted to build a larger 74-gun ship at Milford. The latter was to have been named *Hibernia* but was later christened *Prince of Wales*, a tribute both to the future King George IV (born in August 1762) and to the country where the ship was built; it was the first use of a name that would have an illustrious history in the Royal Navy. However, Neyland's comparative lack of facilities caused problems for the builders. Launching gear had to be brought from Plymouth Dockyard, while shortages of materials caused lengthy stoppages.[6] The *Prince of Wales* was launched in 1765, well after the end of the war. She had a very brief service career, although she did see action in the West Indies in 1778–79 before being broken up in 1783.[7] The Seven Years' War also witnessed a survey of the Haven by an engineer officer, Colonel Bastide, who heaped lavish praise upon the harbour and seems to have been the first to suggest that a dockyard should be established there.[8]

The Dockyard at Milford

The French Revolutionary and Napoleonic wars, commencing in 1793, saw the navy become interested in Milford Haven once again.[1] Messrs Harry and Joseph Jacob of London received orders to build ships there, this time at the new whaling town of Milford rather than upstream at Neyland, but when their business failed following the death of one Jacob and the paralytic stroke of the other, the Navy Board took it on directly, renting the land from Charles Greville.[2] He was the nephew of Sir William Hamilton, who, as noted previously, had inherited extensive Pembrokeshire estates from his first wife, a Barlow of Slebech, where Sir William was ultimately buried. Greville was also the administrator and eventual inheritor of Hamilton's lands, including that along the north shore of the haven, and both men had been involved from the 1780s onwards in developing the new town that came to be called Milford Haven. This explains why, in the summer 1802, Sir William came down to Pembrokeshire with his colourful second wife Emma and her lover, Vice-Admiral Lord Nelson. Their Welsh tour, and Nelson's grandiloquent speech in praise of the Haven, have been described in detail in Chapter 4, and it is possible that Nelson canvassed on Milford dockyard's behalf when he returned to London.[3] Meanwhile the French royalist master shipwright Jean-Louis Barralier had taken up residence in Milford, drew up plans for an extensive private dockyard and was completing the ships originally ordered from the Jacobses, namely the sloop Nautilus, which was launched in 1804, and the frigate Lavinia, launched in 1806. Despite official opposition to Barralier's retention in preference to a native-born shipwright, he subsequently completed the 74-gun Milford, ordered in 1796 but not launched until 1809, the frigate Surprise, two smaller vessels and the 80-gun Second Rate Rochfort, launched in 1814 but broken up only twelve years later. Following the Bourbon restoration in France, Barralier became the master shipwright at Toulon dockyard.[4] Much of the timber for the Milford-built ships was purchased in Herefordshire and the Forest of Dean, then shipped coastwise from Chepstow and Purton; the relatively short distances, compared to those involved in transportation of timber to other dockyards, meant that building costs at Milford were comparatively cheap.[5]

In 1809, the Navy Board decided to buy the land on which the new Milford yard stood and to provide it with the full establishment of a regular Royal Dockyard, thus complying with Charles

Greville's stated wish that it should become for Great Britain what Lorient was for France.[6] The Union flag was hoisted over it on 21 October 1809, the fourth anniversary of Trafalgar. But Robert Fulke Greville, Charles' younger brother (who had just inherited the estate) held out for a better price, only to find his bluff called, while there was also vocal opposition to the employment of the Catholic Barrallier in a state establishment. In August 1810 work on Milford dockyard stopped, and in October 1812 the Navy Board resolved to abandon it in favour of a new site adjoining Pater Fort, upstream and on the opposite shore, by Midsummer 1814, when the *Rochfort* was due to be completed.[7] Nevertheless, the plans for the abortive Milford yard present a remarkable vision. A long range of buildings with classical arcading, centred on a ropery, was to be built on the higher ground (the site of the present Pier Road); sweeping ramps were to lead down to the shore, where the yard would have had three building slips, two dry docks, a basin enclosed by two piers and a mast house with a passing resemblance to a Venetian or Maltese galley dock. A telling proof of the extent of the Admiralty's exasperation with Greville is the amount of building that had already taken place when the yard was abandoned in favour of Pater. A large storehouse, the porter's house, the joiners' shop and several other buildings had already been built; the dry dock had been excavated, the slips laid down and one of the basin piers erected.[8] The remains of Milford Dockyard were so substantial that they remained extant for many years and were still marked prominently on the detailed 1862 map of the town. A few fragments survive to this day.[9]

The Establishment of Pembroke Dock

The new site at Pater, on land purchased from the Meyrick estate, was officially established as a royal dockyard by an order-in-council of 31 October 1815, thus overcoming the somewhat inconvenient fact that until that moment, all the works being carried on there, all the appointments of officers, and all the hirings of workers, were entirely illegal.[17] Initially called Pater, from April 1817 it was referred to officially as Pembroke Dockyard.[18] Its first warships, the small frigates *Valorous* and *Ariadne*, were launched together on 10 February 1816 by Lord Cawdor, the hero of Fishguard, who also suitably christened the *Fisgard* in 1819. That event, along with several other of the early launches, was celebrated with a ball at the Golden Lion, Pembroke, on the same evening.[19] By 1830, Pembroke Dock had launched forty-six ships, including one of 84 guns and two of 74; in 1833 it launched its first first rate, the *Royal William* of 120 guns. However, peacetime retrenchment meant that many of these went straight 'into ordinary', a dismasted, unarmed state of reserve; some Pembroke-built ships, like the frigates *Nemesis*, *Hotspur* and *Leda*, were never even completed.[20] Between 1814 and 1854, the dockyard also broke up many old warships, including the first rates *Windsor Castle* and *Ville de Paris* and 74s like the *Triumph* and *Mulgrave*. Several of these were former lazarettes or quarantine ships, a number of which were moored about half a mile off Angle Point in Milford Haven from 1805 onwards.[21] These also included the Trafalgar veteran *Dreadnought* and the locally built *Milford*, which served as Admiral Fremantle's flagship during the capture of Trieste (1813), but had otherwise seen little naval service.[22] One of the lazarettes' principal tasks was to disinfect cotton bales from Africa in case they were carrying plague. The lazarettes were phased out in the 1840s, the last, the *Hope*, leaving in 1852, but one, *Saturn*, was then converted into a hospital ship for the yard and town, being succeeded in 1866 by the *Nankin*, which served until 1895.[23]

Initially envisaged as a yard with six slips which would be confined to frigate building alone,[24] by 1830 Pembroke Dock had thirteen, numbered from west to east. One of these was covered as early as 1817 and others soon followed, chiefly

because the Welsh and Forest of Dean timber principally
employed at the yard was found to decay unusually quickly if
not placed under cover.[25] By 1830, too, numbers 1 and 2 slips
were capable of building the navy's largest ships, and Pembroke
was no longer confined to frigate construction. But the yard
had no basin, no ropery and, at first, no dry dock or proper
wall either. For some years the only 'storehouse' that it possessed was the old frigate *Lapwing*, which was run aground on
the east end of the Pater shore in 1814, whilst the *Dragon* served
as both the Royal Marines' barracks and the school for dockyard apprentices.[26] Religious services were held on the *Lapwing*
until a temporary chapel opened in 1818, ministered to by the
first chaplain of the dockyard, the Reverend William Griffith
from Caernarfonshire.[27] The dockyard officers had to find
lodgings wherever they could; even Thomas Roberts, the first
master shipwright, lived in quarters through which passed 'a
thoroughfare to a public billiard table'.[28] When proper facilities
were eventually built on the new site, the huge classical building on the clifftop at Milford, which would undoubtedly have
been one of the most astonishing sights in Wales, was discarded
in favour of a row of rather more modest, albeit still substantial, officers' houses. The changed priorities probably reflected
the policy of retrenchment that began towards the end of the
Napoleonic Wars and took hold with a vengeance after the final
defeat of Napoleon. Whereas Milford Dockyard would have
been a grand establishment to rival (and perhaps ultimately
replace) one of the existing yards, Pembroke Dock was clearly
intended from the beginning to be very much a secondary facility. Even so, the yard was expanded westward in 1830 when
a graving dock was added; the construction of the impressive
dockyard wall and substantial row of officers' houses that still
survives was also a consequence of this expansion (the *Lapwing*
had gone to the breakers in 1828). Plans for an even greater
extension to the east in 1850, which would have enclosed West
Llanion Pill and added a large fitting-out basin, were never

proceeded with.[29] As it was, the royal dockyard finally covered an area of some 82 acres, enclosed by an impressive wall which still largely survives. Additionally, in 1875 a torpedo store from which submarine mining experiments were conducted was established at Pennar Point; the site subsequently became a barracks for the Royal Engineers.

The Workforce, the Town and the Garrison

Many of the workers who established Pembroke Dock were transferred from the existing establishment at Milford, and labourers were overwhelmingly local men, but many of the skilled men – shipwrights, caulkers and so forth – were brought in from other yards, especially Plymouth.[30] They included the likes of the shipwright Charles Cozens, born at Churston Ferrers, Devon; Devonport-born mason John Trevena; Richard Tregenna, shipwright, originally of Millbrook, Cornwall; Portsmouth shipwright James Biddlecombe; and John Ostrick Polkinghorn, a shipwright born at Antony, Cornwall, all of whom brought distinctly unfamiliar surnames into Welsh genealogy.[31] Some came from even further afield. John Davidson of Gateshead became a clerk in the yard in 1823, liked it so much that he refused a transfer to Portsmouth, and died in Pembroke Dock thirty years later.[32] Undoubtedly the most remarkable member of the dockyard's workforce in the early years was Joseph King, boatswain of the yard, alias Joaquim Mendoza, a Portuguese subject who had joined the Royal Navy as a boy. In the early 1780s, King was boatswain of the frigate *Boreas* in the West Indies; her captain was a certain Horatio Nelson, who came to regard King as a friend and strongly promoted his career thereafter. They served together during Nelson's commands of *Agamemnon* and *Captain*, and Nelson's recommendation secured for King the post of boatswain of Gibraltar Dockyard. He came to Pembroke in 1821 and died there in 1829, being buried at

Monkton, but like so many of the incomers, he had established a dynasty in his new home. The names of his descendants honoured his old friend: a granddaughter, born at Pembroke in 1826, was christened Ann Horatio Nelson King.[33]

With eighteen boats being required at first to ferry men from their homes at Milford to Pater,[34] the need to erect more convenient accommodation was paramount. The first houses of the new town immediately adjacent to the yard were built in 1814, the first four becoming accommodation for dockyard officials. These buildings formed the first part of what became Front Street. Other houses and streets were built during the years that followed, with the town's first pub being built on the corner of King Street. It was soon followed by others: there were nearly sixty by 1850, ten on Front Street and fifteen on King Street.[35] The new town was laid out on a grid pattern with generous, wide streets, and the navy also sponsored the establishment of a market in 1819. The dockyard church was built in 1832, its bell being the original one fitted aboard HMS *Gibraltar* in 1749 when she was built as the Spanish *Fenix*, subsequently captured at the Battle of Cape St Vincent. As the yard increased in importance, so did the imperative to defend it. The Royal Marines who had arrived in the early days were supplemented by regular soldiers and by a short-lived volunteer Dockyard Battalion, formed in 1846 to man the Pater battery, only to be dissolved in 1857.[36] A huge defensible barracks was built in 1844–45 on the high ground above the dockyard, which meant that the venerable *Dragon* could finally be dispensed with. From 1849 onwards, a series of new fortifications was built to defend the yard. The nearest were the two gun towers at its western and eastern extremities, inaccurately named 'Martello towers' and built between 1848 and 1851; others were built between 1854 and 1871 on Stack Rock and Thorn Island in the entrance to Milford Haven, at Dale, West and East Blockhouses, South Hook, Hubberston, Popton and Scoveston. Another fort was built at Chapel Bay, Angle, in 1891; during the First World

War this acted as the examination battery for Milford Haven, its guns and lights keeping watch over suspected and captured enemy vessels in the anchorage. In 1904, a large new barracks was completed at Llanion, and this continued to be used by the army until 1966.[37] Thus, in many respects, Pembroke Dock was actually more of an army town than a naval one; it was never a naval base where ships were manned and based, lacking even a receiving ship to take in recruits from the local area, so the uniformed naval personnel were always greatly outnumbered by redcoats.

Over the years, dockyard families intermarried and developed into a tightly-knit community; it was said that 'it was no uncommon thing to find a gang of riggers or shipwrights whose foremen and timekeepers were the fathers or uncles or brothers of most of the gang'.[38] Of the children of Benjamin Frise, Torquay-born shipwright who entered the yard from Plymouth in 1822, three married other dockyard workers and another ran a pub in the town; a daughter, Priscilla, lived until 1929, three years after the closure of the dockyard, so just two generations had witnessed almost the entire course of the yard's history.[39] The shipwrights swiftly formed a Friendly Society, the Pembroke Dock Loyal Cambrian Society of Shipwrights, with contributions of 2*d* a week from each member.[40] Like all dockyards, the workers at Pembroke Dock were exposed to industrial injuries that could be of a horrifying nature, even – or perhaps especially – after the yard changed to build ships of iron and steel. John Lewis, aged 56,

> was painting a bulkhead in the port engine room of the new cruiser HMS *Drake* on 30 January 1901 when he slipped and fell thirteen feet onto the engine bearers and then into the crankpit. He fractured his skull 'and is now totally deaf. In addition he has lost his left eye which he states occurred when building HMS *Shannon* on 1st May 1875', wrote Fleet Surgeon Edward Luther.

But Lewis was arguably fortunate when compared with 45-year-old William Williams, a labourer who 'had been greasing cogs in a machine in No. 2 Fitters Shop on the morning of 21 May 1900 when he was caught in the machinery. He was taken to the Surgery with a fractured skull and his right hand amputated "all except his thumb".' Williams died the following day.[41]

Remote and remarkably cosmopolitan by the standards of nineteenth-century Wales, Pembroke Dock quickly acquired something of a 'Wild West' reputation. Within a year of the yard's establishment, Richard Blake, the Timber Master, attacked Edward Wright, chief clerk to the Clerk of the Cheque, 'by wrenching my nose several times', Wright claimed, 'and putting himself in a menacing attitude to strike me with his umbrella'. The relationship between Blake and Roberts, the Master Shipwright, was equally poisonous; the principal officers of the yard spent the best part of six years doing their utmost to undermine and discredit each other.[42] In 1822 Benjamin Isitt, a smith in the dockyard, was accused of raping Mary Morgans of Pembroke. Although he was acquitted, he was convicted forty years later of 'openly, lewdly and obscenely' exposing himself to a woman of the town.[43] In 1824 William Bowen, shipwright, assaulted his workmate Charles May, 'and did then and there violently cast, fling and throw upon and against him the said Charles May divers stones and clods of earth.'[44] The presence of so many dockyard workers and soldiers inevitably attracted prostitutes, and the sheer number of drinking dens led to trouble. The Ship on the Launch pub was particularly notorious for fights, but when the magistrates attempted to shut it down, they were roundly abused in court by the landlady's friends.[45] A particular complication unique to the navy's Welsh yard was the dispersal of many of the workers in communities distant from the dockyard; the town itself was small and many lived in villages several miles away, commuting to and from work by horse, boat or most commonly on foot. The dockyard surgeon had to make his rounds of the outlying villages on horseback.

In springtime, this sometimes led to the surgeon coming across 'sick' workers who were actually moonlighting in the fields to harvest one of Pembrokeshire's most famous assets, its early potato crop.[46]

From 1832, the head of the dockyard was the captain-superintendent, and a large new house was erected to accommodate this august new dignitary. The holders of the office were usually long-serving captains: the first, Sir Charles Bullen, had been flag captain of the *Britannia* at Trafalgar, and among his successors was Sir Watkin Owen Pell, son of a Denbighshire mother, a one-legged martinet who 'is said to have spied with a telescope on his men from Barrack Hill and his donkey, on which he toured his domain, was trained to carry him up the gangways onto the decks of ships under construction'.[47] The superintendents had an uphill struggle against an independent-minded workforce that seems to have known every trick in the book. On 15 July 1898, Captain Burges Watson announced to his assembled dockyard officers that he had discovered

> a hutch in a timber stack, roofed with corrugated iron, and equipped with towels, water and pillows and in which, it seemed, men had been going to skulk, sleep and – worse still – perhaps smoke, for weeks or months previously. The Dockyard Police had later found three men in there and he had discharged them ... Of course, this all caused a great uproar in the local newspaper with complaints that 2,200 men should not be tarred with the same brush as three errant skulkers.[48]

Dockyard apprenticeships were highly sought after. Even if they did not lead to a 'job for life' in the yard, they opened up opportunities for employment in other dockyards, either in Britain or elsewhere in the Empire, or else in commercial shipyards. One of those who benefited was Edgar 'E.P.' Harries, who began a six-year apprenticeship in 1903 at the age of 14 and went on to become one of Britain's most eminent trade unionists, a key figure alongside Ernest Bevin in mobilising the labour force at the beginning of the Second World War.[49] Pembroke Dock was still recruiting apprentices in 1919, with 113 applicants for 43 places, although one suspects that H.G. Roberts, who obtained 22/600 in the examination – the second worst result in any dockyard – was not entirely cut out for such a career.[50] Pembroke was also selected as the first yard to employ women in roles that had traditionally been taken by men, initially as plan tracers. At first, the innovation was greeted with jocularity, as in this vignette from the *Portsmouth Evening News*:

> So we are to have dockyard-women! Lady tracers (not detectives, you must understand, only drawing ladies) will vie with lady polishers in keeping up the King's Navee! A charming idea. The Portsmouth officials are said to be in favour of it. Rather, with good-looking lady tracers on the premises![51]

But as it became clear that the Admiralty was serious, and the plan went into effect, its implications became clearer and led to not a little misogynistic grumbling. The same paper, no longer amused, but fearful that the precedent might spread to the larger yards, warned that women who took such jobs from men 'are not, therefore, likely to receive a very warm welcome', partly because it was likely that they would be paid less: 'they should insist on being paid men's wages if they do men's work.' As it was, the scheme had to be paused at Pembroke Dock because at first there was no suitable accommodation for the 'drawing ladies'.[52]

Shipbuilding: The Era of Wood and Sail

Pembroke was unique among the royal dockyards in that it was exclusively a building yard. Moreover, for much of its existence it did not even fit out the ships it built; after launching, the incomplete hulls were towed to one of the other dock-yards for completion.[53] Nevertheless, the yard developed an extensive range of facilities which included two cambers, a smithery, a mould loft, an oakum store, a mast pond and several storehouses.[54] Most of the slips had timber covers, but in 1844 work commenced on two revolutionary iron roofs over slips 8 and 9, the first in any dockyard, and by 1847 five of the thirteen slips at Pembroke Dock had iron covers.[55] In an age when it was still a relatively new innovation, cast iron was used extensively elsewhere in the yard, for example in the large No. 1 Storehouse and for the spiral staircases of the officers' houses.[56] Pembroke was similarly innovative when it came to the ships it built. Several were 'firsts', 'largests' or 'longests' at the time of construction: the *Gorgon* (1837) was the first really successful steam warship; the *Cyclops* of 1839 was then the world's largest steam man-of-war; while the *Constance*, *Arethusa*, *Octavia* and *Sutlej* (all launched 1846–55) were the largest sailing frigates ever built for the Royal Navy.[57] The *Duke of Wellington* (1852) was the longest battleship afloat and the navy's largest until that time, and the *Orlando* of 1858, the longest wooden warship ever built for the navy, was also the largest frigate in the world at the time.[58] Such was the speed at which nineteenth-century naval technology moved that the yard was soon building 'lasts', too, such as its second HMS *Valorous*, state-of-the-art when ordered in 1847 but obsolete when commissioned in 1853 as the Royal Navy's last major paddle warship. Nevertheless, *Valorous* distinguished herself in the Crimean War, in Arctic exploration and in the relief of famine in Ireland in 1880.[59] Pembroke Dock also built HMS *James Watt*, a 91-gun second rate ordered in 1849 and launched in 1853: the only British warship to bear the name, one of relatively few ever to be named after a scientist, and proof, perhaps, that the Admiralty's adoption of steam power in the second quarter of the nineteenth century was rather more enthusiastic than has sometimes been assumed.

The captain-superintendent of the yard from 1849 to 1854 was Sir Thomas Sabine Pasley, an impoverished Scottish baronet with a surfeit of children.[60] As he put it towards the end of his tenure:

> I am most thankful for this appointment. For a man with a large family, the interests of that family are paramount; and though I shall leave the yard still in debt, and poorer than when I came, yet I shall have educated these expensive boys [*his seven sons*] without quite ruining myself …

Indeed, his daughter claimed that he looked upon the appointment as 'a paradise … no telegraph disturbed his equanimity or harassed his clerks'.[61] Pasley became friendly with the local 'first family', the Earl and Countess of Cawdor at Stackpole, and presided over several of the most memorable ship launches in the entire history of the yard. In September 1852 the *Windsor Castle*, then the longest battleship in the world, went down the ways, having been in gestation for many years; the hull had been cut in half on the stocks so that a steam engine could be fitted into what was originally planned as a pure sailing ship. However, the Duke of Wellington died on the same day and the great ship was renamed after him soon afterwards. Unfortunately, the next major launch, that of the *Caesar* in July 1853, proved to be an unmitigated disaster. At first, all seemed well: 'off went the ship beautifully, but to our dismay stopped, and became immovable, when she had gone nearly her own length.' Successive attempts to complete the launch failed, and in the end it took fifteen days to get the ship into the water.[62] Pasley and every expert he consulted were mystified by the failure, but none of them seem to have been aware of the theory that soon became established in local folklore. According to this account, a local woman called Betty Foggy, who was reputed to be a witch, had tried to enter the dockyard to watch the launch, but was turned away by a policeman who thought her presence would be unlucky.

Eyewitnesses claimed to have heard Betty proclaim that if she could not go in, there would be no launch that day. Her 'curse' seemed to have come true in spectacular fashion.[63]

Shipbuilding: The Era of Iron and Steam

One of Pembroke Dock's proudest moments came on 7 March 1860 when HMS *Howe* went down the slipway into the waters of Milford Haven. Displacing 6,577 tons and designed to mount 121 guns, she was twice the size of Nelson's *Victory* and the largest wooden battleship ever built. She would also be one of the last, for already taking shape in a Thames shipyard was the low, sinister black hull that would render *Howe* and all of her kind obsolete overnight: HMS *Warrior*, the world's first ironclad battleship, which would eventually play her own part in the history of Pembroke Dock and the Milford Haven waterway. The mighty *Howe* never even sailed for sea trials, was never commissioned under her original name, and never carried more than 12 guns during her decades of service as a harbour training ship named successively *Bulwark* and *Impregnable*.[64] The abrupt switch from wood to iron led to the cancellation of seven orders that had been placed with the yard, including that for the 91-gun second rate *Blake*.[65] Pembroke Dock was left with a vast stock of surplus timber and an unfeasibly large number of building slips that had been built to allow several wooden hulls to season simultaneously before launching.[66] There must have been a particular poignancy about the launch of the 91-gun second rate *Defiance* on 27 March 1861; she was the last wooden battleship to be launched in Britain, ending three and a half centuries of tradition and development.[67]

Far from sounding the death knell for the yard, the navy's switch to iron and, later, steel, actually gave Pembroke a new lease of life. It became the second royal dockyard to receive orders for iron ships, building the iron-cased (but wooden-hulled) *Prince Consort* in 1862 and then a succession of ironclads, including the *Inconstant* (1868), *Thunderer* (1873) and *Dreadnought* (1875). The yard built the navy's first steel warships, the despatch cruisers *Iris* and *Mercury* (launched in 1877–78). The metal was supplied by the Landore steel works in Swansea, which was now easily accessible via the railway that had been extended to Pembroke Dock in 1864.[68] The adoption of composite construction (wood planking on iron frames) for smaller ships such as gunboats also benefited the Welsh yard.[69] In 1902 it finally obtained a proper fitting-out facility with the opening of Carr Jetty, supplementing the sheerlegs-equipped tidal wharf at Hobbs Point which had been built in 1829 and used since 1832 by the Irish packet boats. The dockyard served as the training ground for some of the Royal Navy's finest ship designers. Sir Philip Watts, designer of the *Dreadnought* and subsequent classes of battleship and battlecruiser, effectively started his career at Pembroke Dock in the 1870s as assistant constructor during the building of HMS *Shannon*, the first British armoured cruiser.[70] John Harper Narbeth was born in the town, the grandson of the house carpenter who cut the first shaving for the first window frame in the first house in the new town of Pembroke Dock, before later going to work in the dockyard itself.[71] John served as a shipwright apprentice in the yard and went on to work with Watts on the design of *Dreadnought* before designing many classes of warship during the First World War, including some of the first aircraft carriers.[72]

During the first decades of its existence, the dockyard's warships were usually launched by local ladies, the *Prince Consort* by 'Miss Jones of Pantglas, a Carmarthenshire lady' and the mighty *Windsor Castle* by Lady Pasley (who had to break a second bottle on its bow a couple of weeks later, after the ship was renamed *Duke of Wellington*).[73] A rare exception was the launch of the *Clarence* in 1827, which was attended by the Duke of Clarence, Lord High Admiral – the future King William IV – and his old friend Sir Thomas Foley.[74] The greater ease and speed of travel ushered in by the railway era meant that later in the nineteenth century many launches were rather grander affairs, often attended by national and even royal dignitaries. On the other hand, the 'Welshness' of such occasions was given a new emphasis. When the Duchess of Edinburgh, Queen Victoria's daughter-in-law (and sister of the Tsar of Russia), came to Pembroke Dock in 1882 to launch the *Edinburgh*, she was entertained by the Llanelli singer David Andrews, *llew a lan* ('the lion of song').[75] In 1891 another of the Queen-Empress' daughters-in-law, the Duchess of Connaught and Strathearn, came down to launch the battleship *Empress of India*. The band played 'Men of Harlech' and a choir (with soprano soloist) contributed *Hen Wlad Fy Nhadau*, albeit in English.[76] By that time it was also apparently customary for Pembroke-built ships to have leeks mounted upon their mastheads; at her launch in 1893, the cruiser *Cambrian* bore them on each side of her bows 'to symbolise the gallant little country from which she had taken her name'.[77] A number of the dockyard's ships were given Welsh names: the yard built HM ships *Fisgard*, *Druid*, *Dragon*, *Newport*, *Merlin* and no fewer than three *Cambrians*. Launches of the biggest ships at Pembroke Dock were probably some of the largest, if not *the* largest, public occasions in nineteenth-century Wales. The gates of the dockyard were thrown open early in the morning (although as the Betty Foggy incident proved, admission was not necessarily automatic) and thousands turned up, often complete with picnics.[78] The launch of the *Windsor Castle/Duke of Wellington* in 1852 was watched by a crowd of some 20,000, about 2,000 of whom were on boats in the haven. In the early decades, Bristol Channel steamers made special excursions, as in 1833 when the *Palmerston* was diverted from her scheduled service between Bristol and Tenby to carry spectators to the dockyard to witness the launch of the *Rodney*, the first British two-decker to carry 90 guns and eventually the last wooden capital ship on active service.[79]

The royal dockyard was by no means the only shipbuilding yard on the Milford waterway, although it was by far the largest; nor was it the only yard to build warships. In 1874 Edward Reed, former chief constructor of the Royal Navy (who had designed the likes of the ironclad battleships HMS *Devastation* and *Thunderer*), stood as the Liberal candidate for Pembroke, promising that if he was elected, he would establish a private yard to employ men recently made redundant from the royal dockyard. Reed won and duly established the Milford Haven Shipbuilding and Engineering Company at Pennar, swiftly winning an order for a corvette for the Imperial Japanese Navy. This was launched on 19 June 1877 as the *Hiei*; the launch was a grand spectacle attended by the Japanese ambassador and Dr Heinrich Schliemann, the discoverer of Troy. The young lieutenant overseeing the construction of the ship was a certain Heihachiro Togo, who later became Japan's greatest naval hero following his fleet's crushing victory over the Russians at Tsushima in 1905. The *Hiei* served until 1911; the name was subsequently borne by a Japanese battleship sunk at Guadalcanal in 1942 and by a destroyer that served from 1973 to 2011.[80] The shipbuilding yard at Pennar proved rather less enduring. It built several merchant ships as well as HMS *Acorn*, a sloop for the Royal Navy launched in 1884, but the royal dockyard's revival in the 1880s probably contributed to its decline. Reed himself moved on, serving as MP for Cardiff between 1880 and 1895, and again from 1900 to 1906.

Decline and Closure

In many respects, Pembroke Dock was always something of a Cinderella yard. Its lack of comprehensive fitting-out facilities, its inability to refit ships from the active fleet, and its distance from the cosy triangle formed by Whitehall, the Thames/Medway yards and Portsmouth (in other words, within easy distance of the political and, perhaps more pertinently, the social life of the capital), always made it vulnerable.[81] Even in 1851, Sir Thomas Sabine Pasley was convinced that the yard would soon be too small to build the largest ships,[82] and in the same year an MP denounced scandalous mismanagement at the yard and proposed its closure.[83] The same course of action was mooted in 1864, this time in the rather more threatening context of a Parliamentary select committee to consider the future of all the dockyards with a view to making sweeping economies. Pembroke, Deptford and Woolwich were all slated for closure, but while the two Thames yards were duly abandoned, Pembroke survived by the skin of its teeth, albeit only after some acrimonious exchanges in the House of Commons.[84] By the beginning of the twentieth century, though, the yard's workmen and the community that depended upon them were desperately anxious about their futures.[85] Since 1822 the dockyard had launched at least one ship a year, usually several more: but in 1884, 1892, 1898, 1900, 1903 and 1906 it launched none. Repeated attempts were made to demonstrate that Pembroke could build ships more economically than the other dockyards and commercial shipbuilders, with a view to persuading the Admiralty to place more orders there. In 1887, Admiral Richard Mayne, the MP for Pembroke and Haverfordwest, claimed that the battleship *Anson*, launched at Pembroke Dock in the previous year, had cost over 10 per cent less than her sister ship *Benbow*, built on the Thames. In 1906, Mayne's successor, Owen Cosby Phillips, claimed that the Pembroke-built cruiser *Duke of Edinburgh* had cost significantly less than her four sister ships built in commercial yards, but this special pleading was not entirely ingenuous as *Duke of Edinburgh* had been built to a less advanced specification than most of her sisters.[86] Indeed, the campaign to save the dockyard was heavily influenced by local politics, which in turn was influenced by concerns over employment (as had been demonstrated when Edward Reed won the old Pembroke seat in 1874 with his promise to create a new shipbuilding yard). The Pembroke and

Haverfordwest constituency was marginal, changing hands four times between 1885 and 1906, and Tories and Liberals vied to convince the electorate that their opponents were secretly bent on running down or closing the yard.[87]

In the meantime, Pembroke Dockyard continued to build ships for the Royal Navy, although the steady increase in the size of battleships meant that it built no more after the heaviest warship ever built at the yard, HMS *Hannibal*, launched in 1896. In the mid-1850s Pembroke Dock built some of the largest battleships in the world, but such was the extent of its relative decline that fifty years later it was no longer capable of building even the smallest. However, the dockyard continued to build smaller warships during the last twenty years of its existence, notably six heavy cruisers (two of which, *Warrior* and *Defence*, would be sunk at Jutland) together with sixteen light cruisers; the First World War even saw the yard build five submarines. Once the yard was able to fit out the ships it built, sea trials could usually take place in Pembrokeshire waters outside Milford Haven. In wartime, these were inevitably rather more perfunctory than they were in peace: the cruiser *Curacoa* had just two days of trials off Milford, preliminary speed and gunnery trials for six hours on 13 February 1918, and full power trials for four hours the following day, before she sailed to join the fleet.[88]

Pembroke had already built four royal yachts before embarking, in 1897, on the construction of the *Victoria and Albert*, a huge 380ft-long floating palace designed to rival the grand imperial yachts of the Kaiser and the Tsar. She was launched on 9 May 1899 by the Duchess of York (the future Queen Mary), but what should have been one of the dockyard's finest achievements turned into a near-catastrophe outdoing even the launch of the *Caesar*. The launch itself went off successfully, and the early stages of fitting out at Hobbs Point were uneventful, but that berth – then still the yard's only fitting-out facility – was needed for another ship, so the yacht was moved into dry dock for completion. *Victoria and Albert* was to be floated out at dawn on 3 January 1900, but as the dock flooded the ship slipped off her blocks with a list of eight degrees to port. The hull was swiftly sealed, but an 8in dent ran amidships for over 25 feet. Her designer, Sir William White, rushed down from London and oversaw the ballasting of the hull before she was floated out on the next tide, listing ten degrees to port. The press had a field day, questions were asked in Parliament, and an Admiralty enquiry established that although there was no fundamental flaw in the yacht's design, she had been overburdened with decoration and other additions which had made her top heavy. *Victoria and Albert* was taken round to Portsmouth for extensive remedial work, but White was censured and went into an ignominious early retirement. Although hardly the dockyard's fault, Pembroke Dock inevitably suffered by association, its reputation for building good ships as dented as the hull of the yacht. With the future of the dockyard already in doubt, the *Victoria and Albert* calamity could hardly have come at a worse time.

Like all the royal dockyards, Pembroke Dock worked at full capacity during the First World War. Indeed, its efficiency, especially that of the 500 women working there, impressed a middle-ranking American administrator who visited it in July 1918: the Assistant Secretary of the Navy, one Franklin Delano Roosevelt.[89] But in 1921, Sir Eric Geddes, charged by the Lloyd George coalition government with cutting government spending, implemented a series of measures known as the 'Geddes axe', one element of which was sweeping economy in the royal dockyards. This coincided with the Washington naval treaty by which Britain agreed to substantially reduce the size of the Royal Navy, leading to the abandonment of plans for several new classes of warship. Once again consideration was given to closing the dockyard, but it was reprieved, albeit with a much reduced establishment. The workforce at Pembroke Dock was halved in two years, from 2,500 in 1920 to 1,200 by the end of

1922, and the accidental burning in June 1922 of the mould loft – which contained the dockyard's collection of ship models and figureheads – seemed to be a dreadful augury.[90] The rundown of the yard played a significant part in both the 1923 and 1924 elections for the new Pembrokeshire constituency. Not even the intervention of former Prime Minister David Lloyd George could save his son Gwilym, whose exaggerated claims to have saved the yard had been exposed as untrue, from defeat in the second poll.[91]

In reality, though, Pembroke yard very nearly survived: until almost the last minute, a fierce debate raged within government and the Admiralty over whether to close it or Sheerness. At first, a remarkably powerful coalition lined up in support of Pembroke. The Controller of the Navy believed that, regardless of its building role, Pembroke's extensive programme of refitting work on destroyers and other smaller warships made it indispensable; Cabinet secretary Maurice Hankey, Lord President of the Council (and former Prime Minister) Arthur Balfour, the First Lord of the Admiralty (William Bridgeman), and even the head of the newly created Royal Air Force, Sir Hugh Trenchard, all believed that Pembroke's relative invulnerability to air attack made it uniquely valuable, while Bridgeman also observed that it would be 'useful in the event of trouble in Ireland'.[92] Even the Prime Minister, Stanley Baldwin, was surprised that the Admiralty was proposing the closure of Pembroke and Rosyth rather than one or more of the English yards, while Hankey scathingly accused the Admiralty of being so obsessed with the notion that Japan was the only potential enemy that 'nothing will convince them to the contrary' – the contrary, in his view, being the possibility of war with France.[93] But ultimately, the decision taken in 1814 to provide Pembroke yard with slips rather than docks proved fatal. Sheerness was saved because it had a basin and five docks, its equipment was more modern, and thus it could refit submarines, which Pembroke could not. Bridgeman was persuaded to change his mind, the provisional decision to close Sheerness was rescinded, and Pembroke Dockyard was doomed.[94]

The closure of the dockyard, together with that at Rosyth, was finally announced in September 1925, and almost immediately a protest meeting was held in Cardiff with Lloyd George and Ramsay MacDonald sending messages of support.[95] The Mayor of Pembroke Dock wrote at length and in desperation to the Prime Minister, warning that closure would mean 'the bankruptcy of the town and the ruin of 3,000 homes'.[96] But the First Sea Lord, Earl Beatty, responded scathingly:

> Whether these Yards are necessary for naval purposes, the Admiralty is the only competent judge. As to whether they are necessary for political or social reasons is for the Government to decide. The fact is, that so far as the upkeep of the Fleet is concerned, they are entirely redundant.[97]

In Parliament, angry Welsh and Scottish MPs castigated the Admiralty, Lloyd George thundering that it was 'completely obliterating a whole town as though it had been Pompeii or Herculaneum simply buried by ashes coming from the volcano on the Treasury Bench'.[98] (Typically, Lloyd George entirely ignored his own government's part in running down the dockyard in the first place.) But it was to no avail; the yard officially closed on 31 May 1926. Unemployment soared (it was still over 50 per cent in 1937), while many members of the workforce were redeployed to other royal dockyards, leading to the migration of a quarter of the town's population. Many, including three Pembrokeshire county councillors and the Mayor-elect of Pembroke Dock, moved to Portsmouth, where both a Pembroke County Club and a Cymmrodorion Society were established.[99] Richard John Lewis, a fitter, went to Malta (leaving his wife and daughter at St Dogmaels), and in 1940 was awarded the George Medal for his gallantry during some of the early Axis air raids on the island.[100]

No Pembroke-built warship survives. The great *Duke of Wellington* was broken up in 1904, but some of her timbers survive upon the foreshore at Charlton, on the Thames; they lie intermingled with iron plates from the *Ajax*, launched at Pembroke in 1880 as the Royal Navy's last iron-built ship before the supremacy of steel, and also its first battleship with no sailing rig whatsoever.[101] Off the coast of Victoria, Australia, the scuttled Pembroke-built submarines *J3* and *J4* are now popular dives, a fate that also befell the battleship *Empress of India*, launched to the strains of *Hen Wlad fy Nhadau* in 1891 but sunk as a target in Start Bay, Devon, only twenty-two years later. The wreck of HMS *Defence*, launched at Pembroke in 1907 as the navy's last ever armoured cruiser but sunk at Jutland in 1916, was discovered in 2001; she survives, remarkably intact, at the bottom of the North Sea.[102] The cruiser *Curacoa*, launched at the yard in 1917 (as the last surface warship to be built there), was accidentally rammed and sunk by the liner *Queen Mary* in 1942, leading to the loss of 338 men in one of the worst accidents of the Second World War.[103] The last Pembroke-built naval vessel, RFA *Oleander*, was wrecked in Harstad Bay during the Norwegian campaign of 1940, although her remains apparently remained visible for many years.[104] The royal yacht *Victoria and Albert*, centrepiece of the great Spithead fleet reviews of 1935 and 1937, was broken up at Faslane in 1954–55, although many of her fittings made their way into the new royal yacht, *Britannia*. The last surviving Pembroke-built warships of all, the iron screw frigate *Inconstant* of 1868 and the cruiser *Andromeda* of 1898, went to the breakers in Belgium in 1956 after spending many years as harbour training hulks.

Afterlife

The Admiralty maintained the dockyard on a care and maintenance basis until 1 January 1930 when it was transferred to the Air Ministry, although a naval boom defence depot was retained at the western end of the site. The RAF established a flying boat base in the former dockyard; large sloping aprons and two huge new hangars were erected at the eastern end, creating what became for some time the largest flying boat base in the world. From 1938, the base operated the huge Sunderland flying boats.[105] In March 1929, too, a battered old hull was towed into the Haven to become a floating jetty for the Llanion oil fuel depot, a little way upstream from the old royal dockyard. Few probably realised that this unheralded and decrepit new fixture on the Haven was the former HMS *Warrior*, Britain's first ironclad battleship, which had previously been a training hulk in Portsmouth. Just before the Second World War, serious consideration was given to moving HMS *Hornet*, the coastal forces base at Portsmouth, to Pembroke Dock to make it less vulnerable to German bombing, but the scheme was eventually abandoned.[106] The outbreak of war led to a brief renaissance, although the town and its naval facilities also became targets for the Luftwaffe (see Chapter 10). In 1941 a small area at the western end of the yard, alongside the boom defence depot, was re-transferred to the Admiralty for use as a repair base. It employed about 500 people and was principally engaged in refitting Coastal Forces craft, with HMS *Warrior* serving as their base. Assessing the potential for retaining a Coastal Forces base there post-war, one grumpy civil servant commented that 'Pembroke Dock is a miserable hole and would not be liked by naval personnel stationed there in peace time. Compared with the Portsmouth area, the location of a naval establishment at Pembroke would cost the Admiralty a great deal in railway fares.'[107]

After the war, much of the western half of the former dockyard was leased to a commercial ship repair concern, R.S. Hayes, although the westernmost end of the site, centred on Carr Jetty and covering about a quarter of the original dockyard area, continued to serve the navy as an oil fuel, boom defence and mooring maintenance depot. One of the tasks of this small base was to service the moorings and target ships employed on the Aberporth missile range in Cardigan Bay (see Chapter 12); during the 1970s, the frigates *Venus*, *Whirlwind*, *Rapid* and other targets were laid up in the upper reaches of Milford Haven when not in use for target practice.[108] The eastern half of the former dockyard site continued as a Sunderland flying boat base until 1959, when the aircraft was withdrawn from service. Twenty years later, much of the eastern part, including slips 5–7,[109] was cleared and built on to create a new Irish ferry terminal, inaugurated in May 1979. However, the two large Sunderland hangars remained intact and a small RAF Air-Sea Rescue base continued in service at that end of the yard. The officers' houses remained in private ownership, with the captain superinten- dent's house becoming a pub; however, this was ravaged by fire in 2006 and remained derelict thereafter. The dockyard church, too, was derelict for many years until sensitively restored in 2004–05, while several other buildings found new uses. The surgeon's house was renovated to become a visitor centre for the Pembroke Dock Sunderland Trust, promoting the yard's flying boat heritage, while the eastern 'Martello tower' became a museum (until a leaking roof led to its closure, and it was sold off by the local council in 2019).[110] The history of the dockyard is also remembered in six bronze plaques adorning the dockyard wall, the work of local sculptor Perryn Butler. Seemingly run- ning counter to these sensitive treatments of dockyard heritage, though, a large new development of a renewable energy fabrica- tion yard began on the western part of the site in 2022, leading to the infilling of the timber pond and other losses of historic built heritage.

In the mid-1970s, the former royal dockyard site at Pembroke Dock built perhaps one of the most iconic 'fighting ships' of the modern era: the full-size model of Han Solo's spacecraft *Millennium Falcon* used in *The Empire Strikes Back* was constructed in the eastern Sunderland hangar. (The secrecy surrounding it gave rise to local rumours that a UFO was being kept in this unlikely Welsh 'Area 51'.) Meanwhile the Llanion oil fuel depot closed in 1978, making the *Warrior* redundant and finally presenting a golden opportunity to the trust that had already been established to restore her. Britain's first and last iron battleship left her berth of nearly fifty years at Llanion for the final time on 29 August 1979; after restoration at Hartlepool, she opened to the public at Portsmouth in 1987 and remains a popular tourist destination within the Historic Dockyard.[111] The Royal Maritime Auxiliary Service base at the western extremity of the old dockyard lingered on into the new millennium, although the last large warship to be laid up in the haven when not in use as a target at Aberporth, the frigate *Eskimo*, was towed away for scrapping in 1992.[112] With the disbanding of the RMAS and the transfer of its functions to a private company, the blue ensign was finally hauled down on 31 March 2008,[113] ending both two centuries of a continuous naval presence in Milford Haven, and the illustrious history of Wales' only royal dockyard.

Notes

1   Unless stated otherwise, this section is based on J D Davies, 'The Strange Life and Stranger Death of Milford Dockyard', *The Royal Dockyards and the Pressures of Global War, 1793–1815: Transactions of the Naval Dockyard Society*, 13 (2020), 29–53.

2   National Archives of Scotland, GD51/2/950, 953.

3   P Carradice, *Pembroke Dock: the Town Built to Build Ships* (Pembroke Dock, 2006), 19–20.

4   J B Hattendorf et al., *British Naval Documents 1204–1960* (NRS 1993), 473–5. Appointment to Toulon: National Archives of Scotland, GD51/2/1014/2.

5   TNA, ADM106/3186, Barrallier letters, 30 Aug., 5 Sept. 1802, 21 June 1803, 8 Mar., 16 Apr. 1804, 23 July 1807; NAS, GD51/2/950/1.

6   NMM, ADM BP/29B/84; NAS, GD51/2/951/2.

7   L Phillips, 'Pembroke Royal Dockyard' in Modern Pembrokeshire, ed. D Howell (Pembrokeshire County History, IV, 1993), 153.

8   Davies, 'Strange Life', 44, 46–8.
9   Ex info Milford Haven Museum and personal observations, 2011-9.
10   P. Carradice, *Pembroke Dock: The Town Built to Build Ships* (Pembroke Dock, 2006), pp.19–20.
11   J.B. Hattendorf et al., *British Naval Documents 1204–1960* (NRS, 1993), pp.473–5. Appointment to Toulon: National Archives of Scotland, GD51/2/1014/2.
12   TNA, ADM106/3186, Barrallier letters, 30 Aug., 5 Sept. 1802, 21 June 1803, 8 Mar., 16 Apr. 1804, 23 July 1807; NAS, GD51/2/950/1.
13   NMM, ADM BP/29B/84; NAS, GD51/2/951/2.
14   L. Phillips, 'Pembroke Royal Dockyard' in *Modern Pembrokeshire, ed. D. Howell* (Pembrokeshire County History, IV, 1993), p.153.
15   TNA, ADM140/490, 492.
16   Ex info Milford Haven Museum.
17   Phillips, 'Pembroke Royal Dockyard', p.152.
18   NMM, ADM BP/37A/123.
19   R. Rose, *Pembroke People* (Pembroke, 2000), p.189.
20   Lyon and Winfield, p.109.
21   TNA, ADM106/3186, Barrallier letter, 27 Dec. 1805.
22   *The Cambrian*, 4 June, 6 Aug., 8 Oct. 1825; 9 Feb. 1833; 23 Aug. 1834.
23   Peters, Pembroke Dock, p.155; E. Goddard, 'Naval Activity', *Pembrokeshire County History, IV: Modern Pembrokeshire* (1993), p.338.
24   NMM, ADM BP/33C/12. There was a subsequent debate over two rival designs for the yard, one with three docks and two slips, the other with five slips and no docks. The latter evidently won the day: NMM, ADM BP/34B/219.
25   NMM, ADM BP/36B/37.
26   E. Peters, *The History of Pembroke Dock* (1905), pp.9–10.
27   Rose, *Pembroke People*, p.102.
28   Rose, *Pembroke People*, p.91.
29   National Library of Scotland, MSS RHP 1639, 1645; British Library, Additional MS 49,593, fo. 32b.
30   Phillips, 'Pembroke Royal Dockyard', p.153.
31   Rose, *Pembroke People*, pp.115, 121, 123, 132, 161.
32   Rose, *Pembroke People*, p.96.
33   Rose, *Pembroke People*, pp.98–100.
34   NMM, ADM BP/36B/37.
35   Carradice, *Pembroke Dock*, pp.31–4.
36   Carradice, *Pembroke Dock*, pp.45–7.
37   Carradice, *Pembroke Dock*, pp.48–62.
38   Quoted by Phillips, 'Pembroke Royal Dockyard', p.170.
39   Rose, *Pembroke People*, p.125.

40 Rose, *Pembroke People*, p.119.
41 'Important Case Book' of the Surgeon, HM Dockyard, Pembroke:
    Lawrie Phillips collection. (I am grateful to Lawrie Phillips for
    allowing me to cite this source.)
42 Rose, *Pembroke People*, p.91.
43 Rose, *Pembroke People*, p.167.
44 Rose, *Pembroke People*, p.130.
45 Carradice, *Pembroke Dock*, pp.40–1.
46 Phillips, 'Pembroke Royal Dockyard', pp.161–3.
47 Phillips, 'Pembroke Royal Dockyard', pp.167–8.
48 Phillips, 'Pembroke Royal Dockyard', p.169.
49 P. Harries, 'Edgar Phillips Harries, C.B.E. (better known as 'E.P.')',
    Journal of the Pembrokeshire Historical Society, 4 (1990–91), pp.74–89.
50 PRO, HDX/1239/281.
51 *Portsmouth Evening News*, 25 July 1903.
52 *Portsmouth Evening News*, 10 June, 8 July 1904.
53 Phillips, 'Pembroke Royal Dockyard', p.154.
54 British Library, Additional MS 21,139, fo. 15, plan of yard, 1831.
55 D. James, 'The Construction of the Shipbuilding Sheds at Pembroke
    Dock', *MW*, 26 (2005), pp.46–53.
56 Personal observation, Master Shipwright's House, Pembroke Dock,
    May 2008 (my thanks to Tony Mason for facilitating this visit);
    M. Tucker, 'Structural Ironwork at Pembroke Dock: A Microcosm of
    Naval Practice', *Transactions of the Naval Dockyards Society*, ed. R. Riley,
    3 (2007), pp.31–5.
57 For the *Constance*, see L. Phillips, 'An Interesting Frigate from
    Pembroke Dockyard: HMS *Constance*, 1846', *MM*, 73 (1987),
    pp.61–9.
58 Phillips, 'Pembroke Royal Dockyard', pp.157–8; Lyon and Winfield,
    pp.104–5, 150–1, 204.
59 T. Collins, 'HMS *Valorous*: Her Contribution to Galway Maritime
    History', *Journal of the Galway Archaeological and Historical Society*, 49
    (1997), pp.122–42.
60 His life is described by L. Phillips, 'Captain Sir Thomas Sabine
    Pasley Bt RN and Pembroke Dockyard 1849–1854', *MM*, 71 (1985),
    pp.159–65.
61 L.M.S. Pasley, *Memoir of Admiral Sir Thomas Sabine Pasley* (1900),
    pp.151, 172.
62 Pasley, *Memoir of Admiral Sir Thomas Sabine Pasley*, pp.157–8, 160–5;
    Phillips, 'Pembroke Royal Dockyard', pp.164–5.
63 Peters, *Pembroke Dock*, p.18.
64 Lyon and Winfield, p.184.

65 Lyon and Winfield, pp.194, 204–5, 217, 218, 222.

66 www.gwpda.org/naval/pembroke.htm

67 Lyon and Winfield, p.191.

68 D.K. Brown, 'The Introduction of Steel into the Royal Navy', *Journal of Naval Science*, 20 (1995), p.267.

69 www.gwpda.org/naval/pembroke.htm

70 E.L. Carlyle, rev. A. McConnell, 'Watts, Sir Philip (1846–1926), Naval Architect', *ODNB*.

71 D. James, *Down the Slipway!* (Pembroke Dock, 2008), p.49.

72 Rose, *Pembroke People*, p 166; L. Woollard, rev. M. Brodie, 'Narbeth, John Harper (1863–1944), Naval Architect', *ODNB*.

73 Pasley, *Memoir of Admiral Sir Thomas Sabine Pasley* (1900), pp.157–8.

74 British Library, Additional MS 51803, fo. 130. The ship was originally named *Goliath*, but was renamed in honour of its sponsor.

75 Peters, *Pembroke Dock*, p.23.

76 *Western Mail*, 6854, 8 May 1891.

77 *All The Year Round*, 28 Sept. 1889, 304; *Western Mail*, 7395, 31 January 1893.

78 Carradice, *Pembroke Dock*, pp.71–2.

79 A.H. Galvin, *Sea of Change: 19th Century Maritime Activity at Tenby and Saundersfoot* (Coventry 2002), p.172.

80 D. James, 'When the Rising Sun Flew in Jacob's Pill, Pembroke Dock – the Japanese Corvette *Hiei*', *MW*, 23 (2002), pp.51–4.

81 Phillips, 'Pembroke Royal Dockyard', pp.154–5.

82 National Library of Scotland, MS 9871, fo. 160.

83 *Hansard*, HC Deb 10 March 1851 vol. 114 *c*.1203.

84 *Hansard*, HC Deb 21 July 1864 vol. 176 cc1872–3; HC Deb 20 March 1868 vol. 190 cc1036–46.

85 PRO, D/Bush/8/22; *The Times*, 2 June 1906, letter by Thomas G. Meyrick (I am grateful to Alan Phillips for drawing my attention to the latter reference).

86 *Hansard*, HC Deb 17 March 1887 vol. 312 cc627–31; HC Deb 19 March 1906 vol. 154 cc52–3.

87 PRO, D/Bush/8/22.

88 S. Dent, 'HMS *Curacoa*: What's in a Name?', *Warship* (2012), p.173. The name is actually one of many 'spelling mistakes' that became established naval norms.

89 Phillips, 'Pembroke Royal Dockyard', p.170.

90 A. Day, '"Driven from Home": The Closure of Pembroke Dockyard and the Impact on its Community', *Llafur*, 7 (1999), p.83; Phillips, 'Pembroke Royal Dockyard', p.171: D. Pulvertaft, *Figureheads of the Royal Navy* (Barnsley, 2011), p.35.

91   J.G. Jones, 'Major Gwilym Lloyd-George, first Viscount Tenby
      (1894–1967)', *National Library of Wales Journal*, 32 (2001), pp.179–81.
      Gwilym regained the seat in 1929 when the sitting member took the
      blame for the final closure.

92   Controller and First Lord opinions: TNA ADM1/8658/60,
      ADM1/8682/122; Trenchard, Hankey and Baldwin opinions:
      National Archives of Scotland, GD433/2/4/8; Balfour opinion:
      NAS, GD433/2/4/6.

93   National Archives of Scotland, GD/433/2/4/8, 10.

94   TNA, ADM1/8682/122. J D Davies, 'Pembroke Dock, c1900–1926:
      Was the Closure of the Royal Dockyard Really "Inevitable"?',
      Maritime Wales, 35 (2014), 73–94.

95   *The Times*, 44065, 12 Sept. 1925, p.14.

96   National Archives of Scotland, GD433/2/4/3.

97   W.S. Chalmers, *The Life and Letters of David, Earl Beatty* (1951), p.469.

98   *Hansard*, HC Deb 11 Dec. 1925 vol 189 cc854–938; *The Times*,
      12 December 1925.

99   Day, 'Driven from Home', pp.85–6.

100 www.walesonline.co.uk/news/wales-news/2011/12/22/george-
      medal-awarded-to-a-world-war-ii-docks-engineer-returns-to-his-
      home-town-91466-29994039/

101 www.thamesdiscovery.org/frog-blog/charlton-timber-and-iron-
      ships, accessed 29 October 2011; Picture House Television for
      Channel 4, *Time Team Special: Brunel's Last Launch*, first broadcast
      10 November 2011.

102 I. McCartney, 'The Armoured Cruiser HMS *Defence*: A Case-Study
      in Assessing the Royal Navy Shipwrecks of the Battle of Jutland
      (1916) as an Archaeological Resource', *International Journal of Nautical
      Archaeology* 41 (2012), pp.56–66.

103 D.A. Thomas and P. Holmes, *Queen Mary and the Cruiser: The
      Curacoa Disaster* (1997)

104 www.historicalrfa.org/rfa-oleander-ships-details

105 pdht.org/

106 TNA, ADM 116/3894.

107 TNA, ADM 1/19781.

108 Author's personal recollection. *Whirlwind* sank at moorings in
      Cardigan Bay during a gale in November 1974.

109 TNA, DK 1/289.

110 www.westerntelegraph.co.uk/news/17645579.
      regret-disappointment-sale-gun-tower/

111 A. Lambert, *HMS Warrior 1860: Victoria's Ironclad Deterrent* (2011 edn),
      p.53 and passim.

112 A fine 1990 photograph of *Eskimo* moored in Milford Haven in her target role can be found in M. Critchley, *To Sail No More, Part 2* (Liskeard, 1998), p.24.

113 *Dockyards* (the newsletter of the Naval Dockyards Society), 13/1 (2008), p.1.

1. Aberdaron: grave of unknown naval seaman of the First World War. (Author's photograph)

2. Breiddin Hill, near Welshpool: 'Rodney's Pillar'. (Author's photograph)

3. The site of the Battle of Abertywi, 1044, looking towards Llansteffan; at right, the castle built in the early twelfth century to defend the estuary. (Author's photograph)

4. The dock at Rhuddlan Castle. (Author's photograph)

5. Milford Haven in 1595; chart drawn by Paul Ive. (National Maritime Museum)

6. Perhaps the earliest picture of a Welsh sailor from the 'lower deck': John Worley, 'born in Wales 1624' and a pensioner at Greenwich hospital in 1708. (Trustees of the British Museum)

7. Admiral Arthur Herbert, Earl of Torrington, a highly controversial Welsh officer of the seventeenth century. (Trustees of the British Museum)

8. Pwlldu Head, Gower, looking east towards Mumbles Head: site of the wreck of the pressing tender *Caesar,* 1760, with the mass grave being marked by the circle of stones at bottom right. (Author's photograph)

9. Parys Mountain, Anglesey, source of the copper that dramatically improved the performance of British warships from the 1770s onwards. (Author's photograph)

Above left 10. Admiral Thomas Mathews of Llandaff, who was at the heart of one of the most notorious courts-martial of the eighteenth century. (Trustees of the British Museum)

Above 11. Admiral Thomas Griffin of Dixton Hadnock, Monmouth. (Trustees of the British Museum)

Left 12. The 'Naval Temple' on the Kymin, Monmouth. (Author's photograph)

THE WELCH SAILOR'S MISTAKE OR TARS IN CONVERSATION.

Above 13. 'The Welch sailor's mistake: or, tars in conversation' by Thomas Rowlandson, 1808. Five sailors sit together on deck, all smoking or drinking except the Welshman who sits with a hand on each knee, gazing in innocent surprise at a man who leans forward to say: 'And so then do you see, David, we sprung a leak'. The Welshman answers: 'Cot pless us— and save us—did you! and a ferry coot fetchitable it is. I should have liked to have had a pit with you'. (Trustees of the British Museum)

Left 14. Sir Thomas Foley by Henry Edridge, 1807. (National Portrait Gallery)

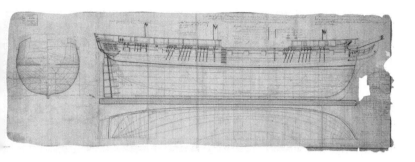

Above 15. Plan of HMS *Owen Glendower*, launched in 1808. (National Maritime Museum)

Left 16. Alexander Raby's furnace, Llanelli, which supplied substantial amounts of ordnance to the navy in the 1790s and 1800s. (Author's photograph)

Below 17. The planned layout of the royal dockyard at Milford Haven prior to its abandonment in favour of Pembroke Dock in 1812. (Author's photograph, reproduced by permission of the National Archives)

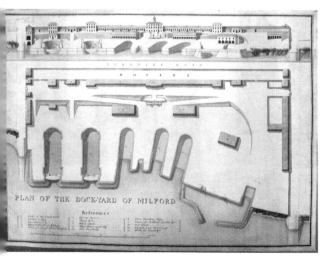

18. The launch of HMS *James Watt* on 23 April 1853 from one of the iron-roofed covered slipways at Pembroke Dock. (Author's collection)

19. HM royal dockyard, Pembroke, *c.* 1896, with the battleship HMS *Hannibal*, the heaviest warship ever built at the dockyard, fitting out at Hobbs Point. In the middle distance is the port guardship HMS *Thunderer*, which had been launched in the dockyard in 1872; the covered building slips can be seen in the distance. (Tenby Museum)

20. The launch of the royal yacht *Victoria and Albert* at Pembroke Dock, 9 May 1899, with her predecessor of the same name (also built in the dockyard) at left. (Tenby Museum)

21. The grave at St Ishmael's church, Ferryside, shared by Lieutenant William Williams of the Brazilian Navy and his brother, the famous radical lawyer Hugh Williams. (Author's photograph)

22. John Lort Stokes of Scotchwell, Haverfordwest, who served with Fitzroy and Darwin during the voyage of the *Beagle*. (National Maritime Museum)

23. An old seaman tells Welsh children about the Battle of Trafalgar, with the poem 'Yn Helynt Trafalgar', published in *Y Darlunydd*, 1876. (Swansea University Information Services and Systems)

24. The memorial to Nelson on the Menai Straits, erected by Admiral Lord Charles Paget in 1873. (Author's photograph)

25. Members of the Royal Naval Reserve battery at Tenby in the late nineteenth or early twentieth century. (Tenby Museum)

26. Naval exercises in Milford Haven, 1886, with Stack Rock Fort 'under attack'. (Author's collection)

27. The cruiser HMS *Carnarvon*, one of many warships named in honour of Welsh towns and counties. Launched in 1903, she served throughout the First World War and was broken up in 1921. (Author's collection)

28. Naval seamen, including presumably several of Welsh origin, behind a blackboard with '*Cymru am Byth*' and a pair of leeks. The presence of seamen of other nationalities, including possibly Frenchmen and Americans, suggests that this might date from the time of the allied intervention in Russia, 1919–21. (Author's collection)

29. Chepstow: a captured First World War U-boat deck gun, now the centrepiece of the memorial to William Williams, VC. (Author's photograph)

30. HMS *Cardiff* leads the line of battleships of the German High Seas Fleet towards the Firth of Forth and internment, 21 November 1918. (Imperial War Museum)

31. A convoy leaving Milford Haven during the Second World War, with balloon protection against low-flying enemy aircraft. (Imperial War Museum)

32. The memorial and mass grave for the crew of HMS *Thetis*, Holyhead.
(Author's photograph)

33. HMS *Welshman*, the only ship ever to bear the name. A fast minelayer
launched in 1940 and sunk off Crete in 1943, she often operated from Milford
Haven. (Author's collection)

34. A wartime sea mine, now forming the centrepiece of Milford Haven's memorial to its wartime role as the navy's principal production site and operational base for minelaying operations. (Author's photograph)

35. John 'Tubby' Linton, VC, of Malpas, the heroic captain of HMS *Thunderbolt* in the Mediterranean during the Second World War.

36. Francis Cromie, a distinguished submarine commander who strayed into the dangerous world of espionage.

37. The crew of HMS *Tenby* marching through the town after the ship received the Freedom of the Borough, 1970. (Tenby Museum)

38. First day cover to mark the decommissioning of HMS *Glamorgan*, 'flagship of the Welsh navy', 1986. (Author's collection)

39. HMS *Dragon* arrives at Portsmouth for the first time, 31 August 2011. (Author's photograph)

7

PIONEERS AND PATAGONIA

THE WELSH NAVAL PRESENCE ABROAD

The Philadelphia shipwright Joshua Humphreys is known as 'the father of the United States Navy'. Between 1794 and 1800 he was largely responsible for the design and construction of six frigates, larger and more powerful than their European counterparts, which formed the backbone of the navy in its early days and particularly distinguished themselves in wars against the Barbary Corsairs and subsequently (1812–15) against the British. Humphreys himself built the *United States*, launched at Philadelphia in 1797, which survived until the American Civil War. The USS *President*, captured by HMS *Endymion* in January 1815, was taken into the Royal Navy, and its name survives as that of the base of the London Division of the Royal Naval Reserve. The most famous ship derived from Humphreys' designs, the USS *Constitution* – nicknamed 'Old Ironsides' – defeated HM Ships *Guerrière* and *Java* during the War of 1812 and survives to this day, the oldest commissioned warship still afloat in the world and one of the most venerated icons of American national identity. But Joshua Humphreys was the grandson of a Quaker who had emigrated from Merionethshire in the 1680s; in turn, his grandmother was a direct descendant of Owain Gwynedd, and Humphreys emphasised his Celtic roots by marrying Mary David, who was also of Welsh parentage.[1] Thus the United States Navy was not quite 'made in Wales', but very nearly so; especially as the President who oversaw the completion of the 'six frigates' and established the US Navy Department, John Adams, was the great-grandson of an Adams from Llanboidy, Carmarthenshire.

Welshmen in the American and Other Navies

Humphreys was not the only American with Welsh blood to play a part in the evolution of the United States Navy. During the early years of American independence, several prominent commanders were descendants of emigrants from the Principality: they included Captain John Harris of the Virginian Navy and Commodore Jacob Jones, who distinguished himself in command of USS *Wasp* during the War of 1812.[2] The true founding father of the United States Navy, John Paul Jones, was a Scot who had added the name Jones to conceal his identity after killing a man, In 1778, Jones and his ship, USS *Ranger*, carried out a daring campaign in the Irish Sea. There is a strong local legend to the effect that during these operations, Jones used Caldey Island off Tenby as a watering place; his supposed anchorage is still called Paul Jones Bay. In later years, William P. Jones of Brecon and Richard Bates, who won the Medal of Honor in 1866, were among those who served in the United States Navy,[3] while a Welshman even seems to have served in the short-lived navy of the independent Republic of Texas. Percy Bolingbroke St John, who went on to be a well-known Victorian journalist and novelist, was the son of another writer, James Augustus St John – who had actually been christened at Laugharne in 1795 as plain James John, the son of a local shoemaker. Details of Percy's service are scant, but he was in Texas in the mid-1840s when it was at war with Mexico, and after his return to Britain he claimed that he had served in the Texan Navy at this time.[4]

Rather better attested are the naval services of some of the Welshmen who served in South American navies during the nineteenth century. Between 1810 and 1830, the Spanish colonies fought a succession of successful wars of independence, then a series of wars against each other sparked by various territorial disputes. Many of the new nations had long coastlines and hastily assembled navies to defend them. They were also keen to recruit skilled personnel, and the end of the Napoleonic Wars in 1815 meant that they could draw on very large numbers of highly experienced, battle-hardened, but now unemployed veterans of the Royal Navy, along with younger men whose dreams of emulating Nelson had been stymied by the coming of peace. William Williams, originally from Machynlleth, was a brother of the radical lawyer Hugh Williams, who sympathised with the Chartists and Rebecca Rioters and became a friend of Cobden, Bright and even Abraham Lincoln. William became 'a lieutenant in the Brazilian Navy', although it is probable that he served in it under the tenuous alias of Joao [John] Williams: if so, he arrived in Rio in May 1823, then served aboard Admiral Cochrane's flagship *Pedro I* in the blockade of Bahia and the capture of San Luis. He then served as a sub-lieutenant on three warships before becoming lieutenant of the brig *Caboclo* in 1826 during the war with Argentina, commanding the schooner *Constança* in the blockade of the River Plate during 1828.[5] Williams subsequently returned to Wales and presumably took up residence with his brother, who by then had a law practice in Carmarthen (where, it was alleged, he later became the secret leader of the Rebecca Riots). When Williams died in 1831, his body was taken down the Tywi from Carmarthen to the ancient church of Saint Ishmael's in a waterborne procession that imitated Nelson's, albeit on a far smaller scale. He was even accorded the posthumous tribute of a poem, 'The Sailor's Grave', penned by Thomas Jenkins of Carmarthen.[6]

The Gower provided the most distinguished of the Welsh naval officers in South American service. Born at Penrice in 1797, James George was a son of the agent to the owner of Penrice Castle. The young man was at sea by 1817, and in the following year he made his way to Chile to join the breakaway country's fledgling navy in its war of independence against Spain. Almost at once he became ensign bearer to the fleet's commander-in-chief, the charismatic and controversial Thomas Cochrane. By 1821 George was a lieutenant, and in 1826 he took command of the corvette *Chacabuco*, one of the four ships that Chile despatched to aid Argentina in its war with Brazil. George's command was the only vessel to survive atrocious weather encountered when rounding the Horn, so, as the senior officer of the reinforcing 'squadron', he became second-in-command of the force attempting to raise the Brazilian blockade of the River Plate. George distinguished himself in a series of actions, during one of which he took four enemy ships. He corresponded occasionally – that is, once every decade or so – with his family on the Gower, and in one letter of 1831 he cryptically informed them that he had added a new surname, that of Bynon. Legend has it that there were some objections to George as a surname (its Spanish equivalent, Jorge, was only a Christian name), so he took the name of the family's shepherd back at Penrice, Beynon being a common name on the Gower.

James George Beynon, or as his adopted countrymen knew him, Santiago Jorge Bynon, commanded merchant ships during the 1830s, but was back in the navy by 1840, taking command of the pride of the fleet, the *Chile*, in 1841. He then held several naval governorships, but in 1850 he was granted permission to go back to the Gower on leave. His mother and father were long dead, and perhaps a sense of imminent mortality made him decide to draft his will at his sister's house in Port Eynon in October 1851. On his return to Chile he was appointed Governor General of the navy, but came back to Britain, and to Gower, one last time, in 1869, when he was tasked with bringing back a new warship that had been built in England. The voyage was disastrous: the new ship was wrecked on her way to Chile, and her Welsh captain's reputation seems to have suffered as a result. He evidently recovered his standing, though, and in 1875 was promoted rear-admiral. Three years later he was acclaimed as one of the three greatest heroes of the Chilean Navy. After his death on 4 August 1883, a statue to his memory was erected in Valparaiso; but either an earthquake or a revolution put paid to it.[7] Another Welshman who became equally, if not more, prominent in his adopted country was William Thomas Lewis, who was recruited into the Russian Navy in 1714, became a captain in 1733, and was first captain of the second flagship in 1734 when the Russian fleet decisively defeated the French off Danzig. He was often given positions of special responsibility, such as escorting Peter the Great's daughter Anna to Holstein following her marriage to its duke, or going to London in 1733 to recruit shipbuilders. During the 1740s he was successively commander at Archangel, Kronstadt and Reval. In 1743 he commanded the White Sea squadron that attempted to leave Archangel to join the fleet moving against the Swedes; the fleet was dispersed in a storm and he was court-martialled, but acquitted. He commanded the Reval squadron that took part in the capture of Memel in 1757, but the arrival of a British fleet in the Baltic led to him being given permission to reside ashore at Memel until the conflict between Russia and Britain was over. In addition to making him Admiral of the Fleet, Catherine the Great also bestowed on him the prestigious Order of Alexander Nevskii, but he retired in 1764 and continued to live in St Petersburg on a full pension until his death in March 1769. In terms of the career he had and the positions he reached, Lewis was undoubtedly one of the greatest Welsh naval officers of all time – yet his name is entirely unknown in his native land.[8]

The American Civil War:
The Confederate Raiders and Wales

The American Civil War broke out when the newly-created
Confederate States of America attacked the federal garrison at
Fort Sumter in Charleston Harbour on 12 April 1861. Within
weeks, the Confederacy established an agency at Liverpool
headed by James D. Bulloch, whose mission was to acquire ships
in Britain that could run the north's blockade of southern waters
or else to serve as commissioned commerce-raiding warships
of the infant Confederate Navy. Welsh waters, and specifically those of Anglesey, became vital to Bulloch's operations.
In October 1861, he went to Holyhead to rendezvous with
the seemingly innocent new Greenock-built, British-flagged
steamer *Fingal*, which was actually carrying a huge arsenal for
the Confederate forces. Unfortunately, the *Fingal* accidentally
rammed and sank an Austrian ship as she entered the harbour;
Bulloch ordered her to return to sea at once, and she proceeded
to Savannah, where she successfully unloaded her cargo. In
1862, Bulloch pulled off an even more audacious coup. A large
barque-rigged steamer, known only by her shipyard number
of 290, was under construction at Laird's yard in Birkenhead,
and in July she sailed for sea trials. She anchored in Moelfre Bay
before heading into the open sea where she rendezvoused with
a barque carrying her guns, coal and crew. Commissioned as the
CSS *Alabama*, she became the most famous Confederate raider
of the civil war, capturing or destroying 65 Union ships before
she was sunk by the USS *Kearsarge* off Cherbourg in June 1864.
The Confederates also acquired a number of ships with Welsh
connections and used them as blockade runners, notably the
former Holyhead ferries *Scotia* and *Anglia*, together with the
Douglas, an excursion steamer that was a familiar sight in the
Menai Strait. Finally, on 6 November 1865, the last Confederate
warship (indeed, the last active southern military unit of the
entire war), the CSS *Shenandoah*, arrived at Point Lynas to take

on a Mersey pilot before proceeding to Liverpool and surrendering to the Royal Navy, no less than seven months after General
Lee's surrender at Appomattox.[9]

The American Civil War:
Cymru of the Blue and the Grey

At least several dozen Welshmen, probably more, served in
the Confederate Navy. The CSS *Virginia*, better known to history by her previous name of *Merrimac*, fought the world's
first ironclad battle against the USS *Monitor* in Chesapeake
Bay on 8–9 March 1862. The man who took over command
of the *Virginia* during the battle was Roger ap Catesby Jones,
but despite the patronymic (which continues in the family
to this day), his Welsh ancestry was remote. Another member
of the *Virginia*'s crew had rather more certain Welsh antecedents, though: William P. Morris, a miner in North Carolina,
later went on to serve in the CSS *Fredericksburg*.[10] The crew of
the legendary CSS *Alabama* included assistant engineer Miles
Freeman, who was probably born in Wales; James Evans, whose
parents had moved to South Carolina when he was five; fireman Edwin Jones of Northop, Flintshire; seaman John Roberts,
who was killed in the action off Cherbourg; and fireman Samuel
Williams, who was wounded and captured in the same action.
David Williams of Llanelli was wounded in the head, jumped
overboard as the ship sank, was rescued and returned to his home
town, having been given a cheque to cover his expenses by the
captain of *Alabama*. The ship's doctor, David Herbert Llewelyn,
was also killed in the *Alabama*'s last fight: he was the son of a
clergyman from Ambleston, Pembrokeshire, who served as
the curate of Easton Royal in Wiltshire. Several Welsh prisoners from ships taken by the *Alabama* were freed on condition
they joined her crew. These were a Hughes from Holyhead and
Thomas Williams, Samuel Roberts and a 'Lieutenant' Morris, all

from Caernarfonshire. Samuel Roberts subsequently returned
to Wales and died in 1916, probably the last surviving crew-
man of the *Alabama*.[11] Welshmen could also be found on other
units of the Confederate Navy. William Morris of Milford was
master-at-arms aboard the CSS *Arctic* in 1863; Henry Isaac Jones
of Tremadog, a medical graduate of Glasgow University, was successively surgeon's steward aboard the CSS *Florida* and *Georgia*,
and later served as a surgeon in the British Army. Finally, there
were at least two Welshmen, Thomas Evans and John William
Jones, aboard the very last operational Confederate warship, the
CSS *Shenandoah*.[12]

An intriguing possible connection between Wales and the
Confederate Navy emerged in a newspaper story which
appeared in the American press in 1883, subsequently finding its
way into the Welsh papers. This was the tale of Pauline Elizabeth
Benjamin, née Harcourt, who turned up in New York claiming to be the widow of Walter P. Benjamin, an officer in the
Confederate Navy and nephew of the CSA's Secretary of State.
She stated that she had been born in Merthyr, the daughter of
Sir Edward Harcourt, 'one of the most brilliant young English
orators', and his actress wife. By the time she was 14, her poetry
was being published in 'the leading magazines of Great Britain'.
Walter Benjamin allegedly met her when she was 17, and despite
the opposition of her family, they married in 1860 when she was
20. After the war Benjamin invested in cotton, made a great deal
of money and left for California with his pregnant wife. When
he and their infant son died, Elizabeth was left destitute and suffered a nervous breakdown. After recovering, she made her way
across the continent, alternately walking and hitching lifts on
trains, narrowly avoiding death on several occasions (once when
sparks from the engine set fire to her dress), all in the hope of
opening a safe deposit box in New York which would contain
the funds 'to take her to her home in Wales'. Unfortunately, this
romantic saga raises a number of awkward questions about the
veracity of 'Mrs Benjamin'. There was no 'Sir Edward Harcourt'

at the time, certainly none with a Merthyr connection; there is no record of poetry published by a youthful Pauline Elizabeth Harcourt; and the only evidence for Walter P. Benjamin's existence seems to come from the newspaper reports of Elizabeth's adventures, which are based solely on her own account.[13] Given her alleged thespian ancestry and self-confessed record of mental illness, it is possible that some or all of her story was fabricated, and there appears to be no record of her fate after her appearance in the newspapers.

Both the limited evidence available and the known political sympathies of the Welsh working and middle classes suggest that significantly more Welshmen served in the Union Navy. Aboard the USS *Monitor* as it sailed into battle against the CSS *Virginia* (and their fellow Welshmen) were coal heaver David Ellis, a trainee teacher from Carmarthenshire, who left a brief memoir of his time on Monitor, eventually published posthumously by his son, and fireman Robert Williams, who later went down with the ship when it sank in a storm in December 1862. A skeleton likely to be that of Williams was discovered when the *Monitor*'s turret was raised in 2002. In 2012, his face was reconstructed by a team from Louisiana State University, and on 8 March 2013 the body believed to be his received a funeral with full military honours at Arlington National Cemetery, Virginia, making him probably the last sailor of the American Civil War to be honoured in this way.[14] On 1 June 1864, the crew of USS *Hartford*, Admiral Farragut's flagship during the crucial Mississippi campaign, included three Welshmen, Daniel Evans, William Stevens and Thomas Williams. At New Year 1864–65 the crew of the powerful steam frigate USS *Minnesota* included 29-year-old David Richard, captain of the forecastle, and 28-year-old Isaac Roberts, while that of the USS *Niagara* included James Early (still on the books despite having deserted in November) and Thomas Morgan, a 26-year-old coal heaver.[15] Harry Evans of 'Llanhydel' (*sic*) served on the USS *Susquehanna*, blockading the coast of the Confederacy, and subsequently settled in Salt Lake

City with his Swansea-born wife.[16] At the end of the war, the Federal Navy included seven Welsh officers, admittedly an insignificant number alongside the 188 Irishmen, 177 Englishmen and 79 Scots; one of them was probably the chaplain Charles W. Thomas, who had joined the US Navy seven years before the civil war began.[17]

However, undoubtedly the most famous Welshman to serve the Union at sea was Henry Morton Stanley, the future discoverer of Doctor Livingstone, who was born and grew up in Denbigh under his real name of John Rowlands before making his way to America and taking the name of a merchant who befriended him. He had already served in both the Confederate army and the Union artillery, as well as spending time on merchant ships, before he enlisted in the United States Navy in June 1864 by blagging his way into a berth on the USS *Minnesota*. According to his own distinctly inventive account, however, Stanley served aboard the screw sloop-of-war USS *Ticonderoga*, where his abundant talents were immediately recognised, leading to his rapid promotion to clerk and then Ensign. In reality, Stanley jumped ship from the *Minnesota* in February 1865 by forging a pass and wearing civilian clothes under his uniform when he went ashore. He swiftly embarked upon a rather more successful career as a journalist, but there was a bizarre sequel to his brief and inglorious service in the US Navy: in 1866 he turned up back in Denbigh wearing his naval uniform and claiming he was on leave from the *Ticonderoga* at Constantinople, and he was thus able to conceal from his Welsh family and friends the truth of the disastrous expedition that he had just undertaken in Turkey.[18]

Y Wladfa: The Patagonian Colony and the Royal Navy

Patagonia is Wales' frontier myth: its Wild West, Outback and North-West Frontier rolled into one. Moreover, it is a myth that still retains a powerful influence on Welsh culture. According to the widely accepted version of the story, on 28 May 1865 the converted tea clipper *Mimosa* sailed out of Liverpool, carrying 160 intrepid settlers. They, and those who followed them, were intent on establishing a new Wales in the inhospitable, barely inhabited territory of the Chubut Valley in Patagonia. This new Wales would be self-governing, democratic, God fearing in the chapel tradition, and pacifist: a land unsullied by the English language, the imperialist pretensions of Victorian Britain, and the British Empire's military and naval might. The reality was rather different.

From its earliest days, the progress of the Welsh colony was a matter of some interest to the officers commanding the Royal Navy's South America station. In July 1866, the paddle sloop HMS *Triton* paid the first visit by a British warship to the new settlement on the Chubut River, and her captain, Richard Napier, sent a detailed report to the commander-in-chief, Rear-Admiral George Ramsay.[19] The visit was prompted by a petition sent to Ramsay, supposedly signed by nineteen colonists and claiming that the whole colony was 'almost in a state of starvation'. Napier's investigations revealed that nine of the signatures were in fact forgeries – six outright, and three the signatures of children aged 11, 6, and 6 months. In truth, the colony was relatively well stocked, well clothed and in good health. Napier went on to provide a detailed history of the genesis of the colony together with his thoughts on its continuance, which suggest that he and Ramsay had at least discussed the possibility of evacuating the entire settlement:

When we weigh all the circumstances of the Welsh emigration to Patagonia and remember that though the settlers suffered much at first, yet they are now comparatively comfortable with every prospect of a good harvest and a general wish to remain; that they have embarked all their means in the venture, and left comfortable homes in Wales for a South

American camp life; it would seem unwise to break up the undertaking … If the strength of the colony were increased by a fresh emigration of some of the labouring, working and agricultural class of Welsh peasants, it would add greatly to their chances of success and give fresh impetus to their labours, the majority of the present population being miners, tradesmen and artificers.

The *Triton* also assisted the colonists in material terms, providing them with large numbers of boots and shoes as well as 1,000 yards of flannel, bought by the sailors themselves from the ship's store.[20]

The *Triton*'s visit was followed by others, initially at intervals of roughly four or five years. From the early 1880s, though, the visits became annual, and each visiting captain sent back detailed reports on what he found. These were usually accompanied by parallel reports from the ships' chaplains, commenting on the spiritual wellbeing of the colonists, and from the surgeons reporting on sanitation and general health. The reports as a whole provide a fascinating alternative history of the *Wladfa*, untouched by the romanticised myth-making that pervades much of the Welsh historiography on the subject.[21] In 1871, for example, the desperate condition of the colonists, who had been without groceries for ten months and news of the outside world for twenty, was relieved by the arrival of HMS *Cracker*, which provided a large quantity of provisions, including bread, potatoes, flour and soap out of her own stores. In 1876, the *Volage* virtually undertook a census of the colony, providing detailed statistics on each household and noting the pressure on resources that had been created by the unexpected arrival of 412 new colonists between September 1875 and January 1876, more than trebling the size of the colony almost overnight. By 1891, though, the overall impression taken away by Captain Lewis Wintz of HMS *Basilisk* was one of prosperity: his report concentrated on the issues of railways and communications, a far cry from the early years when the concern had been overwhelmingly with survival and the state of each harvest.[22]

The report from the chaplain of the Pembroke-built HMS *Flora* in 1900 is remarkably detailed and provides in effect an entire history of the colony. The Reverend David Powell Richards was notably sympathetic towards the original aspirations of the colonists: so much so that his report was 'leaked' to a Welsh MP, who in turn passed it on to the press. He set out to correct the erroneous notion that the colony had been founded 'as a refuge from the tyranny of the British government, and to avoid the oppression of the British flag', as a result of which the colonists 'have forfeited British sympathy and no longer deserve official consideration'. On the contrary, Richards argued, 'the colony was founded … in response to the national aspirations of the Welsh people, and from no animosity against any government'. In fact, the Argentinians were deeply affronted by the fact that most households of the colony contained a portrait, not of *el presidente de la republica*, but of Queen Victoria. Richards criticised some of the leaders of the movement in Wales, whom he claimed had deliberately deluded potential emigrants into believing that they were going to a self-governing territory under British protection when the leaders knew full well that it had been annexed by Argentina: 'they have no excuse for the duplicity and deception which they practised on their misguided fellow countrymen, thus bringing about the stultification and ruin of their national aspirations.' But he was even more damning of past and present Argentinian regimes and their policies towards the colonists, using language that could hardly have been politically correct, even in 1900:

The colonists being honest law-abiding men far superior in intelligence and character to the average population of Argentina and even to those set to 'govern' them, submitted with exemplary patience to the insolence and cruelty of these petty officials … Had they been of the Latin race, accustomed

to the ready use of the assassin's knife or revolver, an official's
life – especially of an alien race – would have been worth a
week's purchase when pursuing such a policy.[23]

There would have been Welsh seamen on board many, if not
all, of the British warships that visited Patagonia, but only
one seems to have left an account of his impressions. This was
George Lloyd of Aberdare, who was serving aboard the cruiser
HMS *Garnet* in 1880 when she was despatched to Puerto Madryn
to monitor a dispute between the Welsh and Argentinians. As
she approached the coast, *Garnet* fired off rockets which could
be seen at Chubut, 30 miles away, to notify the colonists of her
arrival. The settlers flocked to the ship, hoping she had been
sent to rescue them. Lloyd thought they were in a terrible state,
'in rags and some verminous', as a result of drought. The crew
rigged tents for them, set up cooking facilities and gave them
soap, clothing and other basic commodities. The ship returned
to Puerto Madryn in the following year, when Lloyd found
things much improved.[24] The *Garnet*'s chaplain, Samuel Morris
(son of a famous vicar of Llanelli) had his own opinions about
the settlement: 'I think a cultured Welsh-speaking clergyman
(of the Church of England), resident in the valley, would be
of great advantage to the colony.' No doubt such a clergyman
would also have been able to resolve a problem which particularly vexed Morris. As far as he could tell, the marriages being
solemnised in the chapels of the Chubut valley were not legal
under either British or Argentinian law; thus many of the deeply
religious households appeared to be living in sin.[25]

Of course, it was possible to attribute a sinister connotation to
the British naval visits, and in the early years, at least, both some
of the colonists and the Argentinian government were inclined
to do so. The borders of Argentina and Chile were very vague
until they were finally resolved by international treaty in the
mid-1880s; in the interim, the presence of the Welsh colony complicated matters, and both colonists and Argentinian government

officials alike were alarmed that the naval visits might presage a more wholehearted British intervention in the area. The unsympathetic policies of several Argentinian presidents, and the occasional arbitrary excesses of the corrupt functionaries who were sometimes employed within the colony – as David Powell Richards had observed – prompted protests from both the colonists themselves and their supporters in Britain, thus turning the naval visits into rather more than neutral fact-finding missions. Captain Erskine of HMS *Boadicea* hinted at this in his 1879 report:

> the whole administration of this interesting colony, now that it has taken root and is progressing both in wealth and importance, demands serious consideration, and should be carefully attended to. It has, undoubtedly, the germs of British law-abiding propensities, and it is important that it should not be allowed to degenerate under the baneful influence of loose government.[26]

By the 1890s, any residual suspicion of the navy's annual visits had largely evaporated. Indeed, the colonists greatly enjoyed these occasions and the excuses for hunting, shooting and socialising that they provided. It was even claimed that when a British warship docked at Puerto Madryn, the colonists cried '*Duw gadw Sion Darw!*' ('God save John Bull!').[27] Moreover, at least one of the colonists was a former naval man. When the Welsh-speaking chaplain of HMS *Amethyst* reported on the Patagonia colony in 1883, he noted that one of the men he met was a Rogers from Dafen, near Llanelli, 'a blue-jacket in the *Britannia* flagship during the Russian War in the Black Sea, and has the Crimean medals with clasps for Inkerman and Sebastopol.'[28]

Crowns Imperial

The expansion of the British Empire eventually led to the creation of subordinate naval forces which ultimately developed into substantial navies in their own right, and Welshmen played a part in most of these processes. The Indian Navy, for instance, grew out of the maritime service of the East India Company, nominally a merchant service but in practice a navy in all but name. From its foundation in 1600 to its dissolution as a governing entity in 1857, the EIC operated a fleet of ships which were often almost as powerful as the warships of the regular navy. Significant numbers of Welshmen served in the EIC's naval forces, and subsequently in the Indian Navy itself. These included Sir William James (1722–83) from Haverfordwest, who transcended his remarkably obscure origins (his father was probably a miller) to become a commodore in the EIC's Bombay Marine before the age of 30, distinguishing himself in action against the French during the Seven Years' War and returning to Britain a rich man, buying a country estate in Kent and ultimately becoming a governor of the Royal Hospital at Greenwich, an MP and a baronet.[29] John Lloyd from Llanwrtyd also commanded EIC ships during the second half of the eighteenth century, making enough money to retire to his native Breconshire and becoming a substantial figure in society there.[30] John Jones of Swansea (d. 1828) used the profit from his command of a succession of East India ships to return to his hometown in 1792 and acquire the St Helen's estate; however, the outbreak of the French War led him to join the Royal Navy, and he became a commander in 1798.[31] Some Welshmen went into the East India Company's service when it became clear that they were unlikely to obtain further employment in the Royal Navy. Godfrey Lewis of Rhuddallt, Ruabon, entered the navy in 1779, aged 13, and qualified for a lieutenant in 1786, but with no prospect of actually obtaining a commission, he went into the EIC's service instead, dying in 1789, aged 23, as first mate of the *Pitt*.[32] Lieutenant Augustus Aldborough Lloyd Williams of Gwernant, Cardiganshire, made the same career move after the end of the Napoleonic Wars.[33] Others had long careers in the East India service without ever rising to command. Edward

Jacob of Eglwysilan, Glamorgan, slowly worked his way up from midshipman to fifth mate and so through the ranks to first mate by 1832, when he was in his forties.[34]

Welshmen continued to serve in India after 1857, when the Indian Mutiny led to the EIC losing control and the imposition of full-blown British rule. Evan Davies of Cardigan joined the Indian Navy in 1850 and by 1865 was 'commander of the Indus Steam Flotilla', dying in 1896 when in command of the steamer *Jhelum*; one of the Indian Navy's other captains at much the same time was Griffith Jenkins of Penrallt, Cardiganshire.[35] David Edward Evans, son of an Aberystwyth tailor, became a marine chief engineer and moved to India in the mid-1880s, joining the local navy and immediately seeing action in the Burma War of 1886–67. He left with the rank of engineer commander in 1888 and joined a firm operating boats on the River Brahmaputra.[36] Even as late as the time of the Second World War, several Welshmen were still serving in the Royal Indian Navy Volunteer Reserve: they included Neermol Hughes Davies of Ffestiniog and Ralph Stepney Gulston of Derwydd, Carmarthenshire.[37] The establishment of the Royal Australian Navy in 1901 created new opportunities. George Davies Williams, born at St Dogmaels in 1879, went into the mercantile marine but subsequently joined the Royal Naval Reserve in 1909, going 'down under' in 1911 to take command of a training ship. He served as a lieutenant in the RAN during the First World War, initially on the battlecruiser *Australia*, but subsequently returned to the Royal Navy and by 1919 was in command of a minesweeping flotilla in the Aegean and Black Seas, winning the DSO for his service. He went back to Australia in 1920 and subsequently held a series of important posts in maritime administration before rejoining the navy during the Second World War, and taking responsibility for the organisation of convoys sailing from Sydney.[38] Commander Edmund Wybergh Thruston of Pennal near Aberdyfi was second-in-command of the cruiser HMAS *Sydney* when, on 19 November 1941, she fought a battle in the Indian Ocean against the German raider *Kormoran* which led to the sinking of both ships. Many men survived the *Kormoran*, but the *Sydney* was lost with all 645 hands, and for decades, questions were asked about what had caused Australia's worst naval disaster – and, indeed, about the location of the wreck, for the *Sydney* was not found until 2008.[39]

Voyages of Exploration

Welshmen participated in many of the navy's most famous voyages of exploration. Thomas Foley, uncle of Nelson's great friend, sailed with Anson during his circumnavigation of the globe, while Humphrey Edwards, physician of Llanrug, also sailed around the world as ship's surgeon of HMS *Tamar*, part of Commodore Byron's voyage to the South Seas in 1764–66.[40] Some aspects of the career of David Samwell, the colourful surgeon who sailed with Captain Cook, have already been explored (*see Chapter 3*). As he sailed around the world, Samwell always carried a book of Welsh verse, and his antiquarian inclinations led him to take a great interest in the new cultures that the expedition encountered: he translated Maori songs and was the first to properly record the Maori language.[41] But Samwell was not the only *Cymro* to accompany Cook. It has been estimated that perhaps as many as ten of the eighty-five crewmen of the *Endeavour* were Welsh, while John Henry Martin, buried at Ludchurch, Pembrokeshire, in 1823, was one of the last surviving officers who took part in Captain Cook's third voyage.[42] Two of the lieutenants who accompanied George Vancouver on his voyages in the Pacific and on the North American coast in the 1790s, Peter Puget and his friend Joseph Baker (after whom Mount Baker in Washington State is named), settled in Presteigne. Puget lived there only relatively briefly, although a plaque recording his residence adorns the 'Red House' in the town; Baker, who probably originally came from the area and served principally as the expedition's chartmaker, was a longer-term resident and is commemorated by a memorial in the parish church. At much the same time that Samwell, Puget and the others were on their voyages, a Welsh naval officer was playing an important part in the development of Canada. William Owen of Glansevern received a grant of land on Passamaquoddy Island in 1767 and spent the next decade developing a colony there, although he envisaged it as a tenanted aristocratic estate for himself rather than as a self-governing settlement of property owners. He renamed the island Campobello, but his paternalistic, landlord-controlled vision of the colony failed after a few years, partly because William returned to the navy upon the outbreak of the American war, dying in Madras in 1778 when in command of HMS *Cormorant*. Nevertheless, his nephew David (a former naval chaplain) and later his illegitimate son Captain, later Admiral, William Fitzwilliam Owen, a distinguished hydrographer, reasserted the family's control over the island and carried out several surveys of its coast. Campobello eventually became best known as the holiday retreat of President Franklin D. Roosevelt.[43]

John Lort Stokes of Scotchwell, Haverfordwest, belonged to an old established Rees family of Pembrokeshire, his grandfather having changed their surname to Stokes. John entered the navy in 1824, and in the following year, aged 13, he was posted to HMS *Beagle*, serving aboard her until 1836. Thus he was on board throughout the time that Robert Fitzroy commanded her, including the famous cruise of 1831–36 when Charles Darwin was aboard. Stokes remained aboard the *Beagle* when she was recommissioned in 1837, survived being speared by a native and narrowly escaped being eaten by a crocodile, and eventually became her captain, undertaking important surveys in Australian and New Zealand waters.[44] On his return to Britain, he wrote a book describing his experiences. He later returned to undertake further surveys in the same seas before eventually rising to flag rank on the retired list, narrowly missing out on appointment as

Hydrographer of the Navy. Admiral Stokes died at Scotchwell in 1885 and was buried in Prendergast church.[45] The Stokes family was very much a Pembrokeshire naval dynasty: John's brother Henry became a Commander RN, while a second cousin (William) also became an admiral and was followed into the navy by both his son and grandson.[46]

Almost as momentous as the voyage of the *Beagle* was the *Challenger* expedition of 1872–76. *Challenger*'s captain for most of that time was George Nares of Clytha, Monmouthshire, who had joined the navy in 1845 at the age of 14. He took part in one of the missions sent out to try to locate Sir John Franklin's expedition (*below*) and subsequently specialised in training, writing a manual for naval cadets, and then surveying, including a commission as captain of HMS *Newport* on hydrographic work in the Mediterranean. He was thus ideally qualified to take command of HMS *Challenger*, which from 1872 to 1876 undertook the first proper marine survey of the world's oceans. This also included a foray into Antarctic waters and prompted much of the later interest in exploring that continent. His command was widely regarded as an unqualified success, to such an extent that he was recalled early (in 1874) to take command of a major Arctic expedition. Nares was criticised for calling off that mission to prevent loss of life among his men, who were succumbing to scurvy, but, even so, he was knighted and was elected a Fellow of the Royal Society.[47]

Several Welshmen served on Sir John Franklin's ill-fated Arctic expedition of 1845; one of Franklin's two ships, the *Erebus*, had been launched at Pembroke Dock in 1826. William Jerry, Able Seaman aboard the *Terror*, hailed from St David's, while George Williams of the *Erebus* was a native of Rhoscolyn, Anglesey.[48] Another of those who set out aboard *Erebus* in May 1845 was Francis Dunn, a 24-year-old caulker's mate from Kidwelly who had worked in the docks at Llanelli before joining the navy. In the event, both of the expedition's ships, HMS *Erebus* and HMS *Terror*, became icebound off Prince William Island for two

years, forcing the crews to abandon the safety of their vessels
and attempt a trek of over 900 miles, across frozen wastes, to
safety. Rescue missions found hardly any trace of the expedition, but subsequent discoveries led to the shocking realisation
that at least some of the survivors had resorted to cannibalism.
Nothing conclusive of the fate of the expedition was known for
nearly fifteen years, by which time the Admiralty had written
off the officers and men, endorsing the ship's muster book with
the words *'to be considered as having died in the service. Wages are to be
paid to their relatives to that date, as of 1st April 1854.'* The order for
payment to the families was carried out, with the local newspaper, the *South Wales Cambrian*, reporting:

> Sir John Franklin's Expedition. The father of Francis Dunn,
> of Llanelly, one of the seamen engaged in the Arctic expedi-
> tion, has recently received about £300 from the Admiralty,
> the accumulated wages of his son. The family attended Capel
> Newydd on Sunday dressed in deep mourning.

The back pay was sufficient to allow Dunn Senior to buy a pub
in Llanelli, but the mystery that surrounded the disappearance
of his son and his comrades endured, and still continues to
fascinate. In recent years there have been several books and television documentaries on the mystery surrounding the Franklin
expedition an interest given new impetus by the discoveries of
the wrecks of Erebus in 2014 and Terror in 2016. One of the
many theories put forward to explain the expedition's fate has
a particular resonance for the Welshmen on the expedition, and
especially for Francis Dunn. In the 1980s, a theory was developed from three bodies of expedition members discovered in the
Canadian permafrost to suggest that Franklin's men might have
been afflicted by lead poisoning from the solder used in the tin
cans, then a revolutionary new innovation, that the expedition
carried with them. Stephan Goldner, the shady contractor who
provided the cans to the navy might well have obtained them

from one of the few tinplate works then in production: the one in Kidwelly, Francis Dunn's hometown. However, subsequent research has proved that the levels of lead in the bodies were not unusually high by Victorian standards, and that other causes of death would have been more than sufficient to do for Francis and his colleagues: namely, tuberculosis, scurvy, malnutrition, exposure and, perhaps, being eaten by their shipmates.[49]

Over half a century after the disappearance of Franklin's expedition, another British polar expedition ended in tragic but rather better documented circumstances. One of Captain Robert Falcon Scott's most valued assistants during his doomed expedition to the South Pole was Edgar Evans, born at Fernhill or Middleton on the Gower and baptised at Rhossili, the son of a seaman from Oxwich. After attending school and holding several short-lived jobs in Swansea, he joined the navy in 1891, aged 15. He became known to Scott when they both served on the Channel Fleet flagship HMS *Majestic* in 1899–1901, and when Scott organised his first Antarctic expedition in 1901, he requested Petty Officer Evans' release from the navy so that he could take part in it. Evans resumed his naval service in 1904, becoming a torpedo instructor at the Portsmouth training establishment HMS *Vernon*, leading his crew to success in the field gun race at the Royal Navy Tattoos of 1906 and 1907.[50] Evans joined Scott's next expedition in 1910, which had the objective of reaching the South Pole itself. Cardiff played host to Scott's ship, the converted whaler *Terra Nova*, and provided considerable assistance to the expedition.[51] As a South Walian, Evans found himself particularly feted; he was seated between Scott and the Lord Mayor of Cardiff at the valedictory banquet and gave a rousing speech, but afterwards got so drunk that it took six men to get him back to the ship.[52] Evans was one of Scott's own team of four during the desperately difficult journey to the Pole, and Scott paid fulsome tribute to the Welshman's skill and ingenuity. But when they reached the Pole, they found that Amundsen's Norwegian expedition had beaten them to it. During the return journey, Evans fell ill from scurvy, frostbite and an unhealed wound in his hand, and died in the night of 16–17 February 1912. His widow erected a memorial tablet to him in Rhossili church. In 1964, a new accommodation block for Petty Officers at HMS *Excellent*, the gunnery school in Portsmouth, was named the Edgar Evans building. This was demolished in 2010, but a memorial containing his skis and other mementoes was moved into the new building that replaced it.[53]

A Tradition Continues

The Welsh tradition of serving in foreign navies long predated the likes of James George Beynon and Henry Morton Stanley. Some, like the galley slave David Gwyn, were undoubtedly forced into foreign service, but many others went willingly: one such was Jenkin Price, a 'Welsh Englishman' as the Dutch described him, who in 1629–30 was serving under the famous Dutch admiral, Maarten Harpertszoon Tromp.[54] Indeed, and although the numbers might be fewer than in earlier centuries, Welsh men (and, latterly, women) have maintained this long tradition of foreign naval service through the twentieth and on into the twenty-first centuries. Frederick Tuthill, born at Pembroke Dock in 1898, served as a corporal in the Pembroke Yeomanry in the First World War but subsequently emigrated to the United States, becoming a lieutenant in the Naval Reserve. A communications specialist, he served on the staff of the Naval Task Force Commander during the invasion of the south of France in 1944 and ultimately retired as a rear-admiral.[55] Jonathan Rogers of Llangollen served in the Royal Navy during the Second World War but subsequently emigrated to Australia and joined the Royal Australian Navy. He was serving aboard the destroyer HMAS *Voyager* on the night of 10 February 1964 when it was accidentally sliced in two in a collision with the aircraft carrier *Melbourne*. Rogers was trapped in the forward section but helped several men escape through a small hatch before it sank; at the very end, he was heard leading his trapped comrades in a prayer and a hymn. Jonathan Rogers was awarded a posthumous George Cross for his heroism.[56] Four years later, St David's Day was marked aboard HMAS *Queenborough* by 'our two tame Welshmen', CPO 'Taffy' Lloyd and Lieutenant Wally Criddle, who were 'presented with [the] symbol of their heritage – a giant leek'.[57] In 2011, Stephanie Morris from Hengoed qualified as a nuclear propulsion machinist mate in the United States Navy, having joined the service two years earlier thanks to her American parentage and despite her Welsh accent; as one of her former teachers commented, it was hardly the usual career path for a former student of Ystrad Mynach College.[58]

Notes

1   For Humphreys' ancestry, see the article by his great-grandson, H.H. Humphreys, 'Who Built the First United States Navy?', *Journal of American History*, V (1916), pp.49–50.

2   W.D. McCaw, 'Captain John Harris of the Virginia Navy. A Prisoner of War in England, 1777–1779', *The Virginia Magazine of History and Biography*, 22 (1914), pp.160–72; M.M. Cleaver, *The Life, Character and Services of Commodore Jacob Jones* (Wilmington, Delaware, 1906), p.29.

3   *The Cambrian*, 14 Feb. 1835; www.history.army.mil/html/moh/ interawrds.html. (Accessed: 2012)

4   middleton-stjohns.com/wiki/Web:PB-Lectures:Percy_B._ St.John-A_Lecture_on_Texas, citing *The Morning Advertiser*, 28 April 1846; http://john-adcock.blogspot.co.uk/2008/08/percy-bolingbroke-st-john-1821-1889.html. (Accessed: 2012)

5   Personal correspondence (email) from Mr Brian Vale, 7 July 2006. Cf www.irlandeses.org/0607vale1.htm. (Accessed: 2012)

6   The poem, by Thomas Jenkins (1774–1843), is printed in full on my blog, gentlemenand tarpaulins.com/2012/07/03/the-sailors-graves/, using the copy in West Sussex Record Office, Cobden Papers 386.

7   M. Gibbs, 'Don Santiago Jorge Bynon (1797–1883)', *Gower*, 32 (1981), pp.26–36.

8   R Wills, The Jacobites and Russia 1715–50, 149; A Cross, *By the Banks of the Neva: Chapters from the Lives and Careers of the British in Eighteenth*

Century Russia (Cambridge, 1997), 178–9. I am grateful to Trish Newman for the latter reference.

9 I. W. Jones, 'America's Secret War in Welsh Waters', *MW*, 1 (1976), pp.83–101. (Accessed: 2012)

10 David Williams of Llanelli: Llanelly and County Guardian, 14 July 1864. I am grateful to Lyn John for this reference.

11 www.tfoenander.com/csnindex.htm; J. Hunter, *Sons of Arthur, Children of Lincoln: Welsh Writing from the American Civil War* (Cardiff, 2007), pp.259–61. (Accessed: 2012)

12 www.tfoenander.com/csnindex.htm. (Accessed: 2012)

13 The story is reported verbatim in several American papers and finally in *The Western Mail*, 15 Aug. 1883. (Accessed: 2012)

14 R. Field, *Confederate Ironclad vs Union Ironclad: Hampton Roads 1862* (2008), p.38; www.huffingtonpost.com/2012/03/03/faces-of-2-uss-monitor-crew-reconstructed_n_1318584.html; Ellis, *The Monitor of the Civil War* (Lebanon, Pa., 1921). (Accessed: 2012)

15 www.tfoenander.com/minnesota.htm; www.tfoenander.com/niagara.htm; www.tfoenander.com/hartford.htm. (Accessed: 2012)

16 *The Cambrian*, 25 (1905), p.360. (Accessed: 2012)

17 www.tfoenander.com/nationalities.htm; E. Lonn, *Foreigners in the Union Army and Navy* (Baton Rouge, Louisiana, 1951), p.636.

18 *The Western Mail*, 25 March 1866, p.12; F. Driver, 'Stanley, Sir Henry Morton (1841–1904), Explorer and Journalist', *ODNB*; T. Jeal, *Stanley: The Impossible Life of Africa's Greatest Explorer* (2007), pp.52–4, 62–3.

19 Naval Historical Library, Portsmouth, MS 176.

20 W. C. Rhys, *A Welsh Song in Patagonia* (2012 edn.), pp.77–9

21 The most important are collated in TNA, ADM147/1.

22 TNA, ADM147/1.

23 TNA, ADM147/1. A further copy of Richards' report, with associated papers, can be found in NLW, MS 10746E.

24 NLW, MS Facs 777.

25 TNA, ADM147/1.

26 TNA, ADM147/1.

27 Rhys, *Welsh Song in Patagonia*, pp.78–9.

28 *Western Mail*, 9 May 1883.

29 T. H. Bowyer, 'James, Sir William, first baronet (1722–1783), Naval Officer and Director of the East India Company', *ODNB*.

30 K. Jones, 'John Lloyd', *Brycheiniog*, 33 (2001), pp.59–92; *Brycheiniog*, 34 (2002), pp.67–118.

31 H. Bowen, 'Welsh Commanders of East Indiamen: A Case Study of John Jones (1751–1828)', *MW*, 31 (2010), pp.21–36; TNA, ADM9/4/926.

32 TNA, ADM 49/36, PROB 11/1191/15.

33 O'Byrne, iii. 1294.

34 A. Farrington, *A Biographical Index of East India Company Maritime Service Officers* (1999).

35 M.J. Baylis, 'The Makeigs in Cardigan', *Ceredigion : Journal of the Cardiganshire Antiquarian Society*, 7 (1973), pp.201–2; T. Nicholas, *Annals And Antiquities Of The Counties and County Families Of Wales* (1872), i. 197.

36 D.E. Lloyd Jones, 'David Edward Evans', *THSC* (1967), p.134.

37 www.unithistories.com/officers/RINVR_officers.html

38 adb.anu.edu.au/biography/williams-george-davies-9110

39 Memorial in Pennal church; Gwynedd Archives (Dolgellau), Thruston of Pennal MSS.

40 'Edwards, Humphrey (1730–1788), Physician and Apothecary', *WBO*.

41 E.G. Bowen, *David Samwell (Dafydd Ddu Feddyg), 1751–1798* (Cardiff, 1974), p.35; N. Thomas, *Cook: The Extraordinary Voyages of Captain James Cook* (2003), p.269.

42 J. Thomas, 'Captain James Cook and "New Wales"', *THSC* (1970), p.345; L. Phillips, 'John Henry Martin', *MM*, 75 (1989), p.187.

43 W.K.D. Davies, Capt.,'William Owen and the settlement of Campobello', *National Library of Wales Journal*, 31 (1999), pp.189–213; (2000), pp.217–41; www.biographi.ca/ (*Dictionary of Canadian Biography Online*), sv 'Owen, David'.

44 NMM, STK1–78.

45 J.K. Laughton, rev. R.O. Morriss, 'Stokes, John Lort (1812–1885), Naval Officer', *ODNB*.

46 NMM, STK57.

47 R.N. Rudmose-Brown, rev. M. Deacon, 'Nares, Sir George Strong (bap. 1831, d. 1915), Arctic explorer', *ODNB*.

48 R. Lloyd-Jones, 'The Men Who Sailed With Franklin', *Polar Record*, 41 (2005), pp.313, 317

49 J.D. Davies and L.T. John, 'Llanelli's Lost Arctic Explorer', *The Llanelli Miscellany*, 20 (2006–07), pp.76–80 (www.llanellich.org.uk/files/36-llanellis-lost-arctic-explorer.)

50 G. Gregor, 'Edgar Evans', *Gower: Journal of the Gower Society*, 44, (1993), pp.21–33; I. Williams, *Captain Scott's Invaluable Assistant: Edgar Evans* (Stroud, 2012), ch. 1 and passim.

51 A.M. Johnson, 'Scott of the Antarctic and Cardiff', *Morgannwg: Transactions of the Glamorgan Local History Society*, 26, pp.15–25; 'Scott of the Antarctic and Cardiff, Part 2', *Morgannwg: Transactions of the Glamorgan Local History Society*, 27 (1983), pp.25–58.

52 Gregor, 'Edgar Evans', p.26.

53 www.iwm.org.uk/memorials/item/memorial/62642

54 Stadsarchief Rotterdam, MS ONA Rotterdam 190/128/188. Thanks to Professor Steve Murdoch for this reference.

55 L. Phillips, 'Some Pembrokeshire Sea Officers (Part 2)', *Journal of the Pembrokeshire Historical Society*, 9 (2000), pp.17–18.

56 awm.gov.au/exhibitions/fiftyaustralians/40.asp

57 *Royal Australian Navy News*, vol. 11, no. 9, 26 Apr. 1968.

58 www.walesonline.co.uk/news/wales-news/2011/11/05/us-navy-s-newest-recruit-is-stephanie-morris-from-hengoed-91466-29727168/

8

PAX CAMBRENSIS

WALES AND THE VICTORIAN NAVY

Corwen, nestling comfortably in the Dee Valley a few miles west of Llangollen, is not a place where one would expect to find virtually a potted history of the Victorian Navy only a few yards from a bold modern sculpture of local hero Owain Glyndŵr. But just inside the door of the ancient parish church of Saint Mael and Saint Sulien, on the north wall of the nave, is a remarkable *curriculum vitae* in stone. It is, perhaps, one of the most telling correctives anywhere in the British Isles to the notion that the Royal Navy was essentially at peace, and really did very little, for most of the century between 1815 and 1914. The memorial commemorates Captain William Hans Blake RN (1832–74), who entered the navy in 1846, served in the Preventive Squadron against the slave trade, and was in HMS *Edinburgh* during the Crimean War, 'in which ship he commanded a rocket boat at the bombardment of Sweaborg in August 1855 and was gazetted in dispatches – "as maintaining his position with steady gallantry under a smart fire of bursting shells"'. The memorial records how he served on HMS *Cambrian* from 1857–59 during the China War, then went to New Zealand where he was wounded during the Maori War, and promoted for his gallantry. He subsequently commanded ships on the South American, Pacific and Australian stations before captaining HMS *Druid* in West Africa and dying of tropical fever at Cape Coast Castle while commanding the naval brigade during the Ashanti War. The remarkable memorial, erected by his 'sorrowing widow', omits the not unimportant fact that he had married her when he was in Australia, and that she was Sydney-born and bred. A memorial identical to the one in Corwen, and thus bearing the same lengthy inscription, can be found in Saint Matthew's church, Windsor, New South Wales.[1] The Blakes' story truly epitomises the *Pax Britannica*, the heyday of the British Empire, and the great navy that protected it.

Officers and Men: The Steam and Ironclad Eras

During the late summer of 1852, nine harassed Admiralty clerks put in to four hours' overtime a night for two months, working meticulously through individual ships' muster books to record the birthplaces of every man and boy in the Royal Navy. The information that they produced formed a key part of an Admiralty enquiry into the manning of the service, and despite being regarded by their evidently disapproving superior as a 'very voluminous and troublesome return', it provides an invaluable snapshot of the demography of the fleet in the early Victorian period, including the Welsh contribution to it. The returns reveal that there were 340 Welshmen and 32 boys out of a total manpower of 22,343. Pembrokeshire provided 139 men and 19 boys, well over a third of the total, followed by 54 men from Glamorgan and 28 from Caernarfonshire. (By contrast, Montgomeryshire provided five men, Breconshire just two, and Radnorshire none.) Unsurprisingly, the biggest contribution from a single conurbation came from the dockyard town of Pembroke, with 39 men and 10 boys, followed by Milford with 33 and 2, Swansea with 23 men, Haverfordwest and Cardiff with 16 each, Holyhead with 11 and Caernarfon with 10; but there were also individual sailors from such unlikely recruiting grounds as Ruthin, Abergavenny and Merthyr, as well as two from Builth and four from Welshpool.[2] These figures suggest that the Welsh contribution to the navy had declined markedly since Trafalgar. The Welshmen constituted only 1.66 per cent of the fleet's man-power, less than half of the contribution in Nelson's time, and the decline relative to the national population was even more marked. Even so, in relative terms recruitment in Wales was significantly stronger than it was in Scotland; the Admiralty evidently did not regard the former as an issue, but agonised at great length over the latter and investigated various ways of encouraging more Scots into the navy.[3]

There are several possible reasons for the decline in Welsh enthusiasm for naval service. It is possible that the growing influence of the chapels turned some against the entire notion of joining the armed forces of an apparently alien, English-dominated empire; this certainly seems to have been a factor affecting Welsh recruitment for the army, the paucity of which attracted the same levels of concern in government as were displayed towards the shortage of Scots in the navy.[4] The Victorian Royal Navy was one of the very few truly all-British institutions, an indisputable fact that might have attracted and repelled Welshmen in equal measure. The army, with its regimental and regional structures, seemed to offer greater opportunities for comradeship and the projection of Welsh identity, but for much of the nineteenth century the army adopted an explicitly anti-Welsh attitude (for example, banning the use of the language) that the navy as a whole did not emulate.[5] The expanding industries of the southern valleys, and the substantial wages that they paid, might also have provided attractive alternative employment opportunities for young men, while the major improvements to Welsh ports, particularly in the south, and the concomitant growth in long-distance maritime trades to and from them, meant that those who wished to 'see the world' now had viable, non-naval options literally on their doorsteps.[6]

Fifty years later, at first sight the picture appears unchanged. A sample of twenty warships drawn from the 1901 census reveals that Welshmen made up some 1.86 per cent of the crews, although there were some anomalies: there were twenty-seven aboard the battleship *Magnificent* at Gibraltar, some 3.1 per cent of the ship's company, while the cruiser *Amphion* at Vancouver had seventeen Welshmen out of a crew of 312, an impressive 5.4 per cent of the total. These variations are probably accounted for by the fact that most Welshmen joined ships based at Plymouth, the designated manning dockyard for the Principality, so Plymouth-based ships would naturally have a higher proportion than those from Portsmouth or Chatham. Substantial contingents facilitated familiar manifestations of national rivalry: at Bermuda in January 1919 the crew of the cruiser *Devonshire* staged a Wales versus England rugby match (which England won, but only 6-0).[7] At the other extreme, in 1901 Thomas Powell of Tondu was the solitary 'Taff' aboard the gunboat *Redbreast* at Lorenzo Marques in Portuguese East Africa. What had changed markedly since 1852 was the demography of Welsh recruitment. Gone was the traditional dominance of Pembrokeshire; now Glamorgan and Monmouthshire provided over half the Welsh recruits. This is hardly surprising, given the great increase in those counties' populations, but the representation from Anglesey and Caernarfonshire had also fallen sharply in both absolute and relative terms – evidence, perhaps, of a growing antipathy towards apparently English-dominated Imperial institutions in the Welsh-speaking heartland.

On the other hand, the total numbers drawn from individual Welsh towns were often quite significant, and stood comparison with the contribution from roughly equivalent English communities. Between 1853 and 1923, 2,079 Cardiff-born men joined the navy, a figure comparable with the number from Sunderland; so did 1,526 Swansea men and 1,684 from the Milford/Pembroke Dock area, similar to the numbers drawn from Falmouth and Birkenhead, while there were 438 from Llanelli, more than were recruited from Barrow-in-Furness in the equivalent period. Holyhead contributed 217 men and Caernarfon 189, not dissimilar to the numbers from Fowey and Fleetwood.[8] Moreover, even if Welsh recruitment to the navy was relatively unimpressive, it could be argued that it was still rather healthier than the situation in its far more populous Celtic neighbours. In 1913, only 208 of the navy's 12,862 recruits came from Wales, but the figures for Scotland and Ireland were a dire 353 and 360, respectively.[9]

Welshmen joined the navy for many reasons. For George Lloyd, known as 'Georgie Brawd', born at Pembroke Dock but raised in Cardiff and Aberdare, the navy was an escape from a life down the pit that had begun for him before the age of 13. A couple of local lads came home on leave from the navy and persuaded Georgie it was the life for him, so he signed up at the Red Lion, Aberdare, and went off to the training ship *Impregnable* at Devonport. One of his very first experiences at sea was the desperate search for survivors from the Pembroke-built training frigate *Atalanta*, lost with 278 hands (many of them boys under training) during a storm in February 1880. During his time aboard the cruiser *Garnet*, Georgie visited the Welsh colony in Patagonia, as described in Chapter 7, and also called at Rio de Janeiro, where he heard a Royal Marine humming the Welsh hymn tune '*Molwch yr Arglwydd*' and discovered he was from Trecynon. Georgie served as captain's messenger to the *Garnet*'s commanding officer, the Welshman Loftus Francis 'Stinker' Jones, a strict disciplinarian who regretted the fact that he was no longer allowed to flog his men,[*] and went on an expedition up the River Plate with her Welsh navigating officer,

---

[*]   It is interesting that Georgie describes Jones as Welsh, which is presumably how he described himself, as the captain's family had been settled in Ireland since the 1650s. Loftus Francis Jones was the father of Commander William Loftus Jones, VC, who was awarded posthumously for his heroism in command of HMS *Shark* at the Battle of Jutland (and who therefore might perhaps be considered for addition to the roll call of Welsh VC winners).

Lieutenant Gwyne. The third Welsh officer aboard the *Garnet* was the chaplain, Samuel Morris, son of a charismatic vicar of Llanelli. Morris subsequently served as chaplain of the battleship *Victoria* and was lost with 359 other hands when she was accidentally rammed and sunk by HMS *Camperdown* in 1893; a plaque in Llanelli parish church commemorates him. Georgie became friendly with the other Welshman on the *Garnet*'s lower deck, 'Taff' Thomas from Mountain Ash, although he found it difficult to keep up with Taff's prodigious drinking. 'Georgie Brawd' rose to become a gunnery instructor and seemed to have a long naval career ahead of him, but illness led to his being prematurely invalided out of the service.[10]

For some Welsh sailors, a stint in the Royal Navy was merely the preliminary to a much longer career in merchant ships. Thomas Jones, who came from a seafaring family in Borth, served in the navy from 1850 to 1856 and saw action in the Crimean War, but he subsequently passed his master's certificate and owned and skippered the *Pilgrim*.[11] Naval service broadened horizons, both literally and metaphorically. In 1901, 26-year-old Stoker Francis Cardew, from the tiny farming village of Myddfai high in the damp Carmarthenshire hills, found himself aboard the cruiser HMS *Highflyer*, flagship of the East Indies station and based at Trincomalee, Sri Lanka, where 'the thermometer … is seldom below 80 degrees'.[12] That same year the crew of 192 aboard the sloop HMS *Racoon* at Aden included Leading Shipwright Henry Johns of Pembroke, Stoker Richard Milward of Caernarfon and Chief Stoker Arthur Wood of Brecon, whose upbringings presumably would have done little to prepare them for the experience of serving alongside the ship's 'seedies' or local recruits – an eclectic mix of Somalis, Portuguese Goans, Indians, Sri Lankans, Guyanese, Arabs, Sudanese, Sierra Leonean, Malagasy, Socotran, Comoro Islander and Zanzibar crewmen. Other members of the crew were drawn from Whitechapel, Liverpool, Halifax, Tynemouth, Kirkcaldy, Norfolk, Cornwall and Ireland, so the variety of accents aboard such a small ship must have been a veritable Babel.

For officers, the long peace after 1815 proved the graveyard of many once-promising careers, while those of many younger men were effectively still-born. Captain William Webley Parry, who inherited the Noyadd Trefawr estate in Cardiganshire in 1815, had a good war record, having fought at the Nile in 1798 and Copenhagen in 1807, but he held only one peacetime command, which lasted less than three years.[13] Frederick Jennings Thomas of Wenvoe Castle was another who distinguished himself in the war, serving at Trafalgar and during operations at Cadiz during the Peninsular War, but he held no seagoing appointment at all after the war, spending his time on the likes of inventing a new lifeboat and drawing up plans for a pier at Brighton.[14] Like any post-captains who lived long enough, both Parry and Thomas were eventually promoted automatically to flag rank by seniority, but with no serious prospect of actually hoisting their flags at sea. However, Wales now provided other attractions, and alternative routes to fulfilment. Even before the Revolutionary and Napoleonic Wars began, unemployed naval officers had begun to settle in the country, the rugged attractions of which were extolled by the popular 'romantic movement'. One of the earliest converts to the delights of the Principality was Henry Trollope, one of the most spectacularly successful frigate captains of the American War of Independence, who in the 1780s took a lease on Westmead House near Laugharne. For several weeks in 1786 Trollope and his much younger wife entertained the French naturalist, lawyer and diplomat Jean Baptiste Léonard Durand, who had been shipwrecked on nearby Pendine Sands during a return voyage from West Africa. It is probably impossible to prove whether Patrick O'Brian ever read Durand's memoirs, but even if he did not, Trollope and Durand provide an uncanny match for his brilliant fictional creations, Captain Jack Aubrey of the Royal Navy and the Irish/Catalan naturalist and agent Stephen Maturin.[15]

Thanks to the new interest in Wales during the last decades of the eighteenth century and the early nineteenth, Tenby, Ferryside, Swansea and some inland towns in both the north and the south began to develop as resorts, attracting small colonies of naval officers 'put out to grass' on half pay. The new Swansea newspaper, *The Cambrian* (established in 1804), dutifully recorded the frequent arrivals of naval men and their wives in the town, together with the dinners and other social functions that they attended.[16] Swansea briefly even had a 'Classical, Commercial and Naval Academy', run at first by George Hazel, the navy's agent in the port.[17] Others preferred less bustling parts of the country. Captain Hyde John Clark, an ancestor of Olympic Gold medallist and London Olympics organiser Seb Coe, spent much of his retirement at Llangollen.[18] Charles Hamlyn Williams, a younger son of the Edwinsford dynasty, retired as a captain after his ship, HMS *Tribune*, was lost on the Spanish coast in 1839, and spent his latter years at Portiscliff, Ferryside, eventually being promoted to rear-admiral on the retired list.[19] Others settled down as local squires, serving on the magistrates' bench or in other county offices. Having fought throughout the French Revolutionary and Napoleonic Wars, Admiral Sir Charles Thomas Jones retired to his native Montgomeryshire where he served as a JP, deputy-lieutenant and sheriff.[20] Similarly, Thomas Parry Jones-Parry of Llwynon held a couple of small commands at the end of the Napoleonic Wars but then retired to his homeland, becoming a magistrate for Denbighshire and Caernarfonshire as well as deputy-lieutenant and sheriff of the latter.[21]

Some went on to more illustrious political careers. Admiral Sir Charles Paget, brother of the Marquess of Anglesey of Waterloo fame, had used a fortune of £26,000 from prize money to buy an estate in Sussex and was subsequently returned to Parliament for the family's 'pocket borough' of Caernarfon, serving 1806–1826 and 1831–4 before returning to sea to command the North America station.[22] His successor as MP for Caernarfon from

1826–30 was Anglesey's second son, Lord William, who had entered the navy in 1817 and become a post-captain in 1826. He fell out with his father over his choice of wife and extravagant lifestyle, and with his constituents over Catholic emancipation, to which he was a belated convert, so he had to give up the strongly anti-emancipation seat in 1830. By then he was captain of HMS *North Star*, a command marred by the death of a ship's boy, William Heritage, who threw himself over the side rather than face the twelve lashes ordered by Paget for a misdemeanour he had committed. Paget was exonerated by two courts of enquiry and a court martial. He continued to run up vast debts, fought in the Carlist wars in Spain, and served another term as an MP, this time for Andover (1841–46), but he never served at sea again.[23]

Sir Christopher Cole, a Cornishman, served under Thomas Foley early in his naval career and then saw active service from Surinam to Iran and China. In 1810, commanding the *Caroline* (36), he led a small squadron in a surprise attack on the Dutch island of Banda, overrunning the much larger Dutch garrison in a daring exploit that the Prime Minister, Spencer Perceval, declared to be 'an exploit to be classed with the boldest darings in the days of chivalry'. Cole further distinguished himself during the attack on Java in 1811 and was knighted on his return to Britain.[24] Cole effectively retired from active service in 1814 and married his old love, Lady Mary Strangways, the widow of Thomas Mansel Talbot of Margam and Penrice. In 1817 Cole, 'the conqueror of Banda', was persuaded to fill the vacancy in the Glamorgan county seat and, though defeated in 1818, he was returned to it in 1820 in a particularly nasty election: he was stoned as he passed Cyfarthfa ironworks after the declaration. Cole continued to serve as MP until 1830, although he also commanded the royal yacht *Royal Sovereign* from 1828–30 and became Grand Master of the South Wales masons. He was an active MP who strongly promoted the interests of Swansea and the development of roads and railways in Glamorgan, as well as voting to abolish flogging in the navy and campaigning vigorously against slavery.[25] Cole died in 1836, bequeathing £100 to the poor of Penrice on the Gower, where he was buried and where a memorial in the church commemorates him.[26]

For many junior officers, though, the years after 1815 constituted a desperate struggle to secure some form of employment, and the Welsh, geographically so remote from London and opportunities to solicit directly at the Admiralty, were seriously disadvantaged in such a competition. Some, like Lieutenant Valentine Herbert Jones of Anglesey, went into the Customs; his neighbour Lieutenant Henry Paget Jones became commissioner of pilotage at Holyhead; others, like the gloriously named Lieutenant Meyrick Bodychen Sparrow of Beaumaris, seem simply to have given up and gone home.[27] Lieutenant Francis Dornford became dock master for the Glamorgan Canal Company before obtaining the same position at the new Bute Dock in Cardiff in 1841.[28] Some, like Aberystwyth's Trafalgar veteran David Lewis, sought appointment as harbour masters. Such a post was usually a comfortable sinecure, but it proved unexpectedly perilous for John Pasley Luckraft, a Devonian who was appointed harbour master at Llanelli. In September 1843 the Rebecca Rioters, disguised in petticoats, attacked his house, threatening him with a gun and shooting at his windows. Luckraft's 'crime' seems to have been that, as a teetotaller, he had persuaded the Harbour Commissioners to ban their pilots from running pubs as a sideline.[29] The Admiralty packet boats were another possible source of employment, but they paid well and the few commands were highly sought after. One of the lucky ones was Commander John Macgregor Skinner, from an American loyalist family in Perth Amboy, New Jersey. Skinner entered the navy just four months before America declared independence, was examined for lieutenant in 1783 and held several commissions before transferring to the Falmouth packets in 1793. Six years later he obtained the command of the Holyhead packet *Leicester* and swiftly became a prominent figure in local society. He was also an unmistakable one, having lost his right arm shortly after joining the navy and being attended by a remarkably tame pet raven. The high point of Skinner's career came in 1821 when he conveyed King George IV from Holyhead to Howth aboard the steamer *Lightning*. In 1832, the captain was swept overboard by a huge wave, and Holyhead mourned its much-loved adopted son. A subscription in his memory raised over £400, and a large memorial was erected on a hill overlooking the harbour. It remains one of the most prominent landmarks in Holyhead.[30]

Some Welsh officers did manage to sustain active naval careers in the nineteenth-century navy, especially if they had good family and political connections. Henry Warde of Clyne Castle, Swansea, who became a lieutenant in 1811, managed to obtain several seagoing commissions in the post-war navy, thanks primarily to ferocious campaigning on his behalf by his father, a general. Even so, General Warde was convinced that Henry was denied the further promotion that he self-evidently deserved because of the evil machinations of a Scottish naval cabal headed by the First Lord of the Admiralty, Lord Melville.[31] However, connection was not necessarily everything: Henry Warde's brother Charles, who greatly distinguished himself during Lord Exmouth's attack on Algiers in 1816, failed in his attempts to obtain commissions in the post-war navy, while James Davies of Wenvoe, first lieutenant of the *Severn* during the same operation, was promoted to commander as a reward for the ship's heroics.[32] Indeed, it was still just possible for a less well-connected officer to prosper in the Regency and Victorian navies. Lewis Davies of Pembrokeshire, who had served on the 'Fighting *Temeraire*' at Trafalgar, commanded the *Rose* during the Battle of Navarino (1827) and went on to command the *Ariadne* and *Dido*.[33] The total number of Welsh commissioned officers was relatively small. It was claimed that there were only fifty-four in 1849, although this was probably an underestimate. Even in the Victorian era, some considered such personal details as their place of birth to

be no business of some prying busybody writing a directory of
the officer corps. Taken at face value, though, the figure of fifty-
four compares favourably with the numbers produced by the far
more populous kingdoms of Scotland and Ireland, which contributed just sixty-seven and sixty-four, respectively.[34]

A number of Welsh officers went on to achieve considerable
prominence. They included Lord Clarence Paget, whose career
was assisted by his stellar birth: he was a son of the Marquess
of Anglesey, hero of Waterloo, and thus a brother of Captain
Lord William and nephew of Admiral Sir Charles Paget. He
almost threw away these advantages by contracting VD as a
young man, a condition that permanently damaged his eye-
sight. Even so, Clarence Paget served in the Baltic and Black Sea
during the Crimean War, was secretary of the Admiralty from
1859 to 1866 and finally commanded the Mediterranean fleet
before returning home to Anglesey, living at Plas Llanfair just a
short distance from the family home at Plas Newydd. In 1873,
Paget, who was an accomplished amateur sculptor, designed
and had built a statue of Nelson as a seamark on the shore of
the Menai Strait, one side of which bears the Welsh inscription
A laddwyd yn Trafalgar.[35] George Mansel of Swansea entered the
navy in 1808 and, like so many of his contemporaries, eventually crawled to post-rank, in his case in 1840. However, he
then held a succession of important commands, dying in command of the great first rate *St Vincent* in 1854 when she was
transporting French troops to the Baltic during the Crimean
War.[36] Oliver Jones of Fonmon Castle, Glamorgan, fought in
the Indian Mutiny and served as commodore on the China station, eventually becoming a rear-admiral.[37] Perhaps the oddest
claim to fame – or notoriety, depending on both one's point of
view and the view from one's garden – of any Welsh Victorian
naval officer was that of Christopher Leyland of Leighton Hall,
Welshpool, who left the navy as a sub-lieutenant after ten years
of undistinguished service. In his spare time Leyland pottered
in his greenhouse, developing the new species of cypress which

was eventually named after him: that much-reviled scourge of British gardens and cause of countless disputes between neighbours, the dreaded *Leylandii*.[38]

For other officers and men, naval service ended with premature death in some far-flung corner of the world or in one of the many terrible maritime disasters that plagued the Victorian Navy. Edwin Jones of Llanbrynmair, Montgomeryshire, was killed in 1823 in the Ashanti War in what is now Ghana.[39] Charles Oliver Lloyd of Coedmore, Cardiganshire, was 15 years old when he fell to his death from the yard of HMS *Daphne* at Izmir in 1840. A memorial in Tenby's parish church records the death of Bird Allen, captain of HMS *Soudan*, who died at 'Fernando Po' (now Bioko in the Republic of Equatorial Guinea) on 25 October 1841 while 'on an expedition into the interior of Africa', having fallen victim to 'the climate of the River Niger'. In September 1870, the ironclad HMS *Captain* sank in a great storm off Cape Finisterre, taking with her Midshipman Gerald William Trevor of Rhysnant, Llandysilio, aged 20.[41] A memorial in the church of St Nicholas, Churchstoke, Powys, commemorates Commander Philip Nithsdale Wright, who took a year to die from the wounds he received during the Boxer Rebellion in China in June 1900.[42] Richard Evans of Upton Castle, Pembrokeshire, had an astonishingly lucky escape from being just another unfortunate death in some remote corner of the world. In 1881 a mysterious explosion destroyed his command, the gunboat *Doterel*, at Punta Arenas, Chile. Evans was one of only twelve survivors out of a crew of 155.[43] Another lucky escape was that of David Davies of Llantwit Major. During a battle with the ferocious Dyaks of Borneo, he was pinned to the mast by a cutlass and left there while the ship was taken and retaken. Amazingly, Davies survived and eventually retired to his native soil.[44]

No matter how far away a ship might be, Welsh sailors were always able to get letters from home and to write back with accounts of their adventures in exotic climes. In May 1843 Hugh Owens, a seaman aboard HMS *Cornwallis* at Hong Kong, wrote home to his mother at Tyddynsydra near Bangor to say that he had received four letters from her, the last in the previous December; he expected his ship to be ordered home once the 'Chine randsom is paid'.[45] Similarly, Morgan Humphries kept his uncle, a tailor in Abercynon, informed of his activities aboard HMS *Monmouth* at Hong Kong in 1909.[46] Unless one was unlucky, like Tom Powell aboard the *Redbreast*, there was usually at least one fellow *Cymro Cymraeg* aboard, too: G.F. Philipps was one of five Welsh officers aboard the *Barham* at Malta in 1836 (one of them, inevitably, was the chaplain), and one of the others was a Glamorgan man who could speak Welsh, so 'we often have a yarn in our native language, no place like Wales after all – *Cymru dros bith* [sic] is my motto.'[47]

The Crimean War

The war of 1854–56 fought between Russia on the one side and Britain and France on the other is traditionally known as 'the Crimean War', and is best remembered for one of history's greatest military blunders, the Charge of the Light Brigade. But the war was actually much more widespread, with naval action taking place not only in the Black Sea, but also in the Baltic and the Pacific. The last of these theatres of war proved to be the nemesis of one of Wales' most tragic naval men, David Powell Price of Cilycwm, Carmarthenshire. The monument to Captain William Hans Blake at Corwen is unexpected enough, but its incongruity is probably exceeded by the memorial to Price that can be found in his tiny Carmarthenshire village, hidden deep in the remote hills to the north of Llandovery. It is a long way from the sea, but an even longer way from Petropavlovsk on the Kamchatka Peninsula in Siberia:

This tablet was erected to the memory of David Powell Price, Esquire, Rear-Admiral of the White, Knight of the Redeemer

in Greece, and a Magistrate for the County of Brecon ...
His Naval Career Commenced at the Bombardment of
Copenhagen in 1801, and During the Eventful Period from
that Action to the General Peace of 1815, Actively Engaged
in a Series of Brilliant Exploits, in all of which he Displayed
the Skill, Courage and Devotion of the British Sailor ...
He Died While in Command of the Combined English and
French Squadron Before Petropavlovsk, August the 29th
1854, aged 63 Years.

However, the memorial at Cilycwm draws a tactful veil over
exactly how and why its subject perished.

At the beginning of the Crimean War, Rear-Admiral David
Powell Price found himself catapulted into high command
despite the fact that, like so many of his contemporaries, he had
not heard a shot fired in anger in forty years. Again like many of
them, he had not even been at sea for much of that time: between
1815 and 1853 Price commanded just one ship during a commission that lasted only four years (albeit one that brought him his
Greek knighthood). Serving on the Breconshire magistrates'
bench was probably not the best preparation for high command
in a war against the might of the Russian Empire, employing
a new technology – steam power – that was almost unknown
when Price last saw action. Yet when the Crimean War broke
out, David Powell Price was sent out to command a combined
Anglo-French squadron in the Pacific. By 30 August 1854, his
ships lay before the heavily fortified harbour of Petropavlovsk,
and Price held a conference with his French subordinates to discuss a strategy for attacking the enemy. When his visitors had
gone, Price closed the door of his cabin and, at one in the afternoon, shot himself. He aimed for the heart but missed; the bullet
lodged in his lungs, and he lingered until 4.30.[48] The cause of
Price's sudden suicide seemed to be a complete mystery. It has
been suggested that he was overwhelmed by the enormity of
the situation confronting him and painfully aware of his own

inadequacies, notably his lack of recent experience of command and warfare. But it seems that this was not the true cause of Price's sudden breakdown: instead, he apparently found his French allies so exasperating that he decided shooting himself dead was the only way to escape from their incessant niggling.[49]

Other Welshmen fared rather better in the war. John Rees of Llandeilo was surgeon of the flagship and inspector-general of the fleet in the Black Sea. William Robert Mends of Haverfordwest commanded the *Arethusa* and distinguished himself in the bombardment of Odessa on 22 April 1854, attacking the fortifications on the harbour breakwater. Thereafter he became flag captain and chief of staff to the admiral, Sir Edmund Lyons, and successfully organised the naval side of the invasion of the Crimea.[50] John Hughes Lloyd of Cymmer had the war to thank for his one and only command after forty, largely unemployed, years as a naval officer, though it was only of the *Devonshire*, an ancient 74 that had been pressed into service as a prison ship for Russian prisoners of war at Sheerness.[51]

When a new award for bravery in battle, the Victoria Cross, was instituted in January 1856, the first man ever actually to wear the new medal – as the senior member of the senior service present at the first investiture ceremony – had strong Welsh roots. Lieutenant Henry James Raby, RN, was the son and grandson of industrialists domiciled in Llanelli, although his father had fled the town (and his substantial debts) two or three years before Henry's birth at Boulogne in 1827. Young Henry joined the navy in 1842 and on 18 June 1855 was serving ashore as part of the Naval Brigade besieging Sebastopol. Observing a wounded soldier stuck between the lines and crying out for help, Raby and two seamen ran out across 70 yards of open ground under constant enemy fire and successfully brought the soldier back to the British trenches. His Victoria Cross was gazetted on 24 February 1857. The investiture proved to be rather more painful than the action for which he was being rewarded, as the Queen pinned the medal straight into his chest.[52] Raby never forgot his Llanelli connections. At the time of his investiture, he owned thirty-six cottages in the town; he returned there in 1878, visiting the dock, furnace and streets that his grandfather had created, and was greeted everywhere by cheering crowds.[53] Henry James Raby died at Southsea in 1907 and is buried in Highland Road cemetery there, but a plaque in Llanelli Town Hall also commemorates him.

The War Against the Slave Trade

Britain outlawed the slave trade in 1807, but lax policing by Spain and Portugal in particular ensured that it continued on a significant scale. In 1819, therefore, a dedicated unit of the Royal Navy, the Preventive Squadron, was established and tasked with patrolling the west coast of Africa to stamp out the slave trade once and for all.[54] One of the Preventive Squadron's first flagships, in 1823–24, was HMS *Owen Glendower*, and flying his broad pennant in her was a man who would have been well aware of the significance of her name: Commodore Sir Robert Mends of Haverfordwest, uncle of the Crimean War hero. Another officer aboard the ship was Cheesman Henry Binstead, a midshipman who left a vivid diary of *Glendower*'s battle against the slavers. Binstead was often employed in the boat expeditions that went up African rivers, the *Glendower* being too large to navigate upstream. As well as contending with heat and torrential rain, mosquitoes and disease, Binstead and the crew also had to come to terms with the unutterable horror of slavery. A local 'king' told him, 'Suppose you give me musket or coat, I give you good slave man or woman.'[55] But far worse than such casual inhumanity was the spectacle that confronted *Glendower*'s men aboard slave ships and in the slaving stations along the coast.

> [14 May] … at daylight observed the boats board a large Portuguese Brig laying at anchor, she proved to be a slaver

from Rio having on board 320 men, women and children …
I never witnessed a more horrid description than my mess-
mates gave me of the wretched state they were in onboard
actually dying 10–12 a day owing to the confinement below
all the men are in irons and women under them by a small
partition … [4 July] … in less than two hours 181 slaves were
brought off most of them women and children from 3 to 15
years old. I wasn't at the whole proceedings and could not but
feel for the poor creatures, to see them torn from their relations and forced on board to see Father and Mother fighting
for their children was enough to draw pity from the coldest
heart to hear these cries and lamentations were such I never
again hope to see.[56]

Service in the Preventive Squadron took a heavy toll. The
Glendower was ravaged by fever, with sharks trailing her in
the knowledge that yet another body would be thrown overboard sooner rather than later. Mends himself succumbed in
September 1823, followed a few weeks later by his teenage son,
who had been serving as one of his lieutenants. When the ship
returned home in the autumn of 1824, Binstead was one of the
few who had managed to live through the entire commission.

Henry James Raby, VC, commanded HMS *Alecto* in the
Preventive Squadron in the 1860s. In April 1861, he took part
in an attack on the slaving port of Porto Novo in Dahomey.
The naval expedition faced down a local army of some 10,000
men, bombarded the royal palace and ultimately forced the king
to agree to a treaty which ended the slave trade from the port.
Raby was wounded during the action and added a Mention in
Despatches to his Victoria Cross. He stayed on the station for
several years, subsequently commanding the *Adventure*. But the
defeat of the Confederacy during the American Civil War and
the British annexation of Lagos (1861) led to the collapse of much
of the remaining slave trade from West Africa, and ultimately
permitted the abolition of the Preventive Squadron in 1869; its

remit was subsumed within that of the Cape Squadron. During its existence, the squadron had liberated some 160,000 slaves, albeit at the cost of the lives of some 17,000 British seamen.

'Welsh' Warships

Both the second and third HMS *Cambrian* were launched at Pembroke Dock, in 1841 and 1893, respectively (as, indeed, was the fourth, a light cruiser launched in 1916).[57] Another Pembroke ship was the *Dragon* of 1845, a paddle frigate which took part in the bombardment of Sveaborg during the Crimean War.[58] While the previous *Dragon*'s figurehead had actually been St George, that of the 1845 ship was unashamedly 'a full-length winged dragon with its coiled tail running down the trailboards' – in other words, a proper 'Welsh dragon'.[59] The *Merlin* of 1838, also built at Pembroke, was another paddler, employed as a packet boat on the Liverpool station, while her successor of the same name, a sloop launched in 1901, belonged to the last class of Royal Navy warships to be fitted with figureheads. She served as a survey ship in the Far East and was sold at Hong Kong in 1923, but her figurehead survived there until about 1959, when it was apparently 'lost'.[60] The *Severn* of 1856 was the last purely sailing warship to be launched for the Royal Navy, although engines were fitted to her before completion. The next of the name was a relatively early example of a 'second-class cruiser', designed principally for trade protection or interdiction duties on overseas stations.[61] The Victorian Navy had two HMS *Druids*, both of which had undistinguished careers, a *Newport* which served as a survey ship, and the second HMS *Conway*, which saw extensive service in the Americas, East Indies and Africa, including anti-slavery duties, before becoming a training ship for the mercantile marine at Liverpool.[62]

New additions to the Navy List included HMS *Caradoc* and HMS *Llewelyn*, both built as packet boats for the

Holyhead–Dublin service and launched in 1847 and 1848, respectively; but the packet service was 'privatised' soon after they went into service, and *Llewelyn* was sold to an Irish ferry company. *Caradoc*, though, was refitted as a gunboat for Mediterranean service and took part in the Crimean campaign. Curiously, her figurehead – which still survives at the National Museum of the Royal Navy, Portsmouth – portrays 'a turbaned male bust', perhaps suggesting that someone in the Admiralty had a fairly hazy grasp of early Welsh history.[63] Meanwhile, the rapid changes in naval technology had a significant impact on the navy's next *Prince of Wales*, laid down at Portsmouth in 1848 as a great first rate sailing ship of 120 guns, but ordered to be converted for steam propulsion in 1856. Launched in 1860, she never went to sea; her engines were removed in 1867 and she later became a training ship on the River Dart, renamed *Britannia*. She thus gave her name to the purpose-built training college which succeeded her at the beginning of the twentieth century, and which still trains all of the Royal Navy's officers.[64]

From 1900 to 1914, a number of cruiser classes were given geographical names, and some 8 per cent of those were Welsh: a proportion identical to the Scots and Irish names, which arguably should have been rather better represented. The traditional name of *Monmouth* was revived for the namesake of a class of ten large (but severely undergunned) armoured cruisers, while the new name of *Carnarvon* was given to a Devonshire-class armoured cruiser launched in 1903.[65] This was part of a deliberate new policy of 'inclusiveness' towards the non-English components of the United Kingdom and a reflection of the lively national debate in the 1890s and 1900s over the tension between 'Englishness' and 'Britishness'.[66] The name *Prince of Wales* was also employed anew, this time for a battleship launched in 1902. Like all ships of her type, she was rendered obsolete by the launch of HMS *Dreadnought* in 1906, but saw service in the Atlantic and Mediterranean, often as a flagship, before the First World War broke out.

The creation of substantial training establishments at the end of the nineteenth and beginning of the twentieth century reflected the steadily increasing division of the navy into specialist branches. It took some decades before they eventually moved into purpose-built accommodation ashore, and in the interim such establishments were housed in the hulks of retired warships. Two of the most prominent were given Welsh names. *Fisgard* derived its name from the frigate launched at Pembroke Dock in 1819, which spent much of her career as a harbour flagship before being broken up in 1879.[67] Commissioned as a base in 1904, *Fisgard* was initially a torpedo boat depot at Harwich, but in 1905 it became an artificers' training school at Portsmouth, based in a variety of old hulked warships until it moved ashore in 1931. The establishment moved to Torpoint in 1940 and was recommissioned as *Fisgard* in 1946, serving until its closure in 1983.[68] Also hauling down the White Ensign for the last time in that year was HMS *Pembroke*, the naval barracks at Chatham. She had taken her name from the navy's seventh *Pembroke*, a 74-gun third rate launched in 1812 which ultimately became the harbour flagship of the reserve at Chatham.

King Coal

Many factors contributed to the rise of the Welsh coal industry during the nineteenth century: to existing markets like iron, steel and other heavy industries were added new ones like the rapidly expanding railways and the production of gas for urban lighting.[69] But one of the most important reasons for the expansion of the South Wales coalfield was the adoption of its steam coal by merchant shipping and above all by the Royal Navy, which had introduced its first steam ships in the 1820s. The superiority of Welsh steam coal was indisputably one of the most important reasons for the unchallenged dominance of the Royal Navy from 1815 to 1914, when for a long period it was official policy that the navy should be larger than the world's second and third largest navies combined. It was undoubtedly the time when the connection between Wales and the navy was at its strongest, and it shaped the economy, geography and demographics of Wales in ways that still impact the present day.

Initially, the different coalfields of Great Britain competed for naval custom, but in the mid-1840s, when the navy was moving to screw propulsion, a series of independent trials took place. These were conducted on over one hundred coals, a third of them Welsh, and overseen by the geologist Sir Henry de la Beche and the scientist and politician Lyon Playfair. Their three reports, published in 1848, 1849 and 1851, proclaimed the superiority of Welsh steam coal for naval purposes: above all, it was virtually smokeless, an invaluable asset for a warship wishing to approach an enemy unseen. Unsurprisingly, rival interests, particularly the coalowners and MPs from the north-east of England, demurred from this opinion, and their pressure forced further tests and the adoption of a mixture of two-thirds Welsh to one-third northern coal. The opinion of naval officers, however, based on rapidly increasing experience of the merits of the different varieties, together with aggressive counter-lobbying by Welsh MPs (notably Richard Fothergill, the Merthyr ironmaster and coal owner) contributed to Welsh coal's ultimate triumph.[70] By the 1870s and 1880s, Welsh steam coal was universally acknowledged to be by far the best fuel for modern warships, and government policy increasingly reflected this truth.

The consequences of coal mining's expansion for both the economy and appearance of the South Wales valleys were far-reaching. Output rose from 8.5 million tons in 1854 to 56,830,000 in 1913, employment from 26,186 in 1841 to 234,114 in 1914. Before 1848, there were just thirteen collieries in the Rhondda valley; in the following twenty-five years, another fifty opened, and by 1908 there were no fewer than 667 collieries throughout South Wales and Monmouthshire.[71] A select number of these, all within a relatively small area of 150 square miles in East Glamorgan and Monmouthshire, were placed on the 'Admiralty List' of those producing the first-class steam coal that the navy required. The list changed from time to time: in 1876, eleven Monmouthshire coals appeared on it, but in 1903 there were none.[72] By 1904, Admiralty-quality coal accounted for just under half the total production of the South Wales coalfield. By no means all of this went to the Royal Navy; in 1904, for example, the service took just 1,117,000 tons out of the 18 million tons of Admiralty-quality steam coal produced in South Wales, but other significant proportions went to commercial steamship companies and to the French, Italian, Spanish, Russian and other friendly navies.[73] Among those to benefit most spectacularly from the expansion of the coalfield were the Marquesses of Bute, who, despite their Scottish antecedents, had also inherited extensive mineral rights in Glamorgan. The second marquess died in 1848, just before Welsh coal's ascendancy began, but he had already been responsible for the building of the first Bute dock at Cardiff and had a keen interest in the navy; two of his uncles were senior naval officers, and one of them had been MP for Cardiff from 1802 to 1814. The third marquess was the driving force behind the construction of another four docks, which led to an increase in coal shipments through Cardiff – many of them destined for the royal dockyards and the navy's worldwide network of coaling stations – from 44,350 tons in 1840 to 2.2 million in 1870 and 10.7 million in 1913.

The need to get Welsh coal more rapidly to the royal dockyards (and to commercial harbours like Southampton, to meet the demands of increasing numbers of ever larger Atlantic liners) helped shape the development of the railway system in both South Wales, where a bewildering myriad of lines was created to connect the valleys with each other and above all to run down to the coal ports, and the south of England. Providing a more direct route for Valleys coal to Portsmouth and the new fleet base at Portland was one of the key imperatives that drove the construction of the Severn railway tunnel, which was begun in 1873 and finally opened in 1886. Tests took place to see how quickly coal could be moved to the fleet along the new route; for the 1890 fleet manoeuvres, ten trains carrying 3,000 tons of coal ran directly from the Valleys to Portland, taking just twelve hours to get from the colliery to the quayside.[74] But this was only part of the story. The very establishment of the entirely new base at Portland, rather than any other location – a base designed explicitly as a purpose-built coaling harbour – was driven primarily by the transportation costs of South Wales steam coal. In 1857, the cost per ton of moving coal by train to Portsmouth was 12s 6d, to Devonport 14s, but to Portland only 11s.[75] Wars and international crises were good news for Welsh coalowners and miners alike. During the Boer War, the Admiralty's need for coal to supply the additional troopships going out to South Africa greatly boosted demand; during the Russo-Japanese War of 1904–05, both sides acquired large amounts of coal for their navies using third parties to buy it on the Cardiff exchange and using false neutral destinations in Indo-China.[76]

The navy's dependence on coal, and Welsh coal in particular, demanded an elaborate global infrastructure that went far beyond the expansion of the railway network. Fleets of colliers were needed to accompany the fleets, and this made the fortune of several Welsh shipowners and shipping companies like J T Duncan of Cardiff.[77] Welsh coal needed to be constantly available at coaling stations around the globe, meaning that supplies could be found at such locations as Vancouver, Halifax, Bermuda, the Bahamas, Jamaica, Ascension, the Falkland Islands, Gibraltar, Malta, Suez, Aden, Trincomalee, Bombay, Singapore and Hong Kong, as well as at ports not under the British flag such as Luanda in West Africa and Yokohama in Japan. The United States Navy also depended heavily on Welsh steam coal: its intervention in the 1900 Boxer Rebellion in China was hamstrung by the fact that it had to supply its warships with coal from Cardiff, 14,000 miles away.[78] One of the great Welsh 'urban myths' is that the world's first one million pound cheque supposedly changed hands at the Coal Exchange in Cardiff some time in the first decade of the twentieth century, but it has also been suggested that the payer in the colossal transaction was the United States Navy, which experienced great difficulty with coaling President Theodore Roosevelt's 'Great White Fleet' that circumnavigated the globe between 1907 and 1909.[79]

By the first quarter of the twentieth century, miners were perhaps the most organised, powerful and militant of all the major industrial occupations, as demonstrated by the long saga of titanic disputes that culminated in the general strike of 1926; and indeed, the miners were largely to retain this reputation until the strike of 1984–85 and the subsequent virtual demise of the industry. Yet it was deeply ironic that in South Wales, at least in the period until the end of the First World War, the jobs and communities for which the increasingly militant unions claimed to be fighting were sustained largely by the demands of what was then the mightiest war machine the world had ever seen, the British Royal Navy. The pay packets that provided for families from Resolven to Pontypool (and filled the collection plates of the Valleys chapels on Sundays) contained considerable sums that came from Admiralty contracts. Ultimately, the catastrophic contraction in the mining industry in the 1920s and 1930s was due to many factors – underinvestment by the mine owners, outdated methods and equipment, cheap and efficient foreign competition – but one of the most important was the fact that the market which had been one of the mainstays of the southern coalfield since the 1850s had disappeared in just a few short years.

The Royal Navy's decision to switch to oil propulsion did not happen overnight. It had been discussed for many years: trials of oil propulsion took place in 1903 aboard the Pembroke-built battleship *Hannibal* and, significantly, it was a nervous MP for Merthyr Tydfil who asked a parliamentary question about their outcome, 'in respect to freedom from smoke, speed, and cost as compared with best smokeless Welsh coal'.[80] The physical process of coaling ship was dirty, prolonged and essentially impossible to accomplish while under way at sea, despite many attempts to devise a satisfactory method for carrying it out. Oil, on the other hand, was much cleaner and permitted ships to reach higher speeds while also allowing them to be refuelled under way. Against that, coal was from tried, trusted and above all secure domestic sources; oil could only be obtained in far away, inhospitable and frequently hostile lands, with countless political and geographical obstacles in the way of transporting it thousands of miles to the British Isles. When Winston Churchill became First Lord of the Admiralty in 1911, he was swiftly won over to the case for oil, partly due to the persuasion of the former First Sea Lord, Sir John 'Jackie' Fisher. The first class of oil-powered battleships, the Queen Elizabeths, was ordered in 1912. Churchill's decision to go for oil was followed in short order by the outbreak of the First World War. The catastrophic losses of older, coal-powered ships led to their replacement by oil-burners, accelerating a trend that might otherwise have had a less rapid impact on the prospects for the South Wales coalfield.[81]

The switch to oil was a devastating blow to the long-term prospects of the South Wales coalfield: the Royal Navy's demand for coal declined from 1.9 million tons in 1913 to 1,068,000 in 1919 and only 167,000 in 1930, although a small number of naval vessels still used coal propulsion until the end of the 1960s.[82] Other navies that had traditionally provided a significant market for Welsh coal, notably the French, also switched to oil, as did many of the large shipping lines. There were rearguard attempts to persuade the navy to change its mind and, unsurprisingly, several of them originated in Wales: there was a vigorous 'Back to Coal' campaign in the early 1930s, together with brief but illusory hopes that it might be possible to convert coal to oil on a large scale, and these issues were debated in Parliament on several occasions.[83] But it was to no avail. The wisdom of Churchill's decision is still argued over today, given the fact that it made Britain – and ultimately the other western navies and economies

– dependent on oil from the Persian Gulf and thus inexorably bound up with the fragile geopolitics of that region, with consequences that still largely dominate western strategic thinking. Nevertheless, the change to oil brought some limited short-term compensation to South Wales. Between 1918 and 1922, William Knox D'Arcy's Anglo-Persian Oil Company, which was *de facto* under government control, built Britain's first oil refinery near Swansea docks, on a barren patch of upland near Neath which was named Llandarcy after its immodest creator. For a time, the refinery held a monopoly on the supply of refined oil to the Royal Navy. Thus, even in the new age of oil power, Wales continued to play an essential role in propelling the fleet.

The Welsh and Naval Technology

A major new industry was established in the Valleys in 1818 when the Brown, Lenox chain works opened at Pontypridd. While serving as a naval lieutenant, Samuel Brown persuaded the owners of two small North Shields colliers to fit their vessels with iron rigging, and in February 1808 he equipped the merchantman *Penelope* with iron standing rigging and anchor-cables prior to her making a four-month voyage to the West Indies. These trials proved successful, and in 1809 Brown published a monograph advancing the merit of chain cable, including the use of swivels and means of controlling the speed with which it ran out. One reason for seeking a substitute for hemp was Napoleon's attempt, following the Treaty of Tilsit in 1807, to impose an embargo on the export of naval stores from Russia to Britain. In the event, this Continental Blockade was ineffective but it played its part in awakening commercial interest in a substitute for hemp at that particular juncture.[84] In 1812, Brown retired from the navy and with his cousin Samuel Lenox entered into industrial scale manufacture of chain, moving to Pontypridd to be near the plentiful supplies of iron and coal that the South

Wales valleys could provide. Brown, Lenox & Co. had its own
basin on the Glamorganshire canal, from which the chains could
be taken down to Cardiff for onward shipment to the royal dockyards. The firm retained its monopoly on the supply of chain
to the Admiralty well into the twentieth century, and supplied
other fleets too: many ships of the German High Seas fleet in
the First World War were equipped with Brown, Lenox cables.[85]
A 1929 advertisement trumpeted the firm's production of the
world's strongest chain as well as its pedigree in supplying the
navy's largest warships, the *Nelson*, *Rodney* and *Hood*. The factory
also supplied many of the great ocean liners, including the *Great
Eastern*, *Lusitania*, *Mauretania*, *Queen Mary* and finally the *QE2*, its
last major order. The business ultimately closed in 2000.

Muntz metal, an improved form of sheathing with about
60 per cent copper and 40 per cent zinc, was partly developed
at the Middle Bank and Upper Bank works in Swansea from the
1830s onwards. It was much used by the navy and also in merchant ships, most famously the *Cutty Sark*.[86] Robert Griffiths,
of Lleweni in the Vale of Clwyd, developed an improved form
of screw propulsion that was adopted by the navy from 1849
onwards; he was also responsible for the improved propeller that
was fitted to Brunel's SS *Great Britain* in 1853.[87] From his works
at Smethwick he produced the screws for HMS *Warrior*, Britain's
first ironclad, and her sister ship *Black Prince*; at the time of its
manufacture, the 10-ton screw for the *Warrior* was the largest
hoisting propeller ever made.[88] At much the same time, John
Hughes, a former apprentice at the Cyfarthfa ironworks who
had risen to become a director of the Millwall Engineering and
Shipbuilding Company, was responsible for the iron cladding
of many warships of the 1860s and the gun mountings fitted to
them. So impressive was Hughes' reputation that the Russian
government effectively 'headhunted' him, initially to provide
plating for the naval fortress at Kronstadt. In 1869, Hughes went
to the Don basin to set up ironworks and a new town to accommodate the British workers who accompanied him; the town

was named Hughesovka (Yuzovka) after him, although it is now
called Donetsk. Another Welsh engineer who made a significant
contribution to European navies was John Evans, a fitter from
Aberdare who worked for the Russian, Spanish and Ottoman
navies, and ran the Union blockade several times during the
American Civil War, before returning home to become assistant
engineer at Cardiff's Bute Docks.[89] Meanwhile, the Welsh coast
became the graveyard of one of the prototypes of arguably the
most important new naval technology of the nineteenth century: the submarine *Resurgam*, a private venture built by the
Reverend George Garrett in the hope of attracting naval interest, sank some 6 miles north of Rhyl on 25 February 1880. The
wreck remained undiscovered until the 1990s.[90]

Palmerston's Follies

Until the middle of the nineteenth century, Wales was largely
bare of coastal defences against naval attack. There were some
fortifications on Milford Haven, guarding that harbour and the
new royal dockyard (*see Chapter 6*), as well as eighteenth-century
batteries at Fort Belan and Fishguard, but that was all. However,
the rapid expansion of the South Wales coalfield and the ports
that served it, notably Cardiff, was something of a double-edged
sword, for it was immediately apparent that this new prosperity, and above all the importance of Welsh coal supplies to the
Royal Navy, made the south coast a much more likely target for
an enemy attack. A sudden raid by light, fast cruisers of a hostile power (usually unnamed, but of course implicitly assumed
to be France) might lead to the capture or destruction of the
port of Cardiff, which might have untold consequences for the
fleet's ability to operate.[91] Meanwhile, the Crimean War seemed
to teach the lesson that powerful coastal defences could repel,
or at least delay, an attacking fleet. The upshot was a clamour
for greatly enhanced fortifications around Pembroke Dock and

Milford Haven, which led to extensive works there from 1848 to the 1870s (see Chapter 6), and also for new defences in the Bristol Channel. In 1852 the civic authorities at Swansea petitioned for a battery on Mumbles Head, and in 1854 and 1861 reports recommended the construction of fortifications to defend major commercial harbours, including Cardiff and Swansea.[92] Work began on the Mumbles battery, a semi-circular, two storey structure initially equipped with five 80-pounder guns, in 1859. Lavernock and Flat Holm batteries were built between 1866 and 1871 and could provide a cross-fire covering the approaches to Cardiff, while Brean Down and Steep Holm batteries provided similar cover for Bristol. Rapid changes in technology during the latter part of the nineteenth century ensured that the armament fitted to these batteries changed frequently. By 1899, the chief perceived threat was an attack by torpedo boats so smaller calibre, quicker-firing guns were installed, and a new fort, manned by the Royal Garrison Artillery, was built on Penarth Head in 1902.[93] However, the chief claim to fame of the Severn forts turned out to be a peaceful one: on 11 May 1879, Guglielmo Marconi made the first ever wireless transmission over water between Lavernock and Flat Holm. The other new fort designed to protect the Welsh coast from naval attack was that on St Catherine's Island, Tenby, built in 1867 as part of a projected outer ring to guard the southern flank of Milford Haven and Pembroke Dock. The remaining forts at Lydstep, Freshwater Bay and on Caldey Island were never even started, leaving Tenby's fort as an isolated curiosity that has intrigued generations of holidaymakers.

Milford's Mock Wars

By the middle of the nineteenth century, Milford Haven was a regular port of call during the summer cruises of the Channel Fleet; indeed, the anchorage directly opposite the town's foreshore is still known as 'Man of War Roads'. The holding of large-scale annual fleet training manoeuvres began in 1885, and in the following year Milford Haven was used as their base.[94] Thereafter, and for most of the period down to 1914, increasingly elaborate 'war games' were played out around the British Isles every summer, and Milford often played a key role in these. For several days, stretching towards a fortnight by the turn of the century, long lines of battleships, cruisers and smaller ships anchored in the haven, effectively depositing a new town of over 20,000 men into the heart of Pembrokeshire literally overnight. The exercises were important opportunities for the navy to refine its responses to the many new technologies that were introduced in the thirty years before the outbreak of the First World War. The 1886 manoeuvres focused on whether a port could be defended passively, by its fortifications, minefields and torpedo boats; the conclusions were that it could not, and that an aggressive navy could successfully storm it.[95] In 1899, the exercises were concerned principally with the defence of convoys and the potential uses of the wireless in naval warfare.[96] The 1904 manoeuvres demonstrated the potential power of a relatively new weapon, the submarine. Milford Haven played the part of a port under close blockade, and a flotilla of eight submarines was based there. This struck such terror into the 'enemy' fleet that it failed to achieve its aim and impose the blockade, despite the fact that the submarines never left Milford at all; their effect was entirely psychological.[97] Regardless of their long-term impact on strategic thinking, the manoeuvres provided a significant short-term boost to the local economy. Tourists flocked to Milford to watch the war games, officers were billeted in local hotels and houses, and local tradesmen made a killing: in 1899 they were said to have made over £5,000 during the two weeks of the fleet's presence.[98] Although the annual manoeuvres ceased before the First World War, Milford was occasionally used thereafter as a base for naval exercises. In 1930, for

example, the battlecruisers *Renown*, *Repulse* and *Tiger*, together
with fourteen destroyers, anchored in Dale Roads.[99]

Guardships, Training Ships and *Yr Hen Iaith*: The Navy as a Presence in Victorian Wales

The navy had maintained guardships at its dockyards for many
years. An invasion scare in the 1840s led to a report which recommended floating batteries to enhance the defences of the
yards, and as a result the old 74 *Saturn* was deployed to guard
Pembroke Dock.[100] She was later replaced by the *Eagle*, another
distinguished old 74-gun ship-of-the-line; when the latter left
in 1860 she was replaced by the *Blenheim*. The Pembroke-built
Revenge returned to her birthplace to take up the role in 1865.
Subsequent port guardships included *Bellerophon* (1892–93),
Rupert (1893–95), the Pembroke-built *Thunderer* (1895–97) and
the last of all, the *Hood* (1897–1901)[101] But by then Milford was
not the only harbour in Wales with a battleship more or less
permanently moored in its waters. In 1856 the Coastguard was
transformed into a reserve for the navy, and was given a dedicated squadron of old warships based in important commercial
harbours around the British Isles.[102] A guardship was allocated
to the Mersey, but as the port of Liverpool expanded that waterway became ever more congested, so in 1884 the decision was
taken to move it to Holyhead.[103] The *Hotspur* and *Defence* served
there in the mid-1880s, being succeeded by the *Neptune*, which
in turn was replaced in 1893 by the *Colossus*; she was relieved by
Resolution in 1901, with *Edgar* serving until the system of guardships was abolished in 1903. The guardships became a part of
the social life of Anglesey: in October 1895, for example, the
crew of *Colossus* staged a concert for the local community.[104]
Indeed, for the regular naval men assigned to these ships, duties
could be remarkably light – sometimes frustratingly so. Tristan
Dannreuther, commanding *Colossus*' tender HMS *Foxhound* at

Holyhead in 1893–94, described the ship's activities as 'wandering around in general' and 'doing nothing in particular'; occasional voyages to supply coastguard stations with ordnance stores left him plenty of time to climb Snowdon and improve his tennis game, while longer cruises to Stornoway provided perfect opportunities for grouse shooting parties in the Hebrides.[105]

A number of other warships became more or less permanent fixtures in Welsh waters. In 1866 an old frigate loaned by the Admiralty, the Pembroke Dock-built *Hamadryad*, was moored in Cardiff docks as a dedicated seamen's hospital for the growing port. Fitted out for up to sixty-five patients, she was grounded on the foreshore of what became Tiger Bay and financed by contributions of 2 shillings for every 100 tons of registered shipping. Long past the date at which she had become overcrowded and unhygienic, the *Hamadryad* was finally broken up in 1905, but her figurehead has been preserved as an exhibit at the National Museum of Wales. During her time in Cardiff, the ship had accommodated 173,000 patients from all over the world.[106] The notion of training young offenders and other destitute youngsters for service in the royal and merchant navies was a relatively old one, but it was given a new impetus by various acts of Parliament of the 1850s and 1860s which established reformatory schools (for offenders) and industrial schools (for others). Several of these were established in ships around the British coast. HMS *Havannah*, a frigate launched in 1811, became a school ship at Cardiff in 1860, moored just south of Penarth Bridge, and remained there until she was broken up in 1905; a modern housing development, Havannah Quay, commemorates the ship, just as nearby Hamadryad Park remembers the hospital. The third old warship moored in the port of Cardiff in the last decades of the nineteenth century was HMS *Thisbe*, a 46-gun frigate launched in 1824 which was loaned in 1863 to the Missions to Seamen and remained in the West Dock for twenty-nine years, providing meals and shelter for mariners and sending missionaries out into the communities around the docks.[107] In the north, HMS *Clio*, a corvette launched in 1858, became an industrial training ship in the Menai Strait in 1877. The boys aboard her, most of them drawn from the industrial cities of England, were kept busy and followed a strict curriculum which included regular cutlass and gun drill. Changing attitudes to schooling led to the abolition of the 'industrial schools' after the First World War, and the *Clio* was broken up at Bangor in 1920.[108]

The naval presence in North Wales was greatly enhanced after 1862 when a Royal Naval Reserve battery was established at Caernarfon. This was largely at the instigation of Llewelyn Turner, a prominent local dignitary who served as Commodore of the Royal Welsh Yacht Club and had also been behind the previous attempt to establish a naval reserve in the area, the formation in 1854 of a body of coast volunteers. (Turner was later knighted, partly for his sterling efforts in encouraging naval recruitment.)[109] The Caernarfon battery of the RNR proved very popular, possibly because RNR service provided a decent pension of £12 per annum after only twelve years' service. It recruited primarily from the Caernarfon and Bangor areas, but also drew in significant bodies of men from Anglesey and even from the Cardiganshire coast down to Borth and Aberystwyth.[110] The battery continued in service until 1909, when the reserves were reorganised once again.

The Caernarfon battery's involvement in the local community, and indeed its very existence in the traditional heartland of Welsh culture and language, is one of the most telling proofs of a surprisingly positive relationship between 'Welshness' and the Royal Navy. In 1886, for example, the RNR battery provided an honour guard for the Caernarfon Eisteddfod (with music by the band of the 4th Battalion, the Royal Welsh Fusiliers), and in 1897 the prize essay at the Dolgellau Eisteddfod was entitled 'The British Navy', probably not a topic that would have impressed the judges at many future *eisteddfodau*.[111] Indeed, throughout the nineteenth century relations between what

might be termed the Welsh cultural establishment on the one
hand, and the Royal Navy on the other, were often significantly
better than one might assume. There was even a small genre of
naval writing in the Welsh language. In 1826, for instance, the
Reverend William Rees, '*Gwilym Hiraethog*', won the Brecon
Eisteddfod for a poem on Nelson and Trafalgar.[112] The Battle of
Navarino in the following year led to the composition and publication of several poems in Welsh, one of which won second
place at the Brecon Eisteddfod of 1828:

> Magneliau, drylliau (nid oerllyd) – godent
> Ar y gwaedgwn ynfyd;
> Llifai eu gwaed oll hefyd
> Gwnae'r môr yn gochfôr I gyd.

> [Cannons and guns, which were red hot, raised
> Towards the bloody mad dogs;
> All of their blood flowed too,
> Making the sea red all over.][113]

In June 1876, the magazine *Y Darlunydd* published '*Yn Helynt
Trafalgar*', a poem about the battle,[114] and the burgeoning
Welsh-language press frequently carried naval material. *Baner
ac Amserau Cymru*, established under that title in 1859, soon
became a powerful influence in Wales, consistently supporting
Liberal, even radical and Nonconformist principles. But it also
frequently reported on naval matters. Soon after its establishment, in August 1859, it provided a comparison between the
British and French navies, and it invariably printed detailed
coverage of the naval estimates, Parliamentary debates about
the navy and specific naval events, for example by running a
lengthy editorial on the sinking of HMS *Captain* in 1870.[115]
Thus the Victorian Navy and the issues surrounding it would
have been entirely familiar to a Welsh readership, and by the
1890s even the Conservative Party was publishing election

literature on naval matters in Welsh. It is therefore probable that an educated Welsh speaker of the second half of the nineteenth century would have been far better informed about, and possibly more sympathetic towards, the nature and role of the navy than his modern counterpart.[116]

There was even a naval presence in the chapels. In the early 1800s the Wesleyan Methodists at Ludchurch were led by a Mr Tribe, who was said to have served as a coxswain under Nelson.[117] James Oakey, a half-pay Master from the Navy, was a Unitarian and one of the leaders of radicalism at Merthyr Tydfil in the early decades of the nineteenth century. Arthur Augustus Rees of Cilymaenllwyd, Carmarthenshire, was a son of Captain John Rees, RN, and followed his father into the navy, serving as a midshipman in the Mediterranean before leaving the service in 1832 on health grounds. He then went into the Church, became an eminent Nonconformist preacher, and established the huge Bethesda Chapel in Sunderland.[118] Then there was James Hughes of Ciliau Aeron, Cardiganshire, who began work in the royal dockyard at Deptford in 1800, at the age of 21, and remained there for the next twenty-four years. He was converted to Calvinistic Methodism in 1806, began to preach in 1810 and was ordained in 1816, becoming a popular preacher in both London and Wales, a noted commentator on the New Testament and a writer of religious poetry.[119] He also established a Welsh Calvinistic Methodist chapel at Deptford. Indeed, Hughes was eminent enough to merit an entry in the *Dictionary of National Biography*;[120] but it is, perhaps, a comment on an abiding ambivalence towards the navy in certain quarters of Welsh society that when the entry about him was written in 1891, the author, one R.M.J. Jones, excised all mention of Hughes' naval service. By then, admitting that a great preacher might also have been perfectly content to serve that instrument of Satan, the Royal Navy, and to work at fitting out its ships for war, would have been the height of political incorrectness in Welsh chapel culture.

Geoffrey Wheatley Cobb and Naval Training

Geoffrey Wheatley Cobb was the son of Joseph Richard Cobb,
a wealthy Brecon lawyer who in the 1880s spent large sums of
money restoring Manorbier, Pembroke and Caldicot Castles,
the last of which became the family home. Geoffrey inherited
considerable wealth and used this to give expression to his deep
and lifelong passion for the sea. In 1891, the famous old sailing
warship *Foudroyant*, Nelson's flagship at Naples in 1799–1800,
was sold to be broken up, prompting a wave of protests. The
Cobbs responded by purchasing the ship and fitting her out
as a boys' training vessel, taking her around various resorts in
Britain to raise funds to maintain her. In 1897, though, she was
driven ashore at Blackpool in a storm and could not be salvaged.
Undaunted, Geoffrey purchased the sailing frigate *Trincomalee*
from the navy, renamed her *Foudroyant*, and kept her in various
harbours over the years, principally Falmouth but also briefly
at Milford Haven. In 1912 Cobb was given the *Implacable*, originally the French *Duguay-Trouin* that had escaped the Battle of
Trafalgar only to be captured a fortnight later. Throughout
the 1920s Cobb struggled to keep his training fleet afloat; the
upkeep of the large *Implacable* in particular was a constant drain
on his resources. The two ships passed to Cobb's widow after his
death in 1931 and were used once again by the navy as accommodation ships during the Second World War, but thereafter the
Admiralty proved unwilling to pay for the upkeep of *Implacable*
and she was controversially scuttled off the Isle of Wight in
1949.[121] *Foudroyant* survived, however, a permanent fixture in
Portsmouth harbour and one of the highlights of cruises around
the dockyard. She gave generations of youngsters their first
taste of sea life before being taken out of service in 1986. She
was subsequently moved to Hartlepool, restored to her original
condition, and placed on display there under her original name,
HMS *Trincomalee*. She is the oldest British warship afloat, and
Geoffrey Wheatley Cobb is still remembered aboard her: the

first thing that a visitor encounters upon boarding the ship is the legend 'Remember Nelson' on a board affixed to a deck beam, a relic from her days as *Foudroyant* and an evocative reminder of the spirit that Cobb wished to instil in the youngsters who spent time on the ship. Cobb himself is buried at Caldicot church, and a 12-pounder cannon from the original *Foudroyant* still greets the visitor passing through the gatehouse of Caldicot Castle.

Lord Cawdor and HMS *Dreadnought*

Over the years, a number of Welshmen served as Lords of the Admiralty. The third Earl of Carbery, of Golden Grove, Carmarthenshire, was one such, in 1684 and 1689–91; another was John Campbell, MP for Pembrokeshire, from 1736 to 1742. But only four Welshmen ever held the office of First Lord. The first was Arthur Herbert, Earl of Torrington, from 1689 to 1690. Over 200 years passed before the second took office, and he then held it for only eight months. However, the brief tenure of Frederick Archibald Vaughan Campbell, third Earl Cawdor, proved to have an importance out of all proportion to its duration. Cawdor was the great-grandson of the man who led the defence against the French landing at Fishguard in 1797 and thus a direct descendant of John Campbell; despite the Scottish and Shakespearean connotations of his title, his principal seat was at Stackpole Court in Pembrokeshire, and he also owned the Golden Grove estate in Carmarthenshire. Cawdor was an unusual aristocrat in that he enthusiastically embraced the worlds of business and technology.[122] In 1890 he became a director of the Great Western Railway Company, serving as chairman from 1895 to 1905, a role in which he was outstandingly successful. Appointed First Lord of the Admiralty in March 1905, he at once lent his support to the reform programme of the vigorous and highly controversial First Sea Lord, Admiral Sir Jackie Fisher, whose term of office Cawdor arranged to extend until

1910. Extensive correspondence between the two men survives in the archives at Carmarthen,[123] and reveals both the considerable mutual respect that quickly developed between them and Fisher's colourful, outspoken personality which did not suffer fools gladly.

The upshot was that Cawdor enthusiastically supported Fisher's pet project, an all-big-gun battleship that would immediately render obsolete all others (including Britain's). HMS *Dreadnought* was ordered and laid down during Cawdor's time at the Admiralty, and on 30 November 1905 he promulgated a statement of policy which became known as the Cawdor Memorandum and which committed the government to building four Dreadnoughts a year. Despite the misgivings of the Liberal government that came to office in 1906, Cawdor vigorously defended the policy, which ultimately ensured that Britain retained its superiority in battleship numbers during the First World War. His own term of office had ended in December 1905 when Balfour's Conservative government fell. Cawdor became one of the leading figures in the Conservative opposition after 1906 and, had he lived, he might well have regained high office in Lloyd George's wartime coalition; but the third Earl Cawdor died on 8 February 1911 and was buried on the hillside above Stackpole Elidor church. The death just three years later of his son and heir from syphilis presaged a century of incompetence and self-destruction that saw the family ultimately demolish Stackpole, sell all its Welsh estates, and even contrive to lose Cawdor Castle itself.[124]

Officers and Men: The Ironclad Era

A number of younger sons of the Welsh gentry and of the new moneyed industrial plutocracy of the Valleys rose to command during the ironclad era. These included Robert Owen Leach, from an old Castlemartin family, who commanded

HMS *Liverpool* in the 1860s,[125] and John Crawshay Bailey of Glanusk, son of the owner of the Nant-y-Glo ironworks and a great-nephew of the famous ironmaster Richard Crawshay.[126] Price Vaughan Lewes from Felinfach, Cardiganshire, joined the navy in 1878. He won the DSO for his gallantry at Zanzibar in 1893, and when Crete rebelled against the Ottoman Empire in 1898, Lewes' command, the gunboat HMS *Hazard*, was despatched there in order to bring the customs house under international regulation. A mob attacked the British party ashore, so *Hazard* opened fire on the town. Lewes was promoted to commander for his gallantry; his surgeon won the Victoria Cross. At the beginning of the First World War, Lewes was captain of the modern Dreadnought HMS *Superb*, although in reality he was on sick leave at Laugharne, his favourite vacation home. Lewes struggled back to his ship but soon had to be invalided ashore, dying at the naval hospital in Plymouth on 10 November 1914.[127] Algernon Walker-Heneage-Vivian was the son of Henrietta Vivian of Singleton, Swansea, and her soldier husband. In 1900 he was part of the naval contingent sent from HMS *Powerful* to defend Ladysmith against the Boers, and was mentioned in despatches for his gallantry. He subsequently distinguished himself during the Gallipoli campaign in the First World War. Algernon ultimately inherited both Parc Le Breos on the Gower and Clyne Castle from his Vivian relatives and became a prominent figure in Swansea, for example serving as High Sheriff of Glamorgan, chairman of the South West Wales Savings Bank, and becoming the first president of the Gower Society. He died in 1952, after which Clyne Castle was sold to Swansea University.[128]

Another Welsh officer who distinguished himself during the Boer War – and, indeed, most of the others that occurred during his astonishing life – was Walter Henry Cowan, the son of an army officer resident at Crickhowell and his wife, the local doctor's daughter. 'A ferocious midget who loved war so much that he spent his leave periods in the trenches in France and wept when the Armistice was announced,' Cowan's early career reads like a travelogue of Queen Victoria's imperial conflicts.[129] From 1894–97, he was on the coast of Africa, taking part in three bloody punitive expeditions against local tribes on the likes of the Niger and Benin rivers. He then went to Egypt in command of a river gunboat on the Nile and took part in the Battle of Omdurman before confronting a squadron of French gunboats at Fashoda. Cowan effectively had the responsibility for persuading them to retire from the disputed area, thus potentially averting a catastrophic war between the two great powers. In 1900, he went to South Africa to take part in the Boer War as Kitchener's aide-de-camp; unfortunately he had not told the Admiralty that he intended to do this, nor sought their permission to be away from the sea for two years, and their lordships were not amused. Cowan's career did not suffer markedly, though, and he held a succession of commands prior to 1914. During the First World War he commanded the battlecruiser *Princess Royal* at Jutland, where she was severely damaged, and then commanded a cruiser squadron in the North Sea before commanding in the Baltic in 1919 against the Russian Bolsheviks. In 1939, though he was a retired admiral aged 68, Cowan insisted on returning to active service as a mere commander and served in North Africa, being captured at Bir Hakeim in 1942. Freed the following year, he immediately joined commando operations in the Dalmatian Islands, despite then being 72. Cowan retired definitively in 1945 and died in 1956; astonishingly, during almost exactly sixty years of naval and military service he was never wounded.[130]

Despite regularly bumping along at or near the bottom of his class at the naval college in Dartmouth, by 1913 Hugh Heaton of Plas Heaton, near Trefnant in Denbighshire, was a sub-lieutenant aboard the battlecruiser *Indomitable*, which found itself playing host to a particularly controversial First Lord of the Admiralty:

[Heaton] was on the fore bridge from 12.30 midnight to 5.30 am ... at 3.30 however just as I was beginning to pray for a speedy death up rolled Churchill, saw me looking like a lost sheep and came and had a yarn. He is an interesting man and withal possessed of an intense low cunning, whereby he bowled me out rather badly. He was very much interested in the navigation of the ship which I explained to him at some length & then became very much interested in our sounding machine. I also explained this to him, with some beautiful fancy touches of my own, which would I thought sound particularly comic if he ever reproduced them in the House in answer to a question. He however routed me horse and gun at the conclusion of the address by turning round to me & saying 'Let's see, you are fitted with Lord Kelvin's patent machine aren't you?', at which it immediately dawned on me that he was not quite as green as he pretended to be.

It was moments like this that evidently contributed to Heaton's Damascene conversion upon the subject of the future Prime Minister:

I have entirely changed my opinion of Churchill since I have had anything at all to do with the man. I must say that I am still very certain that the man is a knave; but on the other hand I think him a very able one. I always imagined him to be an absolute rotter until I felt his influence in the service. I am convinced that he has done more good in the navy than any two of his predecessors put together … [131]

Notes

1   www.hawkesbury.net.au/memorial/windsor_st_matthews_anglican/ smmw001.html
2   Admiralty committee on manning: *Accounts and Papers of the House of Commons*, xvii (1859), pp.74–5.
3   B. Lavery, *Shield of Empire: The Royal Navy and Scotland* (Edinburgh, 2007), pp.131–53.
4   N. Evans, 'Loyalties: State, Nation and Military Recruiting in Wales, 1840–1918' in M. Cragoe and C. Williams, eds., *Wales and War: Society*,

    Politics and Religion in the Nineteenth and Twentieth Centuries (Cardiff, 2007), p.39.

5   Evans, 'Loyalties', p.43.

6   The Bute West Dock at Cardiff opened in 1839, followed by the town dock at Newport in 1842. Both the north and south docks at Swansea were built in 1852, the year of the survey.

7   WGRO, D/D Z/249/1, 7 Jan. 1919.

8   Analysis based on the returns from TNA, ADM1/139 and 188, searchable online at www.nationalarchives.gov.uk/records/royal-naval-seamen.htm

9   *Hansard*, HC Deb 22 July 1912 vol. 41 c817.

10   NLW, MS Facs 777.

11   T. Davies, *Borth: A Maritime History* (Llanwrst, 2009), p.21.

12   www.royalmarinesfootball.co.uk/early-1900-s-gallery.html

13   *Memoir of William H Webley Parry, Rear-Admiral of the White, CS, GCSS, of Noyadd Trefawr, Cards.* (Carmarthen, 1847), pp.30–1, 34–5, 42–4.

14   O'Byrne, iii. 1167–8.

15   T. James, 'The Loss of the Brigantine *Amiable Martha* off Laugharne, September 1786', *The Carmarthenshire Antiquary*, xxxi (1995), pp.67–74.

16   See e.g. *The Cambrian*, 20 Sept. 1806, 6 June, 9 July 1807, 3 Dec. 1808, 5 Aug. 1809

17   *The Cambrian*, 10 Jan. 1807, 2 Jan. 1808, 1 July 1809, 7 Jan. 1815

18   *Who Do You Think You Are?* BBC, series 8, episode 3, first broadcast 24 August 2011.

19   O'Byrne, iii. 1295.

20   Roberts, *Eminent Welshmen*, i. 218; J.D.K. Lloyd, 'Memorial Inscriptions in the Church of St Nicholas, Montgomery', *Collections, Historical & Archaeological Relating to Montgomeryshire*, 46 (1940), pp.114–5.

21   O'Byrne, ii. 865.

22   J.K. Laughton, rev. A. Lambert, 'Paget, Sir Charles (1778–1839), naval officer', *ODNB*; www.historyofparliamentonline.org/volume/1790-1820/member/paget-hon-charles-1778–1839; http://www.historyofparliamentonline.org/volume/1820-1832/member/paget-hon-sir-charles-1778–1839

23   www.historyofparliamentonline.org/volume/1820-1832/member/paget-lord-william-1803-1873

24   E.I. Carlyle, rev. A. Lambert, 'Cole, Sir Christopher (1770–1836), naval officer and politician', *ODNB*.

25 www.historyofparliamentonline.org/volume/1790-1820/member/
    cole-sir-christopher-1770-1836; www.historyofparliamentonline.
    org/volume/1820-1832/member/cole-sir-christopher-1770-1836

26 memorials.rmg.co.uk/, M3381.

27 O'Byrne, ii. 591, 594–5; iii. 1101.

28 GRO, DXJO 1–2.

29 www.llanellich.org.uk/files/23-rebecca-and-the-harbour-master

30 P.S. Roberts, *The Ancestry, Life and Times of Commander John Macgregor
    Skinner, RN* (Holyhead, 2006), pp.25, 50–3, 93–103 and passim.

31 'A Memoir of Lieutenant Henry Warde, RN', *Minerva: The Journal of
    Swansea History*, viii (2000), pp.52–60.

32 O'Byrne, iii. 1247–8. For Warde's role at Algiers, see S. Taylor,
    Commander: The Life and Times of Britain's Greatest Frigate Captain (2012).

33 PRO, D/ER/4.

34 M. Lewis, *The Navy in Transition, 1814–64: A Social History* (1965),
    pp.36–41.

35 A. Otway, ed., *Autobiography and Journals of Admiral Lord Clarence Paget
    GCB* (1896); A. Lambert, 'Paget, Lord Clarence Edward (1811–1895),
    naval officer and politician', *ODNB*.

36 O'Byrne, ii. 719; *The Cambrian*, 6 Nov. 1841, 5 May, 14 July 1854.

37 GRO, DF16–22.

38 J. Brown, 'Leyland [formerly Naylor], Christopher John (1849–1926),
    Naval officer and Silviculturist', *ODNB*.

39 R. Williams, 'A History of the Parish of Llanbrynmair', *Collections
    Historical and Archaeological Relating to Montgomeryshire* 22 (1888), p.57

40 F. Jones, 'Lloyd of Gilfachwen, Cilgwyn and Coedmore', *Cardiganshire:
    Journal of the Cardiganshire Antiquarian Society*, 8 (1976), p.97.

41 T. Pryce, 'History of the parish of Llandysilio', *Collections, Historical &
    Archaeological Relating to Montgomeryshire*, 32 (1902), p.239.

42 memorials.rmg.co.uk/m1878/

43 PRO, D/TE/228–9, 235–6. There is a surprisingly detailed and
    accurate account of the loss of the *Doterel* on Wikipedia: http://
    en.wikipedia.org/wiki/HMS_Doterel_(1880)

44 T.R. Roberts, *Eminent Welshmen: A Short Biographical Dictionary of
    Welshmen who have Attained Distinction from the Earliest Times to the
    Present* (Cardiff, 1908), i. 31.

45 GAC, XM/2983/1.

46 GRO, D497/1.

47 NLW, Llwyngwain MS 16985.

48 J.D. Grainger, *The First Pacific War: Britain and Russia, 1854–6*
    (Woodbridge, 2008), pp.35–40.

49 I am grateful to Professor Andrew Lambert for this information.

50 J.K. Laughton, rev. A. Lambert, 'Mends, Sir William Robert (1812–1897), Naval Officer', *ODNB*.

51 O'Byrne, ii. 665; threedecks.org/index.php?display_type=show_ship&id=3903

52 W.A. Williams, *Heart of a Dragon: The VCs of Wales and the Welsh Regiments, 1854–1902* (Wrexham, 2006), pp.51–6.

53 Llanelli Highway Rate Book, 1857, Llanelli Library Collection, MS LC6706 (I am grateful to Lyn John for this reference); *Llanelly and County Guardian*, 11 July 1878.

54 S. Rees, *Sweet Water and Bitter: The Ships that Stopped the Slave Trade* (2009), pp.47–51.

55 Rees, *Sweet Water and Bitter*, pp.78–82.

56 www.royalnavalmuseum.org/DiaryextractsChasingFreedom exhibitionroyalnavyandslavery.htm (Accessed: 2012)

57 www.pbenyon.plus.com/18-1900/C/00785.html (Accessed: 2012)

58 www.pbenyon.plus.com/18-1900/D/01453.html (Accessed: 2012)

59 D. Pulvertaft, *Figureheads of the Royal Navy* (Barnsley, 2011), p.128.

60 Lyon and Winfield, pp.167, 292; D. Pulvertaft, *Figureheads of the Royal Navy* (Barnsley, 2011), p.220.

61 Lyon and Winfield, p.104.

62 www.pbenyon.plus.com/18-1900/C/01114.html (Accessed: 2012)

63 Lyon and Winfield, pp.177–8; D. Pulvertaft, *Figureheads of the Royal Navy* (Barnsley, 2011), p.209.

64 Lyon and Winfield, pp.90, 183.

65 *Ex info* Dr Duncan Redford, National Museum of the Royal Navy.

66 J. Rüger, 'Nation, Empire and Navy: Identity Politics in the United Kingdom, 1887–1914', *Past and Present*, 185 (2004), pp.167–73.

67 Winfield 1793–1817, p.186.

68 P.J. Payton, *The Story of HMS Fisgard* (Redruth, 1983), passim.

69 G.M. Holmes, 'The South Wales Coal Industry, 1850–1914', *THSC* (1976), pp.162–5.

70 M. Asteris, 'The Rise and Decline of South Wales Coal Exports, 1830–1930', *Welsh History Review*, 13 (1986), pp.28–30.

71 R.H. Walters, *The Economic and Business History of the South Wales Steam Coal Industry, 1840–1914* (DPhil thesis, Oxford University, 1975; published New York, 1977), pp.346–7, 353–4, 358.

72 J. Elliott, *The Industrial Development of the Ebbw Valleys 1780–1914* (Cardiff, 2004), p.57. W M Brown, 'The Royal Navy's Fuel Supplies 1898–1939; The Transition from Coal to Oil' (PhD thesis, King;'s College London, 2003), 15; S Gray, *Steam Power and Sea*

Power: Coal, the Royal Navy, and the British Empire, c. 1870–1914 (Cambridge 2017).

73 Walters, *South Wales Steam Coal Industry*, pp.321, 325.

74 T.A. Walker, *The Severn Tunnel: Its Construction and Difficulties 1872–87* (Stroud, 2004 edn), p.155.

75 D. Evans, 'Supporting the Steam Navy: The Development of Coaling Facilities at Portland', *MM*, 82 (1996), pp.175–8.

76 Walters, *South Wales Steam Coal Industry* pp.335–6.

77 Brown, 'Royal Navy's Fuel Supplies', 30–32.

78 J H Maurer, 'Fuel and the Battle Fleet: Coal, Oil and American Naval Strategy, 1898–1925', *Naval War College Review*, 34 (1981), p. 63.

79 I am grateful for this point to Huw Williams, chief legal adviser to Senedd Cymru, the Welsh Parliament. There seems to be no documentary evidence for the '£1 million cheque', but one for £5 million was exchanged at the same location in 1919 and reported in the press so the story is not inherently implausible: South Wales Daily Post, 13 September 1919.

80 *Hansard*, HC Deb 11 March 1903 vol. 119 c378.

81 Holmes, 'South Wales Coal Industry', p.206.

82 *Hansard*, HC Deb 23 July 1931 vol. 255 c1687; Asteris, 'Coal Exports', p.42.

83 E.g. *Hansard*, HL Deb 07 Dec. 1932, vol. 86 cc286–92; HC Deb. 12 Mar. 1934, vol. 287, cc.99–159; HL Deb. 16 June 1937, vol. 105, cc.632–66; HL Deb 14 July 1937 vol. 106 cc427–62. 'Back to Coal' campaign: GRO, DCOMC/1/8/110.

84 *Ex info* John Harland, to whom I am very grateful.

85 D. Powell, *Victorian Pontypridd and its Villages* (Cardiff, 1996), pp.32, 91–3.

86 D.O. Evans, 'The Non-Ferrous Metallurgical Industries of South Wales, and Welshmen's Share in their Development', *THSC* (1931, for 1929–30), p.17.

87 J. Burnley, rev. W. Thompson, 'Griffiths, Robert (1805–1883), Inventor of Mechanical Devices', *ODNB*.

88 D.N. Griffiths, 'Robert Griffiths and his Relations: The Migration of a Denbighshire Family', *THSC* (1968, for 1967), p.285.

89 T.R. Roberts, *Eminent Welshmen: A Short Biographical Dictionary of Welshmen Who have Attained Distinction from the Earliest Times to the Present* (Cardiff, 1908), i. 110.

90 R. and B. Larn, *Shipwreck Index of the British Isles: West Coast and Wales* (2000), not paginated.

91 See e.g. NLW, D.A. Thomas (Viscount Rhondda) MSS, A1/60.

92   A. Saunders, C.J. Spurgeon, H.J. Thomas and D.J. Roberts, *Guns Across the Severn: The Victorian Fortifications of Glamorgan* (Aberystwyth, 2001), pp.8, 10–11.

93   Saunders et al., *Guns Across the Severn*, pp.9–15. I am grateful to Huw Williams for the point about Penarth fort.

94   R. Parkinson, *The Late Victorian Navy: The Pre-Dreadnought Era and the Origins of World War One* (Woodbridge, 2008), p.111.

95   *Western Mail*, 5387, 20 Aug. 1886.

96   *Western Mail*, 9411, 24 July 1899.

97   N.A. Lambert, *Sir John Fisher's Naval Revolution* (Columbia, SC, 2002), pp.85–6.

98   *Western Mail*, 5383, 16 Aug.; 5385, 18 Aug. 1886; 9415, 28 July 1899; 9423, 7 Aug. 1899.

99   Goddard, 'Naval Activity', p.342.

100   D.K. Brown, 'The First Steam Battleships', *MM*, 63 (1977), pp.327–9.

101   E. Peters, *The History of Pembroke Dock* (1905), p.154.

102   W. Webb, *Coastguard: An Official History of Her Majesty's Coastguard* (1976), pp.35–6, 39–41.

103   *Hansard*, HC Deb 24 July 1900 vol. 86 cc 1049–50.

104   *North Wales Chronicle*, 3451 (4 Nov. 1893), 4565 (12 Oct. 1895).

105   NMM, DAN/76 (quotations from letters of 16 and 30 Apr. 1893).

106   J.F. Mayberry, 'The Hamadryad Hospital Ship for Seamen', *British Medical Journal*, 281 (1980), pp.1690–2. D Jenkins, 'HMS Hamadryad', WATS, pp. 216–7.

107   J. Richards, *Cardiff: A Maritime History* (Stroud, 2005), pp.67–8.

108   E.W. Roberts, *The 'Clio', 1877–1920: A Study of the Functions of an Industrial Training Ship in North Wales* (Pwllheli, 2011).

109   L. Lloyd, *The Port of Caernarfon 1793–1900* (Caernarfon, 1989), pp.212–4.

110   GAC, XD/30/86-7.

111   *North Wales Chronicle*, 3067 (18 Sept. 1886), 4680 (9 Jan. 1897).

112   E.D. Jones, '"Gwilym Hiraethog" and Giuseppe Mazzini', *National Library of Wales Journal*, 1, (1940), p.149.

113   G. Matthews, '*Gwnae'r môr yn gochfôr I gyd:* The Welsh and the Battle of Navarino', *MW*, 29 (2008), pp.35–42.

114   www.gtj.org.uk/en/small/item/GTJ62579/ (Last Accessed: 2012)

115   *Baner ac Amserau Cymru*, 10 Aug. 1859, 14 May 1870, and sampling of many other editions.

116   FRO, D/GR/563.

117   H.J. Dickman, 'Wesleyan Methodism in Pembrokeshire', *Journal of the Pembrokeshire Historical Society*, 3 (1989), p.101.

118 William Brockie, *Memoirs of Arthur Augustus Rees, Minister of the Gospel at Sunderland* (1884).

119 *The Cambrian*, 21 (1901), n.p.

120 R.M.J. Jones, rev. M.A. Williams, 'Hughes, James [pseud. Iago Trichrug] (1779–1844), Welsh Calvinistic Methodist minister', *ODNB*.

121 Her sternpiece is one of the most prominent exhibits at the National Maritime Museum, Greenwich.

122 Unless stated otherwise, this section is based on R. Williams, 'Campbell, Frederick Archibald Vaughan, third Earl Cawdor (1847–1911), Politician and Railway Administrator', *ODNB*.

123 CAS, Cawdor MSS 1/293.

124 L. Campbell, *Title Deeds* (2007).

125 R. Thorne, 'The Leach family of Castlemartin', *The Pembrokeshire Historian: Journal of the Pembrokeshire Local History Society*, 7 (1981), p.50.

126 O'Byrne, i. 33; www.pdavis.nl/ShowBiog.php?id=831

127 ww1.wales/ceredigion-memorials/henllan-eglwys-dewi-sant-war-memorial/

128 yba.llgc.org.uk/en/s2-WALK-ALG-1871.html

129 A. Gordon, *The Rules of the Game: Jutland and British Naval Command* (1996), p.28.

130 H.G. Thursfield, 'Cowan, Sir Walter Henry, baronet (1871–1956), Naval Officer', *ODNB*.

131 DRO, PH 293, letters to his father of 7 and 20 April 1913.

9

THE WAR TO END ALL WARS

The Welsh narrative of the First World War has essentially been identical to the broader British narrative: in other words, it has been overwhelmingly the story of the trenches. The history of the Welsh on the Western Front – the decimation of the Pals' Battalions, the horror of the 38th (Welsh) Division's assault on Mametz Wood during the Battle of the Somme, individual dramas such as that of Hedd Wyn – has been recounted in heart-breaking detail by many authors and poets in both Welsh and English. Every war memorial in Wales bears witness to the sacrifice of those who answered the call and perished for what they believed to be right, often amid scenes of unimaginable horror. Virtually every Welsh family has its own, often still vividly remembered, link to the tragedy of the trenches. But the war memorials in towns and villages across Wales will often have one or two names that do not fit the usual pattern: an AB rather than a Pte., an LS rather than a Gnr. One might expect this naval presence on the memorials in coastal towns, but it also turns up in unexpected places. Caersws in Powys is about as landlocked as a Welsh village can be, but on its war memorial, among the serried ranks of those who gave their lives in the uniform of the Royal Welch Fusiliers, one name stands out distinctively: Leading Stoker D.J. Trow of the battlecruiser HMS *Indefatigable*, sunk in the Battle of Jutland on 31 May 1916. Thus there is a different Welsh narrative of the First World War: the story of the Welsh in the war at sea.

Your Country Needs You

Despite Wales' strong traditions of religious nonconformity, political radicalism and industrial militancy, men flocked to the colours, setting aside the antipathy to the armed forces that had taken hold in parts of Welsh society.[1] The vast majority went into the army, even in traditional seafaring towns: by January 1916, Barmouth had six officers and twenty men serving in the navy, a respectable number, but there were another 185 in the army. One officer and two men had joined the nascent Royal Naval Air Service.[2] As ever, most Welsh recruits were sent to Devonport-manned ships, some of which enthusiastically embraced the symbols of national identity: in 1914 the cruiser *Carnarvon* even had its own ship's goat, which was paraded in ceremonial attire every Sunday, and large numbers of her crew spoke Welsh to each other as a matter of course.[3]

But the factors that caused men to volunteer for the navy were many and complex. One was local tradition, as at Barmouth; one was an individualistic wish not to follow the herd and join the army. Even in Blaenau Ffestiniog, well inland and a stronghold of the Royal Welch Fusiliers (indeed, it still has a Royal Welch Comrades' club), a few men opted for the navy instead, and the same was true in equally unlikely parts of the country. David Thomas was a 16-year-old woollen carder and church chorister from a farming family in Llanybydder, and had almost certainly never seen the sea when he joined up in 1916; but four years earlier he had been awarded a copy of W.H.G. Kingston's *The*

Three Midshipmen for being 'top boy in his class' at Llanybydder School, and this seems to have been decisive. He became a Wireless Telegraphist and experienced the likes of Rome, Malta, Constantinople and Sebastopol before he returned to Llanybydder in 1919, vastly more worldly-wise.[4] Another motive impelling men into the navy was family or neighbourhood loyalty. William Jenkins of Mumbles was a career naval man who had joined up when he was 13, seeing service in the Boer War and the Boxer Rebellion. He then became a member of the Royal Fleet Reserve and was called up in July 1914 for a month's training which extended into a four-and-a-half-year deployment aboard the cruiser HMS *Leviathan*. But four of his brothers, and a brother-in-law, followed him into the navy (two brothers and the brother-in-law were killed), while a little further up the same street lived Petty Officer E.J. Jones, who was aboard HMS *Majestic* when she was torpedoed at the Dardanelles in 1915.[5] It is likely that workplace discussions also helped make up many men's minds. For example, the proportion of men who went into the navy from the Morlais tinplate works at Llangennech was astonishingly high – exactly half the number who joined up, and they seem to have been reasonably successful in sticking together, with three serving as stokers aboard the Armed Merchant Cruiser HMS *Orvieto* and three more aboard the *Haupiri*. Indeed, all but one of the nineteen Morlais men who served in the navy during the war did so as stokers, which was, unsurprisingly, a particularly common role for men drawn from the heavy industries of the southern valleys.[6]

In several Welsh towns and villages, the first deaths in action that communities suffered during the war were naval ones. On 5 August 1914, only thirty-six hours after war had been declared, the light cruiser HMS *Amphion* struck a mine in the North Sea and sank with the loss of 149 lives. *Amphion* was a Plymouth-manned ship, and thus had a larger Welsh contingent aboard her than those from Portsmouth or Chatham. Among those who died when she went down were Chief Stoker William Bowen

from Carmarthen, a 41-year-old career naval man, Stoker First
Class William Welton of Cardiff, and Stoker First Class Albert
Martin of Milford Haven.[7] The shock and grief felt at the losses
on the *Amphion* were soon multiplied many times over; but
the impact of war was not confined to the endless roll call of
recruits going off to war, of casualties, and the losses of loved
ones suffered by families throughout the land. There were also
more subtle changes to the fabric of society as the old certainties
fractured and assumptions that had long been taken for granted
were discarded. One tiny but telling example of these processes
occurred on a God-fearing Anglesey farm one Sunday in 1916, as
the son of the Calvinistic Methodist household, John Williams
Hughes, recalled many years later:

> Writing and drawing were forbidden on the Lord's day, and
> so were loud talk, whistling and laughter … Experts cannot
> yet decide whether [the battle of] Jutland was a victory or a
> defeat for the Royal Navy, but its real importance lies in the
> fact that it caused the first crack to appear in the forbidding
> edifice of our hated Welsh Sabbath. After much deliberating
> among my elders it was decided that my soul would not be
> eternally damned if I was allowed to see a copy of the previ-
> ous day's English newspaper giving an account of the great
> sea-battle. It was such a momentous occasion that I can still
> visualise the front page of that issue of The Daily Sketch with
> its picture of Jellicoe … One of our dogs was named Jellicoe
> as from that day.[8]

Officers and Men

Welsh naval officers and seamen came from a variety of
social and career backgrounds. Gerald Norman Jones, born
in Denbighshire but brought up in Holyhead, was inspired
to go to sea by his childhood visits to the port guardship

HMS *Colossus*. He spent time on sailing ships before joining the Royal Naval Reserve in 1912, transferring to the navy in 1914 and becoming a lieutenant in the following year. He served in the Dardanelles campaign before commanding torpedo boats during the second half of the war. Jones returned to the merchant service in the inter-war years before becoming a commodore of convoys during the early stages of the Second World War, and subsequently commanded the coastal forces training base at Portland; after the war he served as captain of some of Cunard's largest liners.[9] Another sailing ship veteran who joined the wartime navy was Robert Thomas of Llangybi, who had been captain of the fully rigged *Criccieth Castle* when she was lost off Cape Horn in 1912; Thomas, his pregnant wife and other survivors then made an epic six-day voyage in an open boat through bitter cold and inhospitable seas to reach safety in the Falklands. He volunteered for the navy in 1914, became a Lieutenant RNR and took command of the armed minesweeping trawler *Kelvin* based at Harwich. The *Kelvin* was blown up by a mine on 7 July 1917, and Thomas' body was brought back for interment in the graveyard of Capel Helyg, Llangybi.[10] Rhyl-born Thomas Elwyn Jones had been a mathematics teacher and drill instructor at Carmarthen Grammar School before the war began, but in July 1915 he volunteered for the navy. On 31 May 1916, he was an instructor officer serving aboard the Pembroke-built cruiser HMS *Defence* when she was blown up during the Battle of Jutland with the loss of some 900 of her crew, including dozens of Welshmen.[11]

Evan Rice Hughes of Talwrn, Anglesey, was an unusual recruit to the lower deck. He went into the navy from university, changing 'my habits and conditions of living so much that it seemed like landing suddenly in another world'. Hughes was horrified by what he found, and provided probably one of the most graphic descriptions ever written of the basics of life aboard a large warship. The heads, for example, consisted simply of a space resembling a very narrow corridor. Along one side of it was a platform on which about a dozen seats were fixed. This served remember for over 1000 men … There was absolutely no privacy. Leaning against the partition inside men used to wait in queue and discuss the topics of the day. Insulting remarks were often passed, especially about young boys.

The heads could only be flushed a few times a day when the ship's pumps were in use,

so the water was soon used up and the place could not be flooded. I have seen men treading down the excreta with a sea boot before sitting down … Under such conditions it is impossible to have any refinement. The system coupled with the environs is soul killing … The men become coarse, hardened cynics. The world holds no prospects for them and they feel bitterly that they have been terribly wronged and are only used as a catspaw by their country. The only solace they find is in drink and the pleasures of the flesh. The institution becomes a stronghold of immorality.[12]

Several current or future Welsh rugby internationals served in the navy, notably Cliff Williams, W.J.A. 'Dave' Davies, Melbourne Thomas (a doctor who served as a surgeon officer) and Engineer Captain Charles Taylor, one of the founders of London Welsh RFC, who became the first Welsh international to be killed in the war when the battlecruiser HMS *Tiger* was struck by enemy gunfire during the Battle of Dogger Bank in January 1915.[13] Among the Welsh intellectuals who served was the poet William John Gruffydd, a RNVR officer in the Persian Gulf. At the end of the war he became Professor of Celtic at Cardiff University and won a famous by-election in 1943 as Liberal candidate for the University of Wales parliamentary seat, defeating the founder of Plaid Cymru, Saunders Lewis.[14] Frederick Hill of Pembroke Dock was a medical student when the war began and became a surgeon lieutenant in the navy. In February 1917 he was serving aboard the gunboat HMS *Moth*, part of a flotilla attempting a passage up the River Tigris in Mesopotamia (that is, modern Iraq) while under heavy Turkish fire. Hill crawled out onto deck to try and save a wounded seaman, but was hit himself; even so, he continued to minister to the casualties and was awarded the DSO for his bravery, subsequently becoming a Freeman of Pembroke at the age of only 26.[15]

William Jenkins, the eldest of the five naval brothers from Mumbles, spent a relatively quiet war aboard the *Leviathan*, which served on the North America and West Indies station, often as the flagship. Jenkins remained true to his Nonconformist faith, always seeking out a chapel when he was ashore, and loyal to his roots: in April 1916 he went over to the cruiser *Cumberland* and found half a dozen fellow Mumbles men, so they 'had a good old conflab on Mumbles topics', and in 1918 he met up in New York with various emigrants from the town. Jenkins noted the travails of his countrymen, notably Stoker Sullivan of Swansea, who spent ninety days in prison for striking a Chief Petty Officer. Sullivan was evidently handy with his fists: after his release he entered a boxing match with a Canadian sailor, losing to 'a most unfair decision', in Jenkins' view. Despite his long experience of the navy, Jenkins was a stern critic of its often pointless routines and the quality of some its officers. He regarded *Leviathan*'s first wartime captain as an incompetent martinet who had frequent 'spasms' of rage against the crew and spouted 'senseless twaddle'. One of the ship's first lieutenants 'knew as much about anchors and cables as an elephant does about deer stalking'. Indeed, Jenkins was privately cynical about the cause for which he was fighting. When he learned that the captain of the German cruiser *Blucher* had been buried by the British with full military honours, but that the crew of a sunken patrol boat, which included a friend of his, had been buried in an unmarked grave, he commented 'Oh it's grand to fight for the dear old flag, England never forgets her sons.' A particularly irritating set of impositions by one of the more hated officers led to a nearly treasonous, if tongue-in-cheek, outburst: 'Roll on and let's get under the German Eagle so that we can do the goose step [as well].' But as the conflict dragged on endlessly, Jenkins' principal emotion became war weariness. Every Easter and Christmas he reflected on how many such occasions he had missed sharing with his loved ones back in Mumbles, and wondered when he would celebrate with them again.[16]

Three Welsh seamen won the Victoria Cross, but only one did so during actual service at sea. This was William Williams of Amlwch, who had joined the Royal Naval Reserve in 1914 at the age of 24. On 7 June 1917 he was part of the crew of the Q-ship HMS *Pargust* (a converted Cardiff collier), which continued to fight despite having been torpedoed. Her attacker, *U-29*, was lulled into thinking that the ship had been abandoned, but thirty-six minutes after she had been hit, *Pargust* opened fire, swiftly sinking the U-boat. Williams, who had won the DSM a few months earlier for his actions on another Q-ship, the *Farnborough*, played a crucial part in ensuring victory by propping up the weight of the starboard gun port himself after the blast from the torpedo threatened to throw it open and prematurely reveal *Pargust* for what she was. Williams was awarded the VC under the ballot system then in effect, which meant that the crew voted for one officer and one man to receive the awards on behalf of the entire ship's company, and a couple of months later he won a bar to his DSM for further heroism aboard another Q-ship, the Cardiff steamer *Dunraven*. In later years, Williams' nephews and nieces would ask him *'Am beth y cafoch y VC, Ewythr Wil?'* ('What did you get the VC for, Uncle Will?'), to which he would always reply *'Am fod yn hogyn da i Mam'* ('For being a good boy for Mam'). The Victoria Cross won by 'Wil VC' is now the only one held by the National Museum of Wales.[17] Williams' near-namesake W.C. Williams of Chepstow was a career naval man who had joined the service in 1895 at the age of 15. He was commended for gallantry in three different wars, each time for service on land. Following distinguished service in the naval brigade during the Boer War and in China during the Boxer Rebellion, Williams won the VC for his actions on 25 April 1915 during the Gallipoli campaign. A floating bridge had been built to allow troops to get ashore, but one of the boats crucial to keeping it intact came away. Williams grabbed hold of a rope and secured the boat, even though he and the bridge were under heavy fire for an hour. Finally, a shot struck him and he was killed. Williams became the first naval recipient of a posthumous VC, and he is still commemorated proudly in his hometown.[18] A captured U-boat gun stands in one of the most prominent positions in Chepstow, in Beaufort Square, and is surrounded by a new commemorative pavement; an interpretative panel explains how Williams came to win the illustrious decoration.[*]

Like their contemporaries in the army, decorated Welsh sailors became local celebrities overnight. Jimmy Jones of Pentre, Rhondda, was the first man from the valley to win the Distinguished Service Medal during the war (at Gallipoli), and was feted in a special presentation at the Grand Theatre.[19] Another Rhondda hero was Tom Picton, a miner from Treherbert and stoker aboard HMS *Gloucester* at the Battle of Jutland, who was mentioned in despatches for his part in maintaining the ship's boilers after she was torpedoed. Tom became lightweight boxing champion of the navy in 1917 despite having had his jaw broken in a fight the year before. He later volunteered in the Spanish Civil War and was shot by the fascists in 1938: having been captured, he laid out a guard who was beating a fellow prisoner, and was summarily executed as a result.[20] Among the other Rhondda men who served in the navy during the war were Leonard Edwards, full back for Treorchy and Treherbert, who was killed aboard the battlecruiser *Queen*

---

[*]   The third Welsh naval VC winner of the war, George Prowse, is described shortly.

Mary at Jutland, aged just 22. The same battle also claimed Signaller David George Jones of Heol Fach who went down with the cruiser *Black Prince*, Artificer Engineer John Morgan of Pontygwaith, formerly a collier in the Tylorstown pit, who was lost when the Pembroke-built cruiser *Defence* was sunk, and First Class Stoker David Lewis of Treorchy, killed when the battlecruiser *Indefatigable* blew up. They were just a few of the scores of Welshmen (thirty from Cardiff and eighteen from Swansea alone) who perished at Jutland aboard the battlecruisers and armoured cruisers of the Grand Fleet, the appalling attrition rate of which caused Admiral Beatty to remark, 'There's something wrong with our bloody ships today.' Compared with the dreadful slaughter in the trenches, the numbers killed at Jutland were relatively small; but with the obvious exception of the first day of the Somme, it was very rare for communities to suffer so many fatalities on a single day, so the impact of the battle must have been terrible.*

Enemy action accounted for by no means all of the deaths of Welshmen in naval service. On 30 December 1915 the cruiser HMS *Natal* blew up mysteriously while at anchor in the Cromarty Firth, a disaster that claimed *inter alia* Lieutenants Richard Edward Lewis of Pembroke and William Black of Cardiff, along with Boy First Class Arthur Simpson Protherough of Varteg, Pontypool.[21] Another casualty of the *Natal* was Nurse Maud Edwards from Newport, who was serving on a hospital ship that happened to be in harbour and had fatally accepted an invitation to *Natal*'s wardroom. There is a prominent modern memorial to her at her old school, the

---

* The same was true of the relatively little-remembered loss of the old pre-Dreadnought battleship HMS *Goliath* at Gallipoli on 13 May 1915, which again had a substantial Welsh contingent among her crew (including the chaplain, the Rev. Ivor Lewis of Llanbedr). In 1913–14 Goliath had been based at Milford Haven as flagship of the Third Fleet, a force of five old battleships and one cruiser kept in reserve in the anchorage and manned by skeleton crews.

Haberdashers Monmouth School for Girls, but opinion about her fate was not always so sympathetic: William Jenkins of Mumbles considered the loss of the *Natal* as proof of the old seamen's superstition about the dangers of allowing women onto a warship.[22] The battleship *Vanguard* suffered a similar fate to *Natal* on 9 July 1917, taking with her 22-year-old Owen Wynne Williams of Holyhead, Shipwright Reginald Thomas of Pembroke Dock, Engineer Captain Walter Williams of St David's, and 799 others, including four Cardiff men.[23] As the war drew to its close, some Welsh seamen were particularly unlucky. LS William Bevan of Pembroke Dock, Signalman Edward Jones and Trimmer Thomas Paul of Cardiff, together with two men from the relatively small West Wales village of Pontardulais, Trimmers Matthew Jones and James Price, went down with the minesweeper HMS *Ascot* on 10 November 1918, the day before the Armistice. She was the last British warship to be sunk during the conflict.[24] The last British serviceman to be killed before the Armistice took effect at 11 a.m. the following day might well have been Richard Morgan of Kilgwrrwg, Monmouthshire, serving aboard HMS *Garland*, although there is considerable debate about the criteria for defining the last war death.[25]

The Royal Naval Divisions

Not all of the Welshmen who joined the navy served at sea. When the war began, the navy had too many men and the army too few so, on the order of the First Lord of the Admiralty, Winston Churchill, surplus men were sent into a Royal Naval Division. Although this was serving on land and under army control, it maintained naval procedures and traditions, and its battalions were named after great naval heroes: Nelson, Drake, Hawke and so on. It fought in the Gallipoli campaign and on the Western Front, including the battles of the Somme and Passchendaele. Such was the attrition rate that in the two years 1915 and 1917, exactly one-third of Cardiff's naval fatalities perished, not at sea, but in the trenches or on the beaches of Turkey, fighting in the RND.[26] Stoker James Evans of Camrose, Pembrokeshire, a career naval man, fell at Gallipoli on 4 June 1915 when the Second Brigade of the RND went 'over the top' to storm the Turkish trenches, only to be met by a hail of machine-gun fire.[27] LS Thomas Daniel of Carmarthen served in Hawke Battalion. He was gassed in the Battle of Cambrai during the winter of 1917 and was invalided home, but returned to the RND in April 1918. Gassed again during the Battle of Albert in August, he was sent home once more, but fatally returned to the colours for a third time and was killed on 8 October 1918, just over a month before the Armistice.[28]

The RND provided Wales' third naval Victoria Cross winner of the war. This was Chief Petty Officer George Prowse, originally of Gilfach Goch, who moved to Somerset when very young but returned to Grovesend, Gorseinon, in 1907 to work as a collier. He enlisted in the RNVR in 1915 and won his VC during the Battle of Arras on 2 September 1918, only days after he had won the DCM during the Second Battle of Albert. His citation suggests that he won the VC for several outstanding acts of gallantry over several days, capturing a number of enemy positions, displaying great courage and giving a 'magnificent example and leadership' which were 'an inspiration to all'. But Prowse's moment of glory was short-lived. He was killed on 27 September, during an attack on a German-held sugar beet factory on the road to Amiens. Prowse was the last man to be awarded the VC with a blue naval ribbon, which was subsequently acquired by the Ashcroft Trust, the largest private collection of Victoria Crosses. A blue plaque at his birthplace commemorates him at Gilfach Goch, and in 2003 a building at the Portsmouth training establishment HMS *Collingwood* was named after him.[29]

'Welsh' Warships at War

Many ships that were effectively fixtures in Welsh waters were requisitioned and commissioned as warships. The four fast ferries employed on the Holyhead to Dublin route became armed boarding vessels, with two subsequently becoming hospital ships: *Hibernia*, renamed HMS *Tara*, was sunk in the Mediterranean in 1915, her crew (largely her original complement from Holyhead) subsequently being held prisoner by Senussi tribesmen at a desert oasis before being rescued by an expedition led by no less a figure than the Duke of Westminster.[30] The paddle steamers that made peacetime cruises from the piers of the Bristol Channel were requisitioned as minesweepers, as were the Cardiff and Milford fishing fleets. Many of the fishermen were also members of the Royal Naval Reserve, and were called up with their ships; Milford Haven's war memorial lists the names of those who never returned.[31] Even Lord Tredegar's steam yacht, the *Liberty* – then one of the largest private yachts in the world – was taken into the navy as a hospital ship, initially under the command of her owner, who was given a commission in the RNVR. (Courtney Morgan, Lord Tredegar, was also an important driving force in naval recruitment in South Wales, winning plaudits for his efforts to get men to volunteer for the Royal Naval Divisions.)[32]

The accelerated building programmes in the period leading up to the outbreak of the war, and then during the course of hostilities, brought several new or nearly new Welsh names onto the Navy List. The second HMS *Llewelyn*, a destroyer, was launched in October 1913, spending much of the war based at Harwich. The navy's second *Caradoc* was a light cruiser launched in December 1916, which formed part of the Grand Fleet and later served through the Second World War before being scrapped at Briton Ferry in 1946. *Caradoc*'s near sister ship, the fourth HMS *Cambrian*, was launched at Pembroke Dock in March 1916 but had a quiet war and was broken up as early as 1934. A successor class of cruisers included the navy's fourteenth HMS *Dragon*, completed just three months before the end of the war. The navy's sixth *Druid*, a destroyer launched in 1911, distinguished herself at the battles of Heligoland Bight (1914) and Dogger Bank (1915); her battle ensign from the latter is preserved at the Memorial Institute in Glyn Ceiriog. From 1916 onwards, a class of large minesweepers was built and initially allocated the names of British hunts, although this theme was quickly abandoned and a fairly random cross-section of towns throughout the British Isles suddenly found that a warship had been given their name. Those chosen included *Aberdare*, *Caerleon*, *Penarth*, *Pontypool* and *Prestatyn*. HMS *Penarth* was lost in 1919 when she struck mines off the Yorkshire coast; the rest were disposed of between the wars with the single exception of *Aberdare*, which survived to fight through the Second World War, principally in the Mediterranean. HMS *Chepstow*, launched in 1916, was part of a class of paddle-wheel minesweepers named after racecourses; she was broken up in 1927, but her bell still hangs in Saint Mary's church in the town after which she was named. Meanwhile, one of Wales' most famous but controversial soldiers was commemorated in the name of the monitor HMS *Sir Thomas Picton*, launched in 1915, which shelled Turkish positions from the Dardanelles to Palestine and Egypt. Another monitor, originally built for Brazil, was purchased when the war began and given the name *Severn*, the seventh British warship to bear the name.

Inevitably, war took its toll of this 'Welsh' contingent on the Navy List. A particularly poignant tragedy occurred during its earliest stages, off Coronel on the coast of Chile on 1 November 1914, when a hopelessly undergunned British squadron encountered the vastly superior German Pacific Squadron commanded by Graf von Spee. The cruiser HMS *Monmouth* had been built to a seriously flawed design which meant she was unable to fire many of her guns during the stormy weather on that day, and was quickly overwhelmed and sent to the bottom with the loss of all 678 men aboard. This number included a substantial contingent of Welshmen, including six from Newport, five from Barry, four from Cardiff and many others.[33] The terrible loss of the *Monmouth* so early in the war and with so many casualties had a lasting effect on her namesake town. The new west door of St Mary's priory church was later dedicated to the ship, and a memorial book listing every man killed aboard her still has pride of place adjacent to the door. Another tragic loss was that of HMHS *Llandovery Castle*, a Union-Castle liner requisitioned in 1916 to become a hospital ship, principally manned by Canadian nursing staff and used to ship sick and wounded Canadian soldiers back to their homeland. She was on her way back to Britain on 27 June 1918 when she was torpedoed by *U-86* about 116 miles south-west of the Fastnet Rock. Two hundred and thirty-four, including fourteen nursing sisters, were killed, many of them by gunfire when the submarine ran down and fired on the lifeboats. Only twenty-four of *Llandovery Castle*'s crew survived. Two of the officers of *U-86* were prosecuted in 1921 during the 'Leipzig trials', the first ever war crimes trials. The captain had already fled the country; the other two officers were each sentenced to four years imprisonment, from which they swiftly escaped.[34]

When it was over, and the guns on the Western Front had finally fallen silent, a 'Welsh' warship played the central role in one of the most astonishing naval spectacles ever seen. Following the Armistice on 11 November 1918, arrangements were quickly put in place for the surrender of the German High Seas Fleet and its internment in Scapa Flow. Early in the morning of 21 November, the new light cruiser *Cardiff*, which had been launched on the Clyde in April 1917, slipped quietly out of the Firth of Forth and rendezvoused with the High Seas Fleet, turning to escort the long line of German ships back towards the Forth. Forty miles east of the Isle of May, the *Cardiff* led the surrendered fleet between the two columns of the British Grand Fleet and its French and American allies, all commanded by Admiral Sir David Beatty. When Beatty's flagship *Queen*

Elizabeth came up to her German counterpart, the *Baden*, she and the rest of the allied ships executed an immaculate 180-degree turn, and *Cardiff* then led the three mighty columns of warships back to the Forth.[35] Her role in the proceedings effectively made the *Cardiff* one of the most famous ships in the Royal Navy, a status that was emphasised during the 1942 'warship week' campaign in her namesake city to raise enough funds to formally adopt the ship.

The Jellicoe Specials

Despite the decision to switch to oil propulsion, the great majority of the Royal Navy's ships were still coal powered when the First World War began. In August 1914, the maximum fuel capacity of major warships of the Grand Fleet powered by coal was 136,798 tons, of oil 47,141 tons; by the start of 1918, the figure for oil had increased dramatically to 152,982 tons, but that for coal was still 123,850 tons – totals that reflected the greatly increased size of the fleet.[36] The battlefleet was stationed at Scapa Flow in Orkney, the anchorage best located for bottling up the German High Seas Fleet, so a system had to be devised for transporting huge amounts of Welsh coal to that remote northern harbour. The vulnerability of colliers to U-boat attack, and the inability of the Welsh ports to cope with the number of ships that would be needed, meant that much of the coal was sent by train to Grangemouth on the Firth of Forth, and then taken on by ship to Scapa. Quakers Yard and Pontypool Road formed the hub of what became known as the 'Jellicoe Specials', named after the admiral commanding the Grand Fleet: trains ran from there through Abergavenny, Hereford, Shrewsbury, Wrexham and so on to Warrington and ultimately to Grangemouth. The trains moved by day and night. By the summer of 1915, 200 a month were moving north, a number that grew steadily as the war continued and the system was refined: in September 1918, no fewer than 585 trains made the run. By then the 'Specials' were also having to be run on other lines to reduce the pressure on the track from Pontypool. Thus many coal trains went up the Brecon and Merthyr and Cambrian Railways via Talyllyn Junction, through such isolated mid-Wales communities as Erwood, Llanfaredd, Doldowlod and Pantydwr, before rejoining the main route at Gobowen. In total, 13,631 trains ran carrying a total of over 5 million tons of coal, almost half of which went to Grangemouth, the rest to a number of other naval ports including Plymouth and Holyhead.[37]

Coal's importance to the naval war effort was emphasised by the South Wales miners' strike of July 1915. Denied a pay rise and offered a 'war bonus' instead, the miners walked out. They protested that they were not being unpatriotic; indeed, it has been argued that the miners went on strike because of the strength of their patriotism, with higher wages being seen as the only suitable recognition of their massive contribution to the war effort.[38] Nevertheless, the strike presented the navy with a huge problem. When it began on 15 July, there were 100,000 tons of Welsh coal above ground and another 700,000 held in ships or bunkers ashore, but the navy was burning some 412,000 tons a month, so the Admiralty calculated that if the strike lasted any longer than seventy-one days, the Royal Navy's coal-burning ships – still the vast majority – would either be immobilised or forced to resort to inferior fuel. But the seventy-one day limit took no account of any unexpected deployment of the Grand Fleet, say to meet a German sortie, in which case vast amounts would be expended. On one such day, 15 April 1915, the ships operating from Scapa Flow alone burned 31,500 tons, those from the Firth of Forth another 21,151. The estimate also took no account of the amounts being supplied to Britain's allies, 61,000 tons a month to both the French and Russian navies, 40,000 to the Italian Navy, and another 54,000 to the French railways. Consequently, all fleet commanders were ordered to economise on the use of Welsh coal, for the Grand Fleet to use inferior north country coal whenever possible, and for supplies of Welsh coal to allies to be reduced.[39] In the event, such dire prognostications proved to be unnecessary. Lloyd George used his personal authority to broker a settlement, and the strike ended on 21 July after just six days. But the Admiralty's secret calculations reveal just how important the South Wales coalfield was to the Royal Navy's war effort, and how close the South Wales miners came to placing that effort in serious jeopardy.

Admiral Sir Hugh Evan-Thomas and the Battle of Jutland

Hugh Evan-Thomas' family had been settled at Llwynmadoc, near Llanwrtyd Wells, for generations, and had also acquired the Gnoll estate at Neath and Pencerrig near Builth Wells. Despite being distinctly well-heeled by Welsh standards, the family lacked the sorts of connections normally required for promotion in the Victorian Navy, but Evan-Thomas' career was made by two fortunate coincidences. One was the fact that one of his earliest and closest friends in the navy was the future Sir John Jellicoe, commander-in-chief of the Grand Fleet; the other was his taking a younger cadet under his wing when they were both training at Dartmouth in the 1870s. The younger cadet was Prince George, younger son of the Prince of Wales: in other words, the future King George V. The relationship between the two young men was further cemented when Evan-Thomas' sister married the prince's tutor, John Dalton (their son Hugh Dalton became a notable Labour Chancellor of the Exchequer). Royal patronage benefited Evan-Thomas throughout his career, even into the next generation: at George V's insistence, he commanded the Britannia Royal Naval College at Dartmouth while the king's eldest sons, the future kings Edward VIII and George VI, underwent their naval training. Amiable, well-liked and undoubtedly competent, by 1915 Evan-Thomas was a safe pair of hands to be entrusted with one of the Grand Fleet's plum posts, command of the Fifth Battle Squadron, which consisted of the navy's newest and most powerful battleships of the Queen Elizabeth class. Arguably, however, he lacked the drive and independence of thought necessary for such an important command, and these shortcomings were to prove crucial during the Battle of Jutland.[40] Evan-Thomas was also placed in a difficult position, though. His fast, modern battleships were allocated to the battlecruiser force, and this placed him under the command of the charismatic but controversial David Beatty, Jellicoe's great rival. Evan-Thomas' record as an out-and-out Jellicoe loyalist told against him, and relations between Beatty and his Welsh subordinate were frosty from the outset.[41]

The Battle of Jutland began at about 2.20 p.m. on 31 May 1916 when Beatty's battlecruiser force, steaming north to rejoin Jellicoe, encountered its German opposite number, commanded by Admiral von Hipper, who aimed to lure Beatty into the approaching main body of the High Seas Fleet.[42] At the time, Evan-Thomas's 5BS was about 5 miles north-west of Beatty. The latter now signalled for his ships to turn south-east to meet Hipper, but the signal did not reach Evan-Thomas, who in any case had not been made privy to Beatty's standing orders for such an eventuality. The upshot was that 5BS continued northwest. The great speed of the Queen Elizabeths and Beatty's battlecruisers meant that a gap rapidly opened: 5BS finally turned when it was about 10 miles from Beatty. Thus it was in no position to save *Indefatigable*, which was destroyed by German gunfire just after 4.00 p.m., while Beatty's flagship *Lion* was also badly damaged before 5BS finally got within range at 1615. *Queen Mary* had also been sunk before Beatty, who had now sighted the main body of the High Seas Fleet, turned north at 4.40 p.m. Again, though, there was considerable confusion in the signalling to 5BS, the result being that the latter passed the battlecruisers on the opposite tack before finally turning, thus becoming the rearguard between Beatty and the Germans. From about 6.30 p.m., the two main fleets were in sight of each other and a general fleet action commenced, the upshot of which was the destruction of another battlecruiser (*Invincible*), the Pembroke-built armoured cruisers *Defence* and *Warrior*, and the loss of some 6,000 British and 2,000 German seamen.[43]

By the time the engagement concluded during the night, it was very clear that Jutland had been no Trafalgar. The disappointment of national expectations, together with the extent of the material losses, ensured that the outcome of the battle was soon picked over in the finest detail. During the 1920s, this developed into a vicious propaganda war between the partisans of Beatty and Jellicoe, and inevitably, Evan-Thomas' actions and the role of 5BS were called into question. In particular, he was censured for keeping the squadron's course to the north-west rather than using his initiative and turning much sooner to support Beatty. This was the line taken by Winston Churchill, a firm Beatty supporter, in his influential book *The World Crisis*. Such criticisms stung Evan-Thomas, whose health declined markedly during the 1920s.[44] He died at Cople, Bedfordshire, in 1928,* and to a degree his reputation remains controversial. Much of Andrew Gordon's influential prizewinning book about Jutland, *The Rules of the Game*, focuses on Hugh Evan-Thomas, setting him up as an exemplar of what the author perceives as the rigid, unimaginative Victorian mindset of the senior echelons of the naval officer corps during the First World War . However, the failure to turn south sooner was undoubtedly as much the fault of Beatty and the fleet's signalling, and it can be argued that but for Evan-Thomas and 5BS positioning themselves between the battlecruisers and the High Seas Fleet, taking heavy damage in the process, Beatty's entire battlecruiser force might have been annihilated, in which case Jutland might have become a catastrophic naval defeat.[45] If Britain had lost the battle, then

---

* By coincidence, his grave lies about 3 miles as the crow flies from my office, where I am typing these words.

Churchill's aside about Jellicoe – that he was the only man on either side who could lose the war in an afternoon – might well have been proved true.

Welsh Submariners

The submarine service was still relatively young when the war began, and had a dubious reputation as being both somewhat piratical and distinctly 'un-English'; which supposed traits might have given it a certain vicarious appeal to Welshmen.* One of those who volunteered for submarines was William Hayes Thomas, a leading stoker from Cosheston in Pembrokeshire who was one of only six survivors (out of a crew of 265) when the cruiser *Pathfinder* was sunk in 1914. By August 1915 he was serving aboard HM Submarine *E13*, ordered into the Baltic to attack German shipping and support the Russian Navy. But on 18 August, the vessel ran aground in the Øresund, in Danish territorial waters. Despite this, and the presence of several Danish naval vessels, a German torpedo boat was ordered to destroy the submarine and proceeded to shell and strafe *E13*, continuing to fire even at men in the water. Fifteen men, exactly half of the submarine's crew, were killed in the attack, which caused outrage both in Britain and Denmark.[46] The deaths of the crew of *E13* became one of the many atrocity stories that galvanised the British press and public in the early days of the war. The incident occurred only weeks after the execution of Nurse Edith Cavell, and thus seemed to provide yet more proof of the limitless perfidy of the evil Hun. The bodies were conveyed home by the Danes with full honours, and the dead men were given a spectacular funeral service in Hull. For Thomas, this was followed

---

*   Indeed, to this day Welsh submariners retain a powerful sense of solidarity: see welshsubmariners.com.

by interment in the quiet churchyard of Cosheston, where his sadly neglected grave can still be found.

Another Welshman who saw submarines as a more exciting option than the often boring blockade duties of the Grand Fleet was the young Denbighshire officer Hugh Heaton, presumably recovered from his pre-war embarrassment at the hands of Winston Churchill. When war broke out he shared in the widespread optimism and over-confidence, writing to his mother on 5 August 1914: 'You will laugh uproariously when I tell you all the incidents when I see you next month as there is not much chance of the war continuing after then, whereupon I am coming home for the cub hunting.'[47] The Central Powers proved unexpectedly resilient, so by 1916 Heaton was commanding an antiquated B-class submarine in the Adriatic, fighting against the Austro-Hungarian Navy. On one occasion he had 'seven bells [knocked] out of me' when depth charged off the enemy coast, on another he destroyed an Austrian seaplane that had broken down on the surface.[48] When the Armistice came, Heaton's reaction was frank:

> I've been trying to analyse my feelings about the question of peace. I always imagined myself throwing my hat over the nearest tree & shouting abundantly ... I believe the only remark I made was 'damn'. I suppose I have been looking at this war from a purely selfish point of view. I always hoped that I might make a name for myself out of it. As it is I don't know that I have done any more than thousands of other men.[49]

Francis Cromie almost certainly would not have regarded himself as a Welshman. Born in 1882 in Duncannon, Ireland, to an army officer who had been born in Cincinnati, Ohio (and would die in Dakar, Senegal, as British consul), and his wife, the daughter of the Chief Constable of Pembrokeshire, Cromie belonged to the amorphous, borderless Imperial middle class whose members were usually described by that most all-embracing of monikers, 'Englishmen'. On the other hand, Cromie went to school in Fishguard until the age of 10, moving on to Haverfordwest Grammar School for four years before joining the navy in 1896.[50] In September 1915, a month after *E13*'s fatal attempt to enter the Baltic, Cromie conned his command, *E19*, on an identical voyage. *E19* had better fortune than her sister ship and arrived at the Russian naval base in Reval (Tallinn) on 13 September. Cromie's boat enjoyed considerable success over the following two years, notably when she sank the German cruiser *Undine* in November 1915. But the situation was transformed by the two Russian Revolutions of 1917, particularly the Bolshevik seizure of power in November. The new regime under Lenin and Trotsky swiftly withdrew from the war, and by the following spring an allied intervention intent on ousting the new regime was under way.

It was against this backdrop that, in January 1918, Cromie was suddenly appointed as the new naval attaché at the British embassy at St Petersburg, then renamed Petrograd. He was gradually drawn into the dangerous world of secret intelligence, making contact with members of the opposition and drawing up plans to deploy naval forces on some of the great lakes. On 30 August there was an attempt on Lenin's life which very nearly succeeded in killing the Bolshevik leader. This triggered a ferocious backlash from his followers, and on the following day a party of Red Guards burst into the British embassy. Captain Francis Cromie was shot dead on the stairs. Once the horror and confusion subsided, a funeral was arranged for 6 September at the Smolensky cemetery on Vasilievskiy Island. As the cortege crossed the Nicholas Bridge, the Bolshevik-influenced crews of three destroyers moored in the River Neva were loafing on deck. Suddenly, some of them spotted the Union flag draped over the coffin and realised whose funeral they were witnessing. Caps were replaced, lines were formed, men took up their dressings, and the three crews came smartly and silently to attention. Cromie's memory was preserved in his home county: his name was placed on war memorials in St Mary's church, Fishguard, and in Haverfordwest, where Cromie Avenue and Cromie Terrace were named after him. As a former Pembroke Dock resident who served under Cromie and was one of the last 'to see him alive and shake his hand' put it, he was 'one of Pembrokeshire's greatest sailors and a gentleman'.[51]

RNAS and WRNS

One of the navy's responses to the Germans' first campaign of unrestricted submarine warfare, commencing in February 1915, was to establish Royal Naval Air Service stations in Wales from which airships could operate on anti-submarine patrols. One of the principal airfields was set up on land between Carew, Milton and Sageston in Pembrokeshire; this became known as RNAS Pembroke and provided cover for an extensive area of the Irish Sea and the Bristol Channel.[52] Another airship base, now RAF Mona, was established at Llangefni in September 1915 and was eventually named RNAS Anglesey, responsible for a large sea area from Anglesey to Morecambe Bay in the east and Dublin Bay in the west.[53] The early days of airship operations from Wales were not entirely auspicious. *SS-18*, the first airship based at Llangefni, was crippled when it struck a cow while landing. On another occasion, Thomas Blenheim Williams, CO of the Llangefni-based *Z-35*, had to ditch in the sea and be towed into Llandudno; on another, he landed in the middle of a cricket match in Liverpool.[54] There were many other cases of mechanical failure, a number of the craft operating from both Llangefni and Pembroke were lost, and the airships' achievements were somewhat questionable: they never sank a U-boat, although their deterrent effect – difficult to quantify, as is the case with all deterrents – might have been significant.[55]

By 1916–17, the RNAS was becoming more dependent upon, and well supplied with, increasingly reliable and
effective aeroplanes and seaplanes. Land-based aircraft operated inshore patrols from Pembroke from April 1917, from
Llangefni from that autumn, and a seaplane station was established at Fishguard in the early months of the same year. This
latter had a large wooden hangar and a slipway, with officers
billeted in the local hotel and ratings in the town. The level
of activity varied depending on operational demands and,
inevitably, on the weather. In November 1917, for example,
Fishguard's seaplanes flew thirty-four patrols with a total
duration of over thirty-nine hours, covering 2,591 miles; in
the following month, though, they flew only thirteen patrols
lasting just over thirteen hours and covering just 854 miles.[56]
All of the RNAS bases transferred to the newly established
Royal Air Force on 1 April 1918, although at first there was
very little change and the stations continued to be manned by
naval personnel. The most famous, but also perhaps the least
likely, Welsh recruit into the RNAS was the composer Ivor
Novello (born David Ivor Davies in Cardiff), already famous
for having penned 'Keep the Home Fires Burning' just before
the war began. Novello's flying career was inglorious: after
crashing twice, he was shunted aside to a desk job in London
and continued his theatrical career on the side.[57]

A Women's Royal Naval Service was formed in 1917, primarily to release men from shore tasks for service afloat. They filled
a wide variety of roles, notably as drivers, telegraphists, fitters,
mine cleaners, sailmakers and cipher and intelligence staff. The
arrival of the Wrens, as they were quickly nicknamed, inevitably created something of a stir. This was certainly the case at
Holyhead, where a new senior naval officer discovered that his
coding office was full of them. He blustered 'that if he had his
way he wouldn't have a woman within a hundred miles of any
naval base', and promptly started issuing strict orders about what
the Wrens could and could not do, where they could and could

not go, and so forth. The inevitable happened: a few months later 'the new Senior Naval Officer succumbed and married one of the WRNS on his staff'. Subsequently, when the King's Messenger arrived with secret mails he abandoned the password and replaced it with the scurrilous query, 'Is this the base where the SNO married a WRNS?'[58]

The Naval Defence of Wales

Welsh waters were vitally important to the British war effort. Much of the shipping going to and from Liverpool passed the Welsh coast, while coal shipments from Cardiff in particular were essential to the functioning of the Royal Navy, the fleets of its allies and, as already noted, even the French railways. Consequently, considerable attention was given to the defence of Welsh sea lanes. A naval base was established at Holyhead in 1915, the first commanding officer being Arthur Raby, son of the Victoria Cross winner Admiral Henry James Raby. Six destroyers and sixteen motor launches were initially based there, forming the Irish Sea Hunting Flotilla; towards the end of the war, eighteen American motor launches were also based there.[59] The flotilla had its work cut out, for U-boats regularly operated in the waters around Wales. Thirty-three ships were sunk around Anglesey and Llŷn alone, with the first sinking (that of the *Cambank* by *U-30*, 10 miles east of Point Lynas on 20 February 1915) bringing home to the people of Anglesey the uncomfortable truth that the war could come closer to them than they might ever have imagined.[60] One of the strangest episodes of the submarine war in North Wales waters occurred in August 1915, when two U-boats rendezvoused off Llandudno in an attempt to extract just three escaped prisoners of war: an army officer, U-boat captain Heinrich von Henning, and Korvettenkapitän Hermann Tholens, second-in-command of the cruiser SMS *Mainz*, which had been sunk in August 1914.

On 13 August the three escaped from Dyffryn Aled, a mansion house to the west of Denbigh, and walked overnight to Llandudno, lying low all day to wait for the darkness that would enable them to get on to the Great Orme. Meanwhile the two U-boats had rendezvoused offshore and *U-38* was chosen to make the pick-up. On the three consecutive nights allocated for the operation, the escapees got down to the shore and *U-38* approached, but the two sides were never able to spot each other. Dispirited, the three men went back into Llandudno where they were recaptured on 16 August.[61]

U-boats were also active in southern waters. *U-21* made a pioneering voyage into the Irish Sea in January 1915, and in March *U-28* sank four ships, including the liners *Aguila* and *Falaba*, around Lundy and The Smalls, the treacherous rocks off the approaches to Milford Haven. The forces based at Milford initially included patrol vessels, armed trawlers and minesweepers. In February 1915, Vice-Admiral Sir Charles Holcombe Dare, who had been brought out of retirement, took command of the Milford station, and remained in post for the duration of the war; his headquarters, in Murray Crescent on the Rath, was commissioned as HMS *Idaho*.[62] Among the ships under his command were a number of 'Q-ships', merchantmen fitted with concealed armament, manned by naval crews and commissioned as naval vessels: among them were the Amlwch vessels *Gaelic* and *Cymric*, the first of which fought off a U-boat attack off Kinsale in April 1917. However, the Admiralty was forced to admit that U-boats were generally wise to their tactics, so any successes the decoys obtained were largely down to luck. Perhaps the most illustrious, and thus luckiest, of Milford's Q-ships was HMS *Prize*, formerly the German schooner *Else*, which had been lying at Swansea since 1914 when she became Britain's first German prize of the war (hence her new name, a contraction of *First Prize*), captured off Cornwall four or five hours after war was declared.[63] *Prize* fought a heroic action against *U-93* on 30 April 1917, but was so severely damaged that she had to be towed back to Milford. Her captain, the New Zealander Lieutenant William Edward Sanders, won the VC for the action, but was killed later that year when the *Prize* was sunk by *U-48*. Sanders, still the only New Zealander to win the VC in a naval action, is regarded as one of New Zealand's greatest war heroes, and is also commemorated on the Milford cenotaph.[64]

U-boat activity was not constant. The initial successes of 1915 culminated in the notorious sinking of the *Lusitania*, and the consequent threat of American entry into the war led the Germans to abandon unrestricted submarine warfare. By February 1917 the stakes were higher, however, and the Kaiser and his high command considered the risks of resuming an unrestricted campaign worth taking. The impact was immediate. Six ships were sunk off Bardsey in five days during the second week of February, and others followed in March.[65] In April 1917, a South Western Group took over responsibility for anti-submarine operations in the Western Approaches. By then, the forces at Milford Haven consisted of three yachts, thirty-six armed trawlers, 100 drifters, twelve motor launches and four boom defence vessels.[66] An increase in U-boat activity through that spring and summer led to further refinement. In November 1917 a Milford Haven Group was set up to take responsibility for the Irish Sea, and in March 1918 this was supplemented by a Holyhead Group. The adoption of convoying for both overseas and coastal shipping from the spring of 1917 onwards made the U-boats' task more difficult, forcing them further inshore, but as subsequent events proved, they still possessed considerable potential to wreak havoc.[67]

U-boat activity escalated even more markedly in the last months of 1917 and early months of 1918. For instance, the 7,832 ton *Apapa* was sunk 3 miles off Point Lynas in September 1917 with the loss of seventy-seven lives.[68] She was one of over forty ships sunk off the Welsh coast between November 1917 and March 1918, with the Germans using the likes of Point Lynas and the Skerries as ambush points.[69] Another casualty in the same period, on 2 March, was HM Submarine *H5*, sunk in a collision with a merchant ship about 15 miles south-west of Aberffraw. Her entire crew of twenty-six perished, among them an American liaison officer, Lieutenant Earle Childs, the first American submariner to die in an external, as opposed to a civil, war.[70] The Admiralty responded to the upsurge in U-boat activity by implementing a new policy of combined operations in anti-submarine warfare, with aircraft and warships operating in a more co-ordinated way. Captain Gordon Campbell, VC, who had made his name as a bold and successful Q-ship captain, took command of all anti-submarine forces, both sea and air, from his base at Holyhead. Campbell initially commanded a flotilla of old destroyers, twenty-two motor launches and some other miscellaneous craft, half a dozen airships and a squadron of aeroplanes. He would advise the RNAS station at Llangefni of an inbound convoy in time for them to despatch airships or aircraft to meet it.[71]

Thus, by the summer of 1918 the Welsh ports were at the heart of a sophisticated defence network. In the last week of July 1918, for example, Milford-based warships met one incoming convoy from Gibraltar and escorted to sea the outgoing convoys OM86, consisting of thirty-one ships escorted by four patrol ships and eight trawlers and drifters (and initially by another patrol ship, fourteen more trawlers and two airships), and OM87, with twenty-seven ships escorted by three patrol ships, seven trawlers, and initially by additional escorts which included one aeroplane. During the same week, convoys of between four and seventeen colliers sailed daily from Milford to Rosslare, having assembled there from the other South Wales ports and ultimately going on to various Irish destinations from Galway to Dublin and Cork, and similarly sized convoys went daily in the opposite direction. Meanwhile, other Milford-based armed trawlers and gunboats escorted twenty-one individual ships on a variety of voyages, such as Holyhead and Milford to Barry Roads, Milford to Falmouth, and Milford to the Clyde.[72] These elaborate defensive strategies finally led to a considerable decrease in sinkings during the summer of 1918; by then the Germans were running short of experienced commanders and crews, and eight U-boats were sunk in Welsh waters during the first seven months of 1918. The final sinkings were those of the *Leinster* and *Dundalk* 5 miles north-west of the Skerries in October.[73]

Milford Haven and Holyhead were the navy's principal bases in Wales, but they were not the only ones. A significant number of vessels of the 'Auxiliary Patrol' were based at Swansea: these included armed trawlers and drifters, paddle minesweepers, motor launches and other miscellaneous craft. From June 1918, the Swansea Patrol was supplemented by six submarine chasers from the US Navy. These vessels undertook escort and patrol duties, protected the fishing industry, assisted the crews of sunken ships, and examined incoming vessels, which were compelled to anchor under the guns of the fort at Mumbles. Assistance was also rendered to downed airships, such as *SS Z-37*, which had to make a forced landing at Mumbles. The efforts of the Swansea ships kept sinkings in the area to a minimum but, even so, there were some terrible exceptions. Probably the worst were the sinkings in the Bristol Channel of the hospital ships *Rewa* by *U-55* and *Glenart Castle* by *UC-56* on 4 January and 26 February 1918. Both sinkings caused outrage in Britain, attacks on hospital ships being generally perceived as war crimes.[74]

The United States entered the war in April 1917 and quickly realised the need to establish a secure source of coal for its ships operating in European waters and secure supply lines to its soldiers on the Western Front. A rear-admiral USN was appointed to command a new base at Cardiff, US marines guarded Cardiff docks, and a large fleet of ships was employed to carry Welsh coal to the American forces. The Angel Hotel, Cardiff's beloved port of call for Welsh rugby fans before and after international matches, was commissioned as USS *Chatinouka*, and its bar staff were apparently bemused to learn that they were suddenly serving in a 'warship'.[75] American warships were also based in Welsh

waters. One of these was the United States Coastguard Cutter
Tampa, which regularly escorted convoys to and from Milford
Haven. On 26 September 1918 she was off Land's End, having
brought a convoy safely from Gibraltar, when she lost her com-
panions. That evening, in poor weather, the other ships heard
an explosion, but nothing was found other than a few pieces of
wreckage. It subsequently transpired that the *Tampa* had been
sunk by *UB-91*. There were no survivors from a total of about
130 men on board, making it the United States' worst naval
disaster of the First World War. A large memorial at Arlington
National Cemetery commemorates the sinking. Two bodies
were later washed up in south Pembrokeshire and buried at
Lamphey; one, the only body to be identified, was subsequently
exhumed and returned to America, but the other remains there
to this day. The only identifiable remnant of the *Tampa*, a brass
boat plate, was found on the beach at Rest Bay, Porthcawl, in
April 1924.[76]

Lloyd George and the Admirals

David Lloyd George became Prime Minister on 7 December
1916 and immediately faced a crisis that threatened the very
survival of the nation. Losses of shipping to U-boat attack had
increased steadily from just over 110,000 tons during July 1916
to over 500,000 in February 1917, the month in which Germany
announced its intention to resume the campaign of unrestricted
submarine warfare that it had suspended following the sinking
of the *Lusitania* in 1915. The German change of policy threatened an even greater increase in sinkings; shipyards could not
build enough new merchant ships to replace the losses, whereas
new U-boats were coming down the ways at a rate of eight a
month.[77] If things continued as they were, Britain would be
starved out and would undoubtedly lose the war well before
the end of 1917. Consequently, the new Prime Minister and his

admirals were desperate for a strategy that would enable them to defeat, or at least contain, the apparently unstoppable threat of the U-boats.

The principle of convoy was well understood – indeed, it had been employed for centuries – but in the particular circumstances of the First World War, many at the Admiralty doubted its efficacy. It was believed that a comprehensive convoy system would require many more escorts than were available, that merchant ship crews were incapable of keeping station in such a rigorous way and that, in any case, all convoying did was present submarines with a bigger and slower target. Deep down, the senior echelons of the navy were so focused on the idea of 'the great battle' that all supposedly lesser activities tended to be relegated, a mindset that Lloyd George found 'amazing and incomprehensible'. Over the winter of 1916–17, arguments raged between those who favoured the adoption of convoy and the great majority of senior figures in the navy who were determined to hold out against it. The Prime Minister was characteristically scathing about what he regarded as the hidebound thinking of his opponents:

> The expert advisers of the Admiralty at this time were labouring under a set of surprising delusions. The foremost of these was that the steamers of the mercantile marine could not be relied upon to 'keep station' ... The seamanship of the experienced mariners who steered the tramp steamers through all the weathers across the wild and foggy seas that surround and lead to these islands was completely underestimated.

Lloyd George was even less impressed when he learned that the Admiralty's figures for the numbers of British ships at sea and requiring escort were entirely wrong, the consequence of a simple arithmetical error 'which would not have been perpetrated by an ordinary clerk in a shipping office'.[78]

It is easy to imagine how Jellicoe must have seethed at being lectured on naval strategy by a man who was merely an obscure solicitor in Criccieth when the First Sea Lord was already the assistant director of naval ordnance. But Lloyd George had grown up at Llanystumdwy, less than a mile from a Tremadog Bay still full of brigs, barques and coasting steamers; his constituency included some of the busiest ports and strongest maritime communities in Wales, such as Porthmadog, Pwllheli, Nefyn and Porthdinllaen. Thus he knew the sailing masters and tramp ship skippers of Llŷn as clients and constituents, so when he spoke of their capabilities he had an insight and a confidence in them that the likes of Jellicoe and the proud liner captains could never possess. (Moreover, Lloyd George was an inveterate traveller who had made many voyages in merchant ships, including one as far as Patagonia.) Even so, the story was not quite as clear-cut as the Prime Minister presented it. In reality, the Admiralty was already leaning towards the adoption of convoy before Lloyd George's intervention. Even the particularly reluctant Jellicoe believed that the entry of the United States into the war had transformed the situation and made convoying more feasible. On the other hand, the Admiralty was well aware of the Prime Minister's views long before the meetings of late April when the decision was taken, so it cannot be denied that his strong stance in favour of convoy was a substantial factor in ensuring the adoption of the system: a system which effectively saved Britain from almost inevitable defeat.[79]

Operation Sea Lion

During the spring and summer of 1917, Wales' largest lake, Llyn Bala, witnessed one of the most bizarre attempts of all to counter the U-boat threat.[80] Late in 1916, the Admiralty's scientists began seriously to investigate the possibility of obtaining performing sea lions from the music hall and training them to track enemy submarines. Preliminary tests in swimming pools in Glasgow and Westminster suggested that the scheme had some potential, so plans were made to stage a much larger trial in open water. Sir Herbert Watkin Williams Wynn, seventh baronet and Lord Lieutenant of Montgomeryshire, made Llyn Bala available, and from 30 March to 6 July 1917 a naval trials unit took up residence in the area, the officers being accommodated at Glanllyn. A number of sea lions, many from the music hall but some on loan from London Zoo, were tested to see how well they responded to a variety of underwater noises; trailing them proved problematic, despite the adoption of such surreal expedients as daubing them with luminous paint. Unsurprisingly, the results were inconsistent, and became even more so once the trials moved to the open sea, where the sea lions became increasingly inclined to abscond and follow their own instincts. This revealed the scheme's fatal flaw: as far as any self-respecting sea lion was concerned, a U-boat was neither edible nor sexually attractive. In the Richard Hannay novel *The Three Hostages*, though, John Buchan put forward an alternative explanation for their lack of interest: 'The thing shipwrecked on the artistic temperament. The beasts all came from the music halls and had names like Flossie and Cissie, so they couldn't be got to realise that there was a war on, and were always going ashore without leave.' Before attempts to persuade Britannia's sea lion force to the contrary could make any progress, Lloyd George had convinced the navy to implement a convoy system, a simpler and far more effective solution to the U-boat threat, and the sea lion trials unit was broken up.

The Red Flag

The end of the war seemed to bring a very real threat that the Communist revolution in Russia would spread to western countries, including Britain. To counter the threat, substantial forces were despatched to assist the 'White Russian' opponents of the Lenin regime. British warships were sent into the White Sea, the Baltic and the Black Sea to undertake operations against the Bolsheviks. The situation in the fledgling Baltic states of Latvia, Lithuania and Estonia was chaotic, with British forces trying to hold the line against both the Bolshevik fleet at Kronstadt and their sympathisers ashore, who were intent on turning the Baltic republics into Soviet satellites, and German paramilitary forces equally intent on turning them into colonies of the new Weimar Republic. In January 1919, Crickhowell-born 'ferocious midget' Rear Admiral Walter Cowan was sent to take charge of the squadron operating in the Baltic. The Pembroke-built cruiser *Curacoa* was damaged by Bolshevik mines on 13 May, and on 17 October the navy's twelfth HMS *Dragon* was struck by German fire while providing artillery support for the nascent Latvian army's attempt to win control of Riga.[81] Ultimately, the navy's intervention proved crucial in fending off the Russian and German threats, and the Baltic republics enjoyed twenty years of independence, a state of affairs that was re-established after the end of the Cold War.

In January 1918, the cruiser HMS *Suffolk* was despatched to protect British interests at Vladivostok in the Pacific. One of her officers was a 37-year-old Barmouth-born Lieutenant RNR, Harold Lowe, who had become an overnight celebrity six years earlier when, as Fifth Officer of the *Titanic*, he turned around several of the ships' lifeboats to go back and search for more survivors. Conditions in Vladivostok were undoubtedly reminiscent of the fate of Lowe's previous ship: the *Suffolk* navigated into the harbour through dense ice fields and was swiftly icebound. Relations between the British, American and Japanese crews of the warships in port, and the Bolsheviks ashore, were exceptionally tense and progressively worsened. A new complication was provided in June 1918 by the arrival of a large number of anti-Bolshevik Czech troops, supposedly demobilised now that Russia's war with Germany was over. They swiftly took over the city as Harold Lowe and the guard detail from *Suffolk* that he was commanding looked on, subsequently taking charge of a number of Bolshevik prisoners. Lowe and *Suffolk* remained in Vladivostok for a year, finally leaving on 3 January 1919; the city remained under White Russian and Allied control for another fifteen months before the Bolsheviks resumed control.[82] Harold Lowe rejoined the merchant service later in 1919 and ultimately retired to Deganwy, dying there in 1944.

The intervention in Russia caused considerable resentment, particularly among men who believed that demobilisation was proceeding too slowly and who did not want to take part in what they saw as a campaign against their fellow working men. There had already been several other mutinies on warships around Britain when, on 13 January 1919, the crew of the patrol boat HMS *Kilbride*, at anchor in Dale Roads, Milford Haven, refused to obey orders and hoisted the Red Flag. The mutiny was swiftly quashed, and eight men were court-martialled; seven received sentences ranging from three months to two years and were dismissed from the service.[83] One of them was A.B. Ellis, who had remarked that 'Half the navy are on strike, and the other half will soon be on strike.' But the mutiny on the *Kilbride* also had very specific causes that were unique to the ship. Her commanding officer, Lieutenant Marsh RNR, seems to have been an incompetent bully who provoked the mutiny by ordering the crew to work two watches, rather than the less onerous three.[84] The mutiny on the *Kilbride* was therefore a relatively insignificant event on a markedly insignificant ship in what was, in 1919, something of a naval backwater, but for the Left, the raising of the Red Flag aboard a British warship retains a symbolic importance out of all proportion to the reality.

Kilbride was also by no means the last mutiny in which Wales and Welsh naval men would be involved. On 1 April 1921 the miners began an all-out national strike, with the famously militant South Wales coalfield taking the lead. A state of emergency was proclaimed the battleships Ramillies and Revenge anchored in Milford Haven with large contingents of Royal Marines aboard, the reserves were called up, and a battalion of the Royal Fleet Reserve was despatched from Portsmouth to Newport. The reservists were accommodated in a filthy derelict factory; moreover, many of them were strongly influenced by trade unionism, and had deep qualms about confronting their fellow workers. Consequently, on 29 April most of the battalion refused to obey the order to fall in.[85] Lieutenant A.O. Gillitt of the Royal Marines arrived in Newport on the following day. He noted how 'the bolshies ashore [specifically, 150 miners and a trade union secretary] got hold of them' and how, after refusing to fall in and indulging in some looting, the mutineers finally returned to their duty. A few weeks later a sailor from HMS *Champion* was placed under arrest at Newport for having 'got up at a bolshie meeting ashore and made an awfully seditious speech. I hope he will get about ten years. I think there are extremely few if any at all bolshie sympathisers in the battalion although no doubt bolshie agitators are trying to get at them.' Gillitt was eventually sent to Abertillery and played cricket against the miners, whom he regarded as 'extremely nice chaps and very civil'; he also thought the people of Monmouthshire 'must be pretty well off as there are heaps of beautiful cars about'.[86] Meanwhile, the officer in command of the mutinied reservists, Captain Edward Kennedy, faced a court martial and was dismissed from the service for his failure to handle the situation correctly. He was recalled to service in 1939, but was killed shortly afterwards when commanding the armed merchant cruiser *Rawalpindi* in her heroic but doomed fight against the vastly superior German battlecruisers *Scharnhorst* and *Gneisenau*; his son was the famous broadcaster Sir Ludovic Kennedy.

The most serious mutiny of the inter-war period took place at Invergordon in September 1931, when a large part of the Atlantic Fleet rebelled against a proposed pay cut. Harry Ackland of Cardiff joined the navy in 1926 to escape the intimidation he experienced as an apprentice (who could not walk out) during the General Strike, finding himself one of a large party of Welshmen who were trying to join up at Bristol. In 1931 he served aboard the minelayer-cruiser HMS *Adventure*; he later recalled that she had a large Welsh contingent in her crew, like all Devonport-manned ships, including 'quite a number' from Cardiff and others from Newport and the Valleys. Ackland believed that their background in, and connections with, the severely depressed communities of South Wales made them particularly militant. 'It wasn't a happy time in the navy,' Ackland later recalled. 'This was an unrest you could feel in your bones, something was going to happen.'[87] So it proved. On 15 September the crews of *Hood*, *Nelson*, *Rodney* and *Valiant* disobeyed orders to take the ships to sea for exercises; *Adventure* was one of the ships that joined the mutiny later in the day. The mutiny ended on 16 September with the cancellation of the exercises and the ships sailing for their home ports; the government partially reversed the pay cut, but some two hundred ringleaders were gaoled or dismissed from the service, while the panic that the mutiny engendered on the London Stock Exchange led to Britain coming off the Gold Standard.

A Naval Graveyard [I]

At the end of the First World War, large numbers of surplus warships made their way to shipbreaking yards, many of them relatively newly established, in the harbours and estuaries of South Wales. There was an obvious symbiosis: the large numbers of steel works in or near the coast created a ready and easily accessible market. Thomas Ward had set up a yard at Briton Ferry in 1906, that scrapped the battleship Colossus as early as 1908, John Cashmore established another at Newport in 1909, Cohens began a yard at Swansea, and after the war other yards were established at Porthcawl, Cardiff, Llanelli, Milford Haven and, after the closure of the royal dockyard, Pembroke

Dock.[88] Several ships that had distinguished themselves during the war were opened to the public before being broken up. At Llanelli, crowds flocked to pay 6*d* each to tour HMS *Chester*, aboard which Boy John Travers Cornwell had won a posthumous Victoria Cross at Jutland, aged 16 years and 6 months, the youngest ever naval VC; the proceeds went to Llanelli General Hospital. Similarly, at Newport, John Cashmore donated the proceeds from the public viewing of the battleship *Collingwood* to the Royal Gwent Hospital.[89] Surrendered U-boats, too, were opened for public viewing before going to the breakers: curious crowds flocked aboard *U-112* at Milford Haven and *UB-91* at Pembroke Dock. *UB-91* was broken up at Briton Ferry, and is the likeliest candidate for the source of the gun which forms the memorial to William Williams VC at Chepstow.[90] Another submarine that ended its days in Welsh waters, albeit before its time, was HMS *H47*, sunk in an accidental collision with *L12* 12 miles north of St David's Head on 9 July 1929; twenty-four lives were lost on the two submarines.[91]

Notes

1   G. Phillips, 'Dai Bach y Soldiwr: Welsh Soldiers in the British Army, 1914–18', *Llafur*, 6 (1993), pp.94–105; C. Parry, 'Gwynedd and the Great War, 1914–18', *Welsh History Review*, 14 (1988–89), pp.78–117.

2   L. Lloyd, *Wherever Freights May Offer: The Maritime Community of Abermaw/Barmouth 1565–1920* (Caernarfon, 1993), pp.114–15.

3   IWM, Oral History 12238.

4   J. Rawlins, 'Conflict at Sea: A Llanybydder Boy's Records of Wartime Service in the Royal Navy', *The Carmarthenshire Antiquary*, xxix (1993), pp.103–10.

5   IWM, Documents 12571.

6   www.laugharnewarmemorial.co.uk/page47.htm (Accessed: 2012)

7   www.laugharnewarmemorial.co.uk/page19.htm and the CWGC database. (Accessed: 2012)

8   J.W. Hughes, 'A Red and Green Flavoured Smell on the Wind', *Wales*, 46 (1959), p.30.

9   AA, WD9.

10 A. Eames, *Machlud Hwyliau'r Cymry/The Twilight of Welsh Sail* (Cardiff, 1984), p.81.

11 www.laugharnewarmemorial.co.uk/page19.htm (Accessed: 2012)
12 AA, WM/1041.
13 For Taylor's career see R. Mullock-Morgans, 'Engineer Captain C
   G Taylor, MVO, RN (1863–1915)', *Hel Achau: Clwyd Family History
   Society*, 100 (2009).
14 C.W. Lewis, rev. C.L. Taylor, 'Gruffydd, William John (1881–1954),
   Welsh Writer and University Teacher', *ODNB*.
15 J. Bevan, 'Surgeon Frederick Hill', *Country Quest* (1995), pp.20–1.
16 IWM, Documents 12571.
17 W.A. Williams, *Heart of a Dragon: The VCs of Wales and the Welsh
   Regiments, 1914–82* (Wrexham, 2008), pp.132–43; Eames, pp.519–20.
18 Williams, *Heart of a Dragon*, pp.27–37.
19 *Rhondda Leader*, 28 Oct. 1916.
20 R. Harvard, 'Thomas Picton and Sir Thomas Picton: Two Welsh
   soldiers in Spain', *THSC* (2000), pp.164–5, 180–1.
21 memorials.rmg.co.uk/m3367/, sv M3367; R.G. Gulliford, 'Boy 1st
   Class Arthur Simpson Protherough', *Aberyschan and Garndiffaith Local
   History Group*, 6 (2001), pp.9–10.
22 IWM, Documents 12571.
23 *Ex info* Holyhead Maritime Museum; http://www.pembrokeshire-
   war-memorial.co.uk/page55.htm (Accessed: 2012)
24 www.pembrokeshire-war-memorial.co.uk/page55.htm; www.
   laugharnewarmemorial.co.uk/page65.htm (Accessed: 2012)
25 walesinthefirstworldwar.typepad.com/wales_in_the_first_
   world_/2009/01/able-seaman-richard-morgan-the-last-british-
   serviceman-to-die-in-world-war-one.html
26 Analysis based on the Commonwealth War Graves Commission
   database, www.cwgc.org. The proportion for Swansea in 1917 was
   even higher.
27 www.pembrokeshire-war-memorial.co.uk/page11.htm
   (Accessed: 2012)
28 www.laugharnewarmemorial.co.uk/page19.htm (Accessed: 2012)
29 Williams, *Heart of a Dragon*, pp.257–66; D.G.O. James, 'For Valour:
   George Henry Prowse, VC, DCM, RNVR, Swansea's Forgotten
   Hero', *Morgannwg: The Journal of Glamorgan History*, liv (2010),
   pp.112–26.
30 W. Davies, *The Sea and the Sand: The Story of HMS Tara and the Western
   Desert Force* (Caernarfon, 1988).
31 www.pembrokeshire-war-memorial.co.uk/page47.htm
32 NLW, Tredegar MS P1/83.
33 *Rhondda Leader*, 19 Dec. 1914; www.pembrokeshire-war-memorial.
   co.uk/page55.htm (Accessed: 2012)

34 T. Bridgland, *Outrage at Sea: Naval Atrocities of the First World War* (Barnsley, 2002), pp.176–92.

35 GRO, D198/1.

36 J.T. Sumida, 'British Naval Operational Logistics, 1914–18', *The Journal of Military History*, vol. 57, no. 3 (July 1993), pp.447–80.

37 M. Bodman, 'Coals to Newcastle? The Jellicoe Specials', *Back Track*, 20/8 (2006), pp.498–503.

38 A. Mór-O'Brien, 'Patriotism on Trial', *Welsh History Review*, 12 (1984), pp.76–104.

39 TNA, ADM1/9208.

40 A. Gordon, *The Rules of the Game: Jutland and British Naval Command* (1996), pp.37–42, 216–42, 374–77.

41 Gordon, *Rules of the Game*, pp.54–8.

42 Unless stated otherwise, the account of Jutland that follows is based on Gordon, *Rules of the Game*.

43 One Welsh seaman's account of the battle – that of Frank Smale of Cardiff – is online: www.peoplescollection.wales/items/26154#?xywh=-958%2C-167%2C4242%2C3336

44 Gordon, *Rules of the Game*, pp.546–61.

45 V.W. Baddeley, rev. M. Brodie, 'Thomas, Sir Hugh Evan (1862–1928), naval officer', *ODNB*.

46 T. Bridgland, *Outrage at Sea: Naval Atrocities of the First World War* (Barnsley, 2002), pp.40–58.

47 DRO, DD/PH/293.

48 DRO, DD/PH/293, especially letters to father, 20 Jan 1916, 9 March 1919.

49 DRO, DD/PH/293, letter to father, 13 Nov. 1918.

50 R. Bainton, *Honoured by Strangers: The Life of Captain Francis Cromie CB DSO RN, 1882–1918* (Shrewsbury, 2002), pp.13–16, 23. The remainder of this paragraph is based on Bainton's book.

51 Quoted by Bainton, *Honoured by Strangers*, p.6.

52 A. Phillips, *Defending Wales: The Coast and Sea Lanes in Wartime* (Stroud, 2010), p.25.

53 AA, WM/1609/6-26; G. Jones, *Anglesey at War* (Stroud, 2012), pp.7, 36, 39.

54 IWM, Oral History 313.

55 Phillips, *Defending Wales*, pp.26–42.

56 M. Hale, *Fishguard's Great War Seaplanes* (Pembroke Dock, 2007); Phillips, *Defending Wales*, pp.43–53.

57 J. Snelson, 'Novello, Ivor [real name David Ivor Davies] (1893–1951), Composer, Actor, and Playwright', *ODNB*.

58 G. Campbell, *The Life of a Q-Ship Captain* (2002 edn.), pp.122–3.

59 D. Lloyd Hughes and D.M. Williams, *Holyhead: The Story of a Port* (Holyhead, 1981), p.155.

60 Jones, *Anglesey at War*, pp.32–3. To mark the centenary of the First World War the Royal Commission on the Ancient and Historical Monuments of Wales set up The U-boat Project, which has unearthed new evidence of the naval war in Welsh waters and the wrecks of lost U-boats: see its website, uboatproject.wales/

61 I.W. Jones, *U-Boat Rendezvous at Llandudno* (published privately, Llandudno, 1978).

62 E. Goddard, 'Naval Activity', *Pembrokeshire County History, IV: Modern Pembrokeshire* (Haverfordwest, 1993), pp.339–40. For the U-boat campaign off Pembrokeshire and its impact ashore, see also S. Hancock, 'The Social Impact of the First World War in Pembrokeshire', University of Cardiff PhD thesis (2015), pp. 335–41.

63 TNA, ADM137/1213.

64 Goddard, 'Naval Activity', p.341; www.teara.govt.nz/en/biographies/3s2/1

65 Eames, pp.522–3.

66 Goddard, 'Naval Activity', p.341.

67 P. Armstrong and R. Young, *Silent Warriors: Submarine Wrecks of the United Kingdom*, iii (Stroud, 2010), pp.14–5.

68 Eames, p.525.

69 R. and B. Larn, *Shipwreck Index of the British Isles: West Coast and Wales* (2000), not paginated.

70 Armstrong and Young, *Silent Warriors*, pp.90–6.

71 J.J. Abbatiello, *Anti-Submarine Warfare in World War I: British Naval Aviation and the Defeat of the U-Boats* (2006), pp.120–1.

72 TNA, ADM137/1510.

73 Eames, pp.528–31; Armstrong and Young, *Silent Warriors*, passim.

74 TNA, CAB45/275; T. Bridgland, *Outrage at Sea: Naval Atrocities of the First World War* (Barnsley, 2002), pp.165–75.

75 J. Richards, *Cardiff: A Maritime History* (Stroud, 2005), pp.108–9; www.geocities.ws/fey_uk/Chatinouka.html (Last Accessed: 2012)

76 T. Markes, 'A Pilgrimage in Search of "Lost" Wartime Grave', *Western Telegraph*, 2 Dec. 1992.

77 D.A.H. Wilson, 'Sea Lions, Greasepaint And The U-Boat Threat: Admiralty Scientists Turn To The Music Hall In 1916', *Notes and Records of the Royal Society of London*, 55 (2001), p.430.

78 *War Memoirs of David Lloyd George* (1933), I. 677–96: quotations from pp.677, 681–2 and 682, respectively.

79 J.S. Breemer, *Defeating the U-Boat: Inventing Anti-Submarine Warfare* (Newport, RI, 2010), pp.47–61.

80 What follows is based on D.A.H. Wilson, 'Sea Lions, Greasepaint And The U-Boat Threat: Admiralty Scientists Turn To The Music Hall In 1916', *Notes and Records of the Royal Society of London*, 55 (2001), pp.425–55.

81 www.hmsdragon1919.co.uk/ – an excellent website produced by the granddaughter of one of those killed aboard *Dragon*. (Last Accessed: 2012)

82 I. Sheil, *Titanic Valour: The Life of Fifth Officer Harold Lowe* (Stroud, 2012), ch. 13, passim. I am also grateful to John Lowe, Harold's grandson, for allowing me to study Lowe's photograph albums of his time in Vladivostok.

83 A. Carew, *The Lower Deck of the Royal Navy, 1900–39: The Invergordon Mutiny in Perspective* (Manchester, 1981), p.104.

84 A. Rothstein, *The Soldiers' Strikes of 1919* (1980), p.52.

85 Battleships and Marines at Milford: A J Perrett, *Royal Marines in Wales*, Royal Marines Historical Society, Portsmouth (1992), pp. 10–15.

86 NLW, MS 23133C, fos. 1, 6, 24v, 26, 28.

87 IWM, Oral History 5839.

88 www.naval-history.net/WW1NavyBritish-Shipbreak.htm

89 Chester: *South Wales Press*, 18 Jan. 1922; Collingwood: www.newportpast.com/jd/cashmore.htm

90 K. McKay and G. Springer, *Milford Haven: Waterway and Town* (2011 edn), p.67; information received from Alan Phillips, whose mother toured *UB-91*.

91 P. Armstrong and R. Young, *Silent Warriors: Submarine Wrecks of the United Kingdom*, iii (Stroud, 2010), pp.58–66.

10

TRA MÔR YN FUR I'R BUR HOFF BAU

THE NAVAL DEFENCE OF WALES, 1939–45

When the Second World War broke out in 1939, Wales found itself in the front line to an unprecedented degree. In one sense it remained relatively remote from the main theatres of war, as it had been in the First: the north and east coasts of Scotland were still the front line against the surface ships of the German Navy, and the south-east of England the front line against the Luftwaffe. But the loss of the naval bases in Ireland (which had been of great value in the first war, but were handed over to the Irish Free State in 1938) increased the relative importance of Milford Haven in particular, which became vitally important to the defence of shipping in the Western Approaches. Above all, the improvements in bomber design and range since 1918 meant that Welsh towns, and above all Welsh ports, were now viable targets, particularly after the German conquest of France in 1940, and this truism was demonstrated in particularly devastating fashion during the destruction of the oil tanks at Pembroke Dock on 19 August 1940, the 'three nights' blitz' of Swansea from 19 to 21 February 1941, and the sustained bombing of Cardiff. Enemy aircraft could now attack shipping, or drop mines, right up to the entrances to, or in some cases actually in, Welsh docks and harbours. U-boats also had greater range and could stay on station for longer than they had been able to do in the First World War, making shipping around the Welsh coast even more vulnerable. Welsh shipping was in the front line, too. Of 164 Welsh-owned merchant ships, no fewer than 123 were sunk, and it has been calculated that 'for a town of its size, Barry had proportionately more deaths at sea than any other port in Britain'.[1] Although most of these losses were in the deep seas, a substantial effort had to be devoted to the naval defence of Welsh sea lanes against air and submarine attack. By 1944, though, defence was turning into attack, and Welsh waters were an important marshalling area for part of the largest naval armada the world had ever seen: Operation Neptune, the maritime aspect of D-Day.

The Loss of the *Thetis*

Anglesey was affected by a profound naval tragedy even before the war began. On 1 June 1939, the new submarine HMS *Thetis* sailed from the building yard in Birkenhead for diving trials in Liverpool Bay. She was carrying nearly double her official complement, principally because contractors from the yard were embarked as passengers. She attempted to dive at about 2 p.m., but proved to be too light, so a survey of the water in the tanks and torpedo tubes was carried out. However, when the test cocks on the tubes were opened it was not realised that the one on Tube Five was blocked by enamel paint, so no water trickled out despite the fact that the bow cap was actually open. This and various other confusions aboard led to the fatal opening of the tube's inner door, flooding the forward compartments. The submarine sank, although the stern initially remained above the surface, because rescue attempts took far too long to organise. Four crewmen managed to escape, but the remaining ninety-nine were overcome by carbon dioxide poisoning. The wreck was finally raised on 2 September, the day before war was declared, and towed to Traeth Bychan, Moelfre, where it was beached and the bodies recovered. Forty-four of the victims were buried in November at Holyhead's Maeshyfryd cemetery, where a large memorial was erected over the grave. The *Thetis* herself was refitted, renamed HMS *Thunderbolt*, and was eventually sunk in the Mediterranean in 1943.[2]

Welsh Ports and Sea Lanes under Attack

Shortly before the war began, a naval infrastructure was put in place at the ports of South Wales. Retired Commanders RN were put in charge of Newport, Barry and Swansea (where the base was commissioned as the distinctly sinister HMS *Lucifer*), all under Rear-Admiral R.H.L. Bevan, who was based at Imperial Buildings in Mountstuart Square, Cardiff.[3] This Cardiff sub-command extended as far west as the Tywi Estuary, where the Flag Officer Milford Haven took over. In the early stages of the war its principal responsibility was the despatch of convoys to France, initially those carrying elements of the British Expeditionary Force. A convoy sailed each week until the middle of June 1940, assembling in Barry Roads before sailing for Nantes or St Nazaire with a destroyer escort. A minesweeper flotilla was formed at Swansea to combat the minefields laid in the Bristol Channel by a German U-boat; two merchant ships were damaged by these mines in early October 1939, and several others were sunk or damaged in the early months of 1940. From January 1940, seven converted trawlers operated anti-submarine patrols from Swansea, supplemented by aircraft and depth charge-equipped yachts and motor launches based there and at Barry. By January 1942 the number of mine countermeasures vessels of various sorts based at Swansea had increased to thirty-one.[4] Meanwhile, a Naval Examination Service was set up, and all incoming merchantmen were stopped and checked until they had permission to proceed; the Welsh anchorages used by the Examination Service were the Menai Strait (withdrawn in 1942), Holyhead, Milford Haven, Fishguard (for Port Talbot and all ports westward of it, except Milford) and Barry Roads (for all ports east of Port Talbot), while Swansea was a 'non-search port' where other procedures were followed.[5]

In the north, Abermenai was guarded at first by six patrol boats based at Fort Belan, patrolling out as far as Bardsey. Vice-Admiral Hubert Lynes, a distinguished ornithologist who had organised the Zeebrugge Raid in 1918, was brought out of retirement to become resident naval officer at Caernarfon, commanding two flotillas of six motor launches, which were based at Caernarfon and Menai Bridge. A minefield was laid off Belan Point in March 1941 and the patrol boats were then withdrawn.[6] The First War base at Holyhead was reopened and commissioned as HMS *Torch*; by January 1942 it was the headquarters of the 86th anti-submarine group, a minesweeping group of five Dutch vessels, and a flotilla of eight motor launches. In the south-west, Milford was a discrete command under an admiral, its naval base named HMS *Skirmisher*; the first Flag Officer of the war was Rear-Admiral Philip Esmonde Philips of Crumlin.* Milford was host to an eclectic mixture of ships and nationalities. The Irish Sea Escort Force included several merchantmen that had been converted into anti-aircraft ships, the old AA cruiser *Cairo*, five First World War vintage destroyers, nine sloops (four British, three Free French and two Indian) together with an anti-submarine flotilla consisting of armed trawlers, four of which were named after northern football clubs – one assumes there must have been 'friendly' matches between HMT *Derby County*

---

* An exceptionally detailed account of naval operations from Milford Haven during the war, and of Sunderland flying boat operations from Pembroke Dock, was provided by the respected journalist Vernon Scott (d. 2008) in *An Experience Shared* (Pembroke Dock, 1992).

and HMT *Leeds United*, but regrettably no record of them seems to survive.[7] An old tanker, the *War Hindoo*, was moored in the harbour to refuel the escort ships based there. In January 1942 Milford was also home to two Polish destroyers, one Norwegian and sixteen Dutch Navy minesweepers, together with five Belgian armed motor fishing vessels and various auxiliaries manned by the Free French. A further two flotillas of motor launches were based at Pembroke Dock.[8] One of the units in the Irish Sea Escort Force was the elderly patrol ship *PC74*, which dated from 1918, still occasionally rigged a stay sail, and still included cutlasses as part of her 'armament', much to the delight of her eccentric captain, a bearded, monocled showman named Charles Hughes-White. *PC74*'s doctor, E.V.B. Morton, recalled how she escorted convoys from Barry Roads to Lough Foyle and once spent a month based at Swansea to test a new radar system, her officers spending the weekends on extended drinking sessions with the Polish squadron at RAF Fairwood Common. Milford Haven itself had two naval officers' clubs, one for the more senior and regular RN officers and another, the Starboard Club, for the more junior and RNR/RNVR officers.[9]

The fall of France greatly increased the strategic significance of *Mor Hafren*, the Bristol Channel. Much of the trade of the eastern and southern ports, which were now too exposed to German attack, was diverted there, and the Channel ports became some of the principal termini for the merchant shipping bringing in the arms, munitions and food without which Britain would lose the war. The Germans swiftly realised this, and the first air raid on the Channel took place on 20 June 1940, sinking the SS *Stesso* at her mooring in Bute East Dock, Cardiff. Thereafter raids took place at regular, sometimes daily, intervals on the docks at Cardiff, Swansea, Newport, Penarth and Port Talbot, and during the same period German aircraft also laid new minefields off the Welsh ports. Milford Haven was mined for the first time on the night of 22–23 July.[10] The first Royal Navy vessel to be sunk in the Bristol Channel, the armed trawler

HMT *Oswaldian*, struck a mine near the Breaksea light vessel on 4 August and sank, losing twelve of her crew of seventeen; several merchant ships were also sunk or damaged by mines during the second half of 1940. Over the winter of 1940–41 the focus of the attacks switched to the towns themselves, most notoriously in the 'three nights' blitz' of Swansea, but a less well remembered threat came from the frequent mine laying raids that supplemented the main attacks and which caused serious problems for the naval forces trying to keep the approaches to the ports clear. Several ships evaded U-boat attack and crossed the Atlantic safely only to be mined within sight of their home ports; one was the *Fort Medine*, carrying 7,000 tons of iron ore and en route from Wabana, Newfoundland, to Port Talbot, which struck a mine and sank a mile off the Mumbles lighthouse.[11] Minelaying attacks continued until the end of November 1941, and on several occasions some or all of the South Wales ports had to be closed for a day or more while minesweeping took place. In all, a total of 195 mines were swept by Swansea-based minesweepers.[12] From July 1940 there was also a large defensive minefield, ZME, which covered most of the approach to the Bristol Channel, with shipping being channelled into gaps off the north Devon and Pembrokeshire coasts.[13] Meanwhile, intermittent bombing attacks continued. The destroyer HMS *Puckeridge* was bombed and badly damaged very nearly in the entrance to Milford Haven on 13 December 1941: thirty-two men were killed, most of whom are buried at Llanion Cemetery, Pembroke Dock. It was believed by some that it was a 'friendly fire' incident, and that the ship had been attacked in error by a British aircraft, but the balance of probability suggests that the attacker was German.[14]

From the summer of 1940 onwards, too, naval countermeasures against a potential German invasion were put in place. A line of armed trawlers and other vessels, many of them based at Swansea, patrolled the outer waters of the Bristol Channel to give early warning of any attack. In addition to the anti-landing obstacles placed on beaches, and the defensive lines of pill boxes and other fortifications ashore, a controlled minefield manned by the Royal Marines was laid at the mouth of the Burry Inlet and new gun batteries were established, several of them, like those on Lavernock Point and Flatholm Island, within the footings of older fortifications.[15] When the immediate threats of invasion and the German bombing campaign passed, attention could switch to the establishment of more systematic procedures for naval defence. In April 1941, a system of convoys was instituted between the Welsh ports and those on the south coast of England. Vessels sailed from Barry Roads and were joined by others from Swansea and Milford Haven, each convoy usually escorted by three anti-submarine trawlers. By the time the system ended in June 1944, 530 outbound convoys containing over 6,000 merchant ships had made the passage, suffering relatively light casualties. Larger ocean-going convoys sailed from Barry Roads or Dale Roads in Milford Haven. In all, over 17,000 convoys, with an aggregate displacement of over 63 million tons, sailed from Milford.[16]

There had been intermittent U-boat operations in the Irish Sea and St George's Channel throughout the war, but the effective establishment of allied supremacy in the battle over the Atlantic convoys in 1943 led Admiral Dönitz to change his strategy. The Irish Sea was one of the new theatres of war selected for the U-boats, and their ability to operate there was enhanced by the introduction of *Schnorkel*, which enabled them to obtain fresh air and recharge their batteries while remaining underwater. A sustained campaign took place off the Welsh coast over the winter of 1944–45 and on into the spring.[17] Coastal convoys were re-established, defensive patrols off the South Wales coast were stepped up, and the inshore fishermen of Llanelli, Ferryside and Tenby were recruited to keep a lookout for the tell-tale wisp of smoke that betrayed a *Schnorkel* device in use, because 'Carmarthen Bay appeared to be an ideal funk hole for U-boats preying on shipping entering and leaving the Bristol Channel.'[18] During two days in January 1945, *U-1055* sank four merchant ships in the southern Irish Sea.[19] A few days later, *U-1172* sank two more and also blew the stern of the frigate HMS *Manners*, but this brought a hunting pack after her, and the frigates *Tyler*, *Keats* and *Bligh* sank her in St George's Channel on 27 January. *U-1051* had been sunk off Anglesey the previous day by another group of Captain-class frigates. By the end of February, *U-1302* was on station off the North Pembrokeshire coast, sinking four ships including the *King Edgar*, bound from Vancouver to Milford, which had come safely all the way from the Pacific to be sunk almost within sight of its destination. On 7 March, three Canadian frigates caught up with *U-1302* and sent her to the bottom of Cardigan Bay. Other U-boats were sunk by aircraft or by the anti-submarine minefield laid from Devon to the Irish Coast; for example, *U-242* struck a mine off St David's Head on 5 April and was lost with all forty-four hands. Also in April, warships in Anglesey's waters dealt with *U-246* and *U-1024*, the last U-boat to be captured during the war.[20] The defeat of Germany led to a rapid diminution of the navy's presence in Wales; the base at Pembroke Dock was run down during the summer of 1945, while the Cardiff sub-command was abolished in November 1945, and the naval base there closed in January 1946.[21]

'Warship Weeks'

'Warship weeks', a campaign initially launched on 18 October 1941, was effectively a 'sequel' to the earlier 'war weapons weeks', which attempted to encourage people to save. Communities chose a suitable week during the following few months and were given targets representing the distinct costs of the hulls and fully completed warships, which they were able formally to 'adopt' if they met the target. In a sense the financial targets were hypothetical, as the ships were already 'paid for' (many of them, indeed, had been in service for many years):

the real objective was to discourage spending and attract people instead to savings certificates and 3 per cent Savings Bonds that were specifically aimed at small savers. Like similar campaigns for aircraft, tanks and other war equipment, 'warship weeks' were organised in a highly systematic way. Inevitably, the campaign spawned new committees galore; the first meeting of the Cardiff Docks Committee took place on 12 December 1941 in the presence of the Lord Mayor and the chairman of the overall Cardiff Warship Week Committee, the shipowner Sir William Reardon Smith. In Cardiff and other industrial centres, speakers addressed lunchtime workplace meetings, mobile vans were stationed at key locations to sell bonds, and appeals were placed in workers' pay packets. Special events were laid on, usually at weekends and during evenings so as not to disrupt productivity. There were march pasts, church services, speeches by local dignitaries and, above all, entertainments, at which the emphasis was always on fundraising. These were clearly designed to appeal to all levels of society, but the results were perhaps not entirely what one might expect. In Cardiff, a 'Friday night ball' raised just over £400, easily outdoing the £280 raised at a boxing match, the £235 from a greyhound race meeting and the £207 from the Conservative Association whist drive. Curiously, a football match raised double the amount stumped up by a markedly less generous rugby crowd, and the Llandaff and Barry Conservative Association, which presumably counted among its membership some of the most well-heeled citizens of south-east Wales, contributed only a meagre £2 and 10 shillings.[22]

Elsewhere, Penmaenmawr set out to raise £70,000 for *MTB 223*, initially aiming to raise £25,000 for the hull during its 'warship week' 14–21 March 1942 and the rest of the money by the end of the year. The town organised a full programme of fundraising events, including a 'grand naval dance', and, like many communities, it introduced an element of competition with traditional local rivals, putting up running totals in a ship window so that people could see how Penmaenmawr was doing in comparison with Bangor, Bethesda and Llanfairfechan. The flyer also provided a list of twenty-nine men from the town serving in the navy, the Fleet Air Arm, the Royal Marines and, in one case, the Royal Indian Naval Reserve, together with others in the Merchant Navy; however, several of these were posted as 'missing', including men who had gone down with the carrier *Glorious* in 1940 and the cruiser *Gloucester* in 1941.[23] Even schoolchildren were mobilised for the campaign. In Cardiff, St Peter's School set out to raise £50 towards the adoption of HMS *Cardiff* in January 1942, partly by selling two hundred souvenirs at 3*d* a time. On 19 January, Stacey Infants School was asked to collect £25 for a depth charge, but had double that amount by the end of the afternoon; on the same day ten boys from Hawthorn Mixed visited 'the Exhibition of Warships at the National Museum'. By the end of the week the amounts raised by Cardiff schools varied from £26 12*s* 6*d* at Hawthorn Infants to no less than £1,939 at Gladstone. St Paul's Infants raised four times the school's target; St Illtyd's, ten times. In all, Cardiff's schools raised £33,000, an average of 30 shillings per pupil, and the city as a whole exceeded its target three times over.[24] But not all campaigns were so successful. Anglesey set out to raise £637,000 for a Hunt-class destroyer and a mine-sweeper to be named *Beaumaris*, but raised only just over half of its target; it was suggested that reverses in the Middle and Far East had seriously damaged popular enthusiasm for the fund-raising effort.[25]

Wales as a whole (excluding Monmouthshire) raised £19,432,589 from 'warship weeks' by June 1942.[26] If local targets were met, as they usually were, proud local councils held ceremonies, perhaps combined with those for 'tanks week' and 'wings for victory', at which plaques were exchanged with the new adopted ship and certificates were presented to the parishes, streets, schools and factories that had raised the most money.[27] The upshot was that communities the length and breadth of Wales adopted 'their' ships and followed their war careers with

pride.* Barry adopted the elderly destroyer HMS *Vanessa* in
September 1942. After she sank *U-357* the following Boxing
Day, the mayor sent a message to the ship: 'Heartiest congratu-
lations upon successful encounter with U-boat. Hope you get
many more.'[28] The destroyer *Nubian*, one of Pembrokeshire's
adopted ships, was one of the most decorated British warships
of the entire war, winning no fewer than thirteen battle honours from the Arctic to Crete and Burma. She was only one
of only four ships from the original class of sixteen to survive
until the peace, and was scrapped at Briton Ferry in 1949; she
is still commemorated by a Nubian Crescent in Milford Haven
and a Nubian Avenue in Haverfordwest.[29] However, the loss of
a district's ship had an impact that in some cases is still felt to
this day. A service to commemorate the anniversary of the loss
of HM Submarine *Urge*, the town's adopted vessel, was held in
Bridgend in April 2011, although this was very much a consequence of the sterling efforts of one local campaigner; the local
library had been on the point of throwing out *Urge*'s badge
because the staff had no idea what it was.[30]

Social mores in the 1940s were sometimes very different to
those of the present day. Even so, it is surely a distinct possibility
that at least a few of the more 'macho' miners and metalworkers
of Bedwellty and New Tredegar had some difficulty associat-
ing themselves with their new adopted ship, HMS *Buttercup*,
despite one local poet's attempt to convince them that she would
be 'Bedwellty's battleship'.[31] But some things remain eternal,
the nature of Welsh local authorities being one of them. When
Barry proposed to adopt the *Vanessa*, the civic dignitaries were
uncertain how much to spend on the commemorative plaque
and what size and shape it should be. They discreetly consulted
the clerk to Pontypridd Council, who gladly provided the spec-
ifications of the plaque that they had ordered for their earlier

---

★ A list of known adoptions during Second World War 'warship weeks'
is provided in Appendix 2.

adoption of HMS *Tamarisk*. The clerk concluded by remarking that 'our motto, like that of the navy, is "attack! attack!" – rate-payers for preference!'[32]

Bombs and Butlin's

Although Wales was not exempt from bombing, it was assumed from the outset that it would be less vulnerable to regular, sustained attack than targets nearer to the main Luftwaffe bases on the continent. Moreover, Wales had a substantial unemployed labour force, good transport links (notably the Great Western Railway and the South Wales ports) and immediately adjacent heavy industry and raw materials, notably coal and steel. Consequently, a number of major new naval establishments were set up in Wales during the early years of the war. Construction of a naval propellant works had already begun at Caerwent in 1939, the site having been chosen because it was adjacent to supplies of water pumped out of the Severn Tunnel; this gave it an advantage over the other sites that had been considered, such as Cowbridge, Laugharne and St Clears. Caerwent was operational by 1941, manufacturing cordite for naval artillery, and became one of the largest such sites in Britain, covering some 600 hectares. By 1942, it was producing 250 tons of cordite for the navy every week, a figure which fell to just 17.5 tons after the end of the war. Because all the acids required for the propellants were made on site, Caerwent has been described with some justification as 'without doubt, the most dangerous place of work in Wales'.[33] In 1940, two large armament depots were opened in Pembrokeshire, one at Newton Noyes, Milford Haven, and the other at Trecwn near Fishguard. The construction of the latter, in a remote and beautiful area, was opposed by the local schoolmaster, who wrote a poem to express his feelings on the matter; the gesture would have been insignificant were it not for the fact that the schoolmaster was Waldo Williams,

pacifist and one of Wales' greatest poets of the twentieth century. Newton Noyes, built from 1934 onwards on the site of a
former shipbreaking yard and utilising a huge Victorian railway
pier, was not quite as controversial as Trecwn.[34] It took years to
build because construction involved cutting back the cliffs and
excavating huge underground magazines and railway tunnels.
On opening, it became Britain's principal production plant for
sea-mines; from June 1940, it aimed to turn out 230 Mark IV
mines a day, 1,300 'R' mines a week, and 250 huge 'A' mines
a month.[35] In the early years of the war its principal objective
was the laying of huge minefields in home waters, the Western
Approaches and the Bay of Biscay, with the minelayer-cruiser
HMS *Adventure* and other vessels with mine laying capability
calling regularly in Milford Haven to take on new 'cargoes'.
From 1941, a new class of six fast minelayers came into service,
one of which was HMS *Welshman*, and Newton Noyes became
their principal port of call.[36] A monument in the town – appropriately, a decommissioned sea mine – commemorates the
depot's invaluable wartime service.

In 1943, a Fleet Air Arm stores establishment was built on
a site at Llangennech, north-east of Llanelli.[37] The choice of
Llangennech was determined above all by the expectation that
it would be safe from bombing, and it also had a considerably
larger local workforce available to it than the possible alternative at Margam.[38] From 1944 Llangennech, which then had a
workforce of 800, was responsible for general air stores and for
shipments overseas of material for all Fleet Air Arm aircraft other
than the Swordfish and Walrus; the depot held between 30 and
70 per cent of the airframe spares for most of the service's planes,
including 40 per cent of FAA Spitfire and Seafire spares, and
huge numbers of spare engines.[39] Other Welsh facilities also contributed to the navy's war effort. The Royal Ordnance Factory
at Glascoed, near Usk, built in 1938–40, supplied the RAF and
army as well as producing huge amounts of naval ordnance,
including sea mines; it continued to manufacture torpedoes,

4.5 inch naval shells, and other forms of ordnance after the war. Additionally, in 1942 a large radio station to provide communication between the Admiralty and warships at sea opened at Criggion, Montgomeryshire, while, allegedly, the navy's entire stock of rum was kept in four buildings in Newtown, including the market hall.[40]

Perhaps the most controversial of the new wartime bases in Wales was the large training centre just outside Pwllheli that was commissioned on 1 October 1940 as HMS *Glendower*. The original camp was completed in March 1941, but by then work was already under way on an expansion to the site, which was completed in October. The enlarged *Glendower* accommodated some 4,000 officers and men at a time. The name was an obvious nod to local sensibilities: as the little handbook issued to all those arriving there explained, the name of Glyndŵr (it provided the Welsh spelling as well as the English) reflected the fact that 'his fame lies chiefly in the patience of his strategy, his self-command and tireless energy, and his strength of will and dogged persistence'.[41] Initially, the base was intended primarily for those training to become gunners on DEMS (defensively equipped merchant ships), but in March 1943 it also became the location for a new, faster and more intensive officer selection course.[42] For many, the most abiding memory of *Glendower* was the hideous train journey to adjacent Pen-y-Chain Halt; it took the Geordie Joe Kidger twenty-six hours, with no food or water, to get there from Newcastle.[43] Those who trained at *Glendower* included George Melly and Patrick Macnee, later the star of *The Avengers*. Melly was unimpressed: 'for the first three weeks it rained and drizzled non-stop, and this coincided with more bullshit, discipline and physical unpleasantness than I had yet encountered.' Melly's thoughts wandered elsewhere, notably in the direction of anarchism and surrealism, interests which he first developed properly at *Glendower*.[44] Macnee's schooling at Eton proved good preparation for the Spartan rigours of the base, although his principal memory of his time there was of being violently seasick in Porthmadog Bay.[45] However, the most famous temporary inhabitant of *Glendower* was a young instructor officer who served there for a few months just before the base paid off in 1946: Prince Philip of Greece, the future Duke of Edinburgh.

Many of those who trained at *Glendower* criticised the nature of the training provided there, arguing that it concentrated too much on square bashing and redundant 'sailing navy' skills while giving them virtually no practical experience of what they could expect at sea. Some looked on the experience more positively, though not necessarily for naval reasons. John Arthur, who had been a chemistry student at Imperial College, London, before joining the navy, climbed Snowdon with a colleague. They did so in the depths of winter, with the mountain covered in snow, clad in naval bell-bottoms and oil-skins: 'Looking back on it now,' he said when interviewed in 2001, 'we were absolutely totally bloody mad.'[46] Few of the recruits who passed through *Glendower* remembered much interaction with the locals, but John Mortimer of Norfolk recalled how the Welshmen cleaning the heads (toilets) switched from English to Welsh whenever someone entered the building, reckoning that this reflected their resentment at the 'invasion' of their territory.[47]

The subsequent controversy surrounding HMS *Glendower* stemmed from the way in which it had been established and its intended post-war purpose. When the war began, the entrepreneur Billy Butlin put his holiday camp at Skegness, built in 1936 as the first of his nationwide chain, at the disposal of the navy for the duration of hostilities. The site was commissioned as HMS *Royal Arthur* on 22 September 1939, but a damaging bombing raid exposed the potential vulnerability of the new establishment. Butlin came to the rescue once again, offering to use his own resources to build a new camp at an agreed price which he would then buy back at the end of the war for use as a holiday camp. Butlin had identified 150 acres at Pen-y-Chain, 4 miles east of Pwllheli, and purchased the land in March 1940.

He received authorisation to build the base from the Admiralty in June. The Admiralty was to pay £664,000, of which some £559,375 would be for the 'holiday camp' element; at the end of hostilities, Butlin would be able to buy this back for £318,750.[48] Thus the recruits at *Glendower* were accommodated in typical Butlin's chalets, each containing between three and eight men.[49]

It took some time for horrified local authorities and MPs to realise the full implications of this Faustian deal between the Admiralty and Billy Butlin. The virtual abandonment of normal planning regulations for the duration meant that Butlin had effectively circumvented what were bound to have been furious local objections. The first the county council knew of the camp was when their attention was drawn to the vast excavations that had already been dug. During the early years of the war, the overwhelming sense of national crisis silenced any criticisms, but by the autumn of 1943, with thoughts turning to reconstruction for the post-war world, a concerted campaign began against *Glendower*'s eventual transformation into a Butlin's camp. For many, the preservation of Welsh culture was paramount. The creation of a vast holiday destination, plainly targeted at the populations of the English conurbations of Birmingham, Manchester and Liverpool, on the remote and beautiful Llŷn Peninsula in the very heartland of the purest stronghold of the Welsh language, attracted an outcry that bordered on downright racism: one local councillor thundered that 'we, as Welshmen, should not let an Englishman come here and plant down amongst us an institution which will militate against our culture and traditions'. Llŷn was also an area with a particularly strong temperance movement, where Sunday drinking was banned – until as recently as 1996 – and there was evident disquiet about the prospect of drunken Brummies and Scousers disrupting the quiet of a chapel Sabbath. To some, indeed, there was no limit to the sin that Butlin and the Admiralty were going to inflict on

Llŷn: one councillor was convinced that *Glendower* would end up as a nudist colony.[50]

A 'Lleyn Defence Committee' was duly formed, but the campaign also had some powerful individual supporters. Prominent among them was Thomas Jones, 'TJ', eminent academic, former Deputy Secretary to the Cabinet, founder of the Arts Council and a Companion of Honour. In January 1944, he published an attack on Butlin in *The Observer*, although this was rather more circumspect than it might have been because the censor cut all reference to *Glendower*'s location and role. But his attack, founded on the need to preserve Snowdonia and Welsh culture, opened the protest campaign to accusations of elitism and drew a withering counter-attack from Butlin in the same newspaper a few weeks later. Commenting on Jones' suggestion that the camp would bring 'spoilers' and 'looters' to the area, Butlin asked 'Not, surely, those brave, patient, kindly men and women who answered Mr Churchill's call for toil and sweat and blood? Not, surely, those unsung heroes of the blitz? Definitely not those who fought through Hell from Alamein to Italy? – those who made Wales safe for Dr Jones?' TJ and the Lleyn Defence Committee were also somewhat undermined by the fact that the county council's eminent consulting architect, Clough Williams-Ellis – the creator of Portmeirion, and chairman of the Campaign for the Preservation of Rural Wales – was neutral about the future of *Glendower*, regarding it (rightly) as a fait accompli.[51]

Finally, in October 1945, a delegation of the local MPs met with the First Lord of the Admiralty, A.V. Alexander, and the Minister of Town and Country Planning, Lewis Silkin. The delegation was led by the formidable Lady Megan Lloyd George, daughter of the former Prime Minister and MP for Anglesey.[52] The MPs began by trying desperately to find ways of reneging on the contract with Butlin, suggesting the various alternative purposes for the site that had been mooted by different interest groups since the protest campaign began in 1943: a convalescent home, perhaps, or an educational institution. But it transpired that in 1941 Butlin had also formally applied to the local district council (Llŷn) for permission to use the site post-war as a holiday camp, and had received no answer after two months – a silence which was assumed, at that time, to be consent. (A new act of 1943 reversed this assumption, but that was too late for Pwllheli.) With what must have been growing horror and despondency, the MPs heard from the minister that the decision could not now be reversed without paying Butlin a huge amount of compensation – at least half a million pounds. For his part, Butlin argued that his camp would boost the local economy and create much-needed employment. He tarred all of his opponents with the same brush: 'Heading the attack were the Welsh nationalists. "Butlinisation", they roared, "will ruin one of the most beautiful and unspoilt areas in Wales!"'[53] This charge ignored the fact that all of the MPs who stood against him were Conservatives or Liberals, and that his principal opponent, the man who originally coined the word 'Butlinisation', was none other than the highly respectable 'TJ', certainly no nationalist and as 'establishment' a figure as one could possibly imagine.

The crafty businessman's opponents became increasingly strident in their efforts to find a way of 'getting rid of Butlin', as Lady Megan put it, but, ultimately, all of their suggested alternatives came to nothing. The only sop agreed upon by the meeting was an informal, non-binding enquiry, explicitly intended solely as a means of demonstrating the strength of local opinion. However, the Admiralty and the planning minister also had an awareness of wider public opinion, too – of 'the real need for holidays after the strain of the war years', and the outcry that might ensue 'if the public were deliberately deprived of seaside holiday accommodation of this kind'. Ultimately, the MPs' worst fears were justified. HMS *Glendower* paid off on 1 September 1946 and reopened only a few months later as Butlins' Pwllheli holiday camp. Its initial capacity of 5,000 was soon expanded to 8,000, and it became a popular destination for

English holidaymakers from the Midlands and the north-west. The Queen and Duke of Edinburgh visited it in 1963, and Butlin asked the duke if he could tell him which chalet he had occupied during his time on the site. 'Not bloody likely,' Prince Philip replied. 'You'll only put up a notice on it and charge more!'[54] The camp still exists, albeit renamed Hafan y Môr by its current owner, Haven Holidays, but sadly there is no memorial to its vital wartime service as HMS *Glendower*.

There were relatively few other wartime shore establishments in Wales, certainly when compared with the west coast of Scotland, which had the sea-lochs and wide open spaces to accommodate training bases that served many purposes. However, the vulnerability to bombing of HMS *Daedalus*, the Fleet Air Arm base at Lee-on-Solent, led to the redeployment of Walrus seaplane training to Lawrenny Ferry in the upper reaches of Milford Haven, which was rechristened HMS *Daedalus II*. The officers' mess was established in Lawrenny Castle, and the base was fitted with three seaplane pens and a slipway, which still serves the local boatyard. The final stage of the seaplane course involved the pilots receiving catapult and recovery training in Cardigan Bay aboard the venerable HMS *Pegasus*, which had been built in 1914 as the navy's second *Ark Royal* and its first aircraft carrier.[55] Other Royal Naval air stations were established at Angle (for a few months in 1943), Dale (1943–48) and Brawdy (1945 onwards): the name of HMS *Goldcrest* was passed from one of these bases to another as they commissioned and decommissioned. HMS *Emerald Star* at Fishguard was actually a secretive trials base for the Welfreighter, a midget submarine intended for use by the Special Operations Executive.[56] Some odd incongruities were thrown up by this time-honoured naval tradition of giving warship names to such 'stone frigates'. Perhaps the most bizarre was the grandly named HMS *St Elmo*, commissioned on 1 April 1942, which was actually an accountants' office in the genteel suburb of Uplands, Swansea.

While there were relatively few purely naval shore bases in Wales, the same was not true of the Royal Navy's military arm, the Royal Marines. The cliffs and beaches of Carmarthenshire and Pembrokeshire, and the mountains of Merionethshire, provided excellent training areas for the Marines, and a significant number of camps and other facilities were established during the war. Ystrad Camp, to the south-west of Carmarthen, was in use by Fifth Battalion RM during the second half of 1942 before reverting to the army. A signals training camp was established in Saundersfoot, while further along the coast Marines were also based in Tenby, in Fishguard and adjacent sites, at the Victorian Llanion barracks in Pembroke Dock, and at the large and more permanent camp in Penally which continued in service as an army base until 2022, although it was latterly used to house asylum seekers. Merionethshire had five training camps: Matapan Camp at Tywyn, Gibraltar Camp at nearby Llanegryn, Burma Camp at Llwyngwril, Iceland Camp at Arthog and Crete Camp at Barmouth. Many new wartime recruits passed through them, learning a wide range of skills including boat handling and manoeuvring landing craft.[57]

A Different Kind of Invasion

The German conquests of Denmark, Norway, the Low Countries and France in the spring and summer of 1940 meant that Britain suddenly became the temporary home of several exiled governments and armed forces. Of these, the French presented their hosts with a particularly delicate problem. The pro-Nazi Vichy government that controlled the nominally unoccupied area of France was opposed by the Free French under General Charles de Gaulle, and both competed for control of the still substantial forces of the French Navy. An especially important prize was the *Surcouf*, the largest submarine in the world, which had managed to get away from Brest ahead of the arrival of the Germans and took refuge in Plymouth. Two French-speaking British naval officers were sent aboard her on 3 July to explain to the officers that the vessel was being taken under British control. There was a 'scuffle', and both men were fatally wounded: one was Lieutenant Patrick Griffiths of Llandrinio, Montgomeryshire, a descendant of Sir David Gam of Agincourt fame.[58] About 500 interned French seamen, including the crew of the *Surcouf*, were subsequently billeted in the hotels and lodging houses of Barmouth. They were impressed by the hospitality of the local people; many were rather less impressed with the Gaullist recruiters who were sent to talk them into signing up with the Free French.[59] Another French submarine, the *Créole*, under construction at Le Havre, was towed to Swansea in June 1940 when 70 per cent complete in order to prevent her falling into German hands. She was subsequently seized by the British and remained laid up in Swansea docks until 1946, when she was returned to the French. There was a strong Free French naval presence at Milford Haven throughout the war, but their complex politics caused endless problems: pub brawls were commonplace between supporters of De Gaulle on the one hand and his rivals on the other, with French Canadians happily weighing in to support whichever side they chose to favour on a given night.[60]

In 1940 the *Koninklijke Marine*, the exiled Royal Netherlands Navy, established a base at Holyhead, complementing the newly reopened shore establishment, HMS *Torch*. Operating from the depot ships *Peter Stuyvesant*, *Orange-Nassau* and *Medusa*, the Dutch manned a substantial force of motor torpedo boats and minesweepers. Another large contingent of Dutch ships operated from Milford Haven. Five armed minesweeping trawlers arrived there in October 1940 and were followed by another nineteen, together with a base ship. One of the Dutch minesweepers, the *Caroline*, was sunk with the loss of fifteen lives when she struck a mine in the entrance to the Haven in April 1941, and the graves of the four of her crew who were recovered can be found in the town's cemetery. In all, over 700 Dutch sailors were stationed at Milford, many of them billeted on local families.[61] The Royal Netherlands Navy's sojourn in Wales had a consequence which endures to this day, namely the unexpectedly high incidence of Dutch surnames in the Holyhead and Milford areas. St Cybi's church in Holyhead contains a memorial presented by the Dutch Protestant churches as a gesture of thanks for the town's hospitality, while a memorial to the Dutch naval presence was unveiled on the town's Newry beach in 2014.

As in the Napoleonic Wars, Wales played host to many enemy prisoners of war, including some men of the German and Italian navies. Several prisoner of war camps were established in the country, among them Pabo Hall at Llandudno Junction, Henllan Bridge at Llandyssul, Pool Park at Ruthin, Llanmartin at Magor and Mardy at Abergavenny. The most famous Welsh camp was Island Farm near Bridgend, the scene of the largest ever German breakout from a PoW camp (seventy men, in March 1945). Naval prisoners held there included Vice-Admiral Friedrich Hüffmeier, commander-in-chief of Hitler's forces in Guernsey and a former captain of the battlecruiser *Scharnhorst*, and Admiral Theodor Krancke, who had planned the naval side of the invasion of Norway in April 1940 and later commanded the German naval forces opposing the D-Day landings.[62] A U-boat officer, Johan Oswald Prior, was among those who took part in 'the German Great Escape' and was one of four men who got as far as Castle Bromwich in the Midlands before being apprehended.

Factories and Spies

Both before and during the war, many Welsh industries supplied the navy. A.M. Dickie's boatyard at Bangor built a total of twenty-eight Fairmile motor launches between 1940 and 1945.[63] The Fairfield works at Chepstow built over sixty LCTs

(Landing Craft, Tank) during 1942–45, while South Wales ship repair yards worked on many thousands of ships during the war years. Over 30,000 ships, including 744 British and American warships, were repaired in the Bristol Channel ports; three auxiliary aircraft carriers, *Ruler*, *Emperor* and *Smiter*, were refitted at Newport.[64] The John Williams iron foundry in East Moors, Cardiff, the Glaslyn foundry at Porthmadog, and many other Welsh factories, produced substantial amounts of material for the navy.[65] But one of Wales' naval contractors was also at the centre of one of the most elaborate intelligence operations of the war. Arthur Owens, originally from Pontardawe, ran a company which produced naval batteries. In the 1930s he approached German Intelligence, the *Abwehr*, stating that he was a Welsh nationalist who wished to work for Germany. However, he subsequently went to MI5 and was recruited as a double agent, and attempted to play the two sides against each other in order to make as much money as possible for himself. He was put to work with Gwilym Williams, a former Swansea policeman who pretended to be a nationalist but, unlike Owens, was firm in his loyalty to MI5. Among the operations that they instigated or were involved in was a scheme for a U-boat to land explosives in Oxwich Bay, specifically at a cove in Penmaen, and the landing of three Cuban saboteurs from a fishing boat in Swansea Bay, a scheme that was stymied by atrocious weather which forced the Cubans to throw their arsenal overboard well before they reached the Welsh coast; the boat finally limped into Fishguard harbour, where the crew and the would-be saboteurs were arrested.[66]

D-Day

From 1942 onwards, another group of 'invaders' and their ships poured into Wales. The arrival at Newport on 14 May 1942 of the troopship *Cathay*, carrying large numbers of American troops, marked the beginning of the preparations for the eventual invasion of Western Europe. The build up of American forces in Wales did not go entirely smoothly; when the SS *Henry R Mallory* arrived at Newport on 24 July, an unfortunate misunderstanding between bridge and engine room led to her going full speed ahead in the entrance lock and ramming the inner dock gates, putting the port largely out of action for over a month.[67] American personnel again established a presence in Cardiff Docks, and Penarth became a maintenance base for the US landing craft destined for the Normandy landings.[68] American troops carried out practice landings in Oxwich and Port Eynon bays on the Gower. However, the principal American naval presence was established at Milford Haven, where a USNAAB (United States Navy Advanced Amphibious Base) was set up to service large numbers of LSTs (Landing Ships, Tank). These used the old Ward pier at Castle Pill and were refitted in Milford's dry dock.[69] Hakin wharf in Milford Docks was modified to receive Liberty ships. The arrival of so many Americans added to what was already a potentially combustible multi-national naval presence: they got on particularly badly with the Free French, and there were many fights in the pubs and streets of Milford.[70]

The broad, empty beaches of Carmarthenshire, Pembrokeshire and Cardigan Bay provided ideal training grounds for the invasion of Europe. New technologies could be perfected in these relatively remote areas, well away from prying eyes. Thus DUKWs, American-built amphibious vehicles, practised for the Normandy landings on the beaches of Tywyn, while HMS *Camroux III*, a converted coaster, was used to test-fire rockets into the sands of the Dyfi Estuary and later provided a billet for army officers setting up the Ynyslas testing range. Churchill himself came to Wiseman's Bridge near Saundersfoot in 1943 to watch the largest of Wales' mock invasions, Exercise Jantzen, reputedly refreshing himself with a pot of tea in the local pub. An area of 130 square miles from Laugharne to Tenby and north to the A40 became a 'regulated area', with strict new controls, including a curfew, imposed on the civilian population for the duration. The exercise took place between 21 July and 6 August. Over 16,000 tons of stores were landed, principally from a fleet of coasters that had sailed from Swansea and Port Talbot, together with over 7,000 men and nearly 600 vehicles. But there was much confusion on the beaches, the ferocious tidal range of Carmarthen Bay presented serious difficulties, and it was discovered that the coasters had been loaded poorly, particularly at Port Talbot, because the men who loaded the ships there were 'by profession coal trimmers and not used to ordinary merchandise'. Nevertheless, important lessons were learned, notably in terms of how to manage the logistics of a hastily established bridgehead, and these undoubtedly later con- tributed to the success of D-Day.[71] Most of Jantzen was carried out in good or passable weather conditions, but the fickle nature of the Welsh climate ensured that not all of the preparations for D-Day went so well. On 25 and 26 April 1943 LCG(L) 15 and 16, two Landing Craft Gun (Large) with shallow draughts, were caught in severe weather off Milford Haven. Both sank with a total loss of seventy-three officers and men, and six men of HMS *Rosemary*, which had gone to their assistance, also lost their lives.[72] A memorial and serried ranks of white gravestones in Milford Haven's town cemetery still bear witness to the disaster.

Wales played a full part in Operation Neptune, the naval side of the D-Day landings. Two US army divisions sailed from the Bristol Channel to the Normandy beachhead. Over 130 coasters were loaded at the South Wales ports and those on the English side of the Bristol Channel: ammunition was loaded at Llanelli and Penarth; petrol at Port Talbot; motor vehicles at Barry; troops at Newport, Cardiff and Swansea. The first convoy sailed for the invasion beaches on 30 May, to be followed by fifteen more before 13 June. A gale on 3–4 June caused severe problems for the ships and their embarked troops in Barry Roads and Swansea Bay, but it gradually subsided and sailings could resume on 5 June. Once the army was ashore, the ports switched to turning round merchant ships as quickly as possible to maintain the flow of supplies to the invasion force.[73] The American LSTs and British convoys left Milford Haven for the beaches; a monument to the port's role in D-Day was erected on the Rath in 1994, and is the setting for a memorial service every 6 June. Another part of the D-Day invasion fleet assembled in Benllech Bay, Anglesey, before setting off for Normandy.[74] At the other end of the supply line, an astonishing invention enabled the ships to land their cargoes without the need to secure a port first. The vast prefabricated harbours codenamed 'Mulberry' were designed by Iorys Hughes of Bangor, whose brother, a commander in the Royal Navy, brought the plans to the attention of the Admiralty. Large sections of the prototypes were built on Morfa Conwy opposite Deganwy, where a 1,150ft frontage was given over to their construction.[75] Two Mulberry harbours, one for the Americans and one for the British and Canadians, were towed in sections to the Normandy beachhead, and assembly began within hours of the landings on 6 June. The American harbour was destroyed by storms after only ten days in use, but the British one served for five months and provided a conduit for over two million and over four million tons of supplies. A plaque at Conwy Marina commemorates the parts played in the Mulberry story by Morfa Conwy and local man Iorys Hughes.[76]

Notes

1   Carradice and Breverton, *Welsh Sailors*, pp.240–1; B. Edwards, *They Sank the Red Dragon* (Cardiff, 1987), p.8 and passim.

2   D. Roberts, *HMS* Thetis: *Secrets and Scandal, Aftermath of a Disaster* (1999).

3   Unless stated otherwise, this section is based on TNA, ADM1/17321.

4   www.naval-history.net/xDKWW2-4201-40RNShips3WApproaches.htm#WA.

5   TNA, ADM1/15289.

6   R.C. Jones, *Anglesey and Gwynedd: The War Years 1939–45* (Wrexham 2008), pp.37, 39–40.
7   Scott, *Experience Shared*, pp.106–7.
8   www.naval-history.net/xDKWW2-4201-40RNShips3WApproaches.htm#WA
9   Scott, *Experience Shared*, pp.91–102.
10 Scott, *Experience Shared*, p.65.
11 R. and B. Larn, *Shipwreck Index of the British Isles: West Coast and Wales* (2000), not paginated.
12 TNA, ADM1/17321.
13 Armstrong and Young, *Silent Warriors*, p.17.
14 Scott, *Experience Shared*, pp.129–36.
15 Burry Inlet minefield: TNA, ADM1/12895.
16 Scott, *Experience Shared*, p 70.
17 Armstrong and Young, *Silent Warriors*, pp.17–22.
18 TNA, ADM1/17321.
19 The account of the U-boat campaign which follows is based partly on Scott, *Experience Shared*, pp.259–64, although this is not always accurate; corrections and additional information from uboat.net and other sources.
20 R. and B. Larn, *Shipwreck Index of the British Isles: West Coast and Wales* (2000), not paginated; Armstrong and Young, *Silent Warriors*, pp.84–90, 101–4, 106–117.
21 NMM, MS MGV/35; TNA, ADM1/18394, 18574.
22 GRO, D COMC/1/8/155.
23 www.penmaenmawr.com/historyWarShipWeek.html (Accessed: 2012)
24 K. Strange, 'Cardiff Schools and the Age of the Second World War: The Log Books: A Documentary History', www.ngfl-cymru.org.uk/vtc/ngfl/history/cardiff_schools/Cardiff_schools_and_the_age_of_the_Second_World_War.pdf (Accessed: 2012)
25 Jones, *Anglesey at War*, pp.126–7.
26 *Hansard*, HC Deb 04 June 1942 vol 380 c830W.
27 Programme for Llanelli presentation ceremony, 23 October 1943 (author's collection); GRO BB/C/8/252.
28 GRO, BB/C/8/252.
29 www.naval-history.net/xGM-Chrono-10DD-34Tribal-Nubian.htm
30 www.bbc.co.uk/news/uk-wales-south-west-wales-13200124
31 www.bbc.co.uk/wales/southeast/sites/newtredegar/pages/hmsbuttercup_poem.shtml
32 GRO, BB/C/8/252.
33 www.caerwentcom.com/rnpf01.htm (Accessed: 2012)

34　In addition to other sources cited, information on all of the Welsh depots has been generously supplied by Mr Alan Phillips, formerly of RNSD Llangennech.

35　TNA, ADM1/10953.

36　Scott, *Experience Shared*, pp.163–92.

37　Similarly, in 1940 a military research and testing facility was moved from Shoeburyness in Essex to Pendine in Carmarthenshire; this still remains in use.

38　TNA, ADM 1/28283.

39　MS 'Allocation of Air Store Supply Work to Home Air Store Depots', 14 June 1944, and related documents; Alan Phillips collection.

40　E. Street, 'Royal Ordnance Factory, Glascoed', *Gwent Local History: The Journal of Gwent Local History Council*, 60 (1986), pp.15–18; www. oswestry-history.co.uk/criggion-radio-station.html; www.coflein. gov.uk/en/site/32030/.

41　HMS *Glendower* handbook, April 1945; copy in author's collection.

42　B. Lavery, *Hostilities Only: Training the Wartime Royal Navy* (2011 edn), pp.155, 246–7.

43　IWM, Oral History 23200.

44　G. Melly, *Rum, Bum and Concertina* (1977), pp.42–3.

45　P, Macnee, *Blind in One Ear: The Autobiography of an Avenger* (1988), pp.118–21.

46　IWM, Oral History 21538.

47　IWM, Oral History 18486.

48　TNA, ADM 1/9105.

49　IWM, Oral History 18486, 21575, 23200.

50　NLW, Dr Thomas Jones, CH, Collection, H16.

51　NLW, Dr Thomas Jones, CH, Collection, H16.

52　TNA, ADM 1/9105.

53　B. Butlin, *The Billy Butlin Story: 'A Showman to the End'* (1982), p.156.

54　Butlin, *The Billy Butlin Story*, p.157.

55　M. Hale, *Royal Naval Air Station Lawrenny Ferry* (privately published, 1995).

56　www.welfreighter.info/

57　A. J. Perrett, Royal Marines in Wales, Royal Marines Historical Society (Portsmouth 1992), pp. 17–107.

58　W.A. Griffiths, 'Richard Griffiths of Trederwen Feibion Gynwas (*c.* 1625–1701) and Ann Griffiths the Hymn Writer (1776–1805)', *Collections Historical and Archaeological Relating to Montgomeryshire*, 47 (1942), pp.146–7.

59 C. Smith, *England's Last War Against France: Fighting Vichy, 1940–2* (2009), pp.102–3; N. Atkin, *The Forgotten French: Exiles in the British Isles 1940–4* (Manchester, 2003), p.102.

60 Scott, *Experience Shared*, p.259.

61 Scott, *Experience Shared*, pp.67–9; information from Milford Haven Museum.

62 www.islandfarm.fsnet.co.uk/index.html

63 I.T. Hughes, 'A Brief History of Five Royal Navy Coastal Forces Craft Built at Bangor Between 1940 and 1945', *MW*, 16 (1994), pp.130–8.

64 TNA, ADM1/17321.

65 GRO, D523; GAC, XS3591.

66 J. Humphries, *Spying for Hitler: The Welsh Double Cross* (Cardiff, 2012), pp.13–17, 32, 38, 77, 87–91.

67 TNA ADM1/17321.

68 Richards, *Cardiff: A Maritime History*, p.132.

69 TNA, ADM1/13080, 13157, 17321; Scott, *Experience Shared*, pp.193–208.

70 Scott, *Experience Shared*, pp.202–4.

71 TNA, WO199/2638.

72 A detailed account of the disaster is provided by Scott, *An Experience Shared*, pp.115–28.

73 TNA, ADM1/17321.

74 AA, WM/T/128.

75 Jones, *Anglesey and Gwynedd*, pp.235–42.

76 www.combinedops.com/Mulberry%20Harbours.htm

11

THE WELSH IN CHURCHILL'S NAVY

1939–45

Wales' most famous and charismatic naval sailor of the Second World War was undoubtedly Tristan Jones of Llangareth near Barmouth. His wartime memoir, published as *Heart of Oak*, related how he was torpedoed three times before the age of 18, survived the Russian convoys and the destruction by fire of an armed merchant cruiser, and was present at the sinking of the *Bismarck*. This book, and the accounts of his astonishing peacetime voyages, turned Tristan Jones into a feted celebrity author and TV personality, and so he remained until his death in 1995. Jones span wonderful stories. They would have been even more wonderful if they were true. But there is no such place as Llangareth, a name derived from his real moniker. Jones was born in 1929, not 1924, and was thus too young to serve in the war. In fact, Tristan Jones belonged squarely in another great Welsh tradition, that of the charismatic but not altogether truthful storyteller elaborately intertwining fact and fiction; just as Richard Gwyn and John Dee had done at the time of the Armada, in fact. Jones did indeed serve in the Royal Navy, but he did not enter it until 1946, and then spent fourteen years on unremarkable peacetime duties. But his wholly invented account of his wartime exploits still makes a great read – albeit as fiction – and still deludes some gullible historians to this day.[1] In reality, though, the true stories of the Welshmen who actually served in the navy during the Second World War needed very little embellishment.[2]

Officers and Men

The Welshmen who served in the wartime navy included a remarkable crosssection of the future great and good of post-war Welsh society. As in the first war, a number of current or future Welsh rugby internationals served at sea. These included Gerwyn Williams, full back in the last Welsh team to beat the All Blacks; Rex Willis, a distinguished British Lion and captain of Wales; and Don Tarr, a career naval officer who eventually became a lieutenant commander but whose single cap saw him 'probably [come] closer to dying on the pitch than anyone else ever has in an international match'.[3] Probably the greatest of all rugby journalists, J.B.G. Thomas, served on destroyers and eventually became a lieutenant RNVR, serving on the minesweeper HMS *Saltash* in the vanguard of the Normandy landings.[4] Others who saw wartime service in the navy or its mobilised reserves included the poet T. Harri Jones, the politician Ronald Bell, the radical writer Harri Webb, the historian Ted Ellis, Free Wales Army member Ronnie Williams, the banker Emrys Evans (the man who introduced Welsh language cheques), HTV television presenter Alan Taylor, academic Sir Idris Foster (Jesus Professor of Celtic at Oxford University), anti-apartheid campaigner Bishop Graham Chadwick (both he and Foster served as intelligence officers), and Ivor Rees, Bishop of St David's from 1991 to 1995. Alun Williams, one of Wales' most distinguished broadcasters, served on the minelayer HMS *Adventure* operating from Milford Haven, and later in the

Far East.[5] Others contributed to the naval war effort even if they were not actually members of the service. Evan Williams, a Welsh-speaking Congregationalist stonemason's son from Cwmsychpant and alumnus of Llandyssul County School who had become Professor of Physics at Aberystwyth, became an expert on anti-submarine techniques, initially for the RAF, but from 1943 for the navy as its scientific advisor and subsequently its assistant director of scientific research. His outstanding statistical analyses greatly improved the effectiveness of depth charge attacks from aircraft and were also largely responsible for the so-called 'Bay Offensive' of 1943, a decisive element in the defeat of the U-boats. Williams was not the only Welsh scientist at the heart of the naval war effort: Rhisiart Davies from Corris, who would also hold the Aberystwyth Physics Chair after the war, worked on underwater explosives for the Admiralty.[6]

Many Welshmen joined the navy because it seemed a better option than the limited alternatives available to them at home or in the other services. Indeed, even the most cursory study of Welsh war memorials reveals the basic truth that proportionately, significantly more men served in the navy during the Second World War than in the First. Ron Harry of Cardiff and his friends joined it because they had visions of a repeat of the trench warfare of the First World War and did not wish to be part of yet another army of 'lions led by donkeys', ordered into senseless slaughter.[7] Ken Higgins and James Morton came from Brecon and Penally respectively, both the homes of substantial army establishments, but as a result they had seen enough square bashing and heard enough regimental sergeant majors to decide that the navy was infinitely preferable.[8] Phil Foote of Penclawdd in north Gower could have stayed in a reserved occupation in the local colliery where he worked, but his response was blunt: 'No way, I'm joining the navy.'[9] Joffre Swales of Haverfordwest, who had got married two days before war broke out, played in local bands in peacetime and was attracted to a recruiting advert for Royal Marine bandsmen, so went off to the School of Music at Deal with his instruments and joined up.[10] Family tradition and peer pressure were also important considerations. Doug Watkins of Kenfig Hill went into the navy because an uncle was in the service and several of his friends had already joined it.[11] Four of the Hortop brothers of Barry joined the navy (two others were in the merchant navy and one in the army).[12] Once they were in, Welshmen swiftly experienced the navy's time-honoured obsession with nicknames, usually unoriginal and time-honoured ones. Edgar Nurse of Penclawdd was posted to HMS *Tartar*, where he discovered that 'All the Welshmen were called Taff. I was Taff Nurse.'[13] The vagaries of the naval drafting system sometimes threw up some odd anomalies. The submarine HMS *Phoenix* had a crew of only fifty-three, but both Leading Seaman Oswald Parry and Stoker First Class Christopher Williams hailed from Llanrwst; they were lost on 16 July 1940 when the boat was sunk off Sicily by an Italian warship.

Welsh women also played their part following the re-establishment of the WRNS in 1939. Vera Laughton Mathews, the formidable head of the service, later recounted some of the obstacles she encountered in Wales in the early days of the war. At Newport, the officer in command 'was firmly inveigled into a car alone with me, where he took a deep breath and burst out that he would fight against having Wrens to the last ditch, though he had no doubt that he would be beaten (he was)'. At Swansea, the first batch of twelve recruits was quickly sized up by the local naval officers. One swiftly wrote:

'Commander – presents his compliments to the First Officer and if he is on the list for a typist, he would like the one in the green coat and skirt.' The First Officer replied with 'The First Officer presents her compliments to Commander –. He is not on the list for a typist and in any case the rating in question is a motor driver'. Shortly afterwards her assistant came to her in distress and said, 'Ma'am, we're one Wren short.

The Admiral has pinched that girl in the green coat and skirt
to drive his car'.

Vera Mathews herself toured naval establishments assiduously,
and on one occasion encountered a crisis at HMS *Glendower*
in Pwllheli. At the end of a WRNS concert, the Welsh audience requested community singing, but no-one was available
to accompany it. Mathews herself went to the piano and played
'while the sweet Welsh voices filled the hall with music'. On her
return to London, she immediately ordered the draft of one pia-
nist to *Glendower*.[14]

For many Welsh girls, the WRNS offered more opportunity
and glamour than many of the alternatives available at home.
Kath Bellis of Llandudno, who had been working as a civil servant in Holyhead, joined in 1942 and was posted to Alexandria;
this was something of a backwater after the surrender of Italy,
but it offered a hectic social life, exciting leave opportunities in
the likes of Palestine and the Valley of the Kings, and in Kath's
case, four passionate relationships within the space of eighteen
months.[15] Beryl Jones became a Radio Mechanic and in 1944
worked in the secret Radio Direction Finder stations on the
south coast, communicating with the troops that landed on
D-Day and those who followed them. She was later sent aboard
a Free French warship and was able to hold a tolerable conversation with the Chief Petty Officer assigned to chaperone her, she
talking in Welsh, he in Breton.[16] Muriel Gordon was part of the
naval cipher party on the great liner *Queen Elizabeth*, transporting American troops across the Atlantic, while Lisbeth David
graduated from telegraphist duties at Holyhead to service as an
officer at Trincomalee in Sri Lanka, attending *Eisteddfodau* run by
the Lanka Cambrian Club and 'hymn singing evenings with Sub
Lieutenant Alun Williams playing a prominent part'.[17] Another
wartime Welsh Wren was a girl from Dowlais named Laura
Mountney: she eventually became rather better known under
her married name of Ashley.[18]

Phoney War and Finest Hour, 1939–40

The early months of the war saw Welshmen distinguish themselves in all of the major naval operations, while others were
present during some of the Royal Navy's most catastrophic
losses. The first sinking of a major warship occurred when the
aircraft carrier *Courageous* was sunk by a U-boat on 17 September
1939 with the loss of over 500 men. Casualties included the
likes of Able Seamen George Francis Jones of St Asaph and
Frederick Thomas of Llanelli, together with 17-year-old Boy
First Class Eric Williams of Prestatyn; the captain of *Courageous*,
W.T. Makeig-Jones, was a descendant of an old Cardigan
dynasty. (Other Welshmen, including seven from Cardiff and
nineteen from Newport and the rest of Monmouthshire, were
killed when *Courageous'* sister ship *Glorious* was sunk on 8 June
1940.) The battleship *Royal Oak* was torpedoed in Scapa Flow
on 14 October following an astonishingly audacious attack by
U-47. Among those who perished aboard her were 21-year-old
Leading Seaman Stephen Shaw of Abergele, 20-year-old Supply
Assistant Arthur Bargery of Cardiff, and 17-year-old Boy
First Class Frederick Hughes of Bala. The navy swiftly coun-
tered with the successful destruction of the pocket battleship
Graf Spee during the Battle of the River Plate (13 December).
Nineteen-year-old Albert Gwilliam of Milford Haven won
the Conspicuous Gallantry Medal for his actions aboard
HMS *Exeter*, and on his return to his hometown he was presented with an inscribed plaque.[19] Another 19-year-old, Luther
Meek of Llanidloes, was presented with a gold watch simply
for having been aboard HMS *Ajax* during the battle.[20] With
the army and air force engaged relatively little during the early
months of the war, most of the focus was on the navy, so disasters such as those that befell *Courageous*, *Glorious* and *Royal Oak*,
and the triumph of the River Plate, had particularly powerful
impacts on local communities. As the war dragged on, though, it
became simply impossible regularly to bestow the sort of special

recognition that the likes of Gwilliam and Meek had received in its early days.

Bernard Warburton-Lee of Maelor, Flintshire, was the first of the three Welsh naval VCs of the Second World War. Born in 1895, he joined the navy in 1908 and in 1940 was captain of HMS *Hardy* and senior officer of the Second Destroyer Flotilla. On 10 April 1940, he led his ships into the Ofotfjord leading to Narvik to attack German warships that were supporting the landings there as part of Hitler's invasion of Norway. Using the cover of a snowstorm, Warburton-Lee achieved complete surprise, but as his ships withdrew they encountered five more powerful German destroyers coming up the fjord. As *Hardy* came under the heavy fire that killed him shortly afterwards, Warburton-Lee hoisted a 'Nelsonian' signal: 'Keep on engaging the enemy.' Although his attempts to stop the Germans proved futile, his heroism provided an important morale booster for the British public at a particularly dark time of the war. A large memorial at Whitewell church, Wrexham, commemorates him.[21]

The Battle for the Mediterranean, 1940–43

Italy's entry into the war in June 1940 created a strategic nightmare for Britain. The vital sea-route through the Suez Canal to India was suddenly vulnerable, lying as it did within easy range of Italian airfields in Sicily and Libya, as were the supply routes vital to the Eighth Army in North Africa. The powerful Italian fleet, based at Taranto, could come out at any time and create havoc, and the navy suffered heavy casualties. David Cole-Hamilton of Llangattock, Breconshire, was first lieutenant of the large Tribal-class destroyer HMS *Sikh* when she took part in the sharp engagement with the Italian Fleet off Sirte on 22 March 1942. He survived that engagement but was killed three months later, aged 28; for many years a white ensign from

Sikh hung in St Catwg's church, Llangattock, where David's father was rector for thirty-five years. The enclosed nature of the Mediterranean meant that many more ships were lost to air attack than in other theatres. John Stephens of Abersychan lived through the sinking of *Sikh's* sister ship *Zulu* by Italian bombers off Tobruk on 14 September 1942, the warm Mediterranean waters helping to ensure that most of the crew survived.[22] But Ordnance Artificer Vernon Wait of Llantarnam was one of the seventy-seven men who perished when the destroyer *Lively* was dive-bombed off Tobruk on 11 May 1942, and First Class Petty Officer David Glyndŵr Davies of Upper Cwmtwrch was lost when HMS *Dulverton* was sunk by German glider bombs while attempting to capture the Greek islands of Kos and Leros on 12 November 1942.[23] Well over 700 men were killed when the cruiser *Gloucester* was sunk by Stuka dive bombers off Crete in May 1941: the many Welshmen who perished in her are commemorated from Pontardulais to Penmaenmawr. Lieutenant Vaughan Davies, RNR, of Solva, was one of those attempting to counter the airborne threat, flying with the Fleet Air Arm from the RNAS airfield at Dekheila near Alexandria. He was awarded the DSC for his gallantry but never lived to receive it, lost on 24 January 1942 when his Fairey Albacore went missing between Benghazi and Malta.[24]

The Mediterranean was also one of the principal theatres of operations for British submarines, the Axis convoys sailing from Italy to resupply Rommel's Afrika Korps among their targets. Many Welshmen served in the submarine campaign in the Mediterranean, and it produced a man who undoubtedly ranks as one of Wales' greatest naval heroes of all: Commander John 'Tubby' Linton, born at Malpas in 1905. A fine rugby player, the bearded Linton cut an impressive figure. In 1942 he was given command of the new submarine *Turbulent*, and his achievements in her were remarkable: she sank over 100,000 tons of enemy shipping, including three warships. During the calendar year of 1942 Linton spent 254 days at sea, including nearly 3,000 hours dived, was attacked thirteen times and had 250 depth charges dropped on him. Some time in March 1943 his luck ran out: *Turbulent* was lost between 12 March, when the last contact was made with her, and 23 March, when she failed to return to Malta as scheduled. It is probable that she struck a mine somewhere off Sardinia, but the wreck has never been discovered. Linton's VC was awarded, not for one individual act, but for sustained gallantry over a long period of time. Tubby Linton is still rightly revered as a hero in his hometown (or rather, home city, as Newport became in 2002). A memorial to him was erected by the side of the River Usk, a pub was named after him, and a particularly impressive blog keeps alive his memory.[25] But there is a tragic footnote to the Linton story. His son also became a submariner, and on 16 April 1951 he was a sub-lieutenant under training aboard HMS *Affray* when she failed to make a routine contact report in the English Channel. The wreck was not discovered for two months. Seventy-five men perished in this, the last ever loss of a British submarine.

The Battle of the Atlantic, 1940–45

The Atlantic sea lanes were crucial to Britain's ability to fight and ultimately win the war. Without foodstuffs, fuel and hardware from the United States, Canada and elsewhere, the country would probably have been forced to seek peace terms, so a tremendous effort was put into defending the merchant ships that kept Britain going. Unlike the First World War, there was no debate about the desirability of convoy: an extensive system was put in place at once, and was considerably expanded from the summer of 1940 following the fall of France and the United States' adoption of the 'lend-lease' policy which enabled Britain to circumvent the terms of the Neutrality Acts that Congress had passed in the 1930s. Both coastal and deep sea convoys were allocated codes which were effectively abbreviations of the route. Convoys designated HX were the principal ones from North America to the UK, with ON going in the opposite direction; similarly, HG went from Gibraltar to the UK, OG outbound. In Welsh waters, HM was the designation for convoys from Holyhead to Milford Haven, BB from Belfast to Bristol Channel, PW from Portsmouth to Wales, and so forth.[26]

For those serving on the merchant ships and their warship escorts, the Atlantic convoys were constantly attended by the risk of attack from German U-boats, and the Battle of the Atlantic was essentially a race between the two sides to develop a clear advantage in tactics and technology. For example, the German adoption of wolf-pack tactics in the spring of 1941 (having large groups of U-boats operating together) initially brought them great success, but this was gradually offset by increased numbers of escorts which adopted increasingly sophisticated tactics. By the skill of their crews and sheer good fortune, certain ships developed reputations as successful U-boat hunters. Fred Hortop of Barry was aboard one of them, the destroyer *Hesperus*, which was regularly assigned to convoy duty in the Atlantic. On 7 December 1941, the day of Pearl Harbor, she sank *U-208*, and on 15 January 1942 sank *U-93* off St Vincent. On Boxing Day 1942 she was escorting Convoy HX219 from St John's, Newfoundland, when a submarine was spotted. *Hesperus* and *Vanessa* – coincidentally, the adopted ship of Fred's hometown – attacked her and forced her to the surface, *Hesperus* finishing her off by ramming. Only six members of the crew of *U-357* survived, and Fred felt the mixture of emotions: 'I recall the elation of victory very soon replaced by a feeling of remorse at the killing of our fellow seamen.' *Hesperus* needed extensive repairs after the sinking, so Fred was reassigned to the corvette *Stonecrop*. On 2 April 1943, she was part of the escort for Convoy OS45 when, along with HMS *Black Swan*, she destroyed the highly successful *U-124* and her ace commander, Johann Mohr. The submarine had sunk forty-six merchantmen and two warships, including the cruiser HMS *Dunedin*. Fred was still on *Stonecrop* on 30 August 1943 when she took part in the sinking of *U-634* east of the Azores.[27]

Another Welshman who distinguished himself during the Battle of the Atlantic was Eynon Hawkins. A miner's son from Llanharan who had played rugby for Bridgend, he was one of the Royal Navy seamen deployed on DEMS (defensively equipped merchant ships) to man their armament. On 10 January 1943 he was serving aboard the tanker *British Dominion*, part of a convoy sailing from Malta to the West Indies, when she was attacked and struck by three torpedoes, some 300 miles south-west of Madeira. The oil was burning fiercely, but despite being badly burned himself, Hawkins singlehandedly rescued many of his shipmates from the inferno, gathering them together in safe water not yet reached by the blazing oil. He was awarded the Albert Medal, an award that was subsequently converted to the George Cross. After the war, Eynon played rugby league for Salford, Rochdale and Wales, later returning home to work in the Powell Dufferin and Ffaldau collieries.[28]

If any one man can be singled out for his part in winning the Battle of the Atlantic, it would probably be Sir Max Horton, Flag Officer of the Western Approaches Command, based at Liverpool, from 1942 to 1945. Horton had proved himself as a bold submarine captain during the First World War, and thus had a rare insight into the mentality of the German U-boat commanders and their leader, Admiral Dönitz. By the end of 1942, when Horton took command, the U-boat threat was particularly serious. Dönitz now had many more boats available to him, and the rate of sinkings of merchant ships was fast approaching the unsustainable tipping point at which the allies would not be able to replace their losses quickly enough. As both sides knew full well, this would inevitably presage Britain's defeat. Horton devised a strategy of using support groups of escorts complemented by long-range aircraft, and when these forces went into action in April 1943, the effect was immediate and dramatic: following a series of catastrophic defeats, Dönitz withdrew his boats from the mid-Atlantic in May. Ruthless and highly efficient, but also sensitive and deeply religious, Max Horton also had some Welsh credentials: he was born in 1883 at the Maelog Lake Hotel, Rhosneigr, Anglesey, the son of a London stockbroker who had set up home on the island. His early education took place at a small private school in Llanfairfechan, and he learned to sail in Anglesey waters; a memorial to him was unveiled at Rhosneigr on 14 April 2013.[29] It was therefore entirely fitting that the fleet review commemorating the fiftieth anniversary of the Battle of the Atlantic took place in Moelfre Bay, a wartime convoy anchorage, in May 1993. The weather was also singularly redolent of some of the conditions the merchant ships and warships fighting the Battle had experienced: as the royal yacht *Britannia* passed down the lines of twenty-six British and allied warships during what proved to be one of her last important duties before decommissioning four years later, the heavens opened, the winds reached force eight, and the USS *Devastator* had to belie her name and run for cover.[30]

The Russian Convoys

Hitler's invasion of the Soviet Union (June 1941) entirely changed the nature of the war. Britain was no longer alone, but sending the supplies that its beleaguered Communist ally desperately needed required the setting up of a convoy system to the USSR's only accessible ports, the likes of Murmansk and Archangel in the White Sea. Weather conditions and the ever-present threat from German air and sea forces in Norway made the Russia convoys one of the most appallingly dangerous assignments in the naval war, and many Welshmen perished in the bitter cold of the northern seas. Ellis Wynne Lewis of

Conwy was yeoman of signals aboard HMS *Matabele*, a large Tribal-class destroyer, when she was torpedoed on 17 January 1942 while escorting a Russian convoy; others who perished on her included Able Seaman Vivian Rees of Burry Port, Petty Officer John Webb of Cyncoed, Cardiff, and three Swansea men. For those who survived the Russian convoys, the memories remained vivid. Aran Morris from Borth served aboard the destroyer HMS *Onslaught* and said of his service, 'the crew was advised not to wash as the natural body oils would help against the cold ... there were to be no hammocks used as they were a fire hazard ... we were on constant alert, so we had to sleep where we could and at times this meant sharing sleeping quarters with dead bodies, both German and British.'[31] James Morton of Penally, aboard the cruiser *Glasgow*, remembered the ice in his radio cabin, sleeping on the deck, and eating nothing but sandwiches for a fortnight.[32] Marine Bandsman Joffre Swales, serving on HMS *Norfolk*, once went five weeks without seeing the sun, and remembered how the ship 'bucked like a bronco' in the Arctic Seas.[33] All witnessed terrible losses from German attacks, the sight of men dying hideously in the icy waters, and the barely disguised hostility of their Russian 'allies'. But there were lighter moments, too. Nineteen-year-old trainee teacher John Edwards of Abercynon found himself aboard the cruiser *Jamaica*: his brother Ffrangcon was already aboard her, having lied about his age, which led to the bizarre situation where the younger brother (now allegedly a biologically impossible six months senior) was entitled to draw his rum ration whereas the older brother was not. They were both present at the Battle of North Cape (26 December 1943) when the *Jamaica* delivered the coup de grace to the battlecruiser *Scharnhorst*, John feeling that 'I'd done something towards the war effort, however small.'[34] After a lengthy campaign, a long overdue separate campaign medal, the Arctic Star, was inaugurated in 2012–13, while at much the same time surviving veterans also received Ushakov medals recognising their valour from the Russian government.

Harry Tate's Navy and the War against the Enemy Coast

When the Royal Naval Reserves were mobilised in August 1939, their numbers included many trawlermen and their vessels, which were formed into what became the Royal Naval Patrol Service. This reflected the experience of the First World War, when trawlers, drifters and other auxiliary craft had formed the backbone of the navy's minesweeping and patrol activities. Once again, the Welsh trawler fleets and their crews were called up en masse. Several Milford men were killed in RNPS service, often aboard the trawlers they had crewed in peacetime and which had been requisitioned at the beginning of the war.[35] Others found themselves serving far from Welsh waters. James Lloyd of Dale, Pembrokeshire, went down with the armed trawler *Fifeshire* when she was bombed by German aircraft off Shetland in February 1940.[36] Benjamin Lewis of Clynderwen was lost when the trawler *Kingston Beryl* was mined off Islay on Christmas Day 1943.[37] The headquarters of the RNPS was at Lowestoft, which was also a major base for operations against the enemy-held coasts of the Low Countries, Denmark and Germany itself. Doug Watkins of Kenfig Hill served on motor torpedo boats operating from the port, attacking shipping off the Dutch coast at night.[38]

Following the sinking of the *Bismarck* in 1941, the main German surface threat came from her sister ship *Tirpitz*, and several remarkably dangerous operations were devised to neutralise the vast battleship. On 28 March 1942 a daring raid was launched against the German-occupied port of St Nazaire, which contained the only dry dock on the Atlantic coast capable of docking *Tirpitz*. The training missions for the attack had been carried out in Cardiff docks.[39] The old destroyer

Campbeltown, one of fifty loaned to Britain by the US, was steered into St Nazaire harbour under German colours before ramming the dock gates. After the crew abandoned ship, timed charges concealed in the hull went off, destroying the gates. One of the instigators of the plan was Royal Engineer Captain William Pritchard of Llandaff, whose father was the master of Cardiff docks and who died during the attack; a plaque commemorating him was unveiled in Cardiff in September 2016.[40] *Campbeltown*'s captain during the raid was Lieutenant Commander Stephen Beattie, son of the vicar of Leighton, Montgomeryshire, who won the Victoria Cross for his heroism.[41] The old destroyer was escorted by a flotilla of motor torpedo boats and motor launches carrying the Royal Marines who were to land and cause as much damage as possible to the port infrastructure before evacuating both the Marines and *Campbeltown*'s crew. Thomas O'Leary of Port Talbot was a wireless operator on *ML446* and was lucky to escape unscathed as enemy fire went straight through the wooden hull of the motor launch.[42] The CO of *MTB74* was the charismatic Sub-Lieutenant Micky Wynn of Glynllifon, Caernarfonshire, and Rhug, Denbighshire. If *Campbeltown* failed, he was to launch two delayed-action torpedoes at the dock gate, but Beattie's success meant Wynn fired instead at his secondary target, the old dock entrance; the torpedoes exploded two days later and destroyed it. *MTB74* was sunk on her way back to sea and Wynn was taken prisoner, having lost an eye during the action. He escaped but was recaptured and sent to Colditz, being repatriated shortly before the end of the war. Micky Wynn subsequently became the seventh Lord Newborough, but his involvement in 'naval warfare' was not over: in 1976 he was fined by a magistrates' court for firing from Fort Belan a nine-pound cannonball that went through the sail of a yacht passing through the Menai Strait, apparently during a party to celebrate his mother-in-law's birthday.[43] The memorial that his family erected to him in historic Rug

Chapel near Corwen remembers 'Micky Wynn, courageous in war, a colourful character.'[44]

The Indian Ocean and Far East

As relations with Japan deteriorated towards the end of 1941, a supposedly powerful deterrent force was despatched to the Far East. This consisted of the battlecruiser *Repulse* and the battleship *Prince of Wales*, only in service for eleven months but already famous for her roles in the sinking of the *Bismarck* and carrying Winston Churchill to his meeting with President Roosevelt off the coast of Newfoundland. However, the aircraft carrier that was meant to be the third element of the fleet was damaged, and fatefully never sailed. Bereft of air cover, the British warships were overwhelmed by the huge Japanese airborne force that attacked it on 10 December 1941. The destruction of 'Force Z' was a devastating blow to both the prestige of the British Empire and to families across the British Isles. Among those who went down with the *Prince of Wales* were 18-year-old Signalman John Jones of Tyn-y-Gongl, Anglesey, 19-year-old Roy Walters of Pontypridd and Stoker William Parsonage of Caergwrle.[45] Clive Sutton of Newport, who had been on the *Prince of Wales* when she sank the *Bismarck*, had a lucky escape: 'I jumped over with Fred Tottle from Cwmbran but we lost each other. I felt myself sinking when I was hauled onto a raft by him. We were on it for a few hours and [were] then picked up by the destroyer *Electra*.'[46] The losses on Repulse included four Cardiff men, 20-year-old Stoker William Thomas Wilson of Pontypridd, Ordnance Artificer John Selwyn Thomas of Bargoed, Able Seaman Robert Davies of Tregarth and 17-year-old George Gibbs of Llandudno.[47]

The destruction of Force Z presaged the fall of Singapore in February 1942, and with its major dockyards in the Far East lost to it (Hong Kong having already fallen), the Royal Navy had to withdraw to the Indian Ocean, falling back on such harbours as Trincomalee in Sri Lanka. For much of 1942, one disaster followed another as the seemingly unstoppable Japanese advance continued by both land and sea. On 9 April 1942 the small, old aircraft carrier HMS Hermes had only just put to sea from Trincomalee when she was attacked by an over-whelming force of Japanese dive bombers. Over 300 perished when the ship went down, among them her commanding officer, Captain Richard Onslow; although Hampshire-born and the son of the vicar of the border parish of Bedstone, Shropshire, he is commemorated on the war memorial at Presteigne. Other Welshmen who perished in the attack on *Hermes* included Royal Marines Thomas Griffiths of Marloes and Corporal Tom Williams of Capel Isaac, Llandeilo, and Leading Supply Assistant Arthur Hughes of Wrexham.[48]

In 1944–45 a huge Far Eastern fleet, the largest that the Royal Navy ever sent to sea, was assembled for the war against Japan. More and more ships were transferred to it as operations in Europe were scaled back, and one of them was the aircraft carrier HMS *Illustrious*, which survived a Kamikaze attack before participating in the liberation of the Philippines. Nearly sixty years later, in 2003, one of her crewmen, Able Seaman Glyndŵr Collins of Aberfan, became one of only three Britons to receive the Philippine Liberation Medal when the honour was bestowed on him at the new *Senedd* in Cardiff in a ceremony attended by the First Minister and other dignitaries.[49] Graham Chadwick, the future Bishop of Kimberley and Kuruman, was on the aircraft carri-ers *Indefatigable* and *Formidable* when they, too, were hit by Kamikazes. He also noted how the Welsh and Irish were the ringleaders of a mutiny against the cramped conditions aboard the headquarters ship HMS *Lothian*, which had been sent out without a refit to make her fit for tropical condi-tions.[50] On several ships, official group photographs were organised for all the Welshmen aboard, or for those from particular districts. Thus the nine men from the Swansea and

Llanelli area aboard the escort carrier HMS *Empress* posed for a photograph in March 1945.[51] The defeat of the Japanese was only accomplished at considerable cost, and Welsh sailors continued to perish until the very end: Able Seaman Stanley Robert Price of Pontypridd was one of the seven men killed when the minesweeper HMS *Squirrel* was lost off the Malay Peninsula on 24 July 1945.

'Welsh' Warships

As in the first war, ships that had been engaged in innocuous peacetime activities in Welsh waters suddenly found themselves transformed into warships. The Campbell paddle steamers that ran summer cruises from Penarth, Mumbles and the other piers along the Glamorgan coast were converted into minesweepers, keeping the Firth of Forth and the Tyne clear of enemy mines, while the oldest, *Ravenswood*, became a static anti-aircraft vessel at Belfast and later at Liverpool. Eight of these vessels were involved in Operation Dynamo, the evacuation from Dunkirk; three were lost, but the others managed to bring home over 4,000 men. The survivors became anti-aircraft vessels in 1942, helping to escort coastal convoys, and by the end of the war only four were left.[52] Irish Sea ferries were requisitioned again. *Scotia*, from the Holyhead-Dublin run, was commissioned as HMS *Scotia* but was lost at Dunkirk when a bomb from a Stuka dive bomber went straight down her funnel. Over 300 men were lost, most of them French soldiers.[53] The Welsh trawler fleets were taken into naval service once more. Four Milford Haven trawlers were requisitioned in the earliest days of the war, to be followed by over fifty more.[54] Even smaller craft were called up. The *Lady Drusie*, a motor cruiser owned by Frank Gaccon, Commanding Officer of the Auxiliary Fire Service in Cardiff, was commandeered for minesweeping duties, but struck a mine in the Bristol Channel in November 1940 and was sunk with the loss of eight lives.[55]

The navy's first HMS *Welshman*, completed in August 1941, was
a fast minelayer which spent her first months in service laying
minefields in the Bay of Biscay and the English Channel. In the
spring of 1942 she went to the Mediterranean to run supplies
to the besieged island of Malta, a role for which her high speed
ideally suited her. She carried out several successful runs to the
island, eluding enemy attempts to intercept her, before being
torpedoed and sunk on 1 February 1943 while transporting supplies to Tobruk.[56] Another 'Welsh' warship that played a pivotal
role in the Battle for Malta was HMS *Breconshire*, a merchantman
converted to an auxiliary supply ship. She made more runs to the
beleaguered island than any other cargo-carrying vessel, but in
March 1942 she was part of a convoy from Alexandria to Malta
that came under sustained attack from Axis aircraft and a substantial part of the Italian fleet. The merchantmen were ordered to
break convoy and head for Malta at full speed, but a few miles
off the island *Breconshire* came under air attack once again and was
badly damaged. She was finally brought into harbour under tow,
but a further sustained assault by dive bombers led to her capsiz-
ing in Grand Harbour, where the wreck remained until 1954.

Several veterans of the First World War saw action again in the
Second. HMS *Cardiff*, which had led the High Seas Fleet into captivity, initially served on the Northern Patrol, based at Scapa Flow,
but spent most of the war as a gunnery training ship, based principally in the Firth of Clyde.[57] HMS *Dragon* served in the Atlantic
in 1940–41, then in the Indian Ocean in 1942, before being handed
over to the Polish Navy in 1943; she was sunk off the Normandy
beaches in July 1944. The navy's eighth HMS *Severn* was of a
rather newer vintage. She was a submarine launched in 1934,
seeing service in West Africa, home waters and the Mediterranean
before deploying to the Far East in 1944 and being scrapped in
India in 1946. Another submarine named after a Welsh river, the
navy's first HMS *Usk*, had a much shorter career. Commissioned
in October 1940, she was lost only six months later, probably
striking a mine in the Mediterranean in April or May 1941.

The pressing need for new classes of anti-submarine escorts and minesweepers swiftly added new Welsh names to the Navy List.* The Hunt-class destroyers built from 1939 onwards included *Penylan*, *Talybont* and *Brecon*, the last being only one of two sleek Type IVs to be built; she survived until scrapped in 1962, a year after *Talybont* (which had been adopted by the Isle of Anglesey, despite being the name of a Cardiganshire hunt). *Penylan*'s fate was very different. Adopted by the Borough of Carmarthen, she was commissioned on 25 August 1942 but was sunk by an E-boat off Start Point on 3 December after only thirty days of active service. Meanwhile, in 1940, in dire straits and desperate for more convoy escorts, the Royal Navy acquired fifty old destroyers from the United States under the lend-lease agreement. These were all named after middling British towns, and the list included HMS *Newport* and HMS *Montgomery*, which sank an Italian submarine in 1941; her captain at the time was Bill Puxley, one of the last scions of the famous dynasty from Llanddarog that had also controlled the copper mines of Berehaven, County Cork and been the subject of Daphne DuMaurier's novel *Hungry Hill*. Another lend-lease acquisition was the navy's first HMS *Fishguard*, as opposed to the archaic *Fisgard*, a former US Coastguard cutter which spent much of the war escorting convoys in the Atlantic or to and from West Africa before being deployed to the Indian Ocean in 1944.

Later in the war several new classes of warship took geographical names, including a number of Welsh ones. The River-class frigates built from 1941 onwards included the *Dovey*, *Monnow*, *Taff*, *Towy*, *Usk* and *Wye*; the Bay-class anti-aircraft frigates built from 1943 onwards included the *Cardigan Bay*, *Carnarvon Bay*,

---

★   Perhaps oddly, though, there has never been an HMS *Swansea*, although there was an armed trawler named *Swansea Castle*. However, the frigate HMCS *Swansea*, named after a Toronto suburb which was itself named after the Welsh town, served with distinction during the war, became the Royal Canadian Navy's most successful U-boat hunter, and remained part of the Canadian Navy until 1966.

St Brides Bay and *Tremadoc Bay*. Most of the former had short service careers, but the Bays, almost all of which were completed after the war's end, were not disposed of until 1959–61. The Castle-class corvettes which appeared from 1943 included *Denbigh Castle*, which was torpedoed in the Barents Sea in February 1945, and *Flint Castle*. Meanwhile a new class of minesweepers was designated the Bangor class. The ships included *Beaumaris*, *Rhyl*, *Llandudno*, *Tenby* and *Bangor* herself. Several, including *Tenby*, took part in minesweeping operations during D-Day and the subsequent assault on Cherbourg. All of the 'Welsh' minesweepers were rapidly decommissioned at the war's end. There were also some Welsh connections in other classes of warship. The Captain-class ships were American convoy escorts, transferred to the Royal Navy under lend-lease; they included a HMS *Foley* and a HMS *Tyler*, each of which sank one U-boat before being returned to the United States Navy after less than two years of service.

Notes

1   A. Dalton, *Wayward Sailor: In Search of the Real Tristan Jones* (Camden, Maine, 2003), passim. *Heart of Oak* is still on the shelves of the library at the National Archives, Kew, which contains only a select few particularly significant non-fiction works.

2   Unless stated otherwise, information in this chapter about individual casualties is drawn from the website of the Commonwealth War Graves Commission.

3   www.espnscrum.com/wales/rugby/story/112576.html# (Accessed: 2012)

4   H. Richards, 'Thomas, John Brinley George (1917–1997), Journalist', *ODNB*.

5   Scott, *Experience Shared*, p.178.

6   P.M.S. Blackett, 'Evan James Williams, 1903–45', *Obituary Notices of Fellows of the Royal Society*, 5 (1947), pp.387–405; R.V. Jones, 'Williams, Evan James (1903–1945), Physicist', *ODNB*; 'Davies, Rhisiart Morgan (1903–58), Scientist and Professor of Physics', *WBO*.

7   Carradice and Breverton, *Welsh Sailors*, p.93.

8   Carradice and Breverton, *Welsh Sailors*, pp.114, 163.

9   A. Roberts, *Estuary People: Penclawdd 1900–70* (Langland, 2001), p.271.

10 IWM, Oral History 15108.
11 Carradice and Breverton, *Welsh Sailors*, p.210.
12 Carradice and Breverton, *Welsh Sailors*, pp.336–52.
13 Roberts, *Estuary People*, p.275.
14 V.L. Mathews, *Blue Tapestry* (1948), pp.96, 144.
15 IWM, Documents 15724.
16 Carradice and Breverton, *Welsh Sailors*, pp.127–31.
17 L. Verrill-Rhys and D. Beddoe, eds., *Parachutes and Petticoats: Welsh Women Writing on the Second World War* (Dinas Powis, 1992), pp.89–98.
18 E. Hooson, 'Ashley [*née* Mountney], Laura (1925–1985), Dress Designer and Interior Decorator', *ODNB*.
19 Scott, *Experience Shared*, p.188.
20 NLW, Geoff Charles Collection 003366279.
21 Williams, *Heart of a Dragon*, pp.323–44.
22 Carradice and Breverton, *Welsh Sailors*, p.202.
23 www.cwmbransdead.shaunmcguire.co.uk/W.htm; www.ystradgynlais.info/dg-davies.html (Accessed: 2012)
24 www.pembrokeshire-war-memorial.co.uk/page67.htm (Accessed: 2012)
25 lintonsview.blogspot.co.uk/
26 www.convoyweb.org.uk/
27 Carradice and Breverton, *Welsh Sailors*, pp.343–6.
28 www.guardian.co.uk/news/2001/dec/24/guardianobituaries
29 Schooling: 1891 Census, RG12/4667, accessed via www.ancestry.co.uk; career: W.S. Chalmers, 'Horton, Sir Max Kennedy (1883–1951), Naval Officer', *ODNB*.
30 *Navy News*, July 1993.
31 T. Davies, *Borth: A Maritime History* (Llanrwst, 2009), pp.141–2.
32 Carradice and Breverton, *Welsh Sailors*, p.166.
33 IWM, Oral History 15108.
34 Carradice and Breverton, *Welsh Sailors*, pp.88–90.
35 www.pembrokeshire-war-memorial.co.uk/page48.htm (Accessed: 2012)
36 www.pembrokeshire-war-memorial.co.uk/page20.htm (Accessed: 2012)
37 www.laugharnewarmemorial.co.uk/page22.htm (Accessed: 2012)
38 Carradice and Breverton, *Welsh Sailors*, p.211.
39 D. Morgan, *Cardiff: A City At War* (Cardiff 1998), pp.38–9.
40 https://www.bbc.co.uk/news/uk-wales-south-east-wales-37427432 (21 September 2016)
41 Williams, *Heart of a Dragon*, pp.371–83.
42 IWM, Oral History 11289.

43 Obituary, *The Independent*, 28 Oct. 1998.

44 Personal observation.

45 www.forcez-survivors.org.uk/casualties.html (Accessed: 2012)

46 www.newportpast.com/jd/prince_of_wales.htm

47 www.forcez-survivors.org.uk/casualties.html (Accessed: 2012)

48 www.pembrokeshire-war-memorial.co.uk/page43.htm; www.laugharnewarmemorial.co.uk/page37.htm (Accessed: 2012)

49 wales.gov.uk/newsroom/localgovernment/2003/4038606/?lang=en (Accessed: 2012)

50 Carradice and Breverton, *Welsh Sailors*, pp.66–7.

51 IWM, A27953.

52 Richards, *Cardiff: A Maritime History*, pp.133–4.

53 *Ex info* Holyhead Maritime Museum.

54 TNA, ADM1/17321.

55 D. Morgan, *Cardiff: A City At War* (Cardiff, 1998), p.9.

56 www.naval-history.net/xGM-Chrono-07ML-Welshman.htm

57 GRO, D198/1.

58 www.naval-history.net/xGM-Chrono-10DE-Penylan.htm

59 www.naval-history.net/xGM-Chrono-16CGC-Fishguard.htm

60 'HMS *Tenby*, J34, Remembered' (copy at Tenby Museum).

12

WALES AND THE NAVY

1945 TO THE PRESENT

In November 1981, a brand new warship slipped into Cardigan
Bay to test fire her main weapon system. If any locals were
watching from the Cardiganshire cliffs, or from fishing boats out
of Aberaeron or New Quay, they would have found the scene
entirely familiar: warships had been doing much the same since
not long after the Second World War. The Aberporth range,
originally established in 1939, had been the navy's principal
testing ground for all its main missile systems of the post-war
era. A naval trials unit was established there in 1952 and during
the years that followed, Seaslug, the fleet's first surface-to-air
missile, was test-fired into Cardigan Bay from a purpose-built
simulated ship firing platform. During the 1960s, warships
came onto the range to test their systems for the first time; the
first British warship to be named *Glamorgan* carried out the
first launch of her Seaslug missiles at Aberporth in 1967. More
recently, the surface-to-surface Exocet and the new Seadart
surface-to-air system that was replacing Seaslug were fired in
Cardigan Bay on a number of occasions.[1] The warship herself
would also have been very familiar. She was clearly a Type 42,
one of the new class of destroyers being commissioned into the

Royal Navy. The class included HMS *Cardiff*, which had fired her Seadart system for the first time at Aberporth a year earlier, and (by 1982) seven sister ships, which included HM ships *Sheffield* and *Coventry*. But if a particularly keen-eyed Welsh man or woman was indeed studying the Type 42 destroyer firing her Seadart missile in Cardigan Bay in November 1981, (s)he might have noticed something unusual about her. The ship was not flying the White Ensign; instead, she flew the blue-white-blue colours of the *Armada Republica Argentina*.[2] Perhaps the observer might have found this reassuring. After all, did not Wales and Argentina have a powerful historic connection, thanks to the existence of the Welsh colony in Patagonia? Within twenty weeks, though, Britain and Argentina would be at war, and the officers and men of HM ships *Cardiff*, *Glamorgan*, and every other vessel in the South Atlantic Taskforce would regard the ship moored so innocently in Cardigan Bay, the ARA *Santísima Trinidad*, as one of their deadliest potential enemies.

Officers and Men (and Women)

The end of the Second World War did not see the immediate abandonment of conscription, which was rebranded as National Service in 1948 and continued until its abolition in 1960, with men serving for two years followed by a period in the reserves. Relatively few Welshmen called up for National Service opted for the navy; in the three years 1951–53 only 316 men did so, some 1.3 per cent of the total call-up (compared with 2.1 per cent from England and 1.9 per cent from Scotland).[3] Both during and after the National Service era, the navy continued to attract some who went on to have distinguished careers ashore after their service ended. As in the war years, these included a number of rugby internationals, notably Dewi Bebb, Brian Jones, Lewis Jones, Bryn Meredith, Billy Williams and Malcolm Thomas (the latter being a career naval officer). Others achieved their principal distinction within the service. Rear-Admiral Gwynedd Idris Pritchard, who died in 2012, served as Flag Officer Sea Training and Flag Officer Gibraltar during the 1970s. Rear-Admiral Phillip Edwards was Director of Fleet Support, responsible for logistics during the Falklands War. A Welsh speaker, he subsequently served on the Health Policy Board for Wales.[4] Major General James Louis Moulton of Pembroke Dock (1906–93) joined the Royal Marines in 1924 and ended his career as Chief of Amphibious Warfare from 1957 to 1961, while Surgeon Vice-Admiral Ian Jenkins of Cardiff capped a long career in the navy by serving as Surgeon-General of the armed forces from 2002–06.[5]

Traditional Welsh maritime communities continued to send recruits into the navy. The Borth/Dolybont area, for example, provided the likes of Stoker Gwyndaf Evans; electronic warfare specialist John Cory; naval electrician Stephen Brown, who served in the Falklands War aboard the requisitioned ferry *Rangatira*; Commander Richard Jenkins; and Commander Peter Norrington-Davies, who commanded the submarine HMS *Walrus* before retiring to his home village of Dolybont and becoming the Ceredigion Harbourmaster, responsible for Aberystwyth, Aberaeron and New Quay. When, in 1990, women were finally permitted to serve at sea, Wren Yvette Ellis-Clark of Borth, a radio operator, was one of the first to sign up, joining the crew of HMS *Brilliant* – the first British warship on which women went to sea – and deploying to the Gulf. She subsequently served on HMS *Endurance* in the Antarctic.[6] Another female pioneer at sea was Sally Prendergast of Llandrindod Wells, who rose to the rank of lieutenant-commander and later became a governor of the WRNS Benevolent Trust.[7]

Others joined the Royal Fleet Auxiliary, the organisation that had been founded in 1905 to provide logistical support to the navy's front-line warships. Although it became an indispensable element of the service under the direct operational control of the navy, the RFA was and is officially a part of the Merchant

Navy, crewed by civilians. During the post-war era, the RFA operated a substantial fleet of replenishment tankers, store ships, repair ships and other craft, probably the most famous of which were the landing ships of the Sir class. Built in the mid-1960s, the six ships all bore the names of Knights of the Round Table, a tenuous connection with Wales – or at least, with Welsh myth – that would be reinforced in the most tragic manner possible at Bluff Cove in the Falkland Islands on 8 June 1982 (*see below*). Smaller craft were operated by the Port Auxiliary Service, which merged into the Royal Maritime Auxiliary Service in 1976 and survived until it was privatised in 2008. Several of their vessels were based in Welsh waters and manned locally, while others were given Welsh names. A large class of tenders, built between the 1960s and early 1980s for what became the Royal Maritime Auxiliary Service, included *Aberdovey*, *Beddgelert*, *Criccieth*, *Llandovery*, *Menai* and *Milford*. Meanwhile, a buoy tender based at Pembroke Dock and in service on the Aberporth range from 1976 to 1990 was given the name *Dolwen*, 'after one of the two small beaches at Aberporth'.[8]

The Royal Navy's principal focus after 1945 was the 'Cold War' with the Soviet Union, and many ships were deployed in the Atlantic and Mediterranean, implicitly or explicitly monitoring and deterring Soviet forces. The navy was also heavily engaged in the Korean War of 1950–53. Arthur Jones of Cynwyd, near Bala, served on the carrier HMS *Unicorn*, under almost constant air attack from North Korean and Chinese forces.[9] Otherwise, there were occasional low-level spats, such as the 'Cod Wars' with Iceland, and a number of operations connected with Britain's imperial legacies, such as the Suez debacle of 1956 and the evacuation of Aden in 1967. For many Welshmen of the post-war era, however, naval service was relatively humdrum and certainly not particularly dangerous. Some, though, had more unusual experiences. Wilfred Gordon of Cardiff found himself on a bizarre odyssey which had poignant echoes of the great days of Wales' connection with the navy. In 1956–57 he was a member of the crew of HMS *Foulness*, an ugly, obsolete tank-cleaning vessel which undertook a 12,000-mile voyage from Scotland to Singapore prior to being transferred to the new Malayan Navy. But *Foulness* was also one of the navy's last coal burners, and Gordon must have been one of the last Welsh naval seamen to experience the horrors of coaling ship in the tropics.[10]

As the Cold War continued, the Royal Navy and Royal Marines continued to attract significant numbers of young people from Wales. In 1979–80, for example – the very beginning of the Thatcher era – the service recruited 490 people, compared with 1,389 for the Army and 767 for the Royal Air Force. Intriguingly, this was a marked increase over the previous year, proportionately far greater than that for the army – the RAF even had a slight fall – suggesting perhaps that even prior to the Falklands War and the deindustrialisation of Wales, some young Welshmen saw the navy as a particularly attractive career option. Two hundred and twenty-one of the recruits signed up in Cardiff, 113 in Swansea and 156 in Wrexham.[11] Recruitment fell away dramatically in the 1990s, following the end of the Cold War and substantial cuts in the size of the fleet: in the five years between 1992 and 1997, only 529 joined the navy.[12] In 2003–04, the figure was 176, of whom twenty-nine joined at Cardiff, seventy-three at Swansea and seventy-four at Wrexham. The virtual collapse of naval recruitment from Cardiff and south-east Wales compared with a quarter of a century earlier is particularly marked.[13]

Fighting on the Beaches

When the Cold War began, many top secret contingency plans were initiated. One of these was Operation Sandstone, instituted in 1947, which consisted of a series of surveys of the ports and beaches of the United Kingdom. The intention was that the surveys would provide the raw intelligence for a counter-invasion by the United States if the country were overrun by Soviet forces. The reports, including those on all of the Welsh harbours and beaches, survive at the National Archives, Kew, and provide fascinating insights into both the often alarmist strategic thinking of the Cold War era and the condition of the Welsh coast during the 1950s in particular, when the project was in full swing. (It was eventually disbanded in 1966, by which time the strategic premise underpinning it was long discredited.)[14] The surveys contain detailed charts, photographs and reports which analyse the nature and quality of the anchorages, tides, nature of the sand, beach exits, communications and space available for creating store dumps. Thus, at Pembrey, for example, it was remarked that 'stores could be concealed among the pine trees of Pembrey Forest,' while at Borth, where there was 'a firm sand beach of even gradient', the golf course and caravan park were thought to be suitable sites for the invading US Army's store dumps. At Colwyn Bay, 'in fine weather coasters often anchor temporarily, as there is little tidal stream; the bottom is, however, shingle and therefore bad holding ground.' If the Green Berets had indeed stormed ashore at Colwyn Bay, they would perhaps have been reassured by the information that '[the] A55 is 350 yards inland and can be reached by several roads', thus enabling them to set off on the 58 miles that were said to lie between their landing place and Soviet-occupied Liverpool.[15] Another consequence of the mindset that launched Operation Sandstone was the construction in 1951 of a large new quay at Neyland (at the entrance to the present marina). This, together with the quay at Burton Ferry slightly upstream, was intended for use as a rapid disembarkation point for American forces on their way to reinforce Western Europe. The quay was also supposedly intended to be the evacuation point for the royal family, en route to exile in Canada.[16]

A Naval Graveyard [II]

In 1941 the school ship HMS *Conway*, moored in the Mersey, narrowly escaped destruction by German bombing. As a result, it was decided to move the vessel (originally launched in 1839 as HMS *Nile*) to a safer berth in the Menai Strait, and in 1949 the Marquess of Anglesey provided her with new moorings off his home at Plas Newydd.* In 1953, she began an eastbound voyage through the strait, under tow, with the intention of proceeding to Birkenhead for a refit. This was known to be a complex and dangerous passage, with only very small 'windows of opportunity' when the tides would be right, and those responsible for the tow believed they had researched the issues extensively. Even so, strong north-westerlies on the day of the tow, 14 April, and an unexpected 10-knot tide, complicated matters still further, and shortly before 10.30 a.m. the *Conway* went aground on the rocks known as the Platters.[17] Attempts to refloat her failed, and the strong tides swiftly caused the ship's back to break. The vessel began to be broken up *in situ*, but the process was expedited by a fire on 31 October 1956 which largely destroyed the remains, although much of the hull below the waterline remains on the Platters Reef, and a diving couple from Bangor apparently created an entire fitted kitchen out of her timbers.[18] The *Conway* school moved ashore and survived until 1974, two of its last pupils being England's World Cup winning rugby coach, Sir Clive Woodward, and Conservative minister Iain Duncan Smith. A vigorous old boys' association and a number of displays at Plas Newydd still keep its memory alive.[19]

During the late 1940s and 1950s, the Royal Navy kept a large number of vessels in reserve, cocooning them to keep them

---

* Another school ship from the Mersey, the TS *Indefatigable*, housed in the former cruiser *Phaeton*, also migrated to the Menai Strait in 1941 but was moved ashore to Admiral Lord Clarence Paget's old home, Plas Llanfair, in 1944. The school remained there until closed in 1995: www.anglesey.info/TS%20Indefatigable.htm.

dehumidified. The spacious but now under-used docks of the South Wales ports provided ideal laying-up facilities for many ships of this Reserve Fleet. By 1954 the docks at Cardiff, Penarth and Barry were filled with dozens of destroyers, frigates, minesweepers and other vessels, with the frigate *Derg*, suitably renamed HMS *Cambria*, acting as headquarters ship at Cardiff.[20] Nineteen large Landing Craft Tank (LCT) were laid up at Llanelli, but they were reactivated during the Suez Crisis of 1956 and never returned. By 1959, the reserve fleet presence at the remaining ports was being run down, with Cardiff already earmarked for closure. By then, strategic thinking was increasingly dominated by fears of nuclear attack, and the Cardiff area was felt to be an obvious target. This led to a decision to close the South Wales bases in 1960, the remaining ships being towed away. This affected the eleven ships remaining at Penarth, including the large frigate *Terpsichore*, the netlayer *Guardian* and the small frigates *Loch Killin* and *Loch Dunvegan*; the two old sloops *Snipe* and *Pheasant* at Barry; and the two weather ships, two frigates and three minesweepers at Cardiff. The closures led to only eighty-three job losses, which the Admiralty hoped might mollify the local community: 'political passions are traditionally more easily aroused in South Wales than in most other places, especially when unemployment is concerned.'[21]

As in the period after 1918, many warships ended their days in the shipbreaking yards along the coast of South Wales. Large numbers of old ships were laid up in the upper reaches of Milford Haven, and many were scrapped at the revived Ward yard at Milford.[22] The Rees yard at Llanelli continued to break up escort vessels, submarines and small auxiliaries until its closure in the early 1960s. However, one of Rees' purchases of this era became famous for never reaching the yard at all: the escort destroyer *Cleveland* was wrecked on Rhossili Beach on 28 June 1957 while en route to the breakers. She remained *in situ*, disfiguring one of the Gower's most famous beauty spots, for two and a half years.[23] Thomas Ward's yard at Briton Ferry broke up the likes of the cruisers *Caradoc* (1946) and *Gambia* (1965), the submarines *Seraph* (1965), *Tally-Ho* (1967) and *Taciturn* (1971), the destroyer *Crossbow* (1971), as well as two ships with particularly strong Welsh connections, the destroyer *Cambrian* (1971) and the frigate *Tenby* (1977). The yard lay close to, and was easily visible from, the A48, then the main route along the South Wales coast, so the doomed warships were familiar sights for generations of holidaymakers and Swansea commuters. Slightly further upstream, the Steel Supply Company yard at Skewen broke up the Royal Navy's first gas-turbine propelled frigate, the *Exmouth* (1979) and her sister ship *Palliser* (1983).[24] Finally, until its closure in 1979 the Cashmore yard at Newport, conveniently placed for the steel works at Llanwern, scrapped the likes of the cruisers *Enterprise* (1946), *Suffolk* (1948) and *Devonshire* (1954), several submarines, and the fast minelayer *Manxman* (1970), sister ship of the ill-fated *Welshman*.[25] In the 1970s and 1980s, though, increasingly draconian health and safety regulations, together with aggressive international competition, particularly from Taiwan, the Indian sub-continent and latterly Turkey, led to the virtual demise of the British shipbreaking industry. But economic conditions changed again, and in 2013 HMS Cornwall was broken up at Swansea, although the experiment was not considered to be a success

Sea Lords

Scotland and Ireland produced many Admirals of the Fleet and First Sea Lords; Wales produced none. Nevertheless, three could boast strong Welsh connections, and none of them were anonymous mediocrities. David Beatty, commander of the battlecruisers at Jutland and perhaps the most charismatic British naval officer since Nelson, went to school in Rhyl; Ernle Chatfield, who as First Sea Lord in the 1930s was largely responsible for the expansion of the navy to meet the Nazi threat,

went to school in Tenby.[26] The only one with Welsh blood,
Sir Caspar John, First Sea Lord from 1960 to 1963, was a son
of the bohemian Pembrokeshire artist Augustus John, and seems
to have sought the discipline and certainties of a naval career as
a reaction against his father's chaotic lifestyle. Even so, Caspar
had a bohemian streak of his own; his brusque way of speaking and steely gaze were belied by his love of pubs, parties and
dressing informally, while he always claimed that his father's
influence enabled him to see through the manifold absurdi-
ties and pomposities of the navy.[27] Caspar drove around in a
battered old former London taxi and flew his own planes. He
became a specialist in aircraft carriers and naval aviation, effectively becoming a 'founding father' of the Fleet Air Arm and
being largely responsible for the introduction of the helicopter
into the navy at the end of the Second World War. This experience served him well when he became First Sea Lord, the first
naval aviator ever to hold the position, and he had to defend the
navy's carriers against a ferocious onslaught by the RAF: 'the
atmosphere in Whitehall was at times sulphurous. It was said
that the geographical positions of whole continents were shifted
to accommodate the long-range aircraft which were to replace
the carriers.' John won the argument, although his triumph was
short-lived (the new carrier was cancelled by the Labour government in 1966). The other great issue that he confronted was the
government's decision to adopt Polaris, a submarine-launched
nuclear deterrent. John supported this publicly, despite his deep
misgivings about the project's cost and impact on the balance of
the fleet.[28] To the very end, though, he could not shake off the
shadow of his famous father. Even when Caspar was holding
some of the most senior offices in the navy, Augustus' arrival
in London prompted an aside to his staff, 'my old dad's up in
town and I'd better give him half a pint of beer, so I may be a few
minutes late back,' followed by the disappearance of the admiral
until 5 p.m., when he returned somewhat the worse for wear.[29]
Promoted Admiral of the Fleet in 1962, Sir Caspar John retired

in the following year, spent much of his retirement in a cottage in the Berwyn Mountains and died in 1984.

Having produced only two First Lords of the Admiralty in the previous 300 years, Wales suddenly provided two First Lords very nearly in succession in the decade following the end of the Second World War. George Hall, originally a miner from Penrhiwceiber, served as MP for Aberdare from 1922 to 1946, when he was ennobled as Viscount Hall of Cynon Valley and appointed First Lord, having previously served on the Admiralty board from 1929–31 and later as its Financial Secretary. Hall successfully oversaw the navy's difficult transition to a peacetime footing.[30] When Churchill and the Conservatives returned to power in 1951, the new First Lord was Jim Thomas, born in Llandeilo but MP for Hereford, who held the post from 1951 to 1956, throughout Churchill's second term as Prime Minister and into his friend Anthony Eden's, by which time he had been ennobled as the first and last Viscount Cilcennin. Thomas was the grandson of a naval officer and had served as the Admiralty's financial secretary for two years before he became First Lord. With such advantageous credentials behind him, he took to the office like a duck to water:

> 'There is only one test of a First Lord', he used to remark, 'Will he look well in a yachting cap when visiting the fleet?' Standing over six foot, with boldly cut features and a fresh complexion, Thomas was as much at ease on the lower deck as in the ward room. His popularity was immediate and lasting, his progress round any naval establishment a convivial occasion.

One of his civil servants found him to be

> a handsome bachelor and a marvellous raconteur; he was also very well connected and often accompanied members of the Royal Family to private engagements. He was in great

> demand for dinner parties and other social occasions … Jim
> Thomas was neither an intellectual nor a statesman; and he
> was no eager beaver, slaving over official papers or steeped in
> dogma. But he knew all the right people and had a keen sense
> of what was reasonable and practicable.[31]

Thomas had real problems to resolve, and coped with them
admirably. He ended the system of entry to the naval college
at Dartmouth at the tender age of 13, insisting that entrants
to the profession had to be at least 18. He resisted pressure to
abolish the Fleet Air Arm, managed naval economies sensibly,
and also dealt diplomatically with the visit of the Soviet leaders
Khruschev and Bulganin, notably by playing down the mysterious and potentially explosive disappearance of Commander
'Buster' Crabbe, RN, in the general vicinity of the Soviet
cruiser *Ordzhonikidze* in Portsmouth Harbour.[32] The royal
family's liking for him appears to have been genuine. When he
went to the House of Lords, the Duke of Edinburgh joked that
'it must be a relief to be shot of clamouring constituents;' and
after his departure from the Admiralty, Cilcennin accompanied
the duke on his world tour aboard the royal yacht *Britannia*.
Lord Mountbatten, who owed his position as First Sea Lord
largely to Cilcennin's intervention on his behalf in the teeth
of Eden's opposition, praised the outgoing First Lord in warm
terms: 'the navy has begun to assume its new streamline form
for the atomic age and it was under your guidance that this
was achieved … I have never served a more delightful chief.'[33]
Cilcennin had also promised the young Queen Elizabeth that
when the navy built a new aircraft carrier, it would be named
after her. His promise was fulfilled, albeit only some fifty years
after his premature death in 1960.[34] Despite their very different social backgrounds and politics, Jim Thomas and George
Hall had been united in one thing: they were Welshmen who
were genuinely interested in, and passionately concerned for,
the Royal Navy.

Uncomfortable Bedfellows:
The Royal Navy and Welsh Politics

Naval men had always been involved in Welsh politics. During the nineteenth century such officers as Sir Christopher Cole, Lord William Stuart and Sir Charles Paget had represented Welsh constituencies, with the naval architect Sir Edward Reed joining the list in the last quarter of the century. After the Second World War, two particularly prominent Welsh MPs could claim impeccable naval credentials. Emlyn Hooson, a Denbighshire barrister who had served on a corvette in the North Atlantic, was elected Liberal MP for Montgomeryshire in 1962 and retained the seat until 1979. A candidate for the leadership of his party, he was also a staunch advocate of devolution and an opponent of Britain's involvement in the Falklands War.[35] Meanwhile, in 1944, a sturdily built sub-lieutenant who always cannily wore his naval uniform to political meetings was adopted as the Labour parliamentary candidate for Cardiff South, defeating his nearest rival by one vote. Sub-Lieutenant James Callaghan, the son of a naval Petty Officer, was duly elected at the 1945 election and went on to occupy every great office of state before serving as Prime Minister from 1976 to 1979. He retained a deep and genuine interest in naval matters, something that he inherited from a father who had died when he was only nine: 'by telling his son stories of ships and the sea Callaghan's father also encouraged in the young boy a romantic attachment to all things naval that, although uncharacteristic of his essentially down-to-earth character, remained with him for all his life.'[36]

From its very beginnings in the 1920s, Plaid Cymru, the Welsh nationalist party, had a strong pacifist streak, epitomised by its first president, Saunders Lewis, who was gaoled in 1936 for an arson attack on the Penyberth bombing school on Llŷn. His successor, Gwynfor Evans – famously the victor of the 1966 Carmarthen by-election, the party's first parliamentary triumph – was arguably even more influenced by pacifism, writing popular histories of Wales which emphasised that particular tradition. (On the other hand, even Gwynfor evidently enjoyed playing with the notion of the existence of a 'free Wales navy' in the Middle Ages.)[37] But others in the party were more pragmatic. D.J. Davies, who was one of the founders of the party in 1925, had volunteered for the United States Navy in 1918, serving until 1920 when he returned to his native Carmarthenshire.[38] In 1977, too, Dr Phil Williams, Plaid's then vice-president, was confident enough of imminent electoral breakthrough and thus of independence in the foreseeable future to informally commission members of Plaid's somewhat unlikely Oxford University branch to research the defence policies of small European nations with a view to preparing a strategy for distinctly Welsh armed forces. Contact was made with and information received from the Austrian, Irish, Norwegian and other embassies, and tentative plans for the first independent Welsh armed forces for nearly six centuries – including a small navy, to be based at Pembroke Dock – were drawn up.[39] Only in the first decade of the twentieth century did Plaid Cymru finally and publicly get to grips with the need to develop a coherent defence strategy for its ideal of an independent Wales but, even then, it virtually ignored naval issues and managed to get wrong such a basic, easily accessible fact as the size of the Irish Navy.[40]

One of the most important issues in Welsh politics during the post-war decades was the status of the Welsh language, and surprisingly, the navy found itself the focus of a very early, albeit minor, campaign on behalf of *yr hen iaith*. In 1949, the Welsh Department of the Ministry of Education proposed to the Admiralty that Welsh, 'the national language of a not unimportant part of the United Kingdom', should become an optional subject in the 16+ entrance examination for Britannia Royal Naval College, Dartmouth. The Admiralty considered the matter carefully, examining in detail such questions as how an examination might be administered and how to establish its equivalence with those for other languages. The conclusion was that the inclusion of Welsh was unlikely to lead to more candidates coming forward, and that the few who might benefit would actually have an unfair advantage: 'since Welsh would be the mother tongue of the candidates offering that language, translation from and into Welsh would not indicate the same powers of learning as translation from and into another language.' One of the senior civil servants who signed off the ultimate rejection of the proposal remarked, 'I have a great respect for the Welsh language from a literary and cultural point of view, but I fail to see how the navy would benefit by introducing this further optional subject which is of such limited application.'[41]

Most naval training takes place, as it has done for many decades, in large shore establishments close to the major naval bases. For example, new Welsh recruits join their counterparts from other parts of the country at HMS *Raleigh* in Torpoint, Cornwall, just across the Tamar from Devonport Dockyard, where all of the service's new entry training takes place. In 2007, though, it was announced that in future advanced training for all three services would be consolidated on a huge new £16 billion site at RAF St Athan in the Vale of Glamorgan. The project soon ran into intractable financial difficulties and strong opposition from both local and national organisations, and it was cancelled by the incoming coalition government in October 2010. However, specialist elements of naval training do continue to take place in Wales. The service's Outdoor Leadership Training Centre has been based at Talybont-on-Usk, Powys, since 1962, while potential recruits for the Special Boat Service, the navy's elite Special Forces Unit, undergo their strenuous selection procedure at Sennybridhe in *Y bannau Brycheiniog* (the Brecon Beacons).

With Scotland holding a referendum on independence in 2014, considerable speculation developed about the future of the British nuclear deterrent, consisting of four nuclear-powered Trident submarines based at Faslane on the Gareloch, adjoining the Firth of Clyde. If an independent Scotland ejected the vessels, where in the rump of the United Kingdom could possibly accommodate them? First Minister of Wales Carwyn Jones sparked controversy by stating on 19 June 2012 that the submarines would be welcome at a new naval base on Milford Haven.[42] In fact, it was not the first time that Milford had been proposed for the role: it was one of the sites considered in 1963–64, before the decision was taken to base the submarine deterrent force at Faslane. Indeed, a number of Welsh harbours – Carmarthen Bay, Tremadog Bay, Fishguard and Holyhead – made the original 'longlist' of potential Polaris bases, but all were rejected at a very early stage because of unsuitable geography. Milford Haven made a 'long shortlist' of ten, with plans drawn up for a submarine base at Newton Noyes and a weapons facility at Angle, but it was excluded from the final shortlist of six on safety grounds, due to the proximity of the then new oil refineries.[43] Carwyn Jones' 'invitation' led to a predictable outpouring of opposition. Some, such as the Archdruid of Wales, fulminated against the perceived immorality of *any* military presence in Wales. Others focused on the rather more practical and not unimportant question of the advisability of placing several nuclear reactors and many nuclear warheads immediately adjacent to a number of oil refineries and a huge liquefied natural gas facility; in other words, essentially the very reason why Milford had been rejected as a nuclear submarine base fifty years earlier, writ even larger.[44]

Regardless of the arguments over Milford Haven potentially hosting Britain's nuclear deterrent, Wales had actually long possessed a nuclear submarine 'base' of sorts, namely a 'Z-berth' – a facility in a commercial harbour where such vessels could berth for 'R&R' and which, perhaps, could also be called upon in the (unspoken) event of an attack obliterating one or more of the Royal Navy's principal bases. This briefly caused controversy in the late 1980s when the designated berth was moved from Cardiff to Swansea, with Swansea CND and CND Cymru organising a vocal campaign against the move.[45] Meanwhile, in Parliament the two MPs for Swansea objected vigorously, stressing concerns over the possibility of nuclear accidents, only to be slapped down by a minister in brutal fashion: 'I do not think that I have heard two more whingeing, scaremongering speeches in all my life.'[46] On this, as on many other occasions, Welsh politicians of all hues displayed a consistently woeful ignorance of naval matters. Thus, in 2008 a debate on continuing Llanelli's affiliation with the nuclear submarine HMS *Trenchant* was somewhat diminished by certain councillors' evident confusion between 'nuclear-powered' and 'nuclear armed'.[47]

Peace Dividends: The Disappearance of the Welsh Shore Establishments

With the coming of peace, the chief advantage that Welsh bases had possessed during wartime – their comparative isolation – immediately became a profound disadvantage. This was demonstrated vividly during the notoriously harsh winter of 1947, when both RNAS Brawdy and HMS *Harrier*, the newly-established aircraft direction and meteorological school at nearby Kete, were cut off for days, and the destroyer HMS *Roebuck* had to take emergency supplies from Milford Haven to Brawdy, landing them with difficulty at Solva. *Harrier* was a somewhat curious base: situated on a bleak, windswept peninsula, with beer shipped in from Haverfordwest (14 miles away), most of the personnel were Wrens whose training consisted partly of cycling around the runway on former ice cream tricycles, pretending to be Soviet bombers.[48] Perhaps unsurprisingly, despite its isolation, *Harrier* was a popular posting with its seriously outnumbered male trainees, and the base was responsible for many marriages (and probably far more brief encounters).[49] It survived for only fourteen years before being closed in January 1961, a forerunner of the gradual but ultimately almost total disappearance of the permanent naval presence in Wales during the forty years that followed. In one sense, bases like *Harrier* were clearly too isolated; but in another, they were not isolated enough. The coming of the Cold War, a nuclear arms race and the precepts of 'mutually assured destruction' meant that an establishment in the far west of Wales was now just as vulnerable to obliteration by an inter-continental ballistic missile as those in the south-east of England. And with the Treasury constantly demanding retrenchment of defence spending, the pressure on the navy to aim for economies of scale on fewer and fewer sites inevitably became irresistible.

The existence of the naval bases – like those of the army and the air force – put many Welsh politicians between a rock and a hard place. Those with strong religious or pacifist convictions seemed to have ample cause to see the bases as bastions of warmongering or of an alien imperialism; 'swords into ploughshares' was always a slogan with a powerful appeal in Wales. But equally, the establishments were often major sources of employment – sometimes *the* major source, especially in Pembrokeshire – and contributed substantial amounts of hard cash to local economies.[50] This ambivalence was perhaps demonstrated most markedly in the case of the various incarnations of the base at Brawdy, near St David's. In 1943 the airbase, originally built for the RAF, was transferred to the navy as a night fighting school, commissioning as HMS *Goldcrest II* in 1946 (the first *Goldcrest* was the RNAS airbase at Dale, operational from 1942 to 1948). Brawdy was the home of the Fleet Air Arm's 849 Squadron from 1952 to 1971, and also accommodated many other squadrons while the aircraft carriers from which they usually operated were in refit. In 1960 it worked up the Indian Navy's first front-line squadron, and in 1963 it became the base for advanced and operational flying training.[51] Brawdy developed excellent relations with the local community, notably through annual air displays which became hugely popular events in West Wales. However, the end of fixed-wing flying by the Fleet Air Arm led to the closure of the base on 1 April 1971.[52]

Local concerns over the impact of the airbase's closure on the economy were swiftly offset by announcements both that the RAF would be taking over the airfield and above all that the United States Navy intended to establish a new facility at Brawdy. This was a submarine listening station, part of a worldwide surveillance chain, manned by some 375 US Navy personnel and built next to but separate from the airfield. The station was meant to be top secret (indeed, in the United States most aspects of its work are still classified), but its existence and purpose were common knowledge in the local area. Without a doubt, the personnel of the base went out of their way to establish strong links with their surroundings. During its twenty-one-year existence the base at Brawdy won the US ambassador's award for community relations on no fewer than six occasions: it supported local charities and a special school for disabled children, cleaned beaches and cemeteries, purchased equipment for the local hospital and bought uniforms for Welsh Paralympians. The base contributed significantly to the local economy: it was calculated that it injected at least £1.8 million per annum into Pembrokeshire coffers. But in the era of Thatcher, Reagan and the Greenham Common protests, the base inevitably became a target for those who objected to the American military presence on Welsh soil. In 1982, a women's peace group marched from Cardiff to Brawdy and set up a protest camp at the gates of the base. But USN Brawdy was always intended to have a finite life of twenty years or so, and it was unfortunate that its closure in 1995 nearly coincided with the closures of both RAF Brawdy and the Royal Naval depots at Milford Haven and Trecwn, the last of which closed on 31 July 1995.[53] Both of the depots had been major repositories for Britain's stocks of naval mines, but the end of the Cold War led to the entire abandonment of mining; the United Kingdom discarded its entire stock of mines by 1992.[54] Remote Trecwn, a site of well over 1,000 acres and 3 miles long, had been a self-contained community, with the 400 workers housed on three separate housing estates, and even had its own primary school, Barham. Local MPs, councils and trades unions argued long and hard against the closures, but in vain.[55] As they had predicted, the combined effect on the Pembrokeshire economy was disastrous: unemployment rose steeply, despite the decision to 'recycle' the former RAF/RNAS base at Brawdy once again, this time into an army barracks.[56]

Most of the navy's other establishments in Wales disappeared at much the same time. The vast armament factory at Caerwent was transferred to the Americans in 1967 and closed outright in the 1990s, although the site continues in use as an army training base. The stores depot at Llangennech underwent several metamorphoses: it lost its Fleet Air Arm role in 1973, specialising instead in weapons control, ship's machinery and other tasks, such as repairing ships' furniture. By the 1980s it was still employing over 600 people. However, it ceased to be a Royal Navy stores depot in 1990 and became instead the central repository for all forms, official publications and other paperwork for the armed services. From 1991 the depot also held twentieth-century service personnel records, including those for the navy, Royal Fleet Auxiliary and dockyards, and in 2002–03 much of the material from Devonport Dockyard's historic South Yard was transferred there. But Llangennech closed in 2008 and its contents were transferred to the vast defence facility at Bicester.[57] Criggion radio station, latterly used for communications with Polaris and Trident submarines, closed in 2003. The ordnance factory at Glascoed survives, as does the establishment at Aberporth, although the latter is now outsourced to a private operator.

Naval Reserves and Training Corps

By 2003, only twenty naval personnel were based permanently in Wales,[58] which, in any case, is not a distinct entity as far as the Royal Navy is concerned: it comes under a Naval Regional Officer (Wales and West of England) with his headquarters in Bristol. However, the 'naval presence' in the country was significantly greater, due in particular to various reserve and training units. A Royal Naval Reserve unit for South Wales was commissioned as HMS *Cambria* in July 1947, occupying buildings in Cardiff Docks. Over the years, *Cambria* operated a number of seagoing training ships. A motor minesweeper was replaced in 1954 by the new wooden-hulled minesweeper *Brereton*, which gave way in turn to *Crichton* (1961–76); all of these were rechristened HMS *St David*. A converted trawler, again named *St David*, followed in 1978, to be replaced by the new minesweeper *Waveney*, which did not change her name, in 1984; but a reorganisation of the reserves in 1994 led to the abandonment of the seagoing tenders, and *Waveney* was sold to Bangladesh. Meanwhile, the regeneration of Cardiff's docklands forced the unit to seek a new location, and on 15 October 1980 *Cambria* reopened in new buildings at Sully, on the outskirts of Barry. The unit was granted the freedom of the Vale of Glamorgan in March 2012 but returned to Cardiff docklands and a new purpose-built building in 2020.[59] A Royal Naval Volunteer (Wireless) Reserve unit had been founded at Swansea in 1932, consisting initially of just one person, A.G. Bishop, with its headquarters in the loft of a rented garage in Uplands. The unit expanded (to 48 members by 1970) and moved to a building in King's Dock in 1949. It was commissioned as HMS *Dragon* in 1984, but paid off in 1994.[60] It was subsequently replaced by a satellite unit of *Cambria*, Tawe Division, recruiting from West Wales and West Glamorgan. In 1994, too, a University Royal Navy Unit was established in South Wales, latterly serving Cardiff, Swansea and Glamorgan Universities; the Archer-class patrol vessel *Express* was attached to this and is based at a berth in Penarth Marina.[61] Meanwhile North Wales reservists were and are served by HMS *Eaglet* at Liverpool, established in 1904 and accommodated in training hulks until it moved ashore in 1971.

For many years and in many ways, the Sea Cadet Corps has provided perhaps the most tangible 'naval presence' in Welsh communities, ensuring that naval uniforms are seen, for example, at Remembrance Day services at war memorials up and down the land. Twenty units operate across the country, primarily in the obvious coastal towns but also in Rhondda and Torfaen. A sister organisation, the Girls Nautical Training Corps, was set up during the Second World War, and the first Welsh unit was established at Penarth in 1946, officered by a number of ex-Wrens. By the end of the year it had over fifty cadets, but society's growing emphasis on equality, and the economies that could be achieved by running combined units, led to the GNTC merging into the Sea Cadets during the 1960s.[62] Finally, many independent schools throughout Britain host units of the Combined Cadet Force, and Royal Navy sections have existed for many years at two Welsh public schools, Christ College, Brecon, and Ruthin.

'Welsh' Warships and Auxiliaries

From the 1950s onwards, the Royal Navy embarked on an arguably misguided policy of naming ships after communities throughout the British Isles, even if there was little previous tradition of such names. Thus frigates, by then increasingly important units of the fleet, were named after relatively small seaside resorts, and the Royal Navy gained HMS *Rhyl* and *Tenby*; a class of aircraft direction frigates named after cathedral cities included the only warship ever to be named HMS *Llandaff*.[*] County-class destroyers – actually larger than most previous cruisers – entered service in the 1960s, and most bore traditional cruiser names: but one was HMS *Glamorgan*, an entirely

---

[*]   Sold to the then new navy of Bangladesh in 1976 and commissioned as Umar Farooq, she was not scrapped until 2016..

new name on the Navy List, intended explicitly 'to preserve the naval connections with … Wales'.[63] She was built at Newcastle and launched by Lady Brecon on 9 July 1964; her motto, '*I fyny b'or nod*' (Aim High) was provided by Cynan, the Archdruid of Wales.[64] The main passageway that ran almost the entire length of the ship became known as 'the Rhondda Valley'.[65] But the Counties were too large, awkwardly designed and relatively short-lived (*Hampshire* was scrapped at Briton Ferry in 1979 after only thirteen years in service), and in the 1970s a new class of smaller destroyers bearing city names, albeit traditional ones for warships, was built to replace them. This Type 42 included a new HMS *Cardiff*, built at Barrow-in-Furness and Wallsend, and launched on 22 February 1974. Overall, the Welsh presence on the Navy List was surprisingly impressive. In the classes of major warship given geographical names, Welsh names made up 12 per cent of the total: significantly more than those from Scotland and Northern Ireland, and a sea change from the interwar years when no Welsh names at all had been given to warships.[66]

Geographical names were also used for smaller craft. Welsh names adorned a number of minesweepers: the wooden Ton-class, built in the 1950s, included a clutch of names that were inevitably drawn almost exclusively from the ancient English 'colonies' of south Pembrokeshire and the Vale of Glamorgan, *Clarbeston*, *Hubberston*, *Laleston*, *Letterston*, *Picton* and *Puncheston*. (Unsurprisingly, the navy seems never to have contemplated a 'Llan' class.*) However, the most famous of the entire class of 119 ships, and one of the few still in existence, was *Bronington*, named after the village in Maelor Saesneg near Wrexham. In 1976 she was the command of a young officer not unknown to the Principality, a certain Lieutenant Charles Philip Arthur

---

*   However, a few small warships were built in Wales, by Saunders Roe at Beaumaris, during the post-war years, notably six Dark-class fast patrol boats for the Royal Navy, along with five more for the Burmese, two for the Finnish, and one for the Japanese navies.

George Mountbatten-Windsor; this somewhat tenuous claim to
fame meant that after the navy decommissioned her in the late
1980s, she was acquired by a preservation trust and kept open to
the public on the Manchester Ship Canal into the 2000s, when
the financial collapse of her owners left her facing an uncertain future. The Tons' successors, built in the 1980s and 1990s,
resurrected some older Welsh warship names. They included
a *Brecon*, a *Dovey* and the navy's ninth *Pembroke*, but *Bangor* was
named after the town in Northern Ireland, not the Welsh city.
The name of HMS *St David*, unused since the seventeenth century, was revived (from 1947–83) for the seagoing tenders of the
South Wales division of the Royal Naval Reserve. The navy's
fourth *Anglesey* was a fisheries protection patrol vessel, in service
from 1979 to 2003 when she was sold to the Bangladeshi Navy.
She and her sister ships were replaced by a new River-class which
included the tenth HMS *Severn*, launched in 2002, again maintaining the informal tradition that geographic-themed warship
classes always contain at least one Welsh name.[67]

All of these 'Welsh' warships developed strong links with
their namesake communities. There were port visits whenever
operational commitments permitted, sea cadets from the local
unit went off for short trips to sea, the ships were granted the
freedom of the boroughs and cities concerned (*Severn*, for example, became affiliated to Newport and was granted the freedom
of the city in 2006), while civic dignitaries revelled in invitations
to commissioning ceremonies or wardroom cocktail parties
and reciprocated by hosting lavish lunches when their adopted
ships came to town.[68] Those communities that did not have a
ship bearing their own name were quick to affiliate with others,
perhaps the successors of those they had adopted in the wartime
'warship weeks', or else simply whatever the navy offered them.
Thus Swansea affiliated with the frigate HMS *Arethusa*, which
bore the name of the cruiser adopted during 'warship week' in
1942. The most powerful manifestation of all these connections
between civic Wales and the Royal Navy took place as part of

the celebrations surrounding the Prince of Wales' investiture at Caernarfon Castle on 1 July 1969. Warships visited ports and seaside resorts around the Welsh coast, including several that rarely saw ships of any kind. Thus the minesweeper HMS *Highburton* dropped anchor off Burry Port harbour in Carmarthen Bay, which had been closed to large vessels for decades, and members of the general public were ferried out to her across the frequently choppy waters of the Burry Estuary.[69]

At one time, warships, including the navy's largest, regularly made courtesy visits to the Welsh coast: in 1919 the Second Battle Squadron, consisting of the navy's newest and most powerful battleships (*Barham*, *Malaya*, *Valiant* and *Warspite*), moored off Aberystwyth, and school parties were taken to see it from as far afield as Birmingham. The battleship *Anson* could be seen at anchor in Swansea Bay in 1947, and in 1961, a fairly typical post-war year, eight ships made eleven separate visits to seven Welsh ports and seaside resorts.[70] In 1963 the Admiralty attempted to analyse and increase the frequency of ship visits in order to boost recruitment: that year the destroyer *Cambrian* and frigate *Llandaff* could be seen at Cardiff, the frigates *Keppel* and *Wakeful* at Port Talbot, and the submarine *Grampus* at Barry, while no fewer than four submarines visited Newport simultaneously in August. A schedule of priorities for future visits was established, with Aberystwyth and Holyhead placed ahead of the likes of Abersoch and Aberdyfi which, in turn, were ranked above the likes of Fishguard and Pwllheli. (Curiously, Wales' most famous place name, 'Llanfair PG', also featured on the list.)[71] But as the fleet shrank in size, especially after the end of the Cold War in 1989–90, port visits became relatively few and far between, reducing the contact between the navy and the Welsh public and, crucially, diminishing the latter's awareness of the navy's importance.

The post-1990 defence cuts, and ultimately sheer old age, also gradually diminished the 'Welsh presence' on the Navy List. *Dovey* and *Anglesey* were sold to Bangladesh, while HMS *Cardiff* was decommissioned in July 2005, flying the *Ddraig Goch* as she sailed into Portsmouth harbour for the last time. Tentative proposals to preserve her as a floating museum in her namesake city came to nothing, and the ship was broken up in Turkey in 2008. After making a final visit to her 'home port' of Swansea, *Brecon* left the fleet in the following September, albeit to find a new lease of life as a static training ship for new-entry personnel at HMS *Raleigh*, Torpoint. *Brecon* was a 'casualty' of the peace process in Northern Ireland; from 1998 to 2005 she had formed part of the squadron tasked with patrolling the province's waters, so her decommissioning might have been at least in part a gesture of good faith towards the IRA, which announced the end of its armed campaign that July.[72]

The Falklands, the Gulf and Beyond

The Argentinian invasion of the Falkland Islands (or, as they termed it, the liberation of the *Islas Malvinas*) took place on Friday 2 April 1982. The flagship for the operation was the ARA *Santísima Trinidad*, the same ship that had been on trials in Cardigan Bay only five months earlier. The following day, Lieutenant Keith Mills of the Royal Marines, former head boy of Sir Thomas Jones School, Amlwch, was commanding a detachment of twenty-two men on the island of South Georgia when news was received that the Argentinians were about to invade there, too. London sent instructions to put up only a token resistance; Mills replied 'Sod that, I'll make their eyes water', and proceeded to do so during a two-hour battle, shooting down a helicopter and damaging the powerful corvette ARA *Guerrico*. Despite finally being captured, he was swiftly repatriated and was back in Britain by the end of the month, returning to a hero's welcome in Amlwch.[73] As Mills and his men made their stand, a massive naval response was already beginning to develop. A taskforce that included HMS *Glamorgan* sailed from

Gibraltar, while the aircraft carriers *Hermes* and *Invincible* left Portsmouth on 5 April.

Not only warships set out on the 8,000-mile voyage south: Royal Fleet Auxiliaries were joined by a growing number of merchant ships requisitioned by the government in a variety of roles. These were known by the unfortunate acronym STUFT (Ships Taken Up From Trade) and included the liners *QE2* and *Canberra*, while the old liner *Uganda*, once a regular caller at Swansea to embark Welsh school parties for educational cruises, was converted into a hospital ship. One of the principal reasons for British success in the campaign was the establishment of a lengthy but highly sophisticated supply line, and the navy's Welsh establishments played important roles in this. The stores depot at Llangennech despatched seven storekeepers and clerical officers to the South Atlantic to serve on two Royal Fleet Auxiliaries and one of the STUFT ships. The seven were subsequently presented with South Atlantic campaign medals in a ceremony at the depot attended by a large number of local dignitaries.[74] RNAD Milford Haven and Trecwn also played their parts in supplying the fleet, while several tankers sailed from Milford Haven to transport fresh supplies of oil to the RFAs. The *British Tay*, which sailed from Milford a few days after the Argentinian invasion, was one of the first tankers to sail south, and was subsequently followed by the *British Tamar* and *Scottish Eagle*.[75]

Welsh communities anxiously followed the progress of 'their' ships. On 5 April, not long after the Task Force had begun its journey south, HMS *Glamorgan* received a telegram from one of the new counties whose name she bore: 'The thoughts and prayers of the people of West Glamorgan are with you.' The ship's navigating officer later wrote that 'it was just one line but the very fact that West Glamorgan had taken the trouble to wish us well meant a lot'. Further messages of support came from the likes of the Lord Mayor of Cardiff, and when *Glamorgan* was hit by an Exocet towards the end of the war, Sir Cenydd Traherne,

Lord Lieutenant of Glamorgan, said of her: '[the ship] has a very special place in the hearts of people here. The motto of the ship is *I fyny b'or nod*. They aimed high … very high indeed!'[76] The Type 21 frigate HMS *Ardent* was less fortunate. On 22 May, while covering the British landings at San Carlos, she was bombed and sunk in Falkland Sound with the loss of twenty-two lives. Her sinking had a powerful impact on her affiliated town, Milford Haven; eight days later, 600 people crammed into North Road Baptist church for a service of remembrance. For Britain, though, the defining tragedy of the Falklands campaign was the air attack on the Royal Fleet Auxiliary landing ships *Sir Tristram* and *Sir Galahad* at Bluff Cove on 8 June. A total of fifty-six British service personnel were killed, including thirty-two members of the Welsh Guards.

HMS *Glamorgan* was providing gunfire support off Port Stanley on 12 June when she was struck by an Exocet missile fired from the shore. It was fortunate that the strike was effectively a glancing blow which did not penetrate the hull; even so, fourteen men were killed and others wounded. Meanwhile, on 26 May another 'Welsh' warship had arrived to join the Task Force. HMS *Cardiff* had been redeployed from the Gulf and was soon in action, ultimately shooting down the last Argentinian aircraft lost during the conflict. On 14 June, the day of the Argentinian surrender, *Cardiff* captured the patrol boat *Islas Malvinas*. This was taken into Royal Navy service and wittily renamed HMS *Tiger Bay*, serving until sold a few years later. Meanwhile the damaged *Glamorgan* made her way back to Britain, flying the *Ddraig Goch* from the mainmast as she entered Portsmouth harbour on 10 July.[77] She did not remain in Royal Navy service for very long. In 1984 HMS *Glamorgan* was sold to Chile, a country which had amply aided and abetted Britain during the Falklands/Malvinas war. There she became the *Almirante Latorre*, surviving until 2005, although if the Chilean Navy had a better developed sense of history, it might have regarded *Almirante Bynon* as a more appropriate name.

HMS *Cardiff* continued in service, and in 1991 she played an important role in the next major conflict in which the Royal Navy was involved. The Iraqi regime of Saddam Hussein invaded Kuwait on 2 August 1990, and in September *Cardiff* went to the Gulf to form part of the defensive screen for the American carrier force. On 24 January 1991, her Lynx helicopter spotted three Iraqi minehunters and sank two of them, attacking another group of Iraqi ships a few days later. *Cardiff* was subsequently awarded the battle honour 'Kuwait 1991'.[78] During the second Gulf (or Iraq) War of 2003, British naval efforts centred primarily on keeping the open sea lane to Basra, but the Royal Marines were heavily deployed during the invasion of Iraq itself. One of them was Marine Matt Hughes of Betws-y-Coed, who executed a sniper shot so astonishing that it made the national press and still features as a source of awe on blogs and Internet chat rooms. Ordered to eliminate an Iraqi gunman who was holding up an advance, he aimed 56 feet to the left of the target, to allow for wind, and 35 feet high to allow for a distance of 975 yards. The shot hit the Iraqi in the chest and killed him instantly.[79]

In the twenty-first century, with the possibility of Scottish independence one of the great political issues of the day, a few began to speculate about what the navy of an independent Wales might look like. Three or four ships, perhaps, transferred as part of an independence settlement with the English Navy, but definitely no aircraft carriers, thus dashing the hopes of some optimistic dreamers on the internet.[80] This hypothetical Welsh fleet's role would presumably be similar to that of the current Irish Naval Service (of seven ships), which is concerned principally with the protection of the country's fisheries and the interdiction of drug smugglers. A Welsh navy would have the additional priority of defending Milford Haven, which would presumably continue to be a major port of entry for oil and gas destined for the rest of the former United Kingdom. Welsh independence might still be a far distant prospect, and to many a distinctly unwelcome one, but presumably one of the very few cast-iron certainties about an independent Wales is that it would christen one of its first warships *Owain Glyndŵr*. After all, if the Royal Navy of the United Kingdom twice thought the name good enough, surely so would a Welsh navy, *y Llynges Cymru*?

Notes

1   TNA, AVIA6/23886.
2   *Hansard*, HC Deb 08 April 1982 vol. 21 c457W.
3   *Hansard*, HC Deb 18 May 1954 vol. 527 cc111-2W.
4   www.oxfordpreservation.org.uk/about/trustees.php
5   L. Phillips, 'Some Pembrokeshire Sea Officers', ii , *Journal of the Pembrokeshire Historical Society*, 9 (2000), p.17; www.telegraph.co.uk/news/obituaries/4944779/Surgeon-Vice-Admiral-Ian-Jenkins.html
6   borthmaritimehistory.com
7   Powys Archives, R/SOC/16/NE/4.
8   TNA, AVIA6/23886.
9   www.walesonline.co.uk/news/local-news/bala/2011/07/06/ex-sailor-tells-of-korean-war-ordeal-91466-29000901/ (Accessed: 2012)
10 W. Gordon, *Two Years before the What?* (Milton Keynes, 2008).
11 *Hansard*, HC Deb 17 February 1981 vol. 999 cc98–9W.
12 *Hansard*, HC Deb 17 February 1997 vol. 290 c363W.
13 www.cymdeithasycymod.org.uk/khakidragon.pdf (Accessed: 2012)
14 TNA, administrative history of classmark ADM326.
15 TNA, ADM326/258, 326/282, 326/306.
16 R. Thomas et al., *A Guide to the Military Heritage of Pembrokeshire: Civil War to Cold War* (Narberth, n.d.), p.169.
17 B. McManus, 'The Loss of the Cadet School Training Ship HMS *Conway*', *MW* 20 (1999), pp.84–95; A. Windsor, *HMS Conway 1859–1974* (Livingston, 2008), pp.191–243.
18 www.coflein.gov.uk/en/site/271611/details/HMS+CONWAY/; Windsor, *HMS Conway*, p.259. (Accessed: 2012)
19 www.hmsconway.org
20 I. Buxton and B. Warlow, *To Sail No More, Part 1* (Liskeard, 1997), pp.18–21; M. Critchley, *To Sail No More, Part 2* (Liskeard, 1998), pp.18–19.
21 TNA, ADM1/27050.
22 Goddard, 'Naval Activity', 345.
23 M. Critchley, *To Sail No More, Part 3* (Liskeard, 2000), p.73; D. Rees, 'The wreck of the *Cleveland*', *Wales*, 40 (1959), pp.40–2.

24 Some excellent photographs of ships being broken up at the Briton Ferry and Skewen yards are contained in M. Critchley, *To Sail No More, Part 2* (Liskeard, 1998).

25 www.newportpast.com/jd/cashmore.htm

26 P. Kemp, 'Chatfield, (Alfred) Ernle Montacute, first Baron Chatfield (1873–1967), Naval Officer', *ODNB*.

27 R. John, *Caspar John* (1987), p.15.

28 Obituary of Admiral of the Fleet Sir Caspar John GCB by 'DCEFG', *The Naval Review*, 72 (1984), pp.287–9 (quotation from p.228); D. Williams, 'John, Sir Caspar (1903–1984), Naval Officer', *ODNB*; R. John, *Caspar John*, passim.

29 John, *Caspar John*, pp.198–9.

30 K. Davies, 'Hall, George Henry, Viscount Hall (1881–1965), Trade Unionist and Politician', *ODNB*.

31 www.briansmithonline.com/memoirs/witness21.html

32 briansmithonline.com/memoir/chapter-21.html

33 CAS, Cilcennin MSS 102, 108, 113.

34 The aircraft carrier cancelled in 1966 was to have been named *Queen Elizabeth*: TNA, ADM 1/29044, which also contains the report of Cilcennin's promise to the Queen. The name was eventually allocated to the huge carrier on which construction began in 2009.

35 www.guardian.co.uk/politics/2012/feb/26/lord-hooson

36 R. Hattersley, 'Callaghan, Leonard James [Jim], Baron Callaghan of Cardiff (1912–2005), prime minister', *ODNB*. The opponent he defeated by one vote was George Thomas, the future Speaker of the House of Commons.

37 G. Evans, *Land of My Fathers: 2000 Years of Welsh History* (Talybont, 1998 edn.), p.252.

38 'Davies, David James (1893–1956), Economist', *WBO*.

39 Personal knowledge; or, in the words of Max Boyce, 'I know because I was there'.

40 www.jillevans.net/jill_evans_speeches_keynote_091120.html; S. Jobbins, *The Phenomenon of Welshness: Or 'How Many Aircraft Carriers Would an Independent Wales have'?* (Llanrwst, 2011), pp.176–86. (Accessed: 2012)

41 TNA, ADM1/21386.

42 National Assembly of Wales, Recording of Proceedings, Tuesday 19 June 2012, p.29.

43 TNA, ADM1/28965.

44 www.walesonline.co.uk/news/wales-news/2012/08/07/eisteddfod-archdruid-warns-carwyn-jones-against-nuclear-arsenal-91466-31567157/; National Assembly of Wales, Recording of

Proceedings, Wednesday 4 July 2012, pp.114–41. In the event, in 2021 housing Trident in Milford Haven was again ruled out on virtually identical grounds: Financial Times, 2 September 2021.

45 NLW, Swansea CND and CND Cymru MSS, F1.

46 *Hansard*, HC Deb 19 July 1989 vol. 157 cc 492–500.

47 www.thisissouthwales.co.uk/Council-torpedos-sub-link-critics/story-12444963-detail/story.html

48 PRO, HDX/1831/1.

49 cloudobservers.co.uk, and PDF files accessible from this page.

50 D.H. Blackaby [et al.], 'Defence Cuts, Redundancies and Future Employment Prospects in West Wales', *Contemporary Wales: An Annual of Economic & Social Research*, 6 (1994), pp.49–72.

51 PRO, HDX/1831/1.

52 A. Phillips, *Brawdy: Stronghold in the West* (Stroud, 2009), pp.15, 20, 24, 38, 39–57, 84–101.

53 C. Whitham, 'Sheep, Subs and Showcases: The American Military in Brawdy, 1974–95', *Welsh History Review*, 24 (2008–09), pp.168–86.

54 For a detailed description and photographs of the remains of RNAD Milford, see www.forlornbritain.co.uk/milford.php.

55 *RNAD Trecwn: The Strategic Case against Closure – A Paper Prepared by Dr Chris Smith for Dyfed County Council & Preseli Pembrokeshire District Council, Jan. 1992; The Social and Economic Consequences of the Closure of RNAD Trecwn*, Welsh Affairs Committee, House of Commons, 1992.

56 Speech by Nick Ainger MP, *Hansard*, HC Deb 27 Jan. 1994: vol. 236, cc. 470–3.

57 *Ex info* Alan Phillips, formerly of RNSD Llangennech, and various issues of the *Journal of the Royal Naval Supply and Transport Service* generously supplied by him.

58 *Hansard*, HC Deb 12 Nov. 2003 vol. 413 cc324–5.

59 S. Howarth, *The Royal Navy's Reserves in War and Peace, 1903–2003* (Barnsley, 2003), pp.101, 104–5, 107, 117, 153, 155, 159–60. M Salisbury, ed., HMS Cambria: A Flagship for Wales (Cardiff? n.d.). I am grateful to Huw Williams for providing me with a copy of this resource.

60 West Glamorgan Archive Service, D/D Z 162/1.

61 www.royalnavy.mod.uk/our-organisation/bases-and-stations/training-establishments/university-royal-naval-units/wales

62 GRO, MS D724/1.

63 *Hansard*, HL Deb 11 July 1962 vol. 242 c262.

64 *HMS Glamorgan: The First Two Years* (commission book)

65 I. Inskip, *Ordeal by Exocet: HMS Glamorgan and the Falklands War 1982* (2002), p.159.

66 *Ex info* Dr Duncan Redford, National Museum of the Royal Navy.
67 www.royalnavy.mod.uk/The-Fleet/Ships/Patrol-and-Minehunters/
    River-Class/HMS-Severn.
68 e.g. GRO, MD/C/10/14, 24, 64, lunches for HMS *Glamorgan*.
69 Personal recollection; this was the first time that I ever set foot aboard
    a warship.
70 NLW, MS 4425E; N. Arthur, *Swansea since 1900* (Swansea, 1988),
    picture 125; *Hansard*, HC Deb 01 March 1961 vol. 635 cc1572–3.
71 TNA, ADM1/28723.
72 Northern Ireland Patrol Squadron Decommissioning Book,
    September 2005
73 www.theonlinemail.co.uk/bangor-and-anglesey-news/local-bangor-
    and-anglesey-news/2010/06/16/triumph-and-tragedy-of-anglesey-
    soldiers-in-the-falklands-66580-26654351/ (Accessed: 2012)
74 IWM, Documents 16321.
75 www.naval-history.net/F28weektwo.htm; http://www.
    naval-history.net/F22mnships.htm
76 Inskip, *Ordeal by Exocet*, pp.27, 146, 184.
77 Inskip, *Ordeal by Exocet*, p.218.
78 *Hansard*, HL Deb 24 Feb. 1993 vol. 543 cc15–8 WA.
79 www.telegraph.co.uk/news/uknews/1517045/After-90-years-Army-
    sets-its-sights-on-new-sniper-platoons.html
80 S. Jobbins, *The Phenomenon of Welshness: Or 'How Many Aircraft Carriers
    Would an Independent Wales have'?* (Llanrwst, 2011), pp.181–2, 184–5.

CONCLUSION

Shortly after 8.00 a.m. on 31 August 2011, a huge, sleek modern warship left her mooring at Spithead, sailed briefly to the east, then turned north and west into the main channel towards the entrance to Portsmouth harbour. A few dozen people had gathered at various vantage points along the shore, notably upon the Round Tower erected in 1418 by order of the Monmouth-born King Henry V. Some were the wives and girlfriends of members of the crew; others were local journalists and film crews; most were dedicated 'warship spotters', their long lenses at the ready. As the impressive grey-hulled warship passed Clarence Pier, her escorting tugs discharged their water cannon to welcome the ship to her home port for the first time.[1] When she entered the harbour to waves and cheers from the crowd on the Round Tower, her unique distinguishing feature became clearly apparent. Painted upon the bow of HMS *Dragon*, fourth of the Royal Navy's Type 45 destroyers, was a huge, ferocious red dragon: unmistakably the *Ddraig Goch* of Wales.

Dragon renewed the navy's affiliation with Cardiff, but otherwise the navy's connections with Wales have continued to weaken as the number of warships in service has inexorably declined. HMS *Monmouth*, the 'Black Duke', was prematurely withdrawn from service in 2021 and laid up at Portsmouth. HMS *Pembroke* paid a final visit to her namesake port in July 2023 and returned the Freedom of Pembroke prior to decommissioning. As noted in Chapter Twelve, the number of naval recruits from Wales plummeted after the end of the Cold War, and this trend will undoubtedly have continued; in 2023 the navy had just over 26,000 personnel compared with 62,000 in 1991, the year the Berlin Wall fell. But it is not all doom and gloom. Despite the overall decline in numbers, Welsh men and women continue to serve in the Royal Navy and Royal Marines, and inevitably they continue to be nicknamed Taff, as were generations of their predecessors.[2] They continue to give their lives in the service, too: Marine Nigel Mead of Carmarthen was killed by an improvised explosive device in Helmand Province, Afghanistan, in May 2011, aged just nineteen. In 2020 the impressive new building HMS *Cambria*, the training establishment for the naval reserves in South Wales, opened in Cardiff Bay, while HMS *Express*, the dedicated training ship for the University Royal Navy Units of Cardiff, Swansea and Glamorgan Universities, continues to be based in Penarth Marina. Above all, in 2017 a new HMS *Cardiff* was ordered from a shipyard in Glasgow. The second of the Type 26 frigates, the two halves of *Cardiff*'s hull emerged from the building sheds in the summer of 2023, and the Royal Navy's fourth ship of the name will ensure a Welsh presence in the fleet until the middle of the twenty-first century.

Despite the abiding connections between Wales and the Royal Navy, the broader picture is troubling. Many writers and commentators have suggested that twenty-first century Britain has become 'sea blind': that there is now a lack of awareness, or even complete ignorance, of the role of the navy among the public at large, and a wider lack of understanding of the vital importance of the sea to the British Isles. The last war in which the Royal Navy arguably played the leading role, the campaign in the Falklands, was over forty years ago. For the first two decades of the twenty-first century, the Welsh and British publics, and young people in particular, only knew conflicts in which the Royal Air Force and above all the Army played the principal parts. The navy has not helped itself by frequently conducting its relations with both government and the public in muddle-headed ways.* The virtual withdrawal of the navy from Wales, both in terms of the presence of shore establishments and the frequency of ship visits to Welsh ports, means that for many people, the service is truly out of sight and out of mind. It is almost certain that as the years pass, fewer and fewer people know someone serving in, or who formerly served in, the Royal Navy; fewer and fewer people will have ever seen a warship, let alone been aboard one.

As I suggested in the Introduction, perhaps there are factors unique to Wales at play, too. For example, until at least the middle of the twentieth century, naval officers, like their equivalents in the army, colonial officials, and other functionaries of the British state, were drawn largely from the Welsh middle and upper classes, demographics which have often been ignored or derided in much of Welsh historiography. Therefore, perhaps the lack of awareness of Wales' naval tradition also stems from popular perceptions of Welsh history and the attitudes of Wales' cultural and political (as opposed to social) elites, which have often been antipathetic to anything smacking of militarism or imperialism.[3] On the other hand, this is not just a naval issue, for the neglect of maritime history and heritage as a whole is also glaring. Lack of public interest and the difficulty of attracting

---

* See e.g. www.southwalesargus.co.uk/news/gwentnews/9779035. Newport_sailor_comes_home_aboard_HMS_Severn.

younger generations of volunteers has closed some Welsh mari-time museums and put the survival of others on a knife-edge.*
Local councils afflicted by a dearth of imagination and in thrall to rapacious developers can often think of nothing better to do with old docks than create in them largely empty marinas and populate the quaysides with blocks of ugly flats and national chain restaurants, usually providing little or no interpretation of the original heritage of the area.

Wales is a maritime nation. It is, or has been, a naval nation. But it is a nation that needs to reconnect with the sea that did so much to shape it.

★★★

Relatively few national anthems mention the sea. 'God Save the King' does not; neither does 'Flower of Scotland', that mourn-ful rant against the conqueror of Wales. 'La Marseillaise' and the 'Deutschlandlied' ignore it, as do 'O Canada' and, perhaps surprisingly, the anthems of island nations like Iceland, Malta and New Zealand. 'Advance Australia Fair' merely makes the bland, incontrovertible statement that 'Our Home is Girt by Sea', echoing the equally passing factual mentions in the Danish and Norwegian anthems. In two famous national hymns, the sea is quite explicitly hostile. In the Republic of Ireland's '*Amhrán na bhFiann*' ('The Soldier's Song'), the hated English have come from 'the land beyond the wave', while in 'The Star-Spangled Banner' the sea has brought the British warships attacking Fort McHenry; as the little-sung second verse puts it:

---

* The maritime museum in Porthmadog closed in 2005 (but encouragingly reopened in 2012), the Pembroke Dock Gun Tower Museum closed in 2011 due to storm damage, and Caernarfon Maritime Museum closed permanently in 2012. Llŷn Maritime Museum, which had been closed for some years, has now been re-opened .

On the shore dimly seen through the mists of the deep,
Where the foe's haughty host in dread silence reposes ...

Strangely, perhaps the most explicit reference to the sea in a positive sense, as the principal defence of a nation, comes in the Welsh national anthem, '*Hen Wlad fy Nhadau*' ('Land of My Fathers'). When a capacity crowd at Cardiff's Millennium Stadium bellows out the chorus, the last two lines that they sing, the very climax of the anthem, are:

Tra môr yn fur i'r bur hoff bau,
O bydded i'r hen iaith barhau

which can be translated loosely as:

While seas secure the land so pure,
O may the old language endure.

Taken literally, of course, this is nonsense. The sea does *not* secure Wales, as the very fact of its conquest by way of its long, vulnerable land border – aided and abetted by English seapower – proved all too clearly. But Evan James, who wrote the words of the anthem in 1856, was a native of Pontypridd, and thus he would have been well aware of the importance of the Royal Navy: the town was home to the firm of Brown, Lenox & Co., the principal supplier of iron cables to a fleet that had just emerged victorious from a war against Russia. So James' lyric actually only makes sense in the context of Victorian Wales, and its precious language, being secured by the seas that surround the British Isles *as a whole*, and implicitly by the navy that then dominated those seas. It seems unlikely that any man or woman in the crowd at the Millennium Stadium ever realises that they are actually singing the praises of the Royal Navy, or would respond particularly kindly if this was pointed out to them. But Evan James' words provide a lasting testimony to the abiding connection between Wales and the sea, and to the proud naval heritage of the land of my fathers.

Notes

1   Personal observations, Portsmouth, 31 August 2011.
2   See e.g. www.southwalesargus.co.uk/news/gwentnews/9779035. Newport_sailor_comes_home_aboard_HMS_Severn.
3   H.V. Bowen, ed., *Wales and the British Overseas Empire: Interactions and Influences, 1650–1830* (Manchester, 2011), p.4.

THE WELSH AT TRAFALGAR

It ought to be comparatively simple to provide an exact number for the Welshmen at the Battle of Trafalgar. There are not one but three easily accessible sources that claim to provide comprehensive listings of those who fought in Nelson's fleet: the 'Trafalgar Ancestors' database on the National Archives website;[1] a listing assembled by Dr Reg Davies on the splendid 'Welsh Mariners' website;[2] and the CD assembled by a couple of dedicated amateurs, Derek and Pam Ayshford, in 2004. A simple search for men with Welsh birthplaces on 'Trafalgar Ancestors' reveals 465 names; 'Welsh Mariners' gives 609; and the Ayshfords' CD 622. There are clearly discrepancies and transcription errors in all sources, as indeed there are in the original muster books upon which the listings are based, where English clerks often struggled to cope with Welsh place names (for instance, recording Abersoch as 'Aberstork', Bettws as 'Bettuces' and Amlwch as 'Hamlock'). The raw reliance on the birthplaces recorded in the musters means that a number of men with strong Welsh connections are omitted from one, two or all of the listings. Thus

William Franklin Peter, midshipman of the *Spartiate*, is shown correctly as being born at Falmouth; but he was the son of the Reverend Robert Peter, vicar of Penlline, Glamorgan, from 1786 to 1822. Frederick Jennings Thomas, acting lieutenant of the same ship, is recorded as being born in the New Forest, but he was a son of Sir John Thomas, bart., of Wenvoe Castle; he was the standard-bearer in the first barge during the spectacular waterborne procession that formed the centrepiece of Nelson's funeral.[3] Alexander Dixie, lieutenant of the *Phoebe*, was born in Buckinghamshire and ultimately inherited a Leicestershire baronetcy, but he was raised in Kidwelly by his widowed mother (a Mansel of Stradey) and continued to treat the Carmarthenshire town as his home until his mother's death in 1810.[4] Others acquired their Welsh connections later in life and are thus correctly omitted from all three listings, but are nevertheless still worthy of note. Hugh Entwhistle, first class volunteer aboard the *Bellerophon*, was a Yorkshireman through and through, but after rising to the rank of commander he retired to Marlborough Grange, Glamorgan, dying there in 1867, and is buried in Llanblethian church.[5] William Pryce Cumby of Heighington, Durham, was first lieutenant of the *Bellerophon* in the battle, taking command of her when the captain was killed. He subsequently became captain-superintendent of Pembroke Dockyard, albeit only very briefly before his death in 1837; nevertheless he was buried in the graveyard of the dockyard church at Pembroke Dock. Although the site was cleared in the 1970s, a plaque to his memory was subsequently re-erected there, and in October 2012 the 175th anniversary of his death was marked by a service of commemoration.[6]

There are also significant differences between the three listings, usually reflecting methodological errors or simple slips in one or the other. For example, the 'Trafalgar Ancestors' listing shows William Bunce as carpenter aboard the *Victory*, aged 55 and born in Milford; the Ayshfords and 'Welsh Mariners' give no place of birth at all for him and thus omit him from the 'Welsh' contingent, while the Ayshfords give his age as 25, information repeated on the 'official' Trafalgar roll of HMS *Victory*.[7] The supporting evidence provided by the National Archives shows that their account of Bunce is undoubtedly correct.[8] However, I carried out a detailed cross-check of the three listings of the Welsh contingents from four counties – Cardiganshire, Denbighshire, Merionethshire and Monmouthshire[9] – and found that the bulk of the errors are in the National Archives' 'Trafalgar Ancestors' listing, which thus consistently understates the number of Welshmen in the fleet. The Ayshfords' and the 'Welsh Mariners' databases are generally far more accurate in identifying 'difficult' place names and connecting them to Wales, and usually to the correct county. Thus 'Trafalgar Ancestors' assumes that three men from 'Rixham', 'Nexham' and 'Wraxham' were all from English places with those names; 'Welsh Mariners' identifies two of them, and the Ayshford roll correctly identifies them all, as being from Wrexham. For two individuals, 'Trafalgar Ancestors' supplies 'Derbyshire' instead of 'Denbighshire', and both it and 'Welsh Mariners' fail to assign any nationality at all to Evan Jones of HMS *Prince*, born at 'Landruit, Dyghhrt' – an astonishing name, even by Welsh standards. However, by far the most significant cause of the discrepancy in total numbers between the sources is that 'Trafalgar Ancestors' unaccountably treats Monmouthshire as a part of England. While this was at least partially legally correct in 1805, it seems perverse to apply this archaic definition – which was always highly debatable, even at the time of Trafalgar – in a modern resource, where it will surely serve only to confuse unwitting researchers.

I then took the Ayshford figures for men from the four home nations who were present at the battle (bearing in mind that even these are likely to underestimate the Welsh presence) and compared them with the population figures given in the 1801 census.[10] These were 8,331,434 for England, 1,599,068 for Scotland and 541,546 for Wales; the estimated population of Ireland at the same time was 5.4 million. These figures exclude those already in the armed forces, the merchant navy and the prisons, but it seems probable that the inclusion of the national demographics from these categories would not much alter the balance between the four nations. Not trusting my own limited mathematical skills in a matter of such importance, I had all the calculations re-checked by a Cambridge mathematics graduate who is also a former A-level Chief Examiner in the subject and has over thirty years' experience of teaching it.

The results are as follows:

Nation	Population (1801)	Men at Trafalgar (seamen and marines)	Percentage of national population	Men at Trafalgar (seamen only)	Percentage of national population
Wales	541,546	622	0.115	534	0.099
England	8,331,434	9,644	0.116	7,825	0.094
Scotland	1,599,068	1,358	0.085	1,299	0.081
Ireland	5,400,000	4,100	0.076	3,828	0.071

Notes

1   www.nationalarchives.gov.uk/trafalgarancestors/
2   www.welshmariners.org.uk/index.php
3   'Thomas family of Wenvoe, Glam.', *WBO*.
4   J.D. Davies, 'The Dixies of Bosworth – and Carmarthenshire', *The Carmarthenshire Antiquary*, xlv (2009), pp.49–50.
5   J.F.W. Leigh, 'Glamorgan Men at the Battle of Trafalgar', *South Wales and Monmouthshire Record Society*, publications no. 4, ed. H.J. Randall and W. Rees (Cardiff, 1957), pp.176–7.
6   C. White and the 1805 Club, *The Trafalgar Captains: Their Lives and Memorials* (2005), pp.50–2.
7   www.hms-victory.com (Accessed: 2012)
8   www.nationalarchives.gov.uk/trafalgarancestors/
9   The sample was chosen partly for the manageability of the numbers, but also because it provided a good cross-section of Welsh place names that were likely to have presented varying degrees of difficulty

to both nineteenth-century English clerks and twenty-first-century transcribers.

10 In the case of Ireland, where the first census did not take place until 1841, the comparison was made with the estimate of 5.4 million used on the Public Record Office of Northern Ireland website.

'ADOPTIONS' OF WARSHIPS

BY WELSH COMMUNITIES DURING 'WARSHIP WEEKS', WORLD WAR II

This list has been compiled from a variety of sources, including material from county record offices, online news reports, various websites and above all information received from Peter Schofield, who generously shared with me his knowledge of 'Warship Weeks' throughout the British Isles.

Aberdare	*Aberdare* (minesweeper)
Abergavenny	*MTB 332* (motor torpedo boat)
Abergele	*Hollyhock* (corvette), later *Derg* (frigate)
Abersarn	*MTB 256*
Abertillery	*Nigella* (corvette)
Amman Valley	*Holderness* (destroyer)
Anglesey	*Talybont* (destroyer)
Bangor	*Bangor* (minesweeper)
Barry	*Vanessa* (destroyer)
Bedwas and Machen	*MTB 62*

Bedwellty and New Tredegar	*Buttercup* (corvette)
Betws-y-Coed	*MTB 333*
Blaina and Nantyglo	*Cedar* (armed trawler)
Brecon	*Brecon* (destroyer)
Bridgend	*Urge* (submarine), later *Tudor* (submarine)
Brynmawr	*MTB 104*
Builth Wells	*Cornelia* (armed trawler)
Caerleon	*ML 147* (armed motor launch)
Caerphilly	*Caldwell* (destroyer)
Cardiff	*Cardiff* (cruiser), also *Albury* (destroyer)
Cardiganshire	*Tanatside* (destroyer)
Carmarthen	*Penylan* (destroyer)
Chepstow	*Cape Warwick* (armed trawler)
Connah's Quay	*Tuscan* (destroyer)
Colwyn Bay	*Jackal*, later *Cambrian* (both destroyers)
Conwy	*Erica* (corvette)
Cowbridge	*Gardenia* (corvette)
Crickhowell	*Drangey* (armed trawler)
Cwmbran	*Turquoise* (armed trawler)
Ebbw Vale	*Alresford* (minesweeper)
Glyncorrwg	*MGB 58* (motor gunboat)
Gower	*MTB 18*
Gwendraeth Valley	*MGB 51*
Hay-on-Wye	*MTB 226*
Llandovery	*Cornelian* (armed trawler)
Llandrindod Wells	*Sentinel* (submarine)
Llandudno	*Llandudno* (minesweeper)
Llanelli	*Echo* (destroyer)
Llangan	*Gardenia* (corvette)
Llangollen	*Dianella* (corvette)

Llanrwst	*Othello* (minesweeping trawler)
Llantrisant	*Minuet* (armed trawler)
Llanwrtyd Wells	*ML 137*
Llwchwr	*Unseen* (submarine)
Maesteg	*Mallow* (corvette)
Magor	*Magnet* (boom defence vessel)
Merionethshire	*
Merthyr Tydfil	*Beverley* (destroyer)
Montgomeryshire	*Montgomery* (destroyer)
Monmouth	*Coral* (A/S trawler)
Mountain Ash	*Exe* (frigate)
Mynyddislwyn	*Sapphire* (armed trawler)
Newcastle Emlyn	*Quadrille* (armed trawler)
Newport	*Newport* (destroyer)
Ogmore and Garw	*Quannet* (boom defence vessel) and *MGB 57* (motor gunboat)
Pembrokeshire (north)	*Nubian* (destroyer)
Pembrokeshire (south)	*Argonaut* (cruiser)
Penarth	*Sharpshooter* (minesweeper)
Penmaenmawr	*MTB 223*
Penygroes	*Corena* (armed trawler)
Pontardawe	*Umbra* (submarine)
Pontllotyn and Gelligaer	*Gnat* (gunboat)
Pontypool	*Kittiwake* (patrol vessel)
Pontypridd	*Tamarisk* (corvette)
Port Talbot	*Wishart* (destroyer)

★   There is considerable uncertainty about the status of Merionethshire's adoption. The county clearly aimed for a destroyer, with the publicity poster showing one of the 'four stackers' obtained under Lend Lease from the United States. No such HMS *Merioneth* was ever commissioned, and it seems the county was then promised a new build, HMS *Celt*, ordered in 1942 but which later became HMS *Sword* of the new Weapon-class. This ship, in turn, was cancelled in December 1945, so Merionethshire never got its adopted ship.

Porthcawl	MTB 84
Radnorshire	Scorpion (destroyer)
Rhondda	Velox (destroyer)
Risca	Primrose (corvette)
Sennybridge	ML 136
Swansea	Arethusa (cruiser)
Talgarth	ML 106
Tredegar	Inkpen (armed trawler)
Usk	Tango (armed trawler)
Wrexham	Veteran (destroyer)
Ystradgynlais	Rosalind (armed trawler)

INDEX

ABOUT THE AUTHOR

J.D. DAVIES is a prize-winning author and one of the leading authorities on British naval history of the seventeenth century. He is a former chairman of the Naval Dockyards Society and vice-president of the Navy Records Society, a member of the Council of the Society for Nautical Research and a Fellow of the Royal Historical Society. The author of the naval historical fiction series *The Journals of Matthew Quinton*, his previous naval non-fiction book, *Pepys's Navy*, won the Samuel Pepys prize in 2009.